ROUTLEDGE LIBRARY EDITIONS:
ADOLESCENCE

Volume 4

DEPRESSION IN CHILDREN AND ADOLESCENTS

DEPRESSION IN CHILDREN AND ADOLESCENTS

Edited by

HAROLD S. KOPLEWICZ AND EMILY KLASS

Routledge
Taylor & Francis Group
LONDON AND NEW YORK

First published in 1993 by Harwood Academic Publishers

This edition first published in 2016
by Routledge
2 Park Square, Milton Park, Abingdon, Oxon OX14 4RN

and by Routledge
711 Third Avenue, New York, NY 10017

Routledge is an imprint of the Taylor & Francis Group, an informa business

British Library Cataloguing in Publication Data
A catalogue record for this book is available from the British Library

ISBN: 978-1-138-94766-5 (Set)
ISBN: 978-1-315-64149-2 (Set) (ebk)
ISBN: 978-1-138-95312-3 (Volume 4) (hbk)
ISBN: 978-1-138-95319-2 (Volume 4) (pbk)
ISBN: 978-1-315-66744-7 (Volume 4) (ebk)

Publisher's Note
The publisher has gone to great lengths to ensure the quality of this reprint but points out that some imperfections in the original copies may be apparent.

Disclaimer
The publisher has made every effort to trace copyright holders and would welcome correspondence from those they have been unable to trace.

Depression in Children and Adolescents

edited by

Harold S. Koplewicz and **Emily Klass**

Schneider Children's Hospital
Long Island Jewish Medical Center
New York, USA

harwood academic publishers
Switzerland • Australia • Belgium • France • Germany • Great Britain
India • Japan • Malaysia • Netherlands • Russia • Singapore • USA

Harwood Academic Publishers

Private Bag 8
Camberwell, Victoria 3124
Australia

3-14-9, Okubo
Shinjuku-ku, Tokyo 169
Japan

58, rue Lhomond
75005 Paris
France

Emmaplein 5
1075 AW Amsterdam
Netherlands

Glinkastrasse 13-15
O-1086 Berlin
Germany

5301 Tacony Street, Drawer 330
Philadelphia, Pennsylvania 19137
United States of America

Post Office Box 90
Reading, Berkshire RG1 8JL
Great Britain

Library of Congress Cataloging-in-Publication Data

Depression in children and adolescents / edited by Harold S. Koplewicz and Emily Klass.
p. cm. -- (Monographs in clinical pediatrics ; 6)
Includes bibliographical references and index.
ISBN 3-7186-5317-6. -- ISBN 3-7186-5318-4 (pbk.)
1. Depression in children. 2. Depression in adolescence.
I. Koplewicz, Harold S. II. Klass, Emily. III. Series.
RJ506.D4D46 1993
618.92'8527--dc20
93-28562
CIP

 Printed in Singapore.

CONTENTS

Introduction

Harold S. Koplewicz

The origin of this volume arose from our work at the Schneider Children's Hospital of Long Island Jewish Medical Center. In 1986, we began a study funded by the Leon Lowenstein Foundation of the efficacy of desipramine in the treatment of adolescents with Major Depressive Disorder. At the same time, we established the first Adolescent Depression Service in the New York metropolitan area. This research study and clinical service brought us into contact with hundreds of families whose children had depressive symptoms.

Our interaction with our pediatric colleagues clarified for us the need for early identification of depression in children and adolescents. This goal could only be reached by increasing the pediatrician's awareness of the presence, identification and nature of depressive disorders of children and adolescents. He must possess the clinical skills to differentiate transient moodiness from a depressed mood that is a harbinger of a disorder which can result in dysfunction and possibly suicidal behavior. He must broach the often sensitive matter of explaining to parents the necessity and sometimes the urgency of seeking a psychiatric consultation in the face of lingering prejudice about the stigma of "seeing the shrink". He must answer questions and reassure parents that their depressed child is not "crazy", but has a serious disorder.

Long believed "masked" or absent from childhood, recent research has delineated clear syndromes of depression in all age groups. Depression in children and adolescents can be a chronic, debilitating condition with major impact on family, social and intrapsychic life. Early detection facilitates early treatment, a key to preserving a child's continued growth and development. The presentation of depression can be complicated by co-morbid diagnoses, psychosocial stressors within the family, developmental differences and medical illnesses. This volume seeks to disentangle some threads, weave others together and to generally span the current research in etiology, biology, phenomenology and treatment of depression in children and adolescents.

To do so, we have asked investigators to report on the state-of-the-art in the research of depression in their area of expertise. Beginning with Part One, "Theories of Development and Etiology", Drs. Romano and Schachter of our institution present the essence of the developmental approach to understanding childhood psychopathology in their chapter concerning the varying presentations of depression throughout childhood. Dr. Gurian writes of the "Learned Helplessness" model, laying out the theory and explicating the role of cognitive factors to comprehensibly understand depression. Drs. Anderson and Weissman distill their seminal work in family studies of childhood depression. From a family systems and clinical process-oriented framework, Ms. True and Ms. Kaplan discuss how depression may be part of the family system, how it may express other troubles in the family and how to work with a family to clarify and alleviate the suffering. Dr. Green presents the data and his formulations on the high rates of maltreatment in families in which a child presents with depression and underscores the imperative of investigating for abuse in all cases.

Part Two, "Medical Illness and Depression", is concerned with the complex interplay of medical illness and depression. Dr. Erickson disentangles methodological issues to present what is known about the risks of key pediatric illnesses in the development of depression. Most children with chronic illnesses do not go on to develop major depressions, yet certain subgroups of these children are at higher risk and need to be followed and treated. Drs. Neumann and Inwood outline the impact of acute illnesses on the psychological life of children and adolescents and medication reactions and interactions that appear as depression. Guidelines for intervention are provided by the authors as well. In all of our practices, in pediatrics, psychiatry and psychology, we will be challenged by a child and the family of a child who is dying. Dr. Kriechman takes on this compelling subject by helping the clinician to offer guidance and directions to these children and families.

In Part Three, "Depression and Other Psychiatric Conditions", experts discuss issues of co-morbidity and the interaction between depression and other psychiatric illnesses. Anxiety, conduct problems, substance abuse and eating disorders have significant relationships with depression in terms of etiology, overlapping phenomenology, and family linkage. Dr. Francis surveys the key anxiety disorders preponderant in childhood, as well as the normative and developmental considerations in diagnosing anxiety. Measures of anxiety, it's interaction with affective disorders and treatment strategies are also discussed as well. The co-occurrence of conduct disorder and depression has been documented and Drs. McCracken, Cantwell and Hanna review this phenomenon historically, and, based on their research and that of noted others, theorize in the relation between the disorders, particularly regarding outcome and mechanisms of association.

Among the most common associated symptoms of eating disorders is depression. Drs. Hoffman and Halmi examine prevalence issues, the biological markers and the relationship between the two disorders. In particular, Drs. Piacentini and Pataki discuss the co-morbidity of depression and substance abuse. Depression, these authors indicate, is a potential risk factor for the development of substance abuse and both have been associated with significantly increased rates of suicidal behavior. Given this potentially lethal situation, the primary care physician plays a vital role in detecting either of these disorders.

In Part Four "Treatment Approaches", Drs. Canino and Kestenbaum provide a rich clinical and research-based approach to traditional psychotherapy for children and adolescents. The chapters written by Drs. Schrodt, Klass and Gallagher are "pragmatic" in their approach, providing distinct interventions based on a cognitive-behavioral framework. Dr. Schrodt provides references for clinicians to supply to parents and their children that explain etiology and the process of treatment. Drs. Klass, Kafantaris and myself outline the research on the psychopharmacology of depression for this age group. We delineate guidelines for initiation of pharmacological therapy, note side effects and doses, and formulate the questions that remain about their action.

As editors, we were fortunate to collaborate with experts who were flexible enough to clarify research issues for clinicians, clinical issues for researchers, psychiatric dilemmas for pediatricians and pediatric dilemmas for mental health practitioners. Our goal has been to assist the practitioner on the frontline in the identification, understanding and treatment of childhood and adolescent depression.

The task of coordinating, editing and, at times, cajoling contributing authors can be insurmountable. Dr. Emily Klass, Co-Editor of this volume, made the journey less arduous and even enjoyable at times. I thank her for her perseverance, sense of humor and flexibility.

Our special thanks go to a wonderful staff of Vera Connolly and Patricia Reilly for their tireless efforts in helping to produce this book.

1 Developmental Issues in Childhood and Adolescent Depression

Jayne E. Schachter and Barbara A. Romano

Division of Child and Adolescent Psychiatry, Schneider Children's Hospital of Long Island Jewish Medical Center, New Hyde Park, NY 11042, USA

The practicing pediatrician is usually the first professional to whom parents turn when concerns regarding their children's emotional and behavioral functioning arise. Thus, the pediatrician needs to be well versed in differences between normal developmental phenomena and psychopathology in children. Depression, which was once thought to occur primarily in adulthood, is now generally recognized to present in childhood as well. While it is unusual for parents to report their child is depressed, they will often describe certain behaviors such as lethargy, somatic complaints, and social withdrawal which may be part of a depressive syndrome. In order to identify the problem, pediatricians need to be aware of how depression might appear at various stages in development because a particular behavior at one age may mean something quite different at another age. Research in the area is beginning to help us identify these differences but much remains to be learned.

The study of depression can be dated back to the time of Hippocrates, but the burgeoning of interest in the study of childhood depression is of relatively recent origin. To appreciate the infancy of this area, one need only look at a classic encyclopedic text, Child Psychiatry (Kanner, 1957: 770–777) and fail to find the term "childhood depression" listed in the index. The past 15–20 years has evidenced a growing body of knowledge marked by shifts in theoretical orientation.

The classic psychoanalytic view held that childhood depression could not exist because the necessary psychic structures, i.e. the superego, were not yet sufficiently developed (Rochlin, 1959: 299–315). The initial challenge to the psychoanalytic position came from those positing that depression in children was masked or expressed in depressive equivalents. The view holds that depressive symptoms are not directly expressed by children but must be inferred from other behaviors that mask the underlying depression (Glaser, 1968: 346; Toolan, 1962: 404). Proponents of this view believe that depressive symptomatology as seen clinically in the adult population is rarely seen in children. This perspective does not deny that depressive feelings are common but holds instead that the manifestation of these feelings by children is indirect. Some of the behaviors which have been identified as masking the underlying depression or that are depressive equivalents are hyperactivity, aggressiveness, temper tantrums (Toolan, 1962: 405), somatic complaints such as headaches, stomachaches, enuresis, encopresis (Cytryn and McKnew, 1974: 879–880; Sperling, 1978: 383–394), and school problems such as poor academic performance, truancy, and school phobia (Glaser, 1968: 347). The underlying depression is used to account for the above behaviors even in the absence of dysphoric mood. This perspective has not been widely accepted and numerous criticisms have attacked its logic. One of the major criticisms is that this view has no clinical value because the behaviors identified as masking depression cover the range of childhood psychopathologies (Carlson and Cantwell, 1980: 445; Kaslow and Rehm, 1983: 28) and thus no basis is provided for a differential diagnosis. For example, it is not clear if the hyperactive child is masking depression or is simply hyperactive.

Others have challenged the notion that an actual syndrome of childhood depression exists. Lefkowitz and Burton (1978: 716) argued that depressive features in children reflect a developmental phenomenon rather than a clear clinical syndrome and these dissipate with time. In a rebuttal, Costello (1980: 185–189) argued that while single symptoms of depression may be prevalent and transient in childhood, the syndrome of depression, a cluster of highly correlated symptoms, may not be. For instance, a symptom of depression such as eating disturbance may be prevalent and dissipate with time in six-year olds but the presence of eating disturbance in conjunction with dysphoric mood, anergia, and low self-esteem may not be as transient. Furthermore, even if the syndrome appears to be transient in childhood, it should still be clinically addressed because little is known about the effects of childhood psychopathology on later periods of development.

The consensus view currently held by those researching childhood depression is that depression in children can be diagnosed according to the criteria used in the diagnosis of adult depression. The current diagnostic system in use, DSM-III-R (1987), reflects this view in that there is no separate category for childhood depression. The criteria across ages include affective (dysphoria, weepiness, mood change, and anhedonia), cognitive (low self-esteem, hopelessness, and helplessness), vegetative (sleep and appetite disturbances) and motivational (anergia, decreased social interactions, and avoidance) symptoms with additional specific criteria for young children. Although this view acknowledges possible differences between childhood and adult depression, few studies have systematically investigated the differences.

Nevertheless, serious challenges to this position have been arising from developmental psychopathologists (e.g. Cicchetti and Schneider-Rosen, 1984: 6; Rutter, 1986: 3–30) whose perspective focuses on the continuities and discontinuities between normality and pathology as well as across time, i.e. from one stage of development to the next. As Garber (1984: 37) cogently asserts, if we apply this model to the study of depression, researchers first need to:

1) Determine whether the expression of depressive symptoms varies with development.
2) Identify additional age-appropriate symptoms and areas of dysfunction to include in the diagnostic process.

3) Assess the influence of children's cognitive, affective, and social competence and their physical maturation on the experience and the expression of depressive symptoms (p. 37).

The need to consider depressive symptomatology in relation to what is normal for a particular stage of development becomes quite apparent when we consider specific examples. For instance, frequent tearfulness might be one indication of depression in a 16-year old but would have a quite different meaning if we were instead evaluating a two-year old. Thus the prevalence of particular behaviors in normal children must be considered before attributing these to depression (Digdon and Gotlib, 1985: 165). For example, if poor appetite characterizes 33% of six-year olds (MacFarlane, Allen and Honzitz, 1954: 10), this behavior would not be a particularly significant indicator of vegetative symptoms of depression in assessing a child of that age.

In addition to influencing what we need to measure in assessing childhood depression, development mediates how we should proceed. Young children's limited ability to describe the emotions they are experiencing presents obvious difficulties in assessment.

Instruments have been developed for use with school-age children and have facilitated the study of childhood depression. These include self-report scales, parent, teacher, and clinician rating scales, peer nominations, and interviews (for detailed reviews see Kazdin, 1981: 358–375; Kovacs, 1981: 305–315). There has been increasing recognition of the ability of children to provide information regarding subjective phenomena (e.g. Herjanic, Herjanic, Brown, and Wheatt, 1975: 41–48) and in an area such as depression, where many of the symptoms are manifested intrapsychically, it would appear essential (Puig-Antich, Chambers and Tabrizi, 1983: 160–164). This position is strengthened by the findings that parents and teachers often do not notice depression in youngsters who report it on interview. Thus, self-rating scales such as the Children's Depression Inventory (CDI) (Kovacs 1987) and semi-structured interviews such as the Kiddie-SADS (Puig-Antich and Chambers 1978) have been the most widely used research instruments in the area.

However, developmental variables likely influence both the reporting and manifestations of depression. For example, self-report measures require children to endorse specific behaviors as characteristic of themselves but young children have difficulty distinguishing between sadness and anger (Borke, 1973: 104–106) and are more likely to deny experiencing sadness (Glasberg and Aboud, 1982: 200). In addition, children are unable to provide reliable information on duration of symptoms. Thus, such questions have been omitted from some self-report measures such as the CDI. Because information on symptom duration is diagnostically important, other sources of data are necessary.

Furthermore, because children's natural mood states are elevated as compared to that of adults, it may be more difficult to identify depressed mood in children (Digdon and Gotlib, 1985: 167). These mood states theoretically could manifest as neutral mood and yet be a deviation from normal exuberance. In addition, mood states in children are more likely to shift rapidly in response to environmental stimuli. Due to these difficulties in assessing depression in children, multiple sources of data are required, including child, parent, teacher, and even peer reports.

Keeping these general developmental issues in mind, we will review the state of knowledge regarding depression during four broad stages: infancy, preschool years, school-age, adolescence. We will then consider what is known about the continuity of depression across time. As will become apparent, the literature is fraught with many more questions than answers but hopefully the balance is shifting in favor of a better understanding of affective disorders in childhood.

INFANCY

While much controversy can be found in the literature on the existence of depression in infants, it is important for pediatricians to be aware that infants can present with depressive-like behaviors. Spitz (1946: 113–117) and Bowlby (1960: 89–110, 1980: 9–22) described infant reactions to maternal deprivation or separation in terms similar to the adult symptomatology of depression. Spitz's term, anaclitic depression, referred to the weepiness, withdrawal, apathy, weight loss, sleep disturbance, and developmental decrements observed in six to twelve-month old institutionalized children. Bowlby wrote of the observed sequence of protest – despair – detachment in toddlers, ages six months to four years, separated from maternal caretakers. However, it has been seriously questioned whether this should be regarded as a true form of depression or instead as a parallel to adult grief reactions. It is an understandable response to an actual loss of a loved caretaker and in most cases the infants rapidly recovered following return to the family. Furthermore, similar conditions in infancy can be produced by lack of cognitive stimulation, malnutrition, or organic deficiency diseases. In addition, this reaction obviously lacks the other components of the syndrome such as self-blame, guilt, and decreased self-esteem (Bemporad and Wilson, 1978: 334–336).

While Spitz's and Bowlby's positions stem from anecdotal case studies, Field (1985: 52–55) has demonstrated this pattern of reaction in a more controlled, observational study. She monitored the behavioral and physiological responses of infants and toddlers before, during, and after their mother's hospitalization for the birth of a sibling. While the mothers were hospitalized, and thus separated from their young children, the children were found to be in a state of agitation marked by increases in activity level, heart rate, fussiness, night waking, and nighttime crying. Upon the mother's return home, the children were found to be in a period of "depression" characterized by decreases in activity level, heart rate, active sleep, and positive affect. Parents also reported changes in eating and toileting, sleep disturbances, and increased clinging and aggressive behaviors. Therefore, at routine well-baby visits, pediatricians might hear such complaints from parents concerning older siblings. Even if such problems are not reported, it might be prudent for the pediatrician to inquire about these areas.

Whether or not we choose to consider these reactions "depression" in the sense of a depressive disorder as the term is utilized in older children and adults, it cannot be denied that these infants are experiencing negative affective changes which can be persistent and disabling. For the practicing pediatrician, the theoretical issues may be interesting but of less importance than the fact that infants can experience strong, negative emotional reactions akin to a depressive reaction. Whether or not such a phenomenon should be considered a true depressive disorder, it is nevertheless important to identify the problem and recommend steps toward remediation. A reasonable course of action might be for the pediatrician to initially discuss the problems with the parents and make practical suggestions, e.g. to spend more time with the older sibling. If the problems persist, referral to a child psychologist or psychiatrist would be appropriate.

Another issue of note is the relationship between maternal depression, particularly postpartum depression, and infant affective reactions. While a detailed discussion of this area is beyond the scope of this chapter, it is worthy of mention. Even in nonclinically depressed mothers, it has been suggested that infants' negative affective reactions may be related to the mother's state during this period, as she exhibits more depressed affect, less animation, and exhausted behavior (Field, 1985: 55).

PRESCHOOL YEARS

While much is known about affective and emotional development in the infant and preschool years, less is known about the syndrome of depression in this period as few systematic data are available. This lack of data is a result of researchers' questioning of depression as a true clinical entity.

Clinical observations of depression in preschoolers have been provided by various investigators (Poznanski and Zrull, 1970: 8–15; Ushakov and Girich, 1972: 510–516; Philips, 1979: 512–513; and Herzog and Rathbun, 1982: 115–116). Ossofsky (1974: 20–25) described depressed preschoolers as manifesting mood disturbance (irritability, sadness, and excessive crying), vegetative disturbance (insomnia, decreased appetite) and behavior disturbance (hyperactivity, temper tantrums, absence of normal play). In addition, Ushakov and Girich (1972: 510–515) reported that in their sample of 12 depressed preschoolers, no specific clinical picture was evident. While the children were frequently tearful and appeared sad, symptoms such as motivation to engage in play and psychomotor behaviors appeared to be less stable. Also, in contrast to school-age children, anxiety was a more common feature. Verbalizations of depressed mood and suicidal ideation were not evident. However, most agree that although these symptoms may be present, they are not common among young children.

Researchers have used grief reactions as a model for studying depression. With regard to preschoolers, it has been found that their grief reactions are milder and of shorter duration than in older children. Therefore, some have suggested that depressive reactions in preschoolers may follow this same pattern. Further research is warranted to examine whether the grief reactions model is appropriate for the study of depression in preschoolers.

In an attempt to explain the instability of symptoms in this developmental period, Bemporad and Wilson (1978: 337–338) utilized Piagetian concepts of cognition in the preoperational stage. More specifically, preschoolers have difficulties generalizing from one situation to another and lack understanding of past and future. As an example, a symptom such as hopelessness cannot be experienced by preschoolers because they live primarily in the present. A feeling of hopelessness requires the ability to relate the past to the present and project from the present into the future.

Kashani and Ray (1983: 233–238) were among the first to attempt to systematically investigate the frequency of depressive symptoms and major depressive disorder among a nonclinical population of preschoolers. In their sample of 241 two and a half to six-year old children, parent questionnaires were completed and analyzed utilizing DSM-III criteria. Individual depressive symptoms such as sleep disturbance, appetite disturbance, and agitation or hyperactivity were found while anhedonia and feelings of worthlessness did not occur at all in this group. Furthermore, no case of major depressive disorder was documented. The fact that individual symptoms were not uncommon is not surprising since these behaviors are known to occur frequently at this age. However, this study is quite limited by its unrepresentative sample and single data source, and the authors warn against considering these definitive results on the rates of depression in a normal population of preschoolers.

Some recent data are also available on the incidence and phenomenology of depression in a clinically referred population of preschoolers. Kashani and Carlson (1987: 348–350) looked at a sample of 1000 young children consecutively referred to a child development unit for a variety of reasons including developmental delays as well as emotional and behavior problems. Parent and child interviews were conducted, comprehensive testing was completed, and observations of parent-child interaction were done. Only nine of the children were diagnosed with a major depressive disorder. Thus, even in a clinical population, depression as we currently define and recognize it appears to be uncommon among preschoolers but can be present. Those who were depressed were distinguishable from matched subjects by sadness, appetite loss, sleep changes, fatigue, and somatic complaints. While psychomotor agitation and distractibility were frequently found, these were not distinguishing characteristics as they occurred at an even higher rate in the psychiatric control group. Of particular interest was the finding that 11 of the depressed children had a history of abuse or neglect and lived in broken homes as compared to a much smaller percent of the control group. Furthermore, noting the relatively high rate of somatic complaints, the authors suggest that younger children may be more likely to express their discomfort with physical symptoms. Thus pediatricians should be alerted to young children presenting with frequent, ambiguous complaints and consider depression in their differential diagnosis.

SCHOOL-AGED YEARS

The bulk of the research on childhood depression has focused on the school-aged population. As previously discussed, the consensus is that depression in this period parallels depression in the adult population. While most researchers as well as the

DSM-III-R acknowledge age-specific differences, few studies have directly addressed the developmental issues. In selecting studies for discussion here, we have chosen those which have attempted to do so.

In one attempt to compare symptom patterns across development, Carlson and Kashani (1988: 1222–1225) compared the frequency of depressive symptoms in three studies of four clinic referred age groups: preschoolers, prepubertal children, adolescents and adults. Although they acknowledge the difficulties in comparing across studies, the authors chose the particular studies on the basis of their similarity in methodology. Some symptoms which increased with age included anhedonia, diurnal variation and psychomotor retardation. Those which decreased with age included depressed appearance and somatic complaints. Fatigue, agitation and anorexia were less frequent among prepubertal children and adolescents than they were in the preschool and adult groups. Symptoms such as depressed mood, diminished ability to concentrate, sleep disturbance, and suicidal ideation were consistent across the life span measured.

While Carlson and Kashani looked across the life span, some studies have attempted to examine developmental changes within the prepubertal period. For example, three patterns of depression were identified in a group of six to thirteen year olds (McConville, Boag and Purohit, 1973: 133–138). Symptoms in the six to eight year old group were characterized as the "affectual" type and included dysphoric mood and feelings of loneliness, helplessness and loss. The symptoms in the eight to ten year old group were described as the "self-esteem" type. These included hopelessness and negative self-esteem. The symptomatology in the ten to thirteen year old group was characterized as the "guilt" type.

It has been suggested that the shift from the affectual type to the self-esteem type is due to the ability of the older groups to verbalize their feelings and thoughts about themselves and is a function of their developing cognitive structures. More specifically, children at this point in development are beginning to perceive intentionality in their own behavior as well as in the behavior of others. They are also beginning to misattribute blame which in depressed children, might lead to unwarranted self-blame and guilt (McConville *et al*, 1973: 133–138; Bemporad and Wilson, 1978: 338–339).

On the other hand, young children do not seem to have the cognitive capacity to engage in self denigration by internalizing failure experiences. In a study of the effects of failure on the self-evaluations of children six to eleven years old (Ruble, Parsons and Ross, 1976: 991–996), it was found that failure feedback affected the self-evaluations of the older children (ages eight to eleven) but not the younger children. Additionally, children were given information on the ease with which others completed the task. This affected the self evaluations of the older but not the younger children, suggesting that young children may not engage in self denigration since they are not likely to evaluate themselves negatively (Glasberg and Aboud, 1980: 200). Furthermore, they (Glasberg and Aboud, 1980: 200) found that although both kindergarten and second grade children reported disliking a sad other, only second grade children were able to extend this negative evaluation to themselves. Kindergarten children were unable to evaluate themselves as negatively as they did a sad other. Although young school-age children are cognitively unable to engage in self-denigration, they can exhibit dysphoric mood. It was found (McConville *et al*, 1973: 133–138) that six to eight year old children were able to behaviorally express long periods of sadness but without the accompanying prolonged beliefs that they were bad or inferior. In this period, sadness can be sustained and is usually in response to an external situation. Furthermore, it is seen in overt rather than verbal behavior (Bemporad and Wilson, 1978: 341). Two more recent studies, (Garber, 1984: 29–57, Kovacs and Paulauskas, 1984: 62–77), attempted to overcome the problems of these earlier studies in that they utilized more well-defined criteria and standardized assessment methods. However, their findings are quite contradictory. In Garber's study of seven to thirteen year old clinic-referred females, there was an increase in frequency of depressive syndrome and of individual depressive symptoms. Those symptoms that were found to increase with age were appetite disturbances, hyperactivity, pervasive loss of interest, capacity to have fun, guilt, hopelessness, irritability, fatigue, problems at school, low self-esteem, difficulty concentrating, and depressed feelings. Those symptoms which decreased with age (among the depressed children only) were crying and morbid ideation.

While Garber's results are consistent with the findings of previous studies and with that predicted by developmental changes in cognitive and socioemotional capacities, Kovacs and Paulauska's were contradictory and countertheoretical. For example, in direct opposition to earlier findings, behavior problems and somatic complaints were more evident among the older children in their sample. With regard to other depressive symptoms, the developmental findings were inconsistent, varying with the particular statistical method employed. Furthermore, in contrast to developmental expectations, younger children were found to have the more chronic depressions.

ADOLESCENCE

Unlike earlier points in development, depressive symptoms in adolescence are typically more similar to that in adulthood. Ushakov and Girich (1972: 510–515) found that among 14 to 17 year old depressives, genuine melancholy, psychomotor retardation, difficulty concentrating, and a significant rate of suicidal ideation and attempts were observed. As compared to younger children, crying was less frequent. However, Friedman, Hurt, Clarkin and Corn (1983: 39) found that adolescents experience less self-pity than adults.

In other studies comparing child and adolescent depressives, the frequency and severity of hypersomnia, hopelessness, anhedonia, weight changes, and drug and alcohol use were greater among adolescents than among children (Mitchell, McCauley, Burke and Moss, 1988: 14–18; Ryan, Puig-Antich, Ambrosini, Robinovich, Robinson, Nelson, Iyengar, and Twomey, 1987: 854–861). Furthermore, depressed adolescents with coexisting disorders (eg. anxiety and conduct problems) had higher mean depression severity scores than those adolescents who suffered from depression alone (Mitchel *et al*, 1988: 17). This finding was more significant for adolescents than for children. Another difference found between child and adolescent depressives was the less frequent self-report of anxiety symptoms by adolescents.

Another significant finding differentiating childhood and adolescent depression is the shift in gender differences. Studies of school-age children have found either a slightly greater incidence of depressed males than females or an even distribution. In adolescence, as in adulthood, however, there is a greater incidence of depression in females than in males (Rutter, 1986: 10–14). Similarly, there is a higher incidence of reported depression among adolescents than there is in childhood. For example, in the Isle of Wight study, approximately thirteen percent of ten to eleven year old children showed dysphoric mood, with a smaller percent showing other depressive symptoms, as opposed to forty percent of the children when reassessed at fourteen to fifteen years of age (Rutter and Hemming, 1981: 203–204).

In Carlson and Kashani's comparison of depression across four age groups, suicidal ideation appeared to be consistent. However, suicidal attempts and successful suicides evidence different patterns across development, with adolescence standing out as a particularly vulnerable period. As reported by Rutter (1986: 15–16), United States statistics show that suicide prior to puberty is relatively rare with the rate rising rapidly during midteens and continuing to rise through adulthood. More recently, however, the rates of suicide for the elderly have declined somewhat with a steady increase in adolescence and young adulthood. However, attempted suicide demonstrates a different pattern. It peaks in the midteen years and decreases in adulthood.

In contrast, in a relatively recent study comparing child and adolescent depressives, there was no difference found in the rate of suicidal attempts, nor in the severity of suicidal ideation or seriousness of suicidal intent (Ryan *et al*, 1987: 857). There was a difference in the lethality of the method chosen. Adolescents more often chose gunshots or overdoses as a method to commit suicide.

While adolescent depression is similar to adult depression in many aspects, developmental issues may cloud the diagnostic process. As Garber (1984: 41–42) points out, adolescence is typically a time of emotional turmoil and mood fluctuations as a result of peer pressure, increasing expectations for adult behavior, and physiological changes. The difficult task of the diagnostician is to distinguish between the normal behavior of adolescents and more pathological states. Therefore, he or she must look beyond the mere presence of symptoms and rely more heavily upon duration, severity, and clustering of symptoms than one might at other points in development (Garber, 1984: 41–42).

CONTINUITIES AND DISCONTINUITIES

As mentioned earlier, a developmental model must consider the continuities and discontinuities in psychopathology over time. For example, is a depressed eight year old child likely to be depressed as an adult, even if the specific symptom pattern may change? Or instead, does depression at one stage portend a different form of psychopathology at a later stage? A third possibility is a discontinuity between child and adult disorder so that a depressed child is no more likely to become a depressed adult than is any other child and a depressed adult is unlikely to have a history of childhood depression.

Several studies have provided support for at least short-term stability of depressive symptoms in children. A study (Tesiny and Lefkowitz, 1982: 779) using peer nominations, self-ratings, and teacher ratings, found relatively high stability in depressive symptomatology over a six month period. Poznanski, Krahenbuhl, and Zrull (1976: 492–494) reevaluated ten children who had been diagnosed as depressed an average of six and half years earlier and they found 50 percent to be clinically depressed. Unfortunately, the study lacked methodological rigor, making conclusions extremely tentative, at best. It has been found (Kovacs *et al*, 1984: 645–649) that children who have a depressive syndrome such as major depression or dysthymia are likely to have continuous recurrent bouts with depression.

Regarding the relationship between depression in childhood and adulthood, however, knowledge is more limited. In a review of four retrospective studies (Orvaschel, Weissman, and Kidd, 1980: 9–10), it was concluded that while adult depressive patients were likely to have suffered from family discord and parental abuse, rejection, and inattention, there was no unique clinical picture in childhood.

Robins (1979: 486–510) reviewed follow-up and follow-back studies of childhood psychopathology but these rarely had depression as their focus and preceded the development of consistent diagnostic criteria. Generalizing from the available follow-up data, Robins concluded that neurotic symptoms in childhood, as opposed to psychosis and conduct disorders, were associated with good outcome. Summarizing follow-back studies, he reported that adults with depressive disorders were rarely known to clinics as children. However, among those depressed and anxious adults who were known to clinics as children, symptoms of depression, anxiety and somatic complaints were common in their earlier records.

More recently, it was also found that adult depression was usually not preceded by any kind of psychological disorder in childhood (Zeitlin, 1986: 59–64). Yet of those depressed children who later had psychological disorders as adults, most showed depression as part of their disorder. In addition, Zeitlin found this continuity to be stronger for depression than for any other syndromes, with the exception of obsessive-compulsive phenomena.

While these studies are inconclusive in demonstrating a strong, predictive relationship between childhood and adult depression, there is suggestion that they are not independent clinical phenomena. At this point in our knowledge, the specific nature of the relationship remains to be clarified.

CONCLUSION

A recap of the findings of the extant studies might prove useful by highlighting developmental aspects for the practitioner. There is still much controversy regarding whether or not infants can experience a "true" depression. What is clear is that infants can experience negative affective changes. This may be a reaction to a disturbing experience such as the loss, even the temporary loss, of a primary caretaker, or the negative affective changes in the caretaker.

In the preschool years, the depressive syndrome is still fairly uncommon. However, the manifestation of depressive symptoms in this age period does involve mood, vegetative, and behavioral disturbances. In particular, they are more likely to present with somatic complaints and anxiety. Preschoolers do not typically verbalize feelings of depression and thus, it must be assessed primarily from behavioral observations.

In general, it is not until the school-age years that children begin to verbalize feelings of depression. However, even within this period of development, there are differences with age. It is not until the mid school-age years that children express feelings of self-denigration or guilt. While younger school-aged children can recognize sadness in others, they are too cognitively immature to generalize this evaluation to themselves.

As children mature cognitively, socially, and physiologically into adolescence, depressive symptoms are more typical of that seen in adults. However, an important point to consider is the differentiation between "normal" adolescent turmoil and psychopathology. Thus, more emphasis is placed on duration, severity, and combination of symptoms when diagnosing depression in this age group.

This review may have raised more questions than it has answered. We are still far from fully understanding how the syndrome of depression is influenced by developmental progression. One reason for this is our somewhat limited knowledge base of normal emotional development across the life span. Fortunately, developmental psychopathologists have argued strongly against the assumption that a downward extension of the adult criteria of depression is appropriate for use with children. As we have seen in our review of the manifestation of depressive symptoms across four broad age groups, development certainly impacts on the expression, or even presence, of certain symptoms. Unfortunately, due to the difficulties in conducting developmental research, there is a paucity of systematic controlled studies in this area. However, with increasing methodological rigor and a wider acceptance of the developmental psychopathologic model, there is hope that the tide is changing.

References

American Psychiatric Association. (1987) Diagnostic and statistical manual of mental disorders (3rd Ed.-Revised). Washington, D.C.: American Psychiatric Association.

Bemporad, J.R. and Wilson, A. (1978) A developmental approach to depression in childhood and adolescence. *Journal of the American Academy of Psychoanalysis*, **6**, 325–352.

Borke, J. (1973) The development of empathy in Chinese and American children between three and six years of age. *Developmental Psychology*, **9**, 102–108.

Bowlby, J. (1960) Separation anxiety. *International Journal of Psychoanalysis*, **41**, 89–113.

Bowlby, J. (1980) Attachment and loss, (vol. III): Loss, sadness and depression. New York: Basic Books.

Carlson, G.A. and Cantwell, D.P. (1980) Unmasking masked depression in children and adolescents. *Journal of the American Academy of Child Psychiatry*, **21**, 361–386.

Carlson, G.A. and Kashani, J.H. (1988) Phenomonology of major depression from childhood through adulthood: Analysis of three studies. *American Journal of Psychiatry*, **145**, 1222–1225.

Cicchetti, D. and Schneider-Rosen, K. (1984) Toward a transactional model of childhood depression,

(eds. D. Cicchetti and K. Schneider-Rosen, Childhood depression: New directions for child development, (no. 26), San Francisco: Jossey-Bass.
Costello, C. G. (1980) Childhood depression: Three basic but questionable assumptions in the Lefkowitz and Burton critique. *Psychological Bulletin*, **87**, 185–190.
Cytryn, L. and McKnew, D. H. (1974) Factors influencing the changing clinical expression of depressive process in children. *American Journal of Psychiatry*, **13**, 879–881.
Didgon N. and Gotlib, I. H. (1985) Developmental considerations in the study of childhood depression. *Developmental Review*, **5**, 162–199.
Field, T. (1986) Models for reactive and chronic depression in infancy, (eds. E. Z. Tronick and T. Fields), Maternal Depression and Infant Disturbance, San Francisco: Jossey-Bass.
Friedman, R. C., Hurt, S. W., Clarkin, J. F. and Corn, R. (1983) Primary and secondary affective disorders in adolescents and young adults. Acta Psychiatrica Scandinavica, **67**, 226–235.
Garber, J. (1984) The developmental progression of depression in female children, (eds. D. Cicchetti and K. Schneider-Rosen), Childhood Depression: New Directions for Child Development, (no. 26). San Francisco: Jossey-Bass.
Glasberg, R. and Aboud, F. (1981) A developmental perspective on the study of depression: Children's evaluative reactions to sadness. *Developmental Psychology*, **17**, 195–202.
Glaser, K. (1968) Masked depression in children and adolescents. *American Journal of Psychotherapy*, **21**, 565–574.
Herjanic, B., Herjanic, M., Brown, F. and Wheatt, T. (1975) Are children reliable reporters? *Journal of the Association of Child Psychologists*, **3**, 41–48.
Herzog, D. B. and Rathbun, J. M. (1982) Childhood depression: Developmental considerations. *American Journal of the Disordered Child*, **138**, 115–120.
Kanner, L. (1957) Child Psychiatry, Springfield, IL: Charles C. Thomas.
Kashani, J. H. and Carlson, G. A. (1987) Seriously depressed preschoolers. *American Journal of Psychiatry*, **144**, 348–350.
Kashani, J. H. and Ray, J. S. (1983) Depressive related symptoms among preschool-age children. *Child Psychiatry and Human Development*, **13**, 233–238.
Kaslow, N. J. and Rehm, L. P. (1983) Childhood depression, (eds. R. J. Morris and T. R. Kratochwill), The practice of child therapy: A textbook of methods, New York: Pergamon Press.
Kazdin, A. (1981) Assessment techniques for childhood depression: A critical appraisal. *Journal of the American Academy of Child Psychiatry*, **20**, 358–375.
Kovacs, M. (1978) Children's Depression Inventory (CDI). Unpublished manuscript, University of Pittsburgh.
Kovacs, M. (1981) Rating scales to assess depression in school-age children. *Acta Paedopsychiatrica*, **46**, 305–315.
Kovacs, M., Feinberg, T. L. Crouse-Novak, M. A., Paulauskas, S. L., Pollack, M. and Finkelstein, R. (1984) Depressive disorders in childhood: A longitudinal study of the risk for subsequent major depression. *Archives of General Psychiatry*, **41**, 643–649.
Kovacs, M. and Paulauskas, S. L. (1984) Developmental stage and the expression of depressive disorders in children: An empirical analysis. (eds. D. Cicchetti and K. Schneider-Rosen), Childhood Depression: New Directions for Child Development, San Francisco: Jossey-Bass.
Lefkowitz, M. M. and Burton, N. (1978) Childhood depression. *Psychological Bulletin*, **85**, 716–726.
MacFarlane, J. W., Allen, L. and Honzitz, M. P. (1954) A developmental study of the behavioral problems of normal children between twenty-one months and fourteen years, Berkeley: University of California Press.
McConville, B. J., Boag, L. C. and Purohit, A. P. (1973) Three types of childhood depression. *Canadian Psychiatric Association Journal*. **18**, 133–138.
Mitchell, J. R., McCauley, E., Burke, P. M. and Moss, S. J. (1988) Phenomenology of depression in children and adolescents. Journal of the American Academy of Child and Adolescent Psychiatry, **27**, 12–20.
Orvaschel, H., Weissman, M. M. and Kidd, K. K. (1980) Children and depression: The children of depressed parents; the childhood of depressed patients; depression in children. *Journal of Affective Disorders*, **2**, 1–16.
Ossofsky, H. J. (1974) Endogenous depression in infancy and childhood. *Comprehensive Psychiatry*, **15**, 19–25.
Philips, I. (1979) Childhood depression: Interpersonal interactions and depressive phenomenon. *American Journal of Psychiatry*, **136**, 511–515.
Poznanski, E. O., Krahenbuhl, V. and Zrull, J. (1976) Childhood depression: A longitudinal perspective. *Journal of the American Academy of Child Psychiatry*. **15**, 491–501.

Poznanski, E. and Zrull, J.P. (1970) Childhood depression: Clinical characteristics of overtly depressed children. *Achives of General Psychiatry*, **23**, 8-15.

Puig-Antich, J. and Chambers, W. (1978) Schedule of affective disorders and schizophrenia for school-age children. Unpublished manuscript, New York State Psychiatric Institute and Columbia University, N.Y.

Puig-Antich, J., Chambers, W. and Tabrizi, M. (1983) The clinical assessment of current depressive episoded in children and adolescents: Interview with parents and children, eds. D. Cantwell and G. Carlson, Affective disorders in childhood and adolescence: An update, New York: Spectrum Press.

Robins, L.N. (1979) Follow-up studies, eds. H. Quay and J. Werry, Psychopathological disorders of childhood, New York: Wiley.

Rochlin, G. (1959) The loss complex. *Journal of the American Psychoanalytic Association*, **7**, 299-316.

Ruble, D.N., Parsons, J.E. and Ross, J. (1976) Self-evaluations of children in an achievement setting. *Child Development*, **47**, 990-997.

Rutter, M. (1986) The developmental psychopathology of depression: Issues and perspectives, eds. M. Rutter, C.E. Izard, and P.B. Read, Depression in young people: Developmental and clinical prespective, NY: Guilford.

Rutter, M. and Hemming, M. (1981) Individual items of deviant behavior: the prevalence and clinical significance. Education, Health and Behavior, Huntington, NY: Krieger

Ryan, N.D., Puig-Antich, J., Ambrosini, P., Rabinovich, H., Robinson, D., Nelson, B., Iyengar, S. and Twomey, J. (1987) The clinical picture of major depression in children and adolescents. Archives of General Psychiatry, **44**, 854-861.

Seligman, M.E.P., Peterson, C., Kaslow, N.J., Tannenbaum, R.L., Alloy., L.B. and Abramson, L.Y. (1984) Attributional style and depressive symptoms among children. *Journal of Abnormal Psychology*, **93**, 235-238.

Sperling, M. (1973) The Major Neuroses and Behavior Disorders in Children. NY: Aronson.

Spitz, R. (1946) Anaclitic depression. *Psychoanalytic Study of the Child*, **2**, 113-117.

Tesiny, E.P. and Lefkowitz, M.M. (1982) Childhood depression: A six month follow-up study. *Journal of Consulting and Clinical Psychology*, **50**, 778-780.

Toolan, J.M. (1962) Depression in children and adolescents. *American Journal of Orthopsychiatry*, **32**, 404-414.

Ushakov, G.K. and Girich, Y.P. (1972) Special features of psychogenic depressions in children and adolescents, ed. A. Annell, Depressive states in childhood and adolescence, Stockholm: Almquist and Wiksell.

Zeitlin, H. (1986) The natural history of psychiatric disorder in children, Institute of Psychiatry Maudsley Monograph, London: Oxford University Press.

2 Cognitive and Behavioral Theories of Depression

Anita Gurian

Division of Child and Adolescent Psychiatry, Schneider Children's Hospital of Long Island Jewish Medical Center, New Hyde Park, NY 11042, USA

WHY DO CHILDREN GET DEPRESSED? WHAT DO CHILDREN HAVE TO BE SAD ABOUT?

Thomas Mann, in his short story *Disorder and Early Sorrow* describes Ellie: "the child sitting all pale among her pillows, sobbing and weeping more bitterly than he has ever seen her sob and weep in her life. Her lovely little hands lie on the coverlet in front of her, the nightgown with its narrow lace border has slipped down from her shoulder—such a thin, birdlike little shoulder . . . her head is on one side, with the eyes rolled up to the corner between wall and ceiling above her head. For there she seems to envisage the anguish of her heart . . . her head wobbles as her body is shaken with the violence of her sobs. Her eyes rain down tears. The bow-shaped lips are parted . . . and from them issue long, low wails that . . . rise from the deep extremity of her heart . . ."

Charles Dickens, in *Dombey and Son*: "such spirits as he had in the outset, Paul soon lost . . . but he retained all that was strange, and old . . . he grew more thoughtful and reserved every day . . . he loved to be alone; and liked nothing so well as wandering about the house by himself, or sitting on the stairs, listening to the great clock in the hall. . . . The solitary child lived on, surrounded by this arabesque work of his amusing fancy, and no one understood him. Mrs. Blimber thought him 'odd', and sometimes the servants said among themselves that Dombey 'moped'; but that was all."

Writers have given us accurate and poignant descriptions of children suffering with depressed feelings. However, only recently has there been general agreement in the mental health field that childhood depression, with a set of symptoms constituting a clinical syndrome, does in fact exist. Both parents and professionals, perhaps in an effort to spare their children unhappiness as well as to sustain their own notion that childhood is happy and carefree, seem to pretend that the dark side of human nature does not exist in children.

Research on childhood depression has proliferated during the past 15 years, and numerous studies have expanded our knowledge, but questions remain and the debate continues. Is childhood depression similar to or different from adult depression? Can we diagnose depression in children by the same standards we use for adults? Do depressed children become depressed adults? Is all depression the same? What causes depression in children? Why are some children vulnerable to depression while others, in similar circumstances, cope more adaptively? Despite the absence of definitive answers there is agreement that depression is multidimensional and that all types of depression do not have the same causes or risk factors. This chapter focuses on theories of depression in children: cognitive, behavioral, and psychosocial.

Cognitive theories

Cognitive models of depression are based on the notion that depression is not caused by bad or unfavorable events, but rather by negative thoughts or cognitions in explaining the bad events, the habitual ways we explain trouble to ourselves.

Cognitive theories include the 1) *cognitive distortion model* (Beck, 1967; Kovacs and Beck, 1977) and 2) *learned helplessness model* (Seligman, 1974; Seligman, Peterson, Kaslow, Alloy, and Abramson, 1978), both of which share a common conceptual framework. When applied to children, these theories are most applicable from the age of eight on. By the late elementary school years, children are generally capable of the self-reflection and the causal reasoning which are involved in cognitive theories.

Cognitive distortion model—feelings follow thoughts

Originally formulated in relation to adult depression, studies of children have also provided support for this model. Cognitive style, according to Beck, is rooted in unfavorable life experiences, which eventually result in a tendency to overreact to events, to notice only the unpleasant things, to make pessimistic generalizations about the future. The depressed child exaggerates or misinterprets events, ("Everybody at this party hates me") sees things out of context, ("Suzanne didn't call; my life is awful") distorts experience to confirm his negative view of himself, the world and the future. ("All the other kids got A in chemistry; I'll never be able to learn chemistry".)

The thoughts by which depressed persons interpret their experiences contain elements known as the "cognitive triad".

1) "I am worthless"—I believe I'm deficient and unworthy.

2) "I can't do anything about it"—I believe there is little I can do to change my situation.

3) "It will always be this way"—I believe that things won't improve in the future.

Depressed persons' language makes excessive use of words such as "always, never, must, should." Examples are:

"I must study every day." "I should be able to swim 15 laps." "If I'm not always right, I'm a failure." "I never get anything right."

Any seeming loss, rejection, or disappointment can activate this thought pattern and set off a cycle of distorted thoughts about oneself, the world, and the future, as well as withdrawal and sadness.

This letter was written to a newspaper advice columnist by an eleven-year-old and signed, "Cindy, Sixth Grade Failure."

"I have a huge problem. No matter what I do, I always seem to fail. At school I got an F in science, but it wasn't my fault. I studied, and I thought I understood about earth science, but I guess it's really too hard for me, and I just can't get it.

When I got my report card, my father was really mad. I tried to tell my parents that I really studied, but they didn't believe me. They think I just don't do the work. My brother and sister never listen to me either. I cry a lot. I know it will always be like this; I'll get failing marks and nobody will believe me. I cry all night. I know I'll always be a failure."

Cindy, in fifth grade, has the hallmarks of the "cognitive triad". She exaggerates negative events, views her failure in earth science as typical of her lack of ability, feels nobody values her, and that she'll always be in the same predicament. Feelings of worthlessness, self-rejection, defeatism, and hopelessness characterize her reactions.

Learned helplessness model—giving up

This model is based on the premise that the way we explain things to ourselves about what happens to us affects our ability to cope and renders us vulnerable to depression. Originating in work with animals, the learned helplessness model has spurred much research on depression in humans.

In animal experimental work about 25 years ago (Overmier and Seligman, 1967), dogs were first subjected to inescapable shock situations; they were later placed in shock situations that they could easily escape simply by jumping a simple barrier. However, the dogs rarely tried to escape; they just passively endured shock after shock without a whimper, and even if they did escape once or twice, they did not learn from the experience. This cluster of deficits in motivation, learning, and emotional reactions was described as *learned helplessness* (Maier, Seligman and Solomon, 1969). It was not the shock itself that interfered with the animals' response, but the expectation that they would have no control over it. The dogs had learned to be helpless.

Seligman thought the animals' responses might be a model of human depression, and suggested parallels between helplessness and depression (Seligman, 1974, 1975). Helpless and non-helpless children develop different styles of dealing with problems. A helpless child sees problems as insurmountable; she feels ineffective and unable to influence the events in her life. She does not see a connection between what she does and what happens to her, either good or bad. When something bad does happen, this gives her further evidence that her efforts are useless. Therefore she learns to expect failure no matter what she does. And when she does meet with success, she attributes it to luck or other external causes.

Helpless and non-helpless children cope with failure in different ways. The non-helpless child tries harder. He escalates his efforts and devises alternative strategies for tackling a problem. The helpless child retreats. He becomes passive, demoralized, and essentially incompetent. He punishes himself for failures rather than rewarding himself for success.

Explanatory style

Does the helpless pattern necessarily result in depression? Only for some. Several factors make the difference. One factor is the "attribution" or explanation the child makes to himself about the events—how the child accounts for the causes of bad events—his explanatory style.

According to learned helplessness theory, three dimensions are critical in an explanatory style that predisposes an individual to depression: (Seligman, Kaslow, Alloy and Abramson, 1978)

1) Internal attributions: Bad events are believed to be due to characteristic within the individual, such as worthlessness, incompetence, etc; self-esteem decreases as helplessness increases.

"I can't possibly pass this test; I'm just too dumb." "The teacher doesn't like me because I can't spell." "The other kids are a million times smarter than I am."

2) Stable attributions: Bad events are attributed to facts that persist over time; helplessness is expected to be permanent, so nothing one does can change it. The more stable the attribution, the more chronic the helplessness.

"I know I'll always be a failure." "If the teacher calls on me, I'll be sure to screw up."

3) Global attributions: Bad events are attributed to causes that are present in a variety of situations, rather than in a specific situation. Helplessness is predicted to be pervasive. For example: lack of intelligence is more global than a specific lack of ability in math. The more global the attribution, the more the helplessness is apt to be generalized. The helpless person expects it to seep in everywhere.

"I'm not good at anything." "I'll never know enough to get into college." "Tests in all my subjects bug me."

To the degree that a child attributes bad events to *internal, stable, and global causes,* that child is increasingly likely to be helpless and depressed when a bad event does occur (Abramson, Seligman and Teasdale, 1978). On the other hand, children who explain bad events in terms of *external, unstable, and specific* causes are not likely to become depressed. Numerous studies have shown a correlation between negative explanatory style and depressive symptoms in children, suggesting that this style is associated with depression. The strongest research support has been for the internal attribution concept (for review see Peterson and Seligman, 1984). Criticisms have also been raised. Coyne and Gotlib (1983), reviewing the research on both the cognitive distortion and the learned helplessness models, conclude that neither model has an adequate empirical base and that neither explains the recovery of depressed persons. They believe that negative self-reports would be better understood in relation to their environmental antecedents and consequences.

Nevertheless clinicians have seen many children whose experiences fit the pattern of learned helplessness:

Eight-year-old Matt, an only child, blamed himself for his parents' divorce. He believed his parents split up because he was bad. He said he tried to be good, which meant that he didn't wake in the morning and kept the television sound low, but his parents separated anyway, confirming his feeling that he was really bad and couldn't do anything about it even though he had tried. This simple, negative and defeatist attitude spread to other situations. "When I start feeling bad about something, I know I can't do anything about it," he said. Matt daydreamed in school and his work suffered. His failure offered further confirmation of his worthlessness and inability to succeed in anything. His appetite declined, he became listless and refused to participate in team sports, which he had previously enjoyed, and these factors brought him to the attention of his pediatrician.

Measuring explanatory style

One measure of children's explanatory or attributional style used in numerous studies is the Kastan Revised Children's Attributional Style Questionnaire (KASTAN-R-CASQ, Kaslow, Tanenbaum, and Seligman, 1978). Children are given a possible situation and asked to choose the reason for the situation that seems most true. Some typical situations which tap internal/external, stable/unstable, or global/specific explanations follow.

Your pet gets run over by a car.
A. I don't take good care of my pets. (Internal)
B. Drivers are not careful enough. (External)

Your friend tells you that you look nice.
A. My friend likes the way I looked that day. (Specific)
B. My friend usually likes the way I look. (Global)

A person steals money from you.
A. That person is dishonest. (Specific)
B. People are dishonest. (Global)

You do a project with a group of kids and it turns out badly.
A. I don't work well with people in this group. (Unstable)
B. I never work well with a group. (Stable)

These types of questionnaires have been criticized because the situations are hypothetical. Nevertheless, studies which have looked at the effects of children's negative explanatory style have been informative. Children with this style are especially vulnerable to a number of difficulties. Included are passivity, cognitive deficits, sadness, low self-esteem, lack of self-control, lack of assertiveness and competitiveness. In solving interpersonal problems, they take more time, make more errors, and are less efficient than other children (Mullins, Siegel and Hodges, 1984; Schwartz, Friedman and Lindsay, 1982).

Explanatory style and school achievement

Helpless children may also have problems in academic achievement behaviors; they tend to overestimate failure and underestimate success (Dweck, 1975; Dweck and Repucci, 1973). Studies have shown that the way children explained their performance to themselves influenced whether they gave up or persisted. The spontaneous remarks made by helpless children illustrate their negative explanatory style: "How many more problems are there? I never do well when I'm timed," etc. The comments of nonhelpless children were quite different: "I like anagrams because they're challenging; It's easy once you get the pattern; I'm really smart" (Dweck and Licht, 1980).

Children can learn a negative explanatory style from their parents, particularly the mother (Seligman and Peterson, 1984). When mother and child process information in the same negative style, they create a repetitive interpersonal cycle. The age of the child influences the degree to which the child is affected by the mother's explanatory style, with the preschool age being the most vulnerable.

Sex differences

Female Child A: I guess I'm not smart enough to learn square roots.
Male Child B: I just wasn't paying attention when the teacher explained square roots.

Girls in the upper elementary grades are more likely than boys to show helpless explanatory styles, and they're more likely than boys to make internal and stable explanations for their failures. In one study, girls' and boys' problem-solving strategies were observed (Dweck and Bush, 1976). The girls blamed their own poor ability when they failed. If they succeeded, they attributed it to chance and didn't expect success to continue. Boys, on the other hand, blamed failure on external factors such as bad luck, an unfair test, not having been taught, etc.

One reason for this difference may be that teachers model explanatory style. They respond differently to boys and girls. When elementary school teachers criticize children they use different terms or explanations. In one study 45% of the teachers' negative criticism of boys focused on conduct or other *nonintellectual* aspects of their work, such as lack of neatness, incorrect margins, or insufficient effort. For example: "Robert, you can do it if you try harder with your long division problems" (Dweck and Licht, 1980). In the same study, with girls, almost 90% of the negative feedback to girls related to the *intellectual* quality of their work ("You just don't understand long division"). The girls were likely to attribute failure to a defect in themselves, while boys attributed failure to external factors. For boys negative feedback had little effect on their estimation of their own ability, while for girls it resulted in lowered self esteem.

These interaction patterns over time may contribute to girls' negative perceptions of themselves. Although female depressives begin to outnumber males at adolescence, it is possible that the groundwork for female adolescent and adult depression is laid in the elementary school years, not only in the school setting, but within the larger society.

The concept of learned helplessness has proved to be a fertile ground for research. Recently many intriguing issues have been raised, and the theory is being revised and refined.

The control factor is critical

Child A: I failed the test because I'm stupid. (uncontrollable)
Child B: I failed the test because I didn't study. (controllable)

There's a big difference in the implications of these two explanations. In both cases the child feels the failure was her own fault. Whether the child feels an event is due to a controllable or an uncontrollable situation affects whether or not her explanatory style may lead to depression. When a child attributes bad happenings to *uncontrollable* causes, the connection with depression is positive. However, when the events are attributed to *controllable* causes, there is an inverse relation to depression (Brown and Siegel, 1988).

Children A and B can serve as examples. Child A attributes her failure to an *uncontrollable, personal* cause; she's stupid. On the other hand, Child B attributes her failure to a *controllable personal* cause, her failure to study. She knows that if she changes her study habits she'll do better. In other words, if one believes the negative event to be due to a modifiable aspect of one's behavior, to something within one's control, an optimistic, rather than a depressive, reaction may result. The person may then believe that the bad event might not recur. Thus she alters the depressive character of her explanations to herself for her failure.

Another example: A child who usually plays ball quite well is not asked to play in a ball game on the playground. She may attribute this to an uncontrollable personal cause, that she is basically unlikeable. Or she may attribute it to a controllable personal cause, that she was grouchy on that day, which would alter the depressive character of her explanation. She could then believe she could change and be more agreeable on another day.

Age and explanatory style

The age of the child must be considered in judging children's perceptions of the extent of their control. With a younger child, many stressful life situations are beyond their control. With increasing age and autonomy, however, stress situations are perceived to become more controllable.

5th grade Child A: I'm not as smart as the other kids.
1st grade Child B: I tried hard so that means I'm smart.

Younger children are less susceptible to the sense of helplessness than older ones. Pride in accomplishment can be observed at an early age, as can the effects of failure. By the age of two, children show delight in success and in their own efficacy (Kagan, 1983); they also react with frustration and distress to failure. By the age of four, children seem to have an accurate sense of what they can and cannot do. However, even though young children are aware of their failures, they don't view failure as stable and lasting. Most young children don't make the connection between their abilities and their actual experiences of success and failure. Even when they do make the connection, they don't generalize it to mean that they will fail in all situations.

In addition, young children generally tend to feel competent. They believe that high effort and high ability will result in success, whereas low ability and low effort will result in failure. Older children believe that high effort may compensate for lower ability (Rholes, Blackwell, Jordan and Walters, 1980). Young children don't think much about the future or about distant consequences of their actions. Children as young as four or five are aware that other people are proud or ashamed of them, but it is not until they're about eight that they talk about being proud of themselves. In general, experiences of success and failure have a greater effect on the expectations of older children. Attributional patterns that promote helplessness are not characteristic of children before about 8 or 9 years.

Negative explanatory style – permanent or temporary?

Children whose depressions are largely reactions to environmental stress, such as separation or hospitalization, *do not* maintain a depressive explanatory style after the stress episode subsides (Asarnow and Bates, 1988). As children respond to positive environmental changes, their explanatory style changes and becomes more positive.

Not all children who have a negative explanatory style develop depression; only certain subgroups of depressed children use this style. It can, however, become solidified in children who experience serious, uncontrollable events that affect many areas of their lives over a long period of time.

Whether a depressive explanatory style is dependent on a specific situation or is an enduring attitude or trait of some children is a question to be addressed in future research.

Negative explanatory style – sufficient explanation for depression?

Learned helplessness is a diathesis/stress model of depression; depression results frcm a negative explanatory style *in conjunction* with uncontrollable bad events. Both elements must be present; neither negative explanatory style alone or uncontrollable events alone leads to depression.

The timing of a child's first trauma or serious loss can have a major influence on her explanatory style. The loss of a mother at an early age has both stable and global implications; the mother will never return and almost every aspect of the child's life will be affected. It can, depending on other family circumstances, contribute to further negative effects such as failure in school, loss of friendships, withdrawal, etc. The child may then believe that bad things are likely to happen in many areas and that they are her fault. If the negative style continues it will increase the child's vulnerability to depression when faced with bad events in the future. This may set the pattern for the interpretation of future losses (Nolen-Hoeksema, Girgus and Seligman, 1986).

Stressful life events were found to be even more critical in predicting changes in depression than negative explanatory style, according to a recent study. Children considered at high risk for depression were asked about whether they had experienced changes in their lives that made them upset. Questions dealt with family life, friends, pets, school, health, neighborhood activities, moves, accidents, money problems, problems with the law or other authorities, and major disappointments (Hammen, Adrian and Hiroto, 1988).

Researchers agree that negative cognition is important, but question whether or not it is a cause or an effect of depression. The presence of negative cognitions appear to make it more difficult to overcome depression. The negative explanatory model may be valid only for subtypes of childhood depression. For example, children with mild depression may show different patterns of cognitions than children with major depressive disorders. Negative explanatory style and depression need to be examined in terms of their particular meaning in the context of child's environment. Ongoing research and revision of the theory will shed light on which causes are related to which types of depression.

Implications for treatment

According to cognitive theory the quality of children's responses to failure or misfortune is related to the causes by which they explain events. The helpless child will interpret defeat as permanent, catastrophic, and evidence of personal shortcomings. The non-helpless child will interpret the same misfortune as temporary, under her control, and due to circumstance or bad luck. In treatment, therefore, learned strategies have to be unlearned. Children are taught techniques to help them change their thinking and their explanatory style, correct distorted beliefs, and to attribute their failure to factors over which they have control.

BEHAVIORAL THEORIES

Behaviorists as a rule do not consider the internal causes of behavior. They focus on understanding overt behavior in terms of the events that either precede or follow the behavior, that serve to reinforce it or extinguish it. From the behavioral point of view, changes in reinforcement—either in number or in kind—are seen as the causes of depression (Lewinsohn, Biglan and Zeiss, 1976).

1) Depressed individuals receive less positive reinforcement. In a child's life, there are numerous situations that could result in reinforcement changes; one important event involves the loss of a person who previously supplied the reinforcement—mother, father, or friend. Other stressful life events such as moving, death in the

family, or divorce can all be viewed as situations which result in loss or reduction in sources of positive reinforcement.

2) Depressed individuals elicit fewer reinforcing behaviors from other people. Another important factor is the depressed child's ability, or rather, lack of ability, to actively obtain reinforcements from other people. Some children, even at birth, have outgoing temperaments to which people are more likely to respond. In other cases a child's behavior may not be pleasing to other people; he may be clingy, sullen, needy, whiny, unresponsive, etc. Behaviorists translate the clinical features of depression into learning theory terms. Withdrawal is equated with avoidance behavior. Self-depreciation, crying, irritability and requests for help are seen as behaviors that help the child avoid unpleasant behaviors or to get attention.

If the disturbing behavior persists, it may cause others to avoid the child. He may not get the feedback from the variety of experiences he needs to develop social skills, and receives less positive reinforcement from his peers (Blechman *et al*, 1986; Kaslow *et al*, 1984).

3) Depressed individuals exercise fewer social skills. Many of us have seen a child with a dismal expression hovering on the fringes of a group in a playground, not knowing how to get involved. Although it is obvious that deficient social skills are also common in children with other types of psychiatric disorders, clinical observations show that depressed children are particularly impaired in their social skills. They are ill at ease with the ordinary give-and-take of social interactions. They are awkward in initiating or reciprocating social overtures. They often act impulsively, seemingly insensitive to the consequences of their actions.

Peers of depressed children view them as isolated and unsuccessful in actual social situations. Depressed children view themselves similarly, and are chosen less often than other children as play or workmates. They perform less well on tasks that require interpersonal problem solving. They expect to be unsuccessful; they set more stringent criteria for success and evaluate their own performance unfavorably (Blechman *et al*, 1986; Sacco and Graves, 1984).

Teachers don't enjoy working with depressed children; they feel frustrated by them and keep a distance from them (Morris, 1980). A vicious cycle sets in; the depressed child withdraws, reduces his opportunities to be in social situations, and receives less positive reinforcement from his peers and teachers.

The persistence and pervasive effects of social difficulties are highlighted by the fact that when a depressive episode is over, children do well academically, but often the social problems remain (Puig-Antich *et al*, 1985).

Implications for treatment

Generally treatment is carried out by manipulating reinforcements. Therapy programs range from improving problem-solving abilities, social skills and assertiveness training to increasing the depressed child's involvement in rewarding activities.

PSYCHOSOCIAL FACTORS

Life events and stress

In her five years of life, Sheryl has experienced much suffering. Born to a drug-addicted mother, she went through withdrawal at the age of two weeks. She has lived in two foster homes, and is now back with her natural mother and two older siblings in a one-room apartment.

Vince, now 13, is the older of two children in a middle-class family. His father died when Vince was 8, and Vince and his younger sister grew up in a home headed by his mother. Vince had a poor relationship with his mother and resented the men she dated. He was disruptive in class, often truanted, and had to repeat sixth grade. He started drinking at age 12.

Each person's life contains uncountable numbers of events of varying magnitude, duration, and particular meaning for the individual. Not all life events are stressful. Some, such as the death of a family member, are major, and can cause considerable upheaval. On the other hand, many events are relatively minor and exert relatively less impact (e.g., a child getting a poor grade). Life events affect human development in both positive and negative ways, facilitating positive growth and adaptation as well as contributing to illness and disturbance (Compas, 1987). Major life stresses that require considerable readjustment may lead to reactive and other types of depression.

Of course, what's major to one person may be minor to another. How can one explain the difference? Numerous factors—the quality of early relationships, resources for coping both within the individual and within the family, age, temperament, frequency of stress, and social supports all affect the impact of the event. Recent research suggests that a gender difference may also be present; girls tend to rate events as more stressful than boys and report more major negative events and daily "hassles" or irritations than boys (Lawrence and Russ, 1985; Lewis, Siegel and Lewis, 1984; Burke and Weir, 1978).

There is reasonably strong evidence in adults that stressful life events play a significant role in the onset of depressive conditions and other disorders. Social class, for example, is significant; the rate of depression in the lower socioeconomic classes is significantly higher than in other classes (Brown and Harris, 1975). In contrast to the adult research, there is a paucity of evidence on the impact of stressful life events on psychiatric disorders in childhood. In spite of the considerable variability in measures used, studies do show a relationship between stressful life events and psychological or physical dysfunction in children and adolescents. Evidence for a causal relationship, however, is weak (for a review see Compas, 1987).

Stress has been broadly defined as a stimulus which exerts a *demand* and requires an adaptational response by the child. The child and the event reciprocally influence each other. Sources of stress during childhood and adolescence have been outlined by Compas (1987). He distinguishes between chronic and acute demands.

1) *Chronic stressors*: In triggering psychological distress, chronic stressors, including characteristics of the psychosocial environment (e.g., socioeconomic

status, parental alcoholism, marital discord, family violence, mother's physical or emotional illness, peer group relationships) seem to be more significant than single major life events. Economic factors are critical; more mental illness occurs among poor people, who have to deal with poorer housing, clothing, food, in addition to the psychological stressors. Other chronic stressors may be:

a) Physical disabilities – children with illnesses which entail hospitalization, immobilization and/or pain often have at least one acute depressive episode. Children with chronic disabilities – paralysis, kidney disease, asthma, heart disease – tend to have one or many depressive episodes or a chronic protracted depression. The frequency depends on such factors as family background, personality, and biological makeup. When chronically ill children become depressed, they may give up and not take their medication. Children of parents with a chronic physical illness often suffer episodes of depression either because of losing the parent or because of identifying with the parent's reaction to the physical illness (McKnew and Cytryn, 1973).

b) Learning disabilities – children identified as learning disabled have been found to have higher rates of depression than non-learning disabled children (Brumback *et al*, 1977; Stevenson and Romney, 1984). Depressed learning disabled children were found to have lower self-esteem than non-depressed learning disabled children. The personality traits which characterized the more depressed children were high anxiety, low ego strength, and oversensitivity.

It is sometimes difficult to differentiate between depression and learning disability. In a study of 153 children, 53 of whom were diagnosed in their schools as having a learning disability, it was found that depression, rather than learning disability, was the major factor contributing to poor academics (Colbert *et al*, 1982).

Abused children have been found to have higher rates of depressive symptoms, heightened externality, lowered self-esteem, and greater hopelessness about the future (Allen and Tarnowski, 1989).

2) *Acute stressors*: a) may be specific events, the typical life transitions encountered by most children, such as change of school, etc., or atypical events, such as death or divorce,

b) may also refer to the minor irritations of daily living which have a cumulative effect.

There are times during the life span when the frequency of acute stressors increases. For example, during adolescence many biological and social changes occur, including hormonal changes, school transitions, and different social expectations, all of which may contribute to the increased incidence of depression.

The single most important factor in acute depressive reactions is the sudden loss of a parent, which increases the likelihood that the child will be depressed by a factor of about 2 to 3 (Brown, 1977; Lloyd, 1980). Maternal loss has been shown to be more significant in later childhood. The child who loses either parent when he is 10 to 14 years is considered the most vulnerable for later depression.

Other types of single life events have been studied, several of which are summarized below:

1) Hospital admission – Studies were reviewed by Garmezy (1983) who concludes that hospital admission constitutes short-term distress and disorder in young children but that longer-lasting sequelae are unusual.

2) Birth of a sibling – More than half of forty two-to-three year-olds became temporarily more tearful in reaction to the birth of a sibling; one-fourth had sleeping difficulties; more than half had toileting problems (Dunn *et al*, 1981). Changes in mother/child and family patterns of interaction were considered to be the critical factor.

3) Divorce – For each year during the period from 1972 to 1979, one million children below the age of 18 experienced family divorce (Wallerstein and Kelly, 1980). Although not all children respond adversely, for some divorce can contribute to depression or to aggressive behavior. Wallerstein and Kelly believe that reactions after divorce occur in a stage sequence. The initial stage is profoundly stressful for both parents and children, marked by heightened conflict and sexual and aggressive behaviors. Both parents tend to be inconsistent; in the first year mothers become depressed, self-involved, erratic, less supportive, and more authoritarian. Fathers begin by being indulgent and permissive, but then increase their restrictiveness.

According to Wallerstein and Kelly, after one year, the children showed improvement, typically in advance of the parents, with girls improving faster than boys. For some children, however, the symptomatic responses followed a more chronic pattern, which the researchers attribute to stresses present prior to the separation.

A transition period follows for a span of 2 to 3 years, and by the 5-year mark, some divorced families have achieved stability, while others are still in conflict. Often the reduced status of the divorced family and its negative effect on economic, social and psychological well-being, particularly the heightening of depression, may contribute to the mental health problems of the children. While one-third of the children were lively and well-adjusted at the 5-year mark, the same proportion felt deprived, lonely and rejected.

Many researchers feel that events such as divorce, a loss, entering a new school, or similar experiences do not actually constitute discrete events, but really comprise a series of multiple events. In most cases, the negative event or events stress patterns of family interaction and relationships. The magnitude of the effect of stressful events depends on the coping resources within the child and the family.

Consider Alicia, a depressed 10-year old: Alicia's mother, Mrs R., became depressed and was treated with anti-depressants when her marriage of 15 years ended in divorce. Although she was a college graduate, she could obtain only a routine secretarial job, from which she was often absent because she could not get up on time. At the time of the divorce, Alicia's brother, aged 12, went to live with their father in another city while Alicia remained with their mother. For financial reasons Alicia and her mother moved in with the maternal grandparents and an uncle who was still living at home. They all spent much of their time watching television, seldom leaving the house.

Alicia was brought to a child development center for evaluation at the age of 10 because she was reluctant to go to school where she was failing. During the initial interview, Alicia sat close to her mother and reached out for her hand from time to time. Her downcast features mimicked those of her mother; her voice was monotonous and her movements slow. She described herself as "not much to look at." Alicia said she didn't try to do her work in school because she expected to fail, and that her teachers didn't care about her. Although she said she was interested in making friends, she refused to leave the house to be with other children.

In this family, as in many families of divorce, the daughter remained with the mother during her period of depression. She became overly identified with her mother's sadness, proneness to illness and fatigue, and resistance to leaving the house. The pattern was reinforced by the overly close bonds in the extended family.

Depression is a family affair

Family factors often represent a critical and chronic psychosocial stressor. The most consistent finding in studies of childhood depression is the high incidence of parental depression (McKnew *et al*, 1973; Orvaschel *et al*, 1980; Welner *et al*, 1977). Parental depression can influence a child's emotional development in multiple ways. A child's depression may be the result of a hereditary or genetic vulnerability. It may be due to a child's identification with a depressed parent. It may follow parental rejection or lack of a nurturing relationship over a period of time. It may follow marital discord, intentional separation of a parent and child, or the child's witness of violence. Or it may be a combination of some or all of these factors (Crook and Raskin, 1975; Pfouts *et al*, 1982).

In this chapter we have discussed conceptual models of the causes of depression in children—cognitive, behavioral, and psychosocial.

Other chapters in this volume will address more fully psychodynamic theory, the effects of family interaction patterns, and risk factors.

One theory is not sufficiently comprehensive to account for all aspects of childhood depression. What is clear is that, similar to adult depression, childhood depression is a multidimensional, not a single construct. The theories surveyed in this chapter have numerous points of overlap. Loss of a close and nurturing person, for example, is considered a stress with far-reaching implications in all theories.

Think about the following case of a depressed child, and consider the possible causes of her depression from various theoretical points of view.

Mandy, 9 years old, lives with her mother and grandmother. Her father, an accountant, and mother separated when Mandy was 6. Since her father remarried and moved to another state, visits are confined to school holidays. Mandy's mother recently went back to a secretarial position to supplement the family income. Mandy's teacher reports that Mandy is in danger of failing, that she becomes preoccupied, often looking out of the window, and seldom finishes her work. Mandy has stated that the other children are much smarter than she is. She seldom attends Girl Scout meetings, which she used to enjoy. When she gets home each afternoon, she watches television and eats all the cookies she can find. She usually telephones her mother to make sure she's all right and then goes to bed until her mother comes home. "I don't have any reason to stay up," she said.

From any point of view, there would be concern about Mandy's changed life status (different family composition, lower standard of living), as well as internal changes (low self-esteem, feelings of incompetence, and lack of adaptive coping strategies). All theories would consider her reaction to the loss of her father and the possibility that she might interpret future losses or deprivations as equally irretrievable. A behaviorist might see Mandy's difficulties as stemming from losses in sources of reinforcement. Her father has moved away, her mother has gone back to work, thus reducing her opportunities for positive reinforcement. She has withdrawn from contact ith other children, even further reducing opportunities for reinforcement and development of social skills.

From the cognitive point of view, Mandy sees herself as unworthy, distorts events, feels there is nothing she can do to change her situation, sees her world as gloomy, and therefore withdraws and goes to sleep. Mandy's explanatory style is negative, consisting of internal, stable, and global attributions. She feels she has no control over what happens to her, that she is not smart, that she is incompetent in all situations, and that she always will be. Psychodynamic theorists would focus on the effects of the loss of her father at a critical age, identification with her mother during a time when the mother was depressed, and concern that her mother too may abandon her.

To choose one theory and to interpret Mandy's depression as being due to one cause would obviously be simplistic. The causes of Mandy's depression must be conceptualized from different points of view. Does one explanation invalidate another? Or do they all contribute to our understanding? Current research suggests that childhood depression results from a complex interaction of many factors.

Major questions regarding childhood depression and its causes remain to be answered by future research. Which types of depression are linked to which cause? Do stressful events cause depression or does the presence of depression increase the likelihood of having stressful experiences? Or are both the stress and depression due to a third set of variables? What factors make some youngsters more vulnerable to stress while enabling others to cope more adaptively? And, most importantly, what are the implications for prevention and treatment of depression in children? Since there are probably many etiological factors, it will be important to study childhood depression using the various frameworks of biochemistry, genetics, sex-role expectations, psychosocial stress, behavioral reinforcement, psychodynamics and cognitive development.

References

Abramson, L. Y., Seligman, M. E. P. and Teasdale, J. D. (1978) Learned helplessness in humans: critique and reformulation. *Journal of Abnormal Psychology*, **87**, 49–74.

Allen, D. and Tarnowski, K. (1989) Depressive characteristics of physically abused children. *Journal of Abnormal Child Psychology*, Vol. 17, **1**, 1–11.

Asarnow, J. and Bates, S. (1988) Depression in child psychiatric inpatients: cognitive and attributional patterns. *Journal of Abnormal Child Psychology*, Vol. 16, **6**, 601–615.

Beck, A.T. (1967). Depression: Clinical, Experimental and Theoretical Aspects, New York: Harper and Row.

Blechman, E., McEnroe, M., Carella, E. and Audette, D. (1986) Childhood competence and depression. *Journal of Abnormal Psychology*, Vol. 95, **3**, 223–227.

Brown, G.W. (1977) Depression and loss. *British Journal of Psychiatry*, **130**,1.
Brown, G.W. and Harris, T.O. (1978) Social Origins of Depression, New York: Free Press.
Brown, J. and Siegel, J. (1988) Attributions for negative life events and depression: the role of perceived control. *Journal of Personality and Social Psychology*, Vol. 54, **2**, 316–322.
Brumback, R., Dietz-Schmidt, S. and Weinberg, W. (1977) Depression in children referred to an educational diagnostic center. *Diseases of the Nervous System*, **38**, 529–535.
Burke, R. and Weir, T. (1978) Sex differences in adolescent life stress, social support, and well-being. *Journal of Psychology*, **98**, 277–288.
Colbert, P., Newman, B., Ney, P. and Young, J. (1982) Learning disabilities as a symptom of depression in children. *Journal of Learning Disabilities*, **6**, 333–336.
Compas, B. (1987) Stress and life events during childhood and adolescence. *Psychology Review*, No. **7**, 275–302.
Coyne, J.C. and Gotlib, I.H. (1983) The role of cognition in depression: A critical appraisal. *Psychological Bulletin*, Vol. 94, No. 3, 472–505.
Crook, T. and Raskin, A. (1975) Association of childhood parental loss with attempted suicide and depression. *Journal of Counseling and Clinical Psychology*, **43**, 277–282.
Dickens, C. (1848) Dombey and Son. Edition published in the U.S.A. 1950. New York: Dodd Mead.
Dunn, J., Kendrick, C. and McNamee, R. (1981) The reaction of first born children to the birth of a sibling: mothers' reports. *Journal of Child Psychology and Psychiatry*, **22**, 1–18.
Dweck, C.S. and Repucci, N. (1973) Learned helplessness and reinforcement responsibility in children. *Journal of Personality and Social Psychology*, **25**, 109–116.
Dweck, C.S. (1975) The role of expectations and attributions in the alleviation of learned helplessness. *Journal of Personality and Social Psychology*, **31**, 674–685.
Dweck, C.S. and Bush, E. (1976) Sex differences in learned helplessness: differential debilitation with peers and adult evaluators. *Developmental Psychology*, **12**(2), 147–156.
Dweck, C.S. and Licht, B. (1980) Learned helplessness and intellectual achievement. *Human Helplessness*, (eds. J. Garber and M. Seligman). New York: Academic Press.
Garmezy, N. (1983) Stressors of childhood. *Stress, Coping and Development in Children*, (eds. N. Garmezy and M. Rutter). New York: McGraw-Hill.
Hammen, C. (1985) Predicting depression: A cognitive-behavioral perspective. *Advances in Cognitive-Behavioral Research and Therapy*, Vol. 4, 29–71. (ed. P. Crandall). New York: Academic Press.
Hammen, C., Adrian, C. and Hiroto, D. (1988) A longitudinal test of the attributional vulnerability model in children at risk for depression. *British Journal of Clinical Psychology*, **27**, 37–46.
Kagan, J. (1983) Stress and coping in early development. *Stress, Coping and Development in Children*, 191–216, (eds. N. Garmezy and M. Rutter). New York: McGraw-Hill.
Kaslow, N.J., Tanenbaum, R. and Seligman, M.E.P. (1978) The KASTAN: A children's ASQ, Unpublished manuscript. University of Pennsylvania, PA.
Kaslow, N.J., Rehm, L. and Siegel, A. (1984) Social-cognitive correlates of depression in children. *Journal of Abnormal Child Psychology*, **12**, 605–620.
Kovacs, M. and Beck, A.T. (1977) An empirical-clinical approach towards a definition of childhod depression. *Depression in Children*. (eds. J. Schulterbrandt and A. Raskin). New York: Raven Press.
Lawrence, D. and Russ, S. (1985) Mediating variables between life stress and symptomatology among young adults. Paper presented at annual meeting of the American Psychology Association, Los Angeles, Ca.
Lewinsohn, P.M., Biglan, A. and Zeiss, A.M. (1976) Behavioral treatment of depression. *The Behavioral Management of Anxiety, Depression, and Pain*, (ed. P.O. Davidson), New York Brunner/Maazel.
Lewis, C.E., Siegel, J.M. and Lewis, M. (1984) Feeling bad: Exploring sources of distress amoung pre-adolescent children. *American Journal of Public Health*, **74**, 117–122.
Lloyd, C. (1980) Life events and depressive disorder reviewed. *Archives of General Psychiatry*, Vol. 37, 529–548.
Maier, S., Seligman, M. and Solomon, R. (1969) Pavlovian fear conditioning and learned helplessness. *Punishment*, (eds. B.A. Campbell and R.M. Church), New York: Appleton-Century-Crofts.
Mann, T. (1930) Disorder and early sorrow, *Stories of Three Decades*. Edition published in U.S.A. 1976. (p. 525). New York: A.A. Knopf.
McKnew, D.H. and Cytryn, L. (1973) Historical background in children with affective disorders. *American Journal of Psychiatry*, **130**, 1278.
McKnew, D.H., Cytryn, L. and Efron, A. (1979) Offspring of patients with affective disorders. *British Journal of Psychiatry*, **134**, 145–152.
Morris, M. (1980) Childhood depression in the primary grades: Early identification, a teacher consultation remedial model, and classroom correlates of change. *Interchange*, **11**, 61–75.

Mullins, L., Siegel, L. and Hodges, K. (1984) Cognitive problem-solving and live event correlates of depressive symptoms in children. *Journal of Abnormal Child Psychology*, Vol. 13, **2**, 305-314.

Nolen-Hoeksema, S., Girgus, J. and Seligman, M.E.P. (1986) Learned helplessness in children: A longitudinal study of depression, achievement and explanatory style. *Journal of Personality and Social Psychology*, Vol. 52, **2**, 435-442.

Orvaschel, H., Weissman, M.M. and Kidd, K. (1980) Children and depression: The children of depressed parents. *Journal of Affective Disorders*, **2**, 1-16.

Overmier, J. and Seligman, M. (1967) Effects of inescapable shock upon subsequent escape and avoidance learning. *Journal of Comparative and Physiological Psychology*, **63**, 28-33.

Peterson, C. and Seligman, M.E.P. (1984) Causal explanations as a risk factor for depression: theory and evidence. *Psychological Review*, **91**, 347-374.

Pfouts, J., Schopler, J. and Henley, H. (1982) Forgotten victims of family violence. *Social Work*, **24**, 367-388.

Puig-Antich, P., Lukens, E., Davies, M., Goetz, D., Brennan-Quattrock, J. and Todak, G. (1985) Psychosocial functioning in prepubertal major depressive disorders: II. Interpersonal relationships after sustained recovery from the affective episode. *Archives of General Psychiatry*, **42**, 511-517.

Rholes, W.P., Blackwell, J., Jordan, C. and Walters, C. (1980) A developmental study of learned helplessness. *Developmental Psychology*, Vol. 16, **6**, 616-624.

Sacco, W.P. and Graves, D.J. (1984) Childhood depression, interpersonal problem-solving, and self-ratings of performance. *Journal of Clinical Child Psychology*, **13**, 10-15.

Schwartz, M., Friedman, R. and Lindsay, P. (1982) The relationship between conceptual tempo and depression in children. *Journal of Consulting and Clinical Psychology*, Vol. 50, **4**, 488-490.

Seligman, M.E.P. (1974) Depression and learned helplessness. *The Psychology of Depression*, (eds. F. Friedman, M. Katz), Washington, DC: Winston.

Seligman, M.E.P. (1975) Helplessness: on Depression, Development, and Death, San Francisco: Freeman.

Seligman, M.E.P., Peterson, D., Kaslow, N., Alloy, L. and Abramson, L. (1978) Attributional style and depressive symptoms among children. *Journal of Abnormal Psychology*, **93**, 235-238.

Seligman, M.E.P. and Peterson, C. (1984) A Learned Helplessness Perspective on Childhood Theory and Research *Depression in Young People*, (eds. M. Rutter, C. Izard and P. Read).

Stevenson, D. and Romney D. (1984) Depression in learning disabled children. *Journal of Learning Disabilities*, 579-583.

Wallerstein, J. and Kelly, J. (1980) Surviving the Breakup: How Children and Parents Cope with Divorce. New York: Basic Books.

Welner, Z., Welner, A., McCrary, M. and Leonard, M. (1977) Psychopathology in children of inpatients with depression. *Journal of Nervous and Mental Diseases*, **164**, 408-413.

3 Family Studies of Affective Disorders

Carl E. Anderson and Myrna M. Weissman*

Division of Child and Adolescent Psychiatry New York State Psychiatric Institute, 722 West 168th Street, Box 14, New York, NY 10032, USA

INTRODUCTION

Until recently, the conventional wisdom was that children were not capable of becoming depressed. With the increasing use of systematic diagnostic assessments and direct interviews of children, it has become clear that depression occurs in prepubertal children and is common in adolescents (Weissman, 1988: 143). It is also quite clear from systematic studies that depression runs in families. The offspring of depressed parents and the first-degree relatives of depressed children are at increased risk for depression and other psychiatric disorders. Research efforts are underway to better understand the clinical characteristics, familial aggregation, treatment, and course of depression in children.

The purpose of this chapter is to review recent data concerning the familial nature of major depression and bipolar disorder and to discuss the implications of these findings for pediatricians. This information is of particular importance to pediatricians because they are in a unique position to identify early signs of these disorders in children. They are often the first and, sometimes, the only medical professionals that parents consult concerning their children's psychiatric problems. Parents may consult a pediatrician before anyone else because this relationship is already established and also because it may be too threatening to directly contact a mental health professional.

In addition, some parents may not recognize the signs and symptoms of psychiatric illness in their child. Pediatricians themselves may miss the diagnosis of depression or other psychiatric disorders in children (Chang *et al*, 1988:736–739). As we will demonstrate, depression or bipolar disorder in a parent increases the risk for psychiatric illness in the children and, therefore, it is important for pediatricians to be knowledgeable about the familial aspects of affective disorders.

*Clinical and Genetic Epidemiology, New York State Psychiatric Institute, New York, NY 10032 USA

BACKGROUND

Before we discuss the research findings, we will first describe two basic types of studies which provide information on the familial nature of affective disorders. For a more detailed discussion of family study designs, see Weissman *et al* (1986: 1104–1116). "Top down" studies begin with a depressed or bipolar parent as the patient (called the proband or index case) and study the patient's offspring and spouse. Sometimes the patient's other first-degree relatives (siblings and parents) are also studied. These are also referred to as "high risk" studies since the children are at high risk for psychiatric problems by virtue of the parent's illness.

"Bottom up" studies start with the depressed or bipolar child as the patient (proband or index case) and then study the child's first-degree relatives (parents and siblings). In this chapter we will review some of the more recent "top down" and "bottom up" studies of major depression and bipolar disorder.

To put the recent findings in perspective, it will be helpful to review the changes that have occurred in the methodology of family studies which involve children. Earlier studies were described by Orvaschel (1983: 53–66) in a review of research on the effects of parental depression on psychopathology in children. Many of the studies she described had methodological problems, including small numbers of children, absent control groups, or non-blind interviews.

Methodological differences made it difficult to compare findings between studies. For example, there were differing types of parental affective disorders, differing types of control groups, varying diagnostic criteria and diagnostic methods, differing informants, and varying methods of calculating rates of disorders. Even given these problems, Orvaschel concluded from the available data that the children of depressed parents are at increased risk for depression and behavior problems. In an independent review, Beardslee *et al* (1983: 825–832) reached similar conclusions.

CHARACTERISTICS OF RECENT FAMILY STUDIES

With the increasing availability and use of systematic assessment methods for diagnosing psychiatric disorders in children, there are now a number of well-designed "top down" and "bottom up" studies of major depression and bipolar disorder. In addition, there is a continuing study involving the direct observation and follow-up of the young offspring of parents with bipolar disorder (Zahn-Waxler *et al*, 1988: 506–509).

We will review a subset of these studies which we feel are the best-designed, have reasonable numbers of patients, and use modern diagnostic criteria. Those to be described have used probands, either parents or children, with lifetime histories of either major depression or bipolar disorder. Tables 3.1 and 3.2 present the characteristics of nine selected studies. These studies have looked at children and adolescents (age six and older) and some have included young adults (up to age 23).

In the "top down" studies described in Table 3.1, one parent in each family was chosen as a proband on the basis of having a current episode or lifetime history of

Table 3.1 Characteristics of recent "top down" studies of parent probands with affective disorder

Investigator	*Diagnoses of Parent Probands*	*Diagnostic Assessment Parent*	*Child*	*Ages of Children (Years)*
Breslau *et al.* (1987)	MDD[a] Anxiety Not ill[b]	DIS	DISC	8–23
Gershon *et al.* (1985)	BP[c] Not ill	SADS-L	K-SADS-E	6–17
Klein *et al.* (1985)	BP Other psychiatric disorders	SADS	SADS-L	15–21
Klein *et al.* (1988)	MDD Medical illness Not Ill	SADS	SADS-L	14–22
Orvaschel *et al.* (1988, 1990)	MDD Not ill	SADS-L	K-SADS-E	6–17
Weissman (1988)	MDD Not ill	SADS-L	K-SADS-E	6–23

[a] MDD = major depressive disorder. In this study, only mothers were included and only one child in each family was studied.
[b] No lifetime history of psychiatric illness.
[c] BP = bipolar disorder.

Table 3.2 Characteristics of recent "bottom up" studies of child probands with affective disorder

Investigator	*Diagnoses of Child Probands*	*Diagnostic Assessment Child*	*Adult Relatives*	*Ages of Children (Years)*
Mitchell *et al.* (1989)	MDD Other psychiatric disorders	K-SADS	SADS-L	7–17
Puig-Antich *et al.* (1989)	MDD Anxiety Not ill	K-SADS	SADS-L	6–12
Strober *et al.* (1988)	BP Schizophrenia	SADS	SADS-L	13–17

either major depression or bipolar disorder. Occasionally the co-parent had the same disorder. At least one parent proband in each family, and many of the co-parents, were directly evaluated. The parent proband samples were obtained from outpatient and inpatient settings and also from community derived samples. Therefore, the probands reflect a range of severity of affective illness.

The "bottom up" studies, described in Table 3.2, selected as probands children with current or recent episodes of either major depression or bipolar disorder. The child probands came from both outpatient and inpatient samples.

The parents in these "top down" and "bottom up" studies were directly interviewed using systematic diagnostic interviews, either the Schedule for Affective Disorders and Schizophrenia (SADS) (Endicott and Spitzer, 1978: 773–782) or the Diagnostic

Interview Schedule (DIS) (Robins *et al*, 1981: 381–389). The children were evaluated using the Diagnostic Interview Schedule, Children's Version (DISC) (Edelbrock and Costello, 1984: 286–287), the Schedule for Affective Disorders and Schizophrenia for School-Aged Children, Epidemiologic Version (K-SADS-E) (Puig-Antich *et al*, 1980), or the SADS, lifetime version (SADS-L), used here with adolescents. These interviews yielded diagnoses based upon DSM-III (American Psychiatric Association, 1980: 1–494) or Research Diagnostic Criteria (RDC) (Spitzer *et al*, 1978: 773–779; Endicott and Spitzer, 1979: 52–59).

All of the studies used control proband groups. Studies which do not use control groups cannot demonstrate that the increase in risk of a disorder in relatives is due to the presence of the affective disorder in the probands. The control groups in the "top down" studies consisted of parents with no history of psychiatric illness, with nonaffective psychiatric disorders (e.g., anxiety), or with chronic medical illnesses. In the "bottom up" studies, the control groups consisted of children with no history of psychiatric illness or with nonaffective (e.g., anxiety) psychiatric disorders. Strober *et al* (1988: 255–268) used children with schizophrenia as a control group.

The studies assessed psychiatric illness in the first- and, sometimes, second-degree relatives of the children, either by direct interview or by using the family history method (Andreasen *et al*, 1977: 1229–1235). Diagnoses for most of the relatives of probands were made blindly, without knowledge of the proband's group status (affected or nonaffected). Most of the diagnoses of relatives were made on the basis of the consensus of several clinicians, using all available data from multiple informants. Some of the studies had a follow-up component.

The Breslau *et al* (1987: 285–297) study was not designed for the purpose of studying the familial aggregation of psychiatric disorders, but it does provide some data about the risks to children of having depressed parents. It reports annual, not lifetime, prevalence rates and so the rates cannot be directly compared with those from the other studies, which have used lifetime rates. A "lifetime prevalence rate" for a disorder refers to the number of people/100 who had the disorder at any time in their lives. An "annual prevalence rate" refers to the number of people/100 who had the disorder at any time in a specified one-year time period.

The Hammen *et al* (1987: 736–741) study of children of depressed and bipolar mothers is very well-designed, but it is not included here because the published findings have grouped bipolar and non-bipolar probands. For this review, we are presenting findings separately for the two disorders.

FINDINGS OF RECENT FAMILY STUDIES

Tables 3.3 and 3.4 summarize the findings, from the studies described in Tables 3.1 and 3.2, on the rates of a number of psychiatric disorders in the relatives of probands with affective disorders as compared to the relatives of control probands.

Table 3.3 Comparison of rates of disorders in relatives of depressed probands with rates in relatives of control probands

Investigator	*Any Psychiatric Disorder*	*Major Depression*	*Bipolar Disorder*	*Any Anxiety Disorder*	*Substance Abuse*
Rates of Disorders in Children of Depressed Parent Probands[a]					
Breslau *et al.* (1987)[b]					
8–17 yrs.		N.S.		Increased[c]	
18–23 yrs.		Increased		N.S.	
Klein *et al.* (1988)	Increased	Increased[d]	N.S.		
Orvaschel *et al.* (1988)	Increased	N.S.[e]	N.S.[e]	N.S.	
Weissman (1988)	Increased	Increased		Increased	Increased
Rates of Disorders in First-Degree Relatives of Depressed Child Probands[f]					
Mitchell *et al.* (1989)					
Mothers		N.S.	N.S.	Increased[g]	Increased
Puig-Antich *et al.* (1989)	Increased	Increased	N.S.		Increased[h]

See bottom of Table 3.4 for an explanation of notations.

Table 3.4 Comparison of rates of disorders in relatives of bipolar probands with rates in relatives of control probands

Investigator	*Any Psychiatric Disorder*	*Major Depression*	*Bipolar Disorder*	*Any Anxiety Disorder*	*Substance Abuse*
Rates of Disorders in Children of Bipolar Parent Probands[a]					
Gershon *et al.* (1985)	Increased	N.S.	N.S.	N.S.	N.S.
Klein *et al.* (1985)	Increased	N.S.	N.S., but increased for cyclothymia	N.S.	N.S.
Rates of Disorders in First-Degree Relatives of Bipolar Child Probands[f]					
Strober *et al.* (1988)		Increased	Increased	N.S.	N.S.

[a] A notation of "increased" means that the lifetime prevalence rate of the disorder was significantly higher in children of affected parent probands than in children of control parent probands. "N.S." means that there was no significant difference in rates between children of affected parent probands and children of control probands.
[b] One-year prevalence rates.
[c] Overanxious disorder.
[d] There was a significant difference for RDC major depression, but not for DSM-III major depression.
[e] Rates for affective disorder were increased in children of affected parent probands.
[f] A notation of "increased" means that the rate of the disorder was significantly higher in the first-degree relatives of affected child probands than in the relatives of control probands. "N.S." means that there was no significant difference in rates between the two groups of first-degree relatives.
[g] Panic disorder and/or agoraphobia.
[h] Alcoholism.

Any psychiatric disorder

As can be seen in Table 3.3, the lifetime rates of "any psychiatric disorder" were significantly increased in the children of depressed parents in three studies and in the relatives of depressed children in one study. The rates of "any psychiatric disorder" were increased in both studies of children of bipolar parents.

For the children of parents with major depression or bipolar disorder, the lifetime rates of "any psychiatric disorder" were high (not shown in the tables), ranging from 41/100 (Orvaschel *et al*, 1988: 21) to 76/100 (Weissman, 1988: 150) for the children of depressed parents and from 43/100 (Klein *et al*, 1985: 119) to 72/100 (Gershon *et al*, 1985: 287) for the children of bipolar parents. In the Puig-Antich *et al* (1989: 409) "bottom up" study of depressed children, the rate of "any psychiataric disorder" in first-degree relatives was 64/100. These rates are lifetime prevalence rates and are not age corrected.

While noting the high rates of disorder in the relatives of affected probands, it is important to point out the high rates of disorder, in some of the studies, in the relatives of control probands. The highest rate of "any psychiatric disorder" in relatives of control probands was found in the Weissman (1988: 150) study (57/100). However, when impairment criteria were applied to diagnoses, this rate dropped considerably (Weissman *et al*).

Affective disorders

Table 3.3 presents findings from four studies of children of depressed parents. In three studies, there were increased rates of major depression in the children of depressed parents as compared to the children of control parents. There was a wide variation among the studies in the rates of major depression in the children, ranging from 9/100 (Klein *et al*, 1988: 269) to 28/100 (Weissman, 1988: 150). It is interesting to note that the Breslau *et al* (1987: 290) study found an increased rate of major depression in the older children (age 18–23) of mothers with major depression, but not in the younger children (age 8–17).

As shown in Table 3.3, in one "bottom up" study (Puig-Antich *et al*, 1989: 409), the first-degree relatives of prepubertal depressed children were at increased risk for major depression. However, neither of the two studies demonstrated an increased risk for bipolar disorder in these relatives.

Table 3.4 shows some findings from two studies of children of bipolar parents. The only significant difference in the rates of disorders was in the Klein *et al* (1985: 119) study which found an increased rate of cyclothymia in the children. Cyclothymia is considered to be a mild form of bipolar disorder. As shown in Table 3.4, one "bottom up" bipolar study (Strober *et al*, 1988: 260) found increased rates of major depression and bipolar disorder in the first-degree relatives of the bipolar children.

Anxiety disorders

The findings for anxiety disorders are less clear. The rates of anxiety disorders were increased in the children of depressed parents in two studies, but not in the other two (Table 3.3). Weissman (1988: 150) found a rate of 40/100 for "any anxiety disorder". Breslau *et al* (1987: 290) found an increased rate of overanxious disorder in the younger, but not older, children of depressed mothers. One "bottom up" depression study (Mitchell *et al*, 1989: 354) found an increased rate of panic disorder and/or agoraphobia in the mothers of depressed children. None of the studies of parent or child bipolar probands showed any differences between groups (proband vs. control) in the rates of anxiety disorders in relatives.

Substance abuse

Elevated rates of substance abuse in relatives were reported in one "top down" depression study (Weissman, 1988: 150) and in both "bottom up" depression studies (Table 3.3). There were no significant findings for substance abuse in any of the bipolar studies.

Impairment

In one study (Klein *et al*, 1988: 270) (not shown in Table 3.3), the children of depressed parents had more overall social impairment than did the children of control parents. In another study (Weissman, 1988: 149), they had poorer functioning in school, including more special classes for math and attention problems. This poorer school functioning was not explained by lower IQ scores, since there was no significant difference in IQ scores between the two groups of children.

Suicidal behavior

Of the studies discussed, one "top down" study (Weissman, 1988: 150) reported an increased rate of suicidal gestures or attempts in the children of depressed parents (9/100) (not shown in Table 3.3). Both "bottom up" depression studies had significant findings, although in different directions. Mitchell *et al* (1989: 354) found an increased rate of suicide attempts among mothers of depressed children. On the other hand, Puig-Antich *et al* (1989: 409) found a significantly decreased rate of suicide attempts among first-degree relatives of prepubertal depressed children when compared with relatives of psychiatrically ill controls, and no significant difference when compared with relatives of normal controls. None of the bipolar studies reported data on suicidal behavior.

Psychiatric treatment

There were increased rates of psychiatric treatment in the children of depressed parents in three out of four studies (Klein *et al*, 1988: 270; Orvaschel *et al*, 1988: 22; Weissman, 1988: 150). The lifetime rates of treatment were high, up to 39/100 (Weissman, 1988: 150). Increased rates of treatment among relatives were not found in the "bottom up" depression studies. One possible explanation for this difference is that a parent who is treated for depression may be likely to bring a child in for treatment for psychiatric problems. However, one would not expect that depression in a child would lead to an adult relative being treated.

Developmental and medical problems

The Weissman (1988: 148–49) study found increased rates of a number of developmental and medical problems among the children of depressed parents. These children were born to younger mothers. There was an increased rate of medical problems during pregnancy and an increased rate of adverse perinatal events. The children of the depressed parents were reported by their mothers to be less active and strong, during the first month of life, than the children of the nondepressed parents. They reached several developmental landmarks later, i.e., sitting without assistance and completing urinary and bowel training. In addition, they were at increased risk for seizures and they had an increased rate of surgical procedures requiring hospitalization.

Summary

These findings clearly show that major depression in a parent increases the risk for psychiatric disorders in children, especially for major depression and anxiety disorders and possibly for substance abuse and suicidal behavior. In addition, the children of depressed parents are at increased risk for psychiatric treatment, psychosocial impairment, poor school functioning, and developmental and health problems.

If a parent has bipolar disorder, the children are at increased risk for psychiatric disorder. They are possibly at increased risk for a mild form of bipolar disorder, but elevated risk for other specific psychiatric disorders has not been demonstrated. However, few family studies of bipolar disorder have included children, so the data are limited.

Looking at risk from the point of view of the child's adult relatives, the relatives of depressed children are at increased risk for psychiatric disorder, especially for major depression, anxiety disorders, and substance abuse, but not for bipolar disorder. The findings are mixed concerning suicidal behavior in the adult relatives of depressed children.

If an adolescent has bipolar disorder, there may be an increased risk for major depression and bipolar disorder in relatives. No additional conclusions can be made based upon the studies reviewed because of the small number of bipolar adolescents studied. No conclusions at all can be made concerning the relatives of bipolar prepubertal children because of the absence of data. Moreover, it is unclear if bipolar disorder occurs prepubertally and, if so, what form it takes.

When looking at these findings, one should keep in mind that the absence of significant differences between groups in rates of specific psychiatric disorders does not prove that there were no differences between groups, only that no differences were demonstrated. It is possible that with larger sample sizes, some of the differences in rates between groups might have been significant.

Moreover, even if there is an increased rate of illness in the relatives of depressed or bipolar probands when compared to the relatives of controls, this is not necessarily due to the presence of the affective disorder in the probands. This increased rate may be due to the presence of illness in general (psychiatric or physical) in probands. To determine if the increased rate in relatives is due to the presence of the affective disorder in probands, it is necessary to use control probands who have nonaffective psychiatric illnesses or medical illnesses.

It is not possible from these studies to determine if the affective disorder in the parents caused the children's psychiatric problems or if the children's psychiatric problems caused the parents to become depressed. There may be an interaction of these two processes.

Lastly, while a family study may demonstrate an increased risk for psychiatric problems in the relatives of depressed or bipolar probands, it cannot determine how important genetic factors are, as compared to environmental factors, in producing this increased risk. Most likely, both sets of factors are important. In order to measure the relative contribution of genetic factors, twin, adoption, or genetic linkage studies are necessary.

CLINICAL IMPLICATIONS

Even with the limitations described and recognizing that pediatricians have time constraints and must pay attention to medical problems, these research findings have implications for pediatric practice. Early detection of psychiatric problems in children and referral for appropriate treatment may improve the health of children. More specifically, the findings suggest that if a parent has depression or bipolar disorder, a pediatrician should be watchful for psychiatric problems in all the children in the family. If a child is depressed or bipolar, the pediatrician should suspect psychiatric problems in other family members, especially the parents.

The methods that family studies use to detect psychiatric disorders in the family can also be useful in clinical practice. While the more extended assessments, such as those listed in Tables 3.1 and 3.2, may not be practical in pediatric practice, some self-report questionnaires (completed by the parent, adolescent, or child) may be quite useful as screening tools and can be completed in the waiting room (see Costello and Angold, 1988: 726- 737, for a review of methods).

As pediatricians screen for psychiatric problems, they should keep in mind that psychiatric problems in children will not necessarily be obvious, just as medical illnesses may be hidden. Because of this, a pediatrician should inquire about psychiatric problems in the family, asking the parent about the child, the parent about himself/herself, and the child about himself. In the past, people felt that children were not able to talk with a professional about their psychiatric problems. As a result, professionals did not ask the children about their problems, assuming instead that they could play with the children and learn indirectly about their problems. Now it is clear that children can talk with professionals about their sadness and worries as long as the professionals pay attention to the child's developmental stage, using language and concepts that the child can understand. Many of the newer diagnostic methods take these factors into account and can be used successfully with children to elicit relevant information for diagnostic purposes.

Not only can the child speak about his own problems, but studies which have asked children directly about their problems, and then independently asked the parent, clearly show that the parent may not be aware of the child's psychiatric problems. Moreau *et al* (1989) demonstrated that parents frequently may not be aware of their children's suicide attempts. In addition, parents and children don't always agree about the child's psychopathology. In a study by Weissman *et al* (1987: 747–753) of children of depressed and normal parents, agreement was poor between parents and children concerning the children's psychiatric illnesses. Children were more likely to report psychiatric illness in themselves than parents were likely to report in the children. A child psychiatrist who evaluated both sets of data was more likely to agree with the child's report.

If children or parents are found to have major depression or bipolar disorder, and especially if these problems are severe and cause impairment in functioning, a pediatrician can refer them for further evaluation and treatment. Both parent and child can be referred if both have psychiatric problems. Treatment of a depressed parent may benefit the children and the family. Likewise, treatment of a depressed child may be beneficial for the family as well as for the child.

Acknowledgement

This research was supported in part by NIMH grant #MH36197-09. Dr Anderson was supported by NIMH grant #5-T32-MH16434-09.

Appreciation is expressed to V.E. Anderson, Ph.D., who generously provided comments on this manuscript, and to N. Breslau, Ph.D., C.L.,Hammen, Ph.D., M.B. Keller, M.D. and H. Orvaschel, Ph.D., who generously provided manuscripts and/or articles.

References

American Psychiatric Association (1980) Diagnostic and Statistical Manual of Mental Disorders, 3rd ed., Washington, D.C.: American Psychiatric Association.

Andreasen, N.C., Endicott, J., Spitzer, R.L. and Winokur, G. (1977) The family history method using diagnostic criteria: Reliability and validity. *Archives of General Psychiatry*, **34**, 1229–1235.

Beardslee, W.R., Bemporad, J., Keller, M.B. and Klerman, G.L. (1983) Children of parents with major affective disorder: A review. *American Journal of Psychiatry*, **140**, 825–832.

Breslau, N., Davis, G.C. and Prabucki, K. (1987) Searching for evidence on the validity of generalized anxiety disorder: Psychopathology in children of anxious mothers. *Psychiatry Research*, **20**, 285–297.

Chang, G., Warner, V. and Weissman, M.M. (1988) Physician's recognition of psychiatric disorders in children and adolescents. *American Journal of Diseases of Children*, **142**, 736–739.

Costello, E.J. and Angold, A. (1988) Scales to assess child and adolescent depression: Checklists, screens, and nets. *Journal of the American Academy of Child and Adolescent Psychiatry*, **27**, 726–737.

Edelbrock, C. and Costello, A.J. (1984) Structured psychiatric interviews for children and adolescents, Handbook of Psychological Assessment, ed. G. Goldstein and M. Hersen, New York: Pergamon Press, 276–290.

Endicott, J. and Spitzer, R.L. (1978) A diagnostic interview: The schedule for affective disorders and schizophrenia. *Archives of General Psychiatry*, **35**, 773–782.

Endicott, J. and Spitzer, R. L. (1979) Use of the research diagnostic criteria and the schedule for affective disorders and schizophrenia. *American Journal of Psychiatry*, **136**, 52–59.

Gershon, E. S., McKnew, D., Cytryn, L., Hamovit, J., Schreiber, J., Hibbs, E. and Pellegrini, D. (1985) Diagnoses in school-age children of bipolar affective disorder patients and normal controls. *Journal of Affective Disorders*, **8**, 283–291.

Hammen, C., Gordon, D., Burge, D., Adrian, C., Jaenicke, C. and Hiroto, D. (1987) Maternal affective disorders, illness, and stress: Risk for children's psychopathology. *American Journal of Psychiatry*, **144**, 736–741.

Klein, D. N., Depue, R. A. and Slater, J. F. (1985) Cyclothymia in the adolescent offspring of parents with bipolar affective disorder. *Journal of Abnormal Psychology*, **94**, 115–127.

Klein, D. N., Clark, D. C., Dansky, L. and Margolis, E. T. (1988) Dysthymia in the offspring of parents with primary unipolar affective disorder. *Journal of Abnormal Psychology*, **97**, 265–274.

Mitchell, J., McCauley, E., Burke, P., Calderon, R. and Schloredt, K. (1989) Psychopathology in parents of depressed children and adolescents. *Journal of the American Academy of Child and Adolescent Psychiatry*, **28**, 352–357.

Moreau, D., Walker, M. and Weissman, M. M. (1989) Parents' awareness of child's suicide attempt, poster, American Academy of Child and Adolescent Psychiatry annual meeting.

Orvaschel, H. (1990) Early onset psychiatric disorder in high risk children and increased familial morbidity of depression and anxiety in their second degree relatives. *Journal of the American Academy of Child and Adolescent Psychiatry*, **29**, 184–188.

Orvaschel, H. (1983) Parental depression and child psychopathology, Childhood and Development, ed. S. B. Guze, F. J. Earls and J. E. Barrett, New York: Raven Press, 53–66.

Orvaschel, H., Walsh-Allis, G. and Ye, W. (1988) Psychopathology in children of parents with recurrent depression. *Journal of Abnormal Child Psychology*, **16**, 17–28.

Puig-Antich, J., Goetz, D., Davies, M., Kaplan, T., Davies, S., Ostrow, L., Asnis, L., Twomey, J., Iyengar, S. and Ryan, N. D. (1989) A controlled family history study of prepubertal major depressive disorder. *Archives of General Psychiatry*, **46**, 406–418.

Puig-Antich, J., Orvaschel, H. and Tabrizi, M. A. (1980) The Schedule for Affective Disorders and Schizophrenia for School-Age Children-Epidemiologic Version (Kiddie-SADS-E), 3rd ed., New York: New York State Psychiatric Institute.

Robins, L. N., Helzer, J. and Croughan, J. (1981) The NIMH diagnostic interview schedule: Its history, characteristics, and validity. *Archives of General Psychiatry*, **39**, 381–389.

Spitzer, R. L., Endicott, J. and Robins, E. (1978) Research diagnostic criteria: Rationale and reliability. *Archives of General Psychiatry*, **35**, 773–779.

Strober, M., Morrell, W., Burroughs, J., Lampert, C., Danforth, H. and Freeman, R. (1988) A family study of bipolar I disorder in adolescence: Early onset of symptoms linked to increased familial loading and lithium resistance. *Journal of Affective Disorders*, **15**, 255–268.

Weissman, M. M. (1988) Psychopathology in the children of depressed parents: Direct interview studies, Relatives at Risk for Mental Disorder, ed. D. L. Dunner, E. S. Gershon and J. E. Barrett, New York: Raven Press, 143–159.

Weissman, M. M., Merikangas, K. R., John, K., Wickramaratne, P., Prusoff, B. A. and Kidd, K. K. (1986) Family-genetic studies of psychiatric disorders: Developing technologies. *Archives of General Psychiatry*, **43**, 1104–1116.

Weissman, M. M., Wickramaratne, P., Warner, V., John, K., Prusoff, B. A., Merikangas, K. R. and Gammon, G. D. (1987) Assessing psychiatric disorders in children: Discrepancies between mothers' and children's reports. *Archives of General Psychiatry*, **44**, 747–753.

Weissman, M. M., Warner, V. and Fendrich, M. (1990) Applying impairment criteria to children's psychiatric diagnosis. *Journal of the American Academy of Child and Adolescent Psychiatry*, **29**, 789–795.

Zahn-Waxler, C., Mayfield, A., Radke-Yarrow, M., McKnew, D. H., Cytryn, L. and Davenport, Y. B. (1988) A follow-up investigation of offspring of parents with bipolar disorder. *American Journal of Psychiatry*, **145**, 506–509.

4 Depression within the Family: A Systems Perspective

Fiona True and Laurie Kaplan

Division of Child and Adolescent Psychiatry, Schneider Children's Hospital of Long Island Jewish Medical Center, New Hyde Park, NY 11042, USA
Ackerman Institute for Family Therapy, New York, New York 10021, USA

DEPRESSION WITHIN THE FAMILY: A SYSTEMS PERSPECTIVE

Depression in a child can be terribly frightening to parents. It speaks to a chord sensitive in all of us – that somehow a child is being robbed of his/her "childhood". Depression is usually perceived of as an adult experience with adult emotions such as chronic sadness, apathy, sleeplessness and loss of interest in activities. These feelings are alien to our images of childhood. It might also appear as if a child is seeing life through the eyes of an adult – far too early and not in keeping with his/her developmental life cycle.

Family therapists believe that this is in fact a metaphor for the problem. In systems language, as is aptly described by Virginia Goldner[1] (1985: 539–553), depression in children would be characterized

"As a manifestation of problematic patterns of relationships within a family. It is this pattern that constitutes the 'problem', not the child's symptoms of (depression) alone. A depression, therefore, is not understood in terms of traditional nosological categories (like those of DSM III-R), but in terms of its part in an interactional pattern between that child and the rest of his/her family.

The family therapist, therefore, does not think in terms of 'pathology' located within the child, but in terms of difficulties located within the family system which includes that child. These difficulties are looked at in terms of how the child's depression affects the family and how the family affects the child's depression. This distinction leads to a very different approach to the treatment of (depression) in children." Virginia Goldner.

Underlying family therapy thinking is the belief that all families have strengths and that all families have difficulties. Family therapy seeks to utilize family strengths to overcome problems.

Treatment of the problem

In the individually oriented framework, the child therapist attempts to provide a different "corrective emotional experience" to treat the child's problems. The main

[1]Goldner, V. (1985) Family Therapy, The Clinical Guide to Child Psychiatry, (ed. D. Shafferetal) New York: The Free Press, pp. 539–553.

therapeutic input would be with the child alone—with the parents' perhaps seen as adjuncts to the primary work with the child.

In the family systems framework, the therapeutic intervention always includes the parents, since it is believed that the child's problems cannot be considered apart from the context in which they occur. While therapy might sometimes include sessions with the child alone, the parents are never considered as merely adjuncts to the child's treatment. They are considered to be both part of the problem—and part of its potential solution.

Diagnosis of the problem

The next step for the family therapist is to utilize the initial sessions with the family to accurately diagnose the problem. Central to the diagnostic process, is the ability to differentiate between the symptom and the problem.

The family therapist would ask the following questions: Is the primary problem the child's depression or is the child's depression a symptom of an as yet unnamed larger systems problem within the family?

Similarly, if a child was diagnosed with pneumonia, the pediatrician might ask: "Is pneumonia the primary problem or is the pneumonia a symptom of a larger systemic problem such as cystic fibrosis?"

For the family therapist the means to answering these questions is to develop a hypothesis; that is, a reasoned explanation of how this symptom was developed at this time, in this way, with this family.

Developing an hypothesis

Central to developing an hypothesis is understanding the relationship of the symptom to the problem. If we believed that the symptoms of depression were the primary problem, we would simply treat the symptoms. If, however, we believed that the symptoms were a clue about an underlying problem, we must then find the problem. Family therapists are of the mind that the latter investigation must take place. They believe you must investigate a problem within the context it is located to accurately diagnosis it; namely, the interaction between a child and his/her family, school, friendship network, etc., must be included in a thorough assessment. Like the pediatrician, they include and investigate all relevant material as part of a thorough assessment process.

Impact of family life cycle events

To begin their investigation, they often look to the impact of normal developmental life cycle events on the family in question (i.e., births, marriages, children entering kindergarten, divorces, deaths, older children leaving home, etc.) As depression is often associated with loss, the way a family has handled deaths, illnesses, separations and losses take on a special significance when tackling depression.

Functions of the symptom

The second area of investigation would be to explore the impact of the symptom on the family. Family therapists believe that symptoms can take on important functions within families. For example, symptoms may mask problems that are hard to resolve and distract family members from painful issues. The family therapist looks to investigate all the possible functions a symptom may serve in developing their hypothesis. They would explore how the symptom affects the family and the family affects the symptom.

Case vignette

Suzy, an 8-year old girl, has recently been exhibiting troubling behavior in school. Over the last three months she has been prone to crying in school for no apparent reason, has become more and more withdrawn and is now reluctant to go to school at all. The school psychologist has suggested to the parents that she appears depressed and might need treatment for depression. Unbeknownst to the school psychologist, Suzy's mother, Mrs Johnson, lost her mother five months ago and has been incapacitated by grief. Suzy's depression distracts Mrs Johnson from her grief to active concern about Suzy. She now needs to resume her normal functioning to help her daughter. As Mrs Johnson begins to tackle Suzy's problems (i.e., she is no longer sleeping all day because she is now meeting with teachers, psychologists, her pediatrician, etc.) Suzy's "depression" appears to lift.

In this case example, the family therapist would develop the hypothesis that the life cycle event of grandmother's death precipitated Mrs Johnson's incapacitating grief. Suzy, worried about her mother, becomes depressed and her mother must take care of her. The family therapist would view the function of Suzy's depression as serving to help distract her mother from her grief. By developing this formulation, they are able to bring to light the problem, (i.e., mother's incapacitating grief), and its impact on the entire family; and in particular, the symptoms Suzy has developed in response to her sensitivity to "the problem". The family therapist might explore the meaning of loss for this family and how it has handled other losses in the past and might expect to handle them in the future, attempting to understand why this loss has lead to such incapacitating grief that Mrs Johnson has been unable to function for a number of months.

If, on the other hand, the child's depression were treated as the problem, mother's difficulties might go unnoticed and Suzy's symptoms might increase in an effort to distract her mother from her pain.

Similarly, if the pediatrician with the child with pneumonia treated the pneumonia as the primary problem and it was in fact, a symptom of cystic fibrosis, the cystic fibrosis would go unrecognized until more and more symptoms appeared. When the relationship between the symptom and the problem is diagnosed, treatment efforts are clearly more on the mark and the interaction between symptoms and problems can be understood and treated more accurately.

Consequences of change

Sometimes, however, uncovering the "problem" poses other pitfalls for families. Indeed, learning that your child has cystic fibrosis instead of pneumonia will have a major impact on the family. In the same way, learning the meaning of a child's symptoms of depression and the way it interfaces with other interactive patterns within the family can have a major impact.

Case vignette

John, age 7, was referred to family therapy by his school who were very concerned at his behavior. Since the start of first grade he had been prone to crying in class and more recently to having outbursts directed at peers who teased him, culminating in his saying that he wanted to die. Teachers were concerned enough to lock windows in his classroom.

His biological father, who lived in another state, was dying of cancer. In tracking the onset of John's upset, it became clear that it was directly related to his discovery that his father was ill.

John's mother was living with a man who was very problematic, not contributing to the household expenses and was physically abusive to his mother at times. However, he gave John a lot of attention and each were fond of each other.

John had no plan for suicide; his idea of wanting to die was rather the idea that he wanted to close off the world. He easily engaged in playing with paper airplanes and talking metaphorically about his wish to escape. John's mother often spoke for him no doubt out of a need to protect, but effectively giving him no voice of his own.

The hypothesis the therapist had was that John had the idea that if he behaves badly enough at school, that he would be sent earlier to see his father for the summer vacation. In exploring that hypothesis (i.e., the function of the symptom), John agreed that he had that idea. Thus in diagnosing the origin of John's problems, tackling onset was crucial in understanding John's belief of what would happen if he became worse or better (i.e., the consequences of change) and allowed us to introduce ideas about other changes that would allow him to connect to his father without his having to resort to extremes.

The changes were made by having John write postcards to his father and telephone when that was possible. He also put together an album of photographs of past summer visits, so that he would have a sense of being closer to his dad, as well as a record of those memories after his father's inevitable death.

Coaching John's mother in not speaking for him, both gave validity to his expressions of sadness and allowed her to realize that John would not be overwhelmed by his sadness.

We also hypothesized that by reacting in the extreme way that he had, John had done "a good job" in bringing his mother for help. She was obviously struggling with the decision of asking her lover to leave, in no small part, because of the double loss John would suffer, but also due to her own fear of being alone. The therapist saw the mother individually over a number of sessions and was able to help her make connections in her own family of origin that helped her feel more empowered to take control and evict her lover. Once John saw his mother take charge, he was able to speak of how useless he had felt – knowing he should protect his mother but in doing so, he felt he would be disloyal to her lover. His symptoms abated and he ultimately coped with his father's death in an appropriate way.

Meaning of the symptom

In addition to looking at events in the family life cycle, the function of symptoms and the consequences of change, family therapists are interested in learning about the meaning that a particular symptom may have for a family. Family therapists believe that family premises or beliefs have a profound impact on the way families approach situations – which can, in and of itself, inadvertently sustain a symptom/problem.

Case vignette

Barbara, a 10-year old girl, told her mother that she wished to die, after a year of poor school performance and poor social relationships. Her mother, Margo, terrified by Barbara's symptoms, called a team of family therapists (two social workers trained in family therapy) to help Barbara. Upon further investigation, Barbara did not actually wish to die; rather she felt sad about her poor school performance and her lack of friendships and had often gained attention in the family by being a "sad sack".

The family consisted of two girls: Susan, aged 12 and Barbara, aged 10 and their two parents, Bill and Margo. Bill had lost a younger sister and an aunt, both named Barbara, to suicide. Our hypothesis was that the family believed that 10-year old Barbara, their namesake, was "selected" to be the family member vulnerable to suicide as well. Bill's sense of guilt that he had not stopped his sister – translated into a family belief that he was powerless to intervene around upset and depression.

Margo came from a family where her uncle had been incestuous with her as a little girl. This was a family secret that she had never shared with anyone and her belief was that she and her mother had been powerless to stop him. Since she never confronted anyone in the family about this event, she never challenged these ideas. Therefore, as a mother herself, she too believed that mothers were powerless to intervene and help their daughters with their problems (i.e., in this case, Barbara's suicidal thoughts).

The therapists utilized this hypothesis and intervened by challenging the family's beliefs that they were powerless in the face of their daughter's suicidal thoughts. The parents began to feel more empowered and able to separate their fears from their capabilities.

As they did so Barbara improved and Margo felt less ashamed of her current family "secret" and told her brother about Barbara's past suicidal threats. Her brother became immediately alarmed that the family therapists were not psychiatrists and urged her to go back to her pediatrician for referral to a psychiatrist for a second opinion. Margo, alarmed, followed her brother's advice and took Barbara to a psychiatrist. The psychiatrist told Margo that she thought the child was quite disturbed and while not in need of medication, she certainly needed individual, not family therapy, twice a week.

Margo and Bill discussed together what to do and decided, since Barbara was doing so much better, to stay with the original family therapists. The psychiatrist felt they were absolutely wrong in not giving the child intensive individual psychotherapy and threatened to call the pediatrician to inform him that the parents were endangering the well-being of their child. The old family beliefs of helplessness resurfaced but Bill and Margo were able to face them together. They decided that they could be imprisoned by them no longer. Their ability to believe that they could manage the responsibility of their daughter's welfare themselves was a pivotal point in the therapy.

As they began to own their ability to be in charge, Barbara and Bill relaxed and they were able to deal with the factors that were affecting their daughter's happiness. They intervened in her school, took charge of her disorganized school study habits by giving her a behavioral plan which helped her feel more competent and confident. Over time Barbara's symptoms significantly alleviated (i.e., her friendships increased and her school problems decreased) and she no longer behaved or felt like a "sad sack". As she became less of a patient, Margo began to voice her concerns about Bill—that he was often depressed and that *his* disorganized habits had led to his business partners suggesting that he see a therapist. They could not put up with his messy, unsightly office any longer—they felt it was affecting business. The therapy then shifted to addressing Bill's depression and Margo's anger and disappointment in him. It became clear that Barbara's difficulties had drawn attention away from Bill's problems and the building marital tensions around them.

Bringing the child into family therapy as opposed to individual therapy alone, allowed for the opportunity to treat the depression systemically as it travelled around the family. Similarly, a physician might choose to develop a different treatment plan if he knew there were tumors in several locations as opposed to just one.

Meaning of the symptom and the impact of medication

Occasionally, symptom relief may be all that is required as there is no underlying problem and medication can provide the relief that is needed. Generally, however, family therapists view medication as treating the symptom and not the problem itself. Thus, medication is invariably regarded as an adjunct to the therapeutic process, enabling symptom relief whilst the underlying problem is addressed.

However, medication as part of the treatment process can present problems of its own—mostly in the perception the family has of the problem (i.e., that the problem is caused by a chemical balance or a genetic illness, and therefore feel their efforts are less important than the medication).

Case vignette

This family was seen in an out-patient family therapy clinic. They had a family therapist who was a psychiatrist in a Child Psychiatry Fellowship program. The psychiatrist worked as a member of a family therapy team consisting of social workers and psychiatrists. Keith, 15, was referred for treatment after a number of bizarre outbursts at school and home. Keith was withdrawn and depressed; he would become incoherent, angry, frustrated and generally uncontrollable. Keith had been in the special education track at school since 5th grade and there had been general speculation that he had some neurological disturbance. However, numerous neurological investigations had revealed nothing.

Keith's parents, Bob and Andrea, had always felt him to be different. Keith had one "healthy" sister, three years his junior. The onset of this current crisis had been preceded by Keith's usual stay at a summer camp for disturbed children. Keith had done exceptionally well and experienced none of his outbursts. He returned home with the recommendation that he be mainstreamed into a regular program at school. Keith's explanation of his unproblematic summer was of great interest to the family therapy team. He was able to contain himself at times that he otherwise might have lost control by immediately seeking out a counselor who would listen to him, distract him and generally set very clear boundaries.

Keith's parents, on the other hand, felt powerless to help him. They were unable to set any firm limits and had extreme difficulty insisting that Keith even attend school. Their belief was that their son was "damaged" and taking any firm line was harmful and unjust to a "sick" child. They saw medication as the only realistic treatment.

We hypothesized that Keith faced a real dilemma—by functioning well he was seen as "healthy" and asked to compete in a regular school environment. To avoid that, he had to do poorly and be seen as "handicapped". Neither label fit. We further hypothesized that if Bob and Andrea were able to perceive Keith in a way that would allow them to react firmly, with consistent discipline, they could then contain his outbursts and help *him* to feel more in control—less in a black or white, either/or world. Over a series of sessions, small changes in the handling of Keith were encouraged, noticed and applauded. The family therapist told the family that he believed that their son was not "sick" but was a child who was not living up to his capacities. The parents, seeing the family therapist as an "expert", were ready to go along with the family therapist's recommendations. The family therapist recommended that they devise a system that would set limits with rewards and punishments for acceptable behavior, generally enforcing a plan that they felt would help Keith begin to believe that he could live up to his capabilities. This intervention utilized what the family therapist knew had been effective in another context (i.e., in camp) and utilized the parents' expertise in developing the actual content of the plan, thus heightening the parents' sense of being in control. At its simplest, changing the parents' perception of Keith from a "sick" child to a child whose behavior could be influenced had an immediate and dramatic change on Keith's behavior at home.

Bob and Andrea reported that they had been able to respond firmly and consistently to Keith. Despite the improvements, Keith and his family continued to have difficulty "owning" this new identity. At one point, the parents became alarmed by Keith's voicing thoughts of sadness that he attempted to deal with by ritualized behaviors. Although these ritualized behaviors were nothing new to the family (indeed, Keith had turned the lights on and off, tied his shoes a number of times, etc.

for many years), they had great difficulty sticking with the belief that their boy in fact could overcome these problems. At Keith's request he saw the family therapist individually. In the individual session, Keith revealed a pattern of thoughts and behaviors that was evidence to the therapist that Keith indeed might have an obsessive/compulsive disorder (OCD). Keith was prescribed the medication and immediately his behavior at home deteriorated as well.

The therapist discussed this latest hitch with his team who concluded that medicating Keith at this specific point in time fed into his parents' old view of him that he was "sick". This inhibited them from expecting ordinary behavior and his behavior indeed deteriorated. A family session confirmed this and both parents stated they had again experienced great difficulty in containing his outbursts. In taking a more thorough history it became apparent that the ritualistic type behavior was less intrusive now (even prior to medication) than at any time in the past five years. The family therapy team pointed out this discrepancy to the parents and reassured them about the fairness of their new-found parental control. As the parents regained control, Keith once again improved.

In this case medication was perceived as confirmation that the child was "sick" and for the family, this was an enormous inhibitor to any control being taken by the parents, exacerbating Keith's sense of being out of control. It is thus most important to choose the right timing for use of different treatments as well as choosing treatments that are tailored to be compatible with the ideas and beliefs that are crucial in helping a family treat the problem in question.

Depression and changing family structures

Depression can be a symptom of a child's reaction to changing family structures. Perhaps one of the greatest truisms about the complexities of family relationships is that they are all about the making or breaking of connections. In a family whose boundaries have been blurred by divorce, separation, remarriage or death, the search for those connections is all the harder. Mostly this is true because the family is undergoing change—marital conflict, changed routines, diminished contact with a parent, financial stress, etc. Family therapists can offer much needed education to newly constructed families struggling with new boundaries and establish different connections.

To re-form connections, an understanding of the evolutionary process is necessary to see problems and the inevitable hitches in their context. A child's experience of the disruption involved in divorce or separation is greatly eased by having clarity about who will do what. The typical profile of a depressed child in this context is that of a child caught in a loyalty bind—having to make choices between one parent or the other. Typically the function of a symptom in this case may be to avoid that loyalty bind. For example, if a child is depressed, he does not have to go visit his father on Sunday. If this comes at a time when his mother and his father are in a terrible battle, he can avoid father's probing questions and his mother's distress about his visit. Helping families understand those loyalty binds can alleviate symptoms in children dramatically.

Contact with pediatricians/schools/hospitals

As has been illustrated in the case vignettes, contacts with other agencies or individuals involved in treating or managing a family member is of crucial importance. Obviously a pediatrician responsible for the primary care of a child and who is often the referring source, should both keep and be kept connected with the case as the treatment progresses.

A pediatrician who has had an ongoing relationship with a family often has important insights into that family's patterns and problem. The family therapist is responsible for setting into context any interventions that are to be made so that any strong stance taken should be explained directly to the pediatrician. In hospital settings, pediatrics and psychiatry often utilize each other's expertise to accurately diagnose the physiological and psychological aspects of a child's problem such as an eating disorder, an overdose or any other severe physiological problem requiring hospitalization. It is, however, of crucial import that beyond the diagnosis, the pediatrician and family therapist remain in ongoing contact throughout the treatment process. All too often contact ends after the diagnostic process and the family may find themselves with conflicting views which they have a great deal of difficulty integrating and which then interferes with their ability to follow through on treatment.

When a child's symptoms have been noticed in the school setting, it is also of crucial importance that whatever treatment plan is developed, the school is part of that plan. Otherwise, once again, in this instance, it is the child that may find himself in the midst of conflicting views and treatments which can just perpetuate or even exacerbate the problem.

Indications and contraindications for family therapy

Family therapy is both a way of conceptualizing depression in children as well as being a well-developed methodology for the treatment of children. As parents have the most power in shaping the lives of their children it only makes sense to utilize their beliefs and ideas in understanding and tackling a child's problem. Certainly, at the very least, a family assessment should be an essential part of assessing the child's depressive symptoms—even if an alternative treatment of therapy is seen as being of more value or used in combination with family therapy.

Family therapy has seemed to be most valuable in treatment of physical disorders in which psychological factors play an important part in causing or aggravating the problems—such as asthma, diabetes, epilepsy, recurrent abdominal pain and anorexia nervosa. It is also seen as helpful with physical disorders in which, although psychological factors may not be maintaining the problem, there may be adverse psychological responses. Examples would be illnesses such as congenital heart disease, cystic fibrosis, AIDS, chronic renal disease and malignant disease. It is also seen as valuable with behavioral and emotional problems such as school refusal, separation anxiety, phobias, depression and difficult disruptive behavior. The main contraindication to family therapy is when a family is resistant to help or has low motivation. If a family has very low motivation[2] and appears to be harmful to the child, (i.e., with severe child abuse and neglect) a "corrective emotional experience" outside the family may be indicated instead. In adolescent cases where separation may be an issue, a combination of individual and family may be the best approach. However, for most childhood difficulties, family therapy is an extremely effective clinical strategy, in both the assessment and treatment process.

All families have problems and all families have strengths. In harnessing the family's strengths to battle a child's depression, family therapists can help parents and children alike to utilize the resources they have to resolve the difficulties that have arisen. It is hoped that the skills they gain in mastering this problem can be utilized with other difficulties that will inevitably arise as the family life cycle progresses.

References

Boscolo, L., Cecchin, G., Hoffman, L. and Penn, P. (1987) Milan Systemic Family Therapy, New York: Basic Books.

Carter, E. and McGoldrick, M. (1980) The Family Life Cycle: A Framework for Family Therapy, New York: Gardner Press.

Goldner, V. (1985) Family Therapy, The Clinical Guide to Child Psychiatry, (ed. D. Shaffer *et al.*) New York: The Free Press.

Haley, J. (1976) Problem-Solving Therapy, San Francisco: Jossey Bass.

Hoffman, L. (1981) Foundation of Family Therapy, New York, Basic Books.

Lask, B., Fosson, A. (1989) Childhood Illness: The Psychosomatic Approach, London: Wiley and Sons.

Minuchin, S. (1974) Families and Family Therapy, Cambridge: Harvard University Press.

Minuchin, S. (1978) Psychosomatic Families, Cambridge: Harvard University Press.

Minuchin, S. and Fishman, H.C. (1981) Family Therapy Techniques, Cambridge: Harvard University Press.

Nicols, M. (1984) Family Therapy, New York: Gardner Press.

Palazzoli, M., Cecchin, G., Prata, G. and Boscolo, L. (1980) Hypothesizing, circularity and neutrality: Three guidelines for the conductor of the session. *Family Process*, **19**, 3–12.

Papp, P. (1983) The Process of Change, New York: Guilford Press.

Pierces, F. and Sprenkle, D. (1986) *Family Therapy Sourcebook*. New York: Guilford Press.

[2]Lask, B., Fosson, A. (1989) Childhood Illness: The Psychosomatic Approach, London: Wiley and Sons, p. 120.

5 Child Abuse, Neglect and Depression

Arthur H. Green*

Division of Child and Adolescent Psychiatry College of Physicians and Surgeons of Columbia University, Presbyterian Hospital, 622 West 168th Street, New York, NY 10032, USA

INTRODUCTION

Common sense dictates that maltreated or neglected children are less likely to achieve normal physical and psychological development than children who receive good parenting. A good mother or maternal caretaker is predictable and dependable and is able to provide an infant or young child with a sense of comfort and well-being, and protects the child from abnormal levels of stimulation. An abusing caretaker not only fails to protect the child from noxious stimuli, but inflicts pain and discomfort through physical or sexual abuse. In case of neglect, the parent fails to provide the child with adequate emotional and cognitive stimulation to insure his optimal psychological growth and development.

Depression is one of the most common sequelae of child maltreatment. When a child presents with symptoms of depression, maltreatment should be ruled out. Depression in these children is often accompanied by self-destructive behavior, low self-esteem, apathy and runaway behavior. This chapter will review the research findings linking childhood maltreatment with depression and other forms of psychological distress.

The damaging effect of neglect and maternal deprivation on infants and young children living in institutions has been documented in the pioneering studies of Spitz (Spitz, 1945: 53–74) Bowlby (1951: 355–533), Burlingham and Freud (1944) and Bakwin (1949: 512–521). These children displayed physical and developmental retardation and cognitive impairment, and an impaired capacity to form human attachments. They appeared depressed, exhibiting such signs as listlessness, apathy, unresponsiveness to smiles of adults, withdrawal from others, and a general lack of appetitive behavior. Most often, these symptoms were manifested when the maternal separation took place during or after the second-half year of life and could

*Reprint requests should be directed to the author at the Family Center and Therapeutic Nursery, Presbyterian Hospital, BH 616N, 622 West 168th Street, USA (Tel. (212) 305 6694)

be reversed by restoring the child's relationship within three months. Clearly, the child's behavior was a reaction to the separation. Bowlby (1969: 24–34) describes the responses of toddlers from one to four years to prolonged separation from mother or the primary attachment figure as similar to the adult mourning process. He described three phases: 1) protest: which may last for a few hours to a week or more, in which the child is angry and disturbed, cries loudly and tries to renew contact with the absent parental figures, e.g., runs to the door, makes demands on other adults 2) despair: the child is still preoccupied with mother but appears hopeless and uncertain that mother will return. (In contrast to the first phase, the child may withdraw and become apathetic.) 3) detachment: in which the child appears to lose interest in mother and begins to renew his interest in the environment. If the maternal object returns during this stage, the child may remain remote and apathetic. Insufficient or distorted maternal care, including neglectful and abusive child rearing practices can lead to similar expressions of distress. (Coleman and Provence, 1957: 285–292d; Prugh and Harlow, 1962: 201–221.)

Depression in physically abused and neglected infants and preschool children

When young children are abused or neglected, they develop styles of behaving which interfere with relationships with future caregivers. Gaensbauer and Sands (1979: 236–270) studied a group of 48 abused and neglected infants between 6 and 36 months of age. They discovered that infants who had experienced threatening behavior would "actively" withdraw; those who were neglected evidenced a "passive" withdrawal. Both showed a lack of pleasure, that is, they failed to respond to attempts by others to elicit pleasurable responses and to initiate pleasurable interchanges with others (smiling, cooing). These children often exhibited expressionless, sober faces, indiscriminate superficial attachments to strangers, an ambiguity of affect based on an inability to express subtlety of emotions or a need to mask certain emotional expressions, and a preponderance of negative affects, such as distress, anger and sadness. The authors conclude that these distorted affective communications caused by abuse and neglect may contribute to further maltreatment by making it difficult for the new caretaker to recognize and satisfy their needs, thus causing frustration on the part of the parent and a vicious cycle of parent-child asynchrony.

Pediatricians are able to assess the nature of the parent-child dyad each time mother brings her child into the office. Researchers have used this inroad to understanding by videotaping interactions between mothers and infants to assess behavior.

Wasserman, Green and Allen (1983: 245–252) videotaped 12 abusing and 12 normal mother-infant pairs during free play and demonstrated that the abusing mothers were less verbal, less likely to initiate play and ignored their infants more than the normal mothers. The abusing mothers exhibited more negative behaviors and less positive behaviors than the normal mothers and, interestingly, the abused infants complied less with their mother's attempts to direct their play. The abusing dyad appeared to be locked into a mutually reinforcing negative spiral in which the mother fails to display positive affective behavior to engage the infant, who then responds less positively to her, which in turn, causes the mother to further withdraw. The authors concluded that it is not enough to merely stop the abuse, but the maladaptive mother-infant relationship must also be a focus for intervention.

In thinking about depression and the relationship to maltreatment, Kashani and Carlson (1987: 348–350) reported that all 9 of the 1000 preschool children referred to a child development unit who met criteria for major depressive disorder were found to have been physically abused or severely neglected. Rosenthal and Rosenthal (1984: 520–525) found that of the 16 pre-school children they studied who exhibited suicidal behavior, 81% were unwanted by their parents, and were physically abused or neglected.

Depression in physically abused school age children and adolescents

Similar to the findings in preschoolers, Green (1978: 579–582) found a high incidence of depression in his determination of the incidence of self-destructive behavior in a sample of 59 abused children, 29 neglected children and 30 normal controls. Forty percent of the physically abused children exhibited self-destructive behavior, 17% of the neglected children and 7% of the normal controls were self-destructive. Five of the abused children were suicide attempters, two made suicidal gestures, twelve were self-mutilators and five expressed suicidal ideation. In the vast majority of the cases, the self-destructive behavior was precipitated by parental beatings or occurred in response to actual or threatened separation from key parental figures. According to the author, the abused child's sense of parental assault, rejection and scapegoating formed the nucleus for subsequent self-destructive behavior. The transformation of the child's self-hatred into self-destructive behavior was catalyzed by ego deficits such as impaired impulse control.

Other researchers have obtained comparable findings; (Allen and Tarnowski, 1989: 1–11; Kazdin *et al*, 1985: 298–307; and Martin and Beezely, 1976: 105–111) all found that measures of depression, hopelessness, self-esteem, negative expectations of the future were elevated for these children.

Abused children do not feel that their actions have an impact on environmental events and have lowered feelings of self-reliance and feelings of belonging (Reidy *et al*, 1980: 284–290). It can be concluded that physically abused children are an at-risk population for depressive symptoms and that when a child is first seen, and the question of depression is raised, abuse and neglect should be questioned immediately.

Depression in sexually abused children

In light of what has been postulated, it is not surprising that depressive symptoms have been widely observed by numerous clinicians involved in the evaluation and treatment of sexually abused children as well. (Kempe and Kempe, 1978: 25–42; Nakashima and Zakins, 1977: 696–701; Rosenfeld *et al*, 1977: 327–339; McVicar, 1979: 343–353) indicated that adolescent sexual abuse victims were more vulnerable to depression than those of latency age. Other researchers have described depression, guilt and low self-esteem, along with a sensation of permanent physical damage ("damaged goods" syndrome) as almost universal issues facing victims of child sexual abuse. Suicidal behavior has been reported in sexually abused girls particularly following the disclosure of incest (Kaufman, Peck and Tagiuri, 1954: 266–279; Lukianowicz, 1972: 301–313; Sgroi, 1982: 112–120).

Within inpatient psychiatric facilities, and chemical dependency treatment programs, sexually abused adolescents have been found to be more depressed, have psychotic features with depression, and seem to be more suicidal, fearful, inhibited, and overcontrolled than other adolescent psychiatric and substance abusing adolescents (Cavaiola and Schiff, 1989: 181–188; Livingston, 1987: 413–415; Sansonnet-Hayden *et al*, 1987: 753–757; Freidrich, Urquisa and Beilke, 1986: 47–57).

Depression in adults with a history of sexual abuse during childhood

Retrospective analyses of adults with a history of sexual abuse during childhood constitute another approach to understanding this psychological situation. This longitudinal approach has the benefit of contributing understanding of the impact of maltreatment on the lifetime. Adult women who were sexually abused as children have been frequently reported to exhibit depression (Bagley and Ramsay, 1986: 33–47; Sedney and Brooks, 1984: 215–218; Briere and Runtz, 1988: 51–59) suicidal behavior (Sedney and Brooks, 1984: 215–218; Herman, 1981: 99), and low self-esteem (Briere, 1984). Briere and Runtz (1988: 51–59) also compared the symptomatology of adult males and females attending a crisis center who were molested as children with those without a history of prior sexual abuse. Fifty-five percent of the abused sample of men and women made prior suicide attempts compared to 20% of the nonabused males and 24% of the nonabused females. The sexually abused sample also demonstrated a higher incidence of depression and sleep disturbance than the nonabused sample. No differences were found between the male and female subjects with a history of sexual abuse.

Krug (1989: 111–119) described case histories of 8 men who sought psychotherapy and had been sexually molested by their mothers during childhood. Seven of them fit criteria for Dysthymic Disorder (chronic depression). According to Krug, the depression resulted from anger "turned in on the self" because the men were unable to direct it towards their mothers. Five of these men were involved in drug abuse during or shortly after the sexual abuse as a means of dealing with anxiety associated with the incest.

Psychobiological correlates of abuse and neglect in children

Child abuse and neglect may cause the young victims to become vulnerable to subsequent stress because of a learned predilection for psychological and physiological hyperarousal. According to Field (1985), the mother classically serves as a mediator of soothing and arousal in the child. By this modelling, the child learns to soothe herself by using symbols and fantasy. Failure in the development of synchronicity between the mother and the child leads to physiological disorganization, which in turn leads to extremes of under and overarousal. These children are vulnerable to experiencing subsequent stresses as somatic states, since they have difficulty mediating the environment, which may take the form of psychosomatic symptoms, panic attacks, rage reactions, or behavioral reenactments.

The biochemical changes in the central nervous system underlying these processes have been described by van der Kolk (1988: 273–290) using the animal model of inescapable shock. Like their animal counterparts, maltreated children are traumatized by their inability to escape from their physically or sexually abusing environment. According to this model, the excess trauma depletes norepinephrine and dopamine which renders the relevant receptors hypersensitive to subsequent norepinephrine stimulation. van der Kolk proposes that depression, emotional constriction, and numbing in these children are a result of the norepinephrine depletion, while the symptoms of hyperarousal coincide with the chronic noradrenergic hypersensitivity associated with excessive activation of noradrenergic pathways emanating from the locus coeruleus to the hippocampus and amygdala of the temporal lobe. This produces startle reactions, intrusive thoughts, repetitive nightmares and psychophysiological symptoms so often seen in these children. This trauma induced noradrenergic stimulation can set up hyperpotentiated pathways which are reactivated at times of subsequent arousal.

A similar model is proposed for children who experience early separation from a primary caretaker. (This is work based on primate research.) Infants who are separated from their mothers show changes in hypothalamic serotonin, adrenal gland catecholamine synthesizing enzymes, plasma cortisol, and immunoresistance, which persist over time. Separations lead to a decrease in serotonin and a high cerebrospinal fluid norepinephrine response to subsequent social stressors, suggesting that the behavioral responses of the infant to separation and loss of the primary caretaker, such as depression, apathy and withdrawal rest on long-term neurobiological alterations (van der Kolk, 1989: 401).

van der Kolk (1989: 399–402) also proposes a role for endogenous opiates in stress syndromes. High levels of stress activate endogenous opioid systems. Animals exposed to inescapable shock develop stress-induced analgesia when re-exposed to stress shortly afterward. In humans, elevations of enkephalins and plasma beta endorphins have been reported following a large variety of stressors. This endogenous opiate response may produce both dependence and withdrawal phenomena resembling those of exogenous opioids. van der Kolk suggests that traumatized individuals may reexpose themselves to traumatic situations to evoke an endogenous opioid response, producing the same effect as ingesting endogenous opioids, to neutralize their hyperarousal and produce an anxiolytic and tranquilizing action. He cites this as a possible explanation for abused children to seek victimization. Physically abused children often injure or mutilate themselves, and a study by Coid *et al* (1983: 545–546) found increased levels of metenkephalins in habitual self-mutilators during the active stage of self-harm, but not 3 months later. Opioid receptor blockade with naloxone has been found to decrease self-mutilation.

Drugs can reduce autonomic arousal at different levels in the nervous system by inhibiting noradrenergic activity. Tricyclic antidepressants and monoamine oxidase inhibitors cause a down regulation of sensitivity to norepinephrine in the post-synaptic cell. Clonidine, which blocks alpha-two receptors in the locus coeruleus has been useful in reducing startle responses, explosiveness, intrusive reexperiencing and nightmares. Beta blockers, like propanalol, have a selective sympatholytic action on the peripheral nervous system which reduces the somatic symptoms of anxiety. Benzodiazepines exert an anxiolytic action due to their central inhibitory effect on the central nervous system GABAergic system.

Discussion

Depression is frequently observed in children who have been maltreated within their family environment. While depression and impaired self-concept might represent a prototypical reaction to grossly aberrant parenting and caretaking practices during infancy and childhood, it is important to hypothesize about more specific pathological elements operating in different types of maltreatment. For example, the depression occurring in the aftermath of physical and sexual abuse might be associated with the child's inability to cope with an excessive amount of pathological and noxious stimulation from which there is no escape. On the other hand, the depression resulting from neglect, deprivation, and separation from caretakers is likely to be based on a deficiency of positive physical and psychological stimulation and a lack of contingent responsiveness to the child's needs by the parent.

With respect to physical abuse, Green (1981: 435–446) theorized that the underlying pathological parent-child interaction not only fails to soothe and protect the child from abnormal levels of stimulation, but adds physical assault, scapegoating, and rejection to his environment. This contributes to a core affective disturbance which forms the nucleus of depressive symptoms and a negative self-image. The abused child attempts to exclude the negative imagery and painful affects from awareness by using defense mechanisms such as denial, splitting, projection, dissociation and provocative self-blaming behavior in order to preserve the fantasy of having a "good parent", so vital to the child's need for security and survival.

In this sort of case, a young child, desperate to preserve the "image" of the parent as being a caretaker may find reasons to blame herself for the abuse (or may unconsciously deny that it happened.) It is often perplexing to the clinician when this child, (or spouse) acts protectively toward the abusive parent. Green (1978: 579–582) also posited that the abused child's feeling of "badness" and self-hatred derived from the parental assault, rejection and scapegoating forms the nucleus for subsequent depression and self-destructive behavior. ("I'm so bad, I have to kill myself".) Green feels that the depression and self-destructive behavior manifested by abused children do not appear to be primarily related to self-punishment out of a sense of guilt but rather correspond to more primitive learned behavior patterns originating in the earliest painful encounters with hostile caretakers during the proverbial period of life. Self-hatred and self-destructive behavior might also represent the child's compliance with the rejecting and destructive parental attitudes directed towards him. "If Daddy thinks I'm bad, I probably am."

Finkelhor and Browne (1986: 180–198) offer a comprehensive conceptual framework for understanding the effects of specifically sexual abuse on children. They hypothesized four traumatic processes inherent in the sexual abuse. 1) Traumatic sexualization: this refers to a process in which a child's sexuality is shaped in a developmentally inappropriate and dysfunctional fashion as a result of the sexual abuse (not dealt with here, but important to consider). 2) Betrayal: by a trusted parent upon whom the child is dependent. 3) Powerlessness: as a result of the child being repeatedly physically and psychologically overwhelmed by a parental figure, and 4) Stigmatization: which refers to the negative connotation communicated to the child about the sexual experiences. Betrayal exposes the child to the realization that the trusted figure will not act in his best interest. The ensuing loss of the trusted figure may lead to a grief reaction. Powerlessness imparts a sense of impotence and expectation of re-victimization leading to despair and depression. Stigmatization produces feelings of badness, shame and guilt which become incorporated into the child's self-image. Stigmatization is increased if the child is blamed for the molestation or if others are shocked by the disclosure, and if the child is pressured for secrecy.

It is clear that the methods of assessing maltreatment, confronting the people concerned, accessing treatment and following-up are sensitive and difficult interventions. Often, it is the pediatrician who is placed in the position of maintaining a relationship with all parties while engineering changes. The issues laid out in this chapter might then serve as guidelines for assessment and intervention in these complicated, emotionally charged, sorry situations.

References

Allen, D. M. and Tarnowski, K. J. (1989) Depressive characteristics of physically abused children. *Journal of Abnormal Child Psychology*, **17**, 1–11.

Anderson, L. (1981) Notes on the linkage between the sexually abused child and the suicidal adolescent. *Journal of Adolescence*, **4**, 157–162.

Bagley, C. and Ramsay, R. (1986) Sexual abuse in childhood: psychosocial outcomes and implications for social work practice. *Journal of Social Work and Human Sexuality*, **4**, 33–47.

Bakwin, H. (1949) Emotional deprivation in infants. *Journal of Pediatrics*, **35**, 512–521.

Bowlby, J. (1951) Maternal care and mental health. *Bulletin of the World Health Organization*, **31**, 355–533.

Bowlby, J. (1969) Attachment and Loss: Volume 1, Attachment, New York: Basic Books.

Briere, J. (1984) The long-term effects of childhood sexual abuse: defining a post-sexual-abuse syndrome, Paper Presented at the Third National Conference on Sexual Victimization of Children, Washington, D.C.

Burlingham, D. and Freud, A. (1944) Infants Without Families, London: Allen and Unwin.

Cavaiola, A. and Schiff, M. (1988) Behavioral sequelae of physical and/or sexual abuse in adolescents. *Child Abuse and Neglect*, **12**, 181–188.

Coid, J. *et al* (1983) Raised plasma metenkephalin in patients who habitually mutiliate themselves. *Lancet* **2**, 545–546.

Coleman, R. and Provence, S. A. (1957) Developmental retardation (hospitalism) in infants living in families. *Pediatrics*, **19**, 285–292.

Field, T. (1985) Attachment as psychobiological attunement: being on the same wavelength.

Psychobiology of Attachment and Separation, (eds. M. Reite and T. Field). Orlando, Florida: Academic Press.
Finkelhor, D. and Browne, A. (1986) Initial and long-term effects: a conceptual framework, A Sourcebook on Child Sexual Abuse, (ed. D. Finkelhor). Beverly Hills, Sage Publications.
Friedrich, W. *et al* (1986) Behavior problems in sexually abused young children. *Journal of Pediatric Psychology*, **11**, 47-57.
Gaenesbauer, T. (1982) Regulation of emotional expression in infants from two contrasting environments. *Journal of the American Academy of Child Psychiatry*, **21**, 167-171.
Gaenesbauer, T. and Sands, K. (1979) Distorted communication in abused/neglected infants and their parents and their potential impact on caretakers. *Journal of the American Academy of Child Psychiatry*, **18**, 236-250.
Green, A. (1978) Self-destructive behavior in battered children. *American Journal of Psychiatry*, **135**, 579-586.
Green, A. (1981) Core affective disturbance in abused children. *Journal of the American Academy of Psychoanalysis*, **9**, 435-446.
Kashani, J.H. and Carlson, G.D. (1987) Seriously depressed preschoolers. *American Journal of Psychiatry*, **144**, 348-350.
Kaufman, I. *et al* (1954) The family constellation and overt incestuous relations between father and daughter. *American Journal of Orthopsychiatry*, **24**, 266-279.
Kazdin, A.E. *et al* (1985) Depressive symptoms among physically abused and psychiatrically disturbed children. *Journal of Abnormal Psychology*, **94**, 298-307.
Kempe, R. and Kempe, C. (1978) Child Abuse, Cambridge: Harvard University Press.
Krug, R.S. (1989) Adult male report of childhood sexual abuse by mothers: case descriptions, motivations and long-term consequences. *Child Abuse and Neglect*, **13**, 111-120.
Livingston, R. (1987) Sexually and physically abused children. *Journal of the American Academy of Child and Adolescent Psychiatry*, **26**, 413-415.
Lukianowicz, N. (1972) *Incest, British Journal of Psychiatry*, **120**, 301-313.
Martin, H.P. and Beezley, P. (1976) Personality of abused children. *The Abused Child*, (ed. H.P. Martin), Cambridge: Ballinger.
MacVicar, K. (1979) Psychotherapy of sexually abused girls. *Journal of the American Academy of Child Psychiatry*, **18**, 342-353.
Nakashima, I. and Zakins, G. (1977) Incest: review and clinical experience. *Pediatrics*, **60**, 696-701.
Oates, K. (1986) Child Abuse and Neglect: What Happens Eventually?, New York: Brunner/Mazel.
Prugh, D.G. and Harlow, R.D. (1962) Masked deprivation in infants and young children, Deprivation of Maternal Care: A reassessment of its Effects, Geneva: World Health Organization.
Reidy, T.J. *et al* (1980) Abused and neglected children: the cognitive, social, and behavioral correlates, Traumatic Abuse and Neglect of Children at Home, G.J. Williams and J. Money eds. Baltimore: John Hopkins University Press.
Rosenthal, P.A., Rosenthal, S. (1984) Suicidal behavior by preschool children. *American Journal of Psychiatry*, **141**, 520-525.
Sansonnet-Hayden, H. *et al* (1987) Sexual abuse and psychopathology in hospitalized adolescents. *Journal of the American Academy of Child and Adolescent Psychiatry*, **26**, 753-757.
Sedney, M.A. and Brooks, B. (1984) Factors associated with a history of childhood sexual experience in a nonclinical female population. *Journal of the American Academy of Child Psychiatry*, **23**, 215-218.
Sgroi, S. (1982) Handbook of Clinical Intervention in Child Sexual Abuse, Lexington MA: Lexington Books.
Spitz, R.A. (1945) Hospitalism: an inquiry into the genesis of psychiatric conditions of early childhood. *Psychoanalytic Study of the Child*, **1**, 53-74.
van der Kolk, B.A. (1988) The trauma spectrum: the interaction of biological and social events in the genesis of the trauma response. *Journal of Traumatic Stress*, **1**, 273-290.
van der Kolk, B.A. (1989) The compulsion to repeat the trauma: re-enactment, revictimization, and masochism. *The Psychiatric Clinics of North America*, **12**, 389-411.
Wasserman, G. *et al* (1983) Going beyond abuse: maladaptive patterns of interaction in abusing mother-infant pairs. *Journal of the American Academy of Child Psychiatry*, **22**, 245-252.

6 Pediatric Illness as a Risk Factor in Depression

Candace J. Erickson

Department of Psychiatry College of Physicians and Surgeons of Columbia University, New York, NY 10027, USA

Epidemiological surveys have shown that the prevalence of chronic physical disorders in children range from 5 to 20 percent depending on the criteria used for defining a chronic physical illness (Pless and Roghmann, 1971: 351–359). The presence of illness in a child can produce enormous stresses on the child and family alike. It has been a commonly held assumption that children with physical illnesses are more likely than healthy children to have psychological problems. However, Tavormina *et al* (1976: 99) and others have questioned this assumption, remarking that the vast majority of physically ill children demonstrate no psychological problems. This chapter will review the research evidence assessing whether psychological maladaptation, and specifically, depression, is more prevalent in chronically ill children; outline how physical illness can be expected to impact on normal emotional and cognitive development; and discuss approaches to working with children and families who must cope with chronic pediatric disorders.

SUMMARY OF RESEARCH

Before summarizing the results of the large body of research which has accumulated over the last twenty-five years, it is important to consider some of the methodological issues which impact on the quality of that research and on the validity and generalizability of the findings. There are four issues which are particularly important: the definition and measurement of depression; the definition and measurement of chronic illness; controlling for confounders or other factors influencing the outcome; and the basic study design. Each will be discussed in turn.

Definition of depression

As has been discussed elsewhere in this book, the understanding of childhood depression has been undergoing significant re-evaluation during the last ten years. While it was once believed that children did not manifest the same symptoms of depressions as adults (such as decreased appetite, sleep disturbance and anhedonia), it is now clear that at least some children do demonstrate these traditional symptoms of depression. Meanwhile, the concept of "masked depression" in children has lost its former popularity. However, it remains true that the symptoms of depression may vary somewhat at different ages. Agreement on the symptoms of depression in children is still not complete. However, diagnostic classification systems have been developed which permit researchers to be more consistent in selecting populations for study (APA, 1987: 213–234).

Even when the symptoms of a major depressive disorder can be delineated, other, less severe depressive disorders such as dysthymia, adjustment disorders with depressed mood or grief reactions may also be important reactions to illness and may merit professional concern and possible intervention. Since there is great variability among studies, it is important to know precisely what is being assessed, be it major depression or simply sad feelings.

Once it is specified that which is being assessed, this outcome needs to be accurately measured. Standardized instruments for measuring depression have only recently been developed. Some of them yield psychiatric diagnoses, but many yield scores which are sums of symptoms of depression without regard to whether or not the patient meets the criteria for a psychiatric disorder. Whether the instrument used has well documented psychometric properties and the type of "score" it yields, both dramatically influence the interpretation of the results of a study.

In short, the state of the art in research on childhood depression has been rapidly evolving over the last decade. In the past it was difficult to do methodologically sound research on childhood depression because of these issues of definition and measurement. These problems are further complicated in assessing depression in children with illnesses, since many of the symptoms used to define depression, such as poor appetite, sleep disturbances, and lack of energy, may also be symptoms of the physical illness. It becomes difficult to determine whether these symptoms are due only to the physical disorder, or if they are, in fact, symptoms of depression. Using criteria to define an outcome variable (depression) which are intrinsic aspects of the independent variable (physical illness) will produce an apparent association between the two even if none exists.

Few of the studies of the psychosocial consequences of chronic illness have specifically measured depression. The majority have assessed more global indicators of psychiatric disorder, psychological adaptation, behavior problems and self esteem. The problems affecting the definition and measurement of these other psychological variables are similar to those described for depression. For the most part, each study defines psychological outcome in its own way and uses different methods of assessment. In addition, many studies use unstandardized instruments to measure outcome. This makes summarizing the research and assessing its implications difficult.

One further problem in doing research on mental health in children is determining who should provide the information about the child's symptoms. Often it is the parent who is asked to do this. However, particularly for disorders such as depression, many of the symptoms are feelings and thoughts which the child may not have shared with the parent. Meanwhile, children may not be particularly accurate observers of their own behaviors. Teachers are sometimes the informants. While they may have a better knowledge of what behaviors are normal at a specific age, they see the child in only one very specific setting for only a portion of each day. Unfortunately, research has demonstrated (Achenbach *et al*, 1987: 213–232) that there is often little agreement between the information provided by parent, child and teacher. At the moment, there is no good solution to this problem. Using a single informant may compromise the validity of the results while using multiple informants may yield conflicting results which are hard to interpret.

Defining illness

Defining illness is similarly problematic. There is evidence that psychological outcome is not illness specific, but is related to such aspects of the illness as severity, functional disability, predictability, and visibility (Stein and Jessop, 1982: 361). However, most studies have looked at psychological outcome for groups of children having the same diagnosis, without regard for range of severity, disability and the like. When a number of chronic illnesses are grouped together, the characteristics of each illness in the group must be considered. In certain epidemiologic studies, when all chronic illnesses are grouped together, the inclusiveness of the definition of chronic (how long) and illness (should disorders such as hayfever at one end of the spectrum and mental retardation at the other end of the spectrum be included) will influence both the prevalence of chronic illness in the population and the prevalence of psychological problems in the ill children. Other aspects of the illness, such as the age of onset (how early the illness interrupts the developmental sequence), duration (there appears to be adaptation to illness over time), presence of central nervous system involvement, and whether the child is acutely ill at the time of evaluation, will all influence the prevalence of psychological dysfunction.

Controlling for confounders

In any study it is important to remember that variables which are related both to the independent variable (illness) and to the dependent variable (depression or psychological dysfunction) can bias the results unless controlled for either statistically or through the research design. Social class is one such variable. It has been repeatedly demonstrated that the prevalence of a variety of psychological problems, including depression, is different in different social classes. When there is also a differential prevalence of illness across social classes, (as, for example, in sickle cell anemia), it may appear that there is an increase in the prevalence of psychological problems among children with this illness when, in fact, the cause of the increase in psychopathology is social class differences. Matching the children with sickle cell disease with healthy controls from the same social class would prevent this from happening. Similarly, controlling for social class statistically can often be used if there are sufficient numbers of subjects of the relevant social classes in both the ill and control groups. Studies in which standardized norms rather than control groups are used are particularly problematic because there is no way to assess the impact of possible confounding variables.

Other variables which must be considered possible confounders in studies of psychological functioning in chronic illness include age at evaluation, sex, intelligence, parental psychopathology, and poor family functioning. Some of the research on psychological problems in illness control for social class. Others exclude children who are mentally retarded. Most studies restrict the age range of children included in the study. A number report the results separately for males and females. However, few studies consider the possible confounding effect of parental dysfunction or disturbed family functioning on the relationship between illness and psychological functioning of the child.

Study design

Nolan and Pless (1986: 201–216) have presented an excellent critique of the types of studies done to assess the relationship between chronic illness in children and psychological functioning. They include tabulated summaries of a good proportion of the studies done between 1970 and 1985. They note that there are basically five types of studies done in this area. These include 1) case series without controls, 2) case series with controls, 3) prevalence studies, 4) cohort studies, and 5) intervention studies. Definitions over strengths and weaknesses of each type of study are outlined below, followed by a summary of the findings.

Case series without controls

This type of study evaluates a group of children who are diagnosed as having a specific illness or one of a group of illnesses. There is, by definition, no evaluated control group. This design is very weak for two reasons. First there is no control group with which to compare the prevalence of psychological problems of the physically ill group. There is no way to determine whether the score for the ill group is different than should be expected. The exception to this statement is when the measures of emotional functioning have standardized norms. In this case, at least the scores in the ill group can be compared to these norms. But, as noted above, one must assess whether the group on which the measure was standardized is an appropriate control group for the population of ill children in question. Differences between the standardization group and the ill group on possible confounding variables should be considered to determine whether there may be significant bias. It is also important to consider whether there are a large number of health related items on the measure of psychological functioning. When there is, these items will confound the results.

The second reason why these studies are weak is that the data is cross sectional. This requires that the assumption be made that the emotional problems found in the study did not exist prior to the onset of the physical condition. With physical disorders which are present from birth, this is not a consideration. Otherwise, even when the association is very strong, the opposite direction of causality must always be considered.

One other time when this study design is not weak is when the study explores differences between subgroups. Looking at differences between males and females, between different levels of severity or differing visibility of illness may yield very useful information.

In the present survey of the literature, there were fifteen case series without controls which did not use standardized measures of functioning[1] and twelve case series without controls which used standardized measures[2]. Of the fifteen studies not using standardized measures, twelve (80%) found children with chronic illness to have psychosocial problems, one (7%) did not, and two (13%) had equivocal results. Of these studies, seven assessed depression and two assessed related concepts of "misery" and "isolation". All of these studies found that ill children were depressed. Of the twelve studies which used standardized measures of psychological functioning, ten (83%) found that ill children scored as having more problems than the norms while two (17%) did not. Three of these studies specifically assessed depression, one assessed alienation and two assessed emotional disturbance as distinct from behavior or conduct problems. All of these showed ill children to be more depressed than the norm.

Case series with controls

In this type of study, psychological functioning is assessed in one group of children who have chronic illness and in a control population. These control groups are usually matched for age, and often for sex and social class. Occasionally, there is matching for variables such IQ and sib rank. The important question with these studies is who are appropriate controls. Several approaches have been used, each of which has its own drawbacks. Many studies use clinic controls, that is children attending well child care clinics at the same center where the chronically ill child attends a specialty care clinic. Children attending well care clinics often differ from the children attending specialty clinics at the same institution in age, ethnicity and social class. Other studies have used healthy siblings of the ill children as controls arguing that this will also control for family environment as well as social class and ethnicity. However, it is often difficult to find a sibling who is the same sex and close in age to the ill child. A sampling bias is also introduced if one eliminates from the ill sample those children without siblings. But the most important difficulty is that the siblings of chronically ill children may not be psychologically normal themselves. There is evidence that these siblings have an increased prevalence of psychological problems secondary to having an ill sibling (Drotar and Crawford, 1985: 355–362). Some studies have had ill children nominate like sex and age friends to serve as controls. Here there is concern about overmatching for personality characteristics which contributed to the formation of the friendship. One other alternative has been to use sex matched controls from the ill child's classroom. This approach is logistically difficult for the researcher because it requires cooperation from many different schools. However, the only methodological concern with this type of control group is the inevitable difference of home environment.

It should be recognized that these case series with controls are not case control studies. In a case control study, the cases refer to cases of a specific outcome, in this instance children with psychological maladaptation. The controls are a sample of nondisturbed children drawn from the population of origin of the cases. Assessment is then made regarding exposure to a risk factor, in this case chronic illness, in both the cases and controls. There have been no case control studies of chronic illness as a risk factor for psychosocial dysfunction. However, a case control study of hospitalization as a risk factor for psychological disturbance among children on the Isle of Wight and in an inner London borough (Quinton and Rutter, 1970: 447–459) demonstrated that repeated or prolonged hospitalization in early childhood was a risk factor for later psychiatric disorder.

In the present survey of the literature, there were twenty four case series which had a comparison group[3]. One of these studies did not compare the psychological functioning of the ill and healthy children. Of the twenty-three remaining studies, thirteen (57%) found that the ill children had more psychological problems than the controls, four (17%) showed mixed results, and six (26%) found no difference between the ill and healthy children. Of these studies, three specifically assessed depression, one measured negative self comments, one isolation, and three looked at affective disorders under the classification of emotional disorders. All of these studies found children with chronic illness to have more depressive symptomatology than well children.

Prevalence studies

Prevalence studies involve evaluating a representative sample of a defined population to determine which subjects in the sample have a chronic illness and which subjects have psychological disorders. Assessing a defined population eliminates the problem of selection bias. This type of study also permits accurate estimation of the relative risk. However, these studies are very expensive, and, because of the relative rarity of chronic illness in childhood, there is a risk of having very few cases of chronic illness in the sample unless the sample is very large.

There have been four prevalence studies evaluating the association of psychosocial dysfunction with chronic illness[4]. The sample sizes in these studies range from 1700 to 3300 children. All four studies showed an increase in psychological problems in children with chronic illness, with relative risks of 2.2 or greater. None of these studies looked specifically at depression. However, two of them assessed a category classified as neurotic or emotional disorders in addition to a category of antisocial or conduct disorders. Both of these studies found increases in both types of disorders in children with chronic illnesses.

Cohort studies

There are three types of cohort studies. one begins with a group of chronically ill children (exposed) and a comparable group of healthy children (unexposed) and follows them longitudinally until the events of interest (development of psychological disorder) occurs. A second begins with a birth cohort and follows the children over time until all of the events of interest (diagnosis of chronic illness and development of psychological disorder) occur. This type of study requires a very large sample because of the relative rarity of chronic illness in children. The third, a historical cohort, looks back to ascertain presence of chronic illness and development of psychological disorder after all of the events have occurred. In these studies the investigator must rely on information which has already been collected, and which may not be optimal for the study's purpose. However, all three of this variety of study have the advantage of being longitudinal and therefore providing the time sequence of events. They eliminate the possibility of the psychological disorder predating the onset of the illness. This makes this type of study particularly strong for causal inference.

There have been eight cohort studies on the effect of chronic illness on psychological functioning[5]. Three of these studies had no control group so that comparisons of psychosocial dysfunction between ill and healthy children cannot be made. However, the five studies with control groups all found an increase in psychological problems in children with chronic illness. None of the cohort studies specifically assessed depression.

Intervention studies

Nolan and Pless (1986: 201–216) point out that the randomized controlled trial is the gold standard of research design. However, it is obvious that children cannot be randomized to the ill and healthy groups. They suggest an interesting alternative. They argue that if there is an hypothesized causal pathway with an intervening variable (e.g. illness leads to poor self esteem which leads to depression), and a treatment is developed to affect the intervening variable, subjects can be randomly assigned to treatment groups. Then if the treatment affects the intervening variable and decreases the psychological dysfunction, this evidence supports the hypothesized mechanism. Also, if the illness also decreases in the intervention group, this gives evidence for reversed causality. This is an interesting new approach to studying the psychosocial consequences of chronic illness.

There are a number of intervention studies in the literature on psychosocial adaptation in chronic illness[6]. The majority indicate an improvement in the psychosocial dysfunction in the treatment group. However, the interventions in all of these studies are rather general (such as supportive counseling) and not specifically directed at an hypothesized intervening variable. So that while this approach is promising, there are at present no research findings using this approach which contribute to our understanding of the psychosocial consequences of illness in children.

Summary of research

As can be seen from the review above, the research evidence consistently demonstrates that children with chronic illnesses are at an increased risk for developing psychosocial problems. From the prevalence studies cited, it appears that the relative risk is approximately 2 across categories of illness. There is also consistent evidence from studies which look specifically at depression, that chronically ill children exhibit more signs of depression than do healthy children. It must be kept in mind, however, that while the prevalence of psychosocial problems is greater for ill children, still most studies indicate that fewer than 30% of chronically ill children actually have psychological disorders. This means that the vast majority of these children and their families find ways to cope with the additional stresses which arise from the child's physical disorder.

Several of the cohort studies looked at the persistence of psychological problems over time (Ahnjso *et al*, 1981: 321; Breslau and Marshall, 1985: 199; Heller *et al*, 1985: 257; Kovacs *et al*, 1985: 827; Orr *et al*, 1984: 152). While most of them showed that there was some adaptation to the illness with improvement in psychological functioning, it appears that the increased risk of psychological problems persists when the illness persists. There is more controversy about whether there are long term emotional consequences after the illness has resolved. Although young adults who had persistent chronic pediatric disorders had an increase in psychological problems, Pless found that psychological functioning was no different in young adults who had previously had chronic pediatric disorders than in healthy controls. Similarly, in an uncontrolled study of young adults who were five year survivors of juvenile Hodgkins disease, Wasserman *et al* (1987: 626–631) found the prevalence of psychiatric diagnoses to be similar to that expected in normal community samples. However, O'Malley and Koocher (1979: 608) in their study of long term survivors of childhood cancer, found that 59% had some psychological problems and 12% had severe problems in young adulthood. It may be that disease characteristics such as severity of disorder or invasiveness of treatment regimens account for the differences in these findings.

There are certain risk factors which increase the likelihood that a child with a chronic illness will show psychological problems. The severity of the illness, particularly when there is significant functional disability, appears to increase the prevalence of psychological problems (Steinhausen and Schindler, 1981: 74; Daniels *et al*, 1987: 295–308; Cadman *et al*, 1987: 805–813). In the Ontario Child Health Study, presence of disability increased the relative risk of neurotic disorders and attention deficit disorder from 2.2 to 5. It did not alter the relative risk of conduct disorders. Involvement of the central nervous system also dramatically increases the risk of psychological disorder (Rutter *et al*, 1970; Breslau, 1985: 553). In the Isle of Wight study, Rutter found that while 17% of children with chronic illness but without brain involvement had psychological problems, 36% of children whose illness involved the brain demonstrated psychiatric problems. Both of these were compared with only 6.6% of physically healthy children who had psychological disorders.

There are several other risk factors which appear to increase the risk of psychological maladaptation. It appears that the less visible the illness, the more likely the child is to have emotional problems (McAnarney *et al*, 1974: 523; Jessop and Stein, 1985: 993). It is postulated that this results from the child attempting to pass for "normal" while living in fear of not being successful because of his "secret" disability. Meanwhile, the child is never forced to confront and deal with the illness in the same way as children who have more visible or more disabling disorders. There is a great deal of uncertainty in this marginality. Uncertainty may also influence adjustment in another way. Children with illnesses where symptoms are episodic and unpredictable may live in anticipation of their next "attack". Again, the child and family cannot fully enjoy the periods of normalcy, and yet do not have the opportunity to adjust to a day to day pattern of coping with the disorder. There is mounting evidence that children with illness who have a parent with psychological problems are at greater risk for psychosocial problems. Family dysfunction similarly increases the risk (Steinhausen and Schindler, 1981: 74; Daniels *et al*, 1987: 295–308; Lewis and Khaw, 1982: 636). There is also some evidence that the presence of other stressful life events in addition to the illness can increase the risk of psychological problems in an ill child (Daniels *et al*, 1987: 295–308).

AN APPROACH TO UNDERSTANDING THE IMPACT OF ILLNESS ON CHILD DEVELOPMENT

It can be useful to develop a theoretical understanding of how illness can interfere with the normal cognitive and psychological development of children. From this perspective, one can begin to predict the types of problems ill children may develop and perhaps begin to develop true preventive intervention strategies to circumvent or diminish the potential problems. Needless to say, the theoretical models and proposed interventions must be empirically validated before they can become more than working hypotheses. In this section, one approach to understanding the impact of illness on child development will be described. This approach is based on the theory of psychosocial development described by Erik Erikson (1963: 247–274) and on the theory of cognitive development originally described by Jean Piaget (1969). For each age grouping, normal psychosocial and cognitive development will be described briefly. Ways in which illness can interfere with this development will then be delineated. Certain preventive intervention strategies present themselves as obvious outgrowths of this approach to understanding the genesis of psychological problems associated with chronic illness. It must be kept in mind, however, that these theories are describing potential problems which can arise because of an illness' interference with normal psychosocial development. There is a strong likelihood that at least some of the psychiatric problems seen in children with illnesses are direct consequences of biologic effects of the illness on the functioning of the central nervous system.

Infancy

For the purposes of this discussion, infancy can be defined as the first 18 months of life. During this period, the child moves from being completely dependent on the environment to a stage where he can begin to get around under his own power and begins developing independence. This coincides with the Eriksonian stage of Trust vs. Mistrust. To move through this stage, the infant must come to see the environment as a safe, stable place and to see others as reliable, nurturing and predictable. The child must trust that the environment will respond to the needs which he is as yet unable to meet for himself. Developing this trust requires consistency in the child's environment so that he can predict events and learn through experience that when needs arise, the environment will respond appropriately. The infant, who has no concept of time, feels each need as complete and overwhelming. Since the baby's only reality is the sensations of the moment, each need threatens survival. The child must learn to trust himself, that he can survive until the need is met. To do this, the child relies on signals from the environment that he can survive and on the repeated experience that the discomfort predictably resolves before the child is overwhelmed. Establishing this sense of trust provides the child with a stable base from which he can move out and explore. Piaget described this period as the "sensorimotor" stage of cognitive development. During this stage, the child is practicing and combining various patterns of acting on his environment in order to define its reality and begin to develop a concept of cause and effect. Cognitive development during this stage is very dependent on the child's ability to experience and act upon his physical environment. Early on the child's reality is defined only by what is in his perceptual field. If he cannot see an object, it no longer exists. However, during this stage, by games such as peek-a-boo, the child begins to develop a primitive symbolic capacity which allows him to hold an object in mind even when it is no longer visible. Repeated physical and temporal links between the child's actions and their consequences permit a primitive understanding of cause and effect to emerge.

Illness interrupts the predictability both of the environment and of internal sensations and responses to the environment. Often, caregivers are required to administer treatments which may be frightening or uncomfortable. Routines are disrupted. Things are no longer as they were. Meanwhile, internal sensations caused by the illness, such as pain, may be new and may come at "inappropriate" times, e.g. eating may cause pain rather than dispel hunger. Meanwhile, the child's responses to environmental efforts to help may also be disrupted, e.g. rocking which normally soothes does not relieve the pain. All of these disruptions may render the child's internal and external worlds unpredictable.

Illness may also disrupt the parents' ability to bond with the child. Particularly with chronic illness, parents often grieve the loss of the healthy child they had hoped for. This grief may make it difficult for the parents to be emotionally available to the ill child. In addition, an ill child does not provide the normal positive reinforcement to parents for their parenting efforts. When a child smiles, alerts to the parent or calms when consoled, the parents feel good about their interaction with the child and repeat the behaviors which were successful. They also feel good about their own ability as parents. However, because of the illness, a sick child may not smile, may not be alert, may not respond to comforting. This lack of response provides no reinforcement either for the parents' behaviors or for their self image as parents. These difficulties may make it harder for parents to be available to their ill children in a nurturing way.

The presence of illness in an infant may also disrupt the parents feeling of confidence in parenting. This may happen because of the ill child's lack of response to parenting efforts. However, most parents are also unsure of how to help their ill child and rely upon medical personnel to do this for them. The parents' inexperience with illness and lack of a knowledge base for making health care decisions, leaves the parents feeling helpless and anxious. They may then be unable to give the child the message that things are under control.

Restrictions on physical movement may occur as the consequence of illness in a child. This may be a consequence of the illness itself, such as when braces are needed or when fatigue may diminish physical activity. Overprotective parents or health care professionals may also unnecessarily limit the activity of ill children because of exaggerated concern about the physical welfare of the child. This restriction of activity can interfere with the child's ability to interact with his physical environment and may thus limit the opportunity for developing certain important cognitive skills.

When a child is sufficiently ill to require hospitalization, separation from home and parents may be added to the problems outlined above. Since the infant relies on his parents as his major coping mechanism, such a separation can be quite traumatic, especially since the child is sick and may be unable to mobilize whatever internal resources he may have. This leaves the child quite alone and defenseless in a strange and threatening environment.

In view of these predictable disruptions of normal development caused by illness, it would seem reasonable to develop guidelines for preventive intervention based upon these expected difficulties. A number of such preventive intervention strategies are listed below.

1) Discuss with parents how to increase predictability of the child's environment. This should include such things as developing and maintaining routines that define the rhythm of daily life. Daily activities such as mealtimes, naptime, bathtime and bedtime should follow a routine schedule as much as possible. Association of rituals with certain activities, such as bedtime rituals, can also help the child learn that one thing consistently follows another. Consistent use of the same objects or techniques to comfort a child can enhance both the predictability of the situation and the association of the object or technique with the expectation of comfort.

2) Maintain similar consistency during uncomfortable procedures. Practices such as only doing procedures in a treatment room, always wearing the same apron to do a procedure, or always using the same ritual to administer medication, can allow the child to mobilize his anxiety only when it is necessary and appropriate, rather than having to maintain a constant vigilance in case of attack. Predictability of uncomfortable experiences make even those experiences easier to handle.

3) Treat pain and other symptoms of the illness as well as is possible. This may seem obvious, but there is considerable evidence that pain in children is significantly undertreated (Schecter, 1989: 791–794). Adequate treatment of these symptoms will

mean less unpredictability in the child's internal sensations, and may allow the child to reinforce his parents in more normal ways.

4) Warn the parents about child behaviors which are expected consequences of the illness, such as irritability or fatigue. This will help the parents to use their own cognitive abilities to prepare for and accept the child's behaviors rather than perceive them as indications that the parents are ineffective or the baby is bad.

5) Emphasize the baby's positive attributes. This may help the parents remember and focus on those things which elicit warm and nurturing responses rather than those things which disappoint them.

6) Support the parents in their role and ability as parents. Stress the importance of the parents' role in maintaining both the child's physical and emotional wellbeing. A safe haven of comfort and care is something that only the parents can provide. Many parents also want to participate directly in the child's health care, and they should be incorporated into the health care team as much as possible. It is also important to remember to acknowledge the parents' successes and to reinforce them for the good care and the warm nurturing which they provide for their child.

7) Counsel parents regarding whatever realistic limitations the child might have and then encourage them to permit the child to explore fully within these limits. It is important to remember that parents are often anxious and insecure with regard to their child's illness and will require continued reassurance and encouragement.

8) When a child requires hospitalization, recommend rooming-in to prevent separation whenever this is possible.

9) Provide parents with the opportunity and the forum to grieve the loss of their hoped-for, healthy child. Chronic illness or disability in a child is a terrible loss for child and parent alike. Parents often have more difficulty with this loss than the child because the parents are able both to project forward to future difficulties and to compare what lies in store for their child with what would be "normal" if the child were healthy. Parents often find it helpful to discuss this issue with their pediatrician or subspecialist, a mental health professional, or as a part of a parent support group.

Toddlers

Toddlerhood lasts from about 18 months to three years of age. During this period, as the child's neurological system continues to mature, the child develops increasing control over locomotion, fine motor control, sphincter control and begins to develop language as a form of symbolic thought.

This age corresponds to Erikson's stage of Autonomy vs. Shame and Doubt. During this stage, the child begins to master her own body as she learns to walk, run, climb, feed herself, dress herself, go to the bathroom by herself and express herself verbally. This is an age where the child is developing an ever increasing sense of autonomy and self-control, and wants to do everything for herself. She also wants to make her own decisions, saying "no" to everything suggested by the parent and resisting, often through tantrums, the will of her elders. At this stage, parents need to allow the child to take progressively more responsibility without having excessive expectations. It is important for the child to experience success as she attempts to master her body. Failure leads to a sense of being unready (shame) and a fear of failure in mastering the task (doubt). To succeed, the toddler needs to attempt tasks truly within her power. She needn't succeed every time, but sufficiently often to consolidate her sense of mastery and encourage her continued efforts. Parental reinforcement of effort and success enhances the toddler's self esteem. Parental approval also allays the child's fear that if she becomes independent she will anger and lose her parents. Unrealistic parental expectations may lead the child to experience repeated failure and thus begin to doubt her own emerging capacities. Overprotective parents prohibit her from facing challenges that would expand her capabilities.

This age is still a part of Piaget's sensorimotor stage described above. The child continues to act upon her environment, developing ever more sophisticated patterns of action which allow her to be more effective in her activities. Experimentation continues to enhance the toddler's understanding of physical cause and effect.

Children who are ill often need to go back to being fed, wearing diapers, being carried or staying in bed. Through pain, immobility, hospitalization, dietary restrictions, etc., illness often prohibits the toddler from developing or maintaining normal mastery over bodily functions. Being unable to do things for oneself leaves the child with a sense of thwarted mastery and doubt about her competence.

As during the previous stage, parents may have difficulty discovering realistic expectations for an ill child. This may lead them to expect more than the child is able to do. Such excessive expectation can, through repeated failures, lead to poor self-esteem. Meanwhile, parents who are overprotective curtail the child's opportunities for mastery and communicate to the child her fragility and inability to perform.

Parents are also often reluctant to set appropriate behavioral limits for an ill child. They often feel sorry for the child and become overindulgent. However, the toddler needs consistent parental limits in order to incorporate them and establish self control. Overly permissive parents do not provide the toddler with the help that she needs in determining when to rein in her behavior.

Many of the suggestions for preventive intervention listed under Infancy are also applicable during the toddler stage. The following interventions are of particular importance in this age group.

1) Encourage parents and health care providers to allow the toddler to do as much for herself as she can. Provide her with as many opportunities as possible to master her body and her environment.

2) Advise parents regarding realistic expectations for a toddler with the specific illness involved. This will permit them to help the child to succeed and reward the successes, without demanding more of the child than she can possibly do. It is also useful to explore with the parents activities in which the child is talented and can be successful.

3) Counsel parents regarding appropriate behavioral limits and how to set them with an ill child. It will be very important to support the parents through their effort in limit setting, as setting limits is difficult even under the best of circumstances. Guilt, anxiety and pity make it even more difficult for the parents of ill children.

Preschool child

The preschool years run from age 3 years to 5 or 7 years. Erikson called this age the stage of Initiative vs. Guilt. During the previous stage, the child learned to control his own body. During this stage, he learns to manipulate his environment and the people in it. While energetically trying to influence his environment, the preschooler may overstep his bounds and infringe on the rights of others. The restrictions placed on this behavior becomes incorporated into the child's newly developing conscience. It is through this process that the child begins to master his social environment and learns social values from family and peers.

During this period, the child also has a heightened body awareness and concern over body integrity. The child now requests a bandaid for the slightest cut and wants to be sure that he will not lose any important part of his body. This is likely related to the child's expanding consciousness of his own sexuality and the differences between boys and girls.

Piaget calls this stage preoperational. Piaget described this age as the period when symbolic thought begins to develop. The child can now think about things which are not present, and he has become aware that events have causes. However, he does not yet understand complex interrelationships and thus uses associative logic. Events that are temporally or spatially close together are seen as cause and effect. Perceptual cues are used as the most powerful determinants of categorization. Thus age is determined by height, sex by hair length or dress, and amount by length or height.

Children at this stage exhibit an incredible egocentrism and omnipotence. They believe that they cause everything and that the world revolves around them and their needs. This gives them a sense of power, but this power can be a double edged sword. While allowing the child to believe he can do anything, this sense of omnipotence can also be frightening. Angry thoughts or wishes are seen as being as dangerous as actions. The magical thinking of this age results in the belief that these wishes will cause the thoughts to happen. Being able to see things only from his own perspective, the child assumes that everyone else thinks and feels the same things as he does. The child will therefore expect the parent to know his thoughts and feelings without being told about them.

As was true in the other stages, the limitations imposed on a child by illness can restrict his mastery of the developmental tasks appropriate to his age. Fatigue, hospitalization, and being kept at home can limit the child's exposure to social settings. Irritability or lethargy may alter the types of social interchanges experienced by the child. Being infantilized and overprotected in social situations compromises mastery. Lack of limit setting teaches the child incorrect social boundaries and may alienate him from adults and peers.

Because of their egocentrism, preschoolers often feel that they have caused their own illness or that pain and other unpleasant aspects of the illness are punishments for bad behavior. Since the illness has no real relationship to the child's behavior, the child can never be good enough to avoid the bad consequences. This may lead the child to conclude that he is bad, and deserving of punishment. The inability to control the illness through his behavior may also leave him feeling helpless and hopeless.

The child may get many cues about "bad" which relate to the illness and not just to transgressing social boundaries. The illness is often seen by the child as a part of who they are ("a part of them that is sick"), but a part over which have relatively little control. It is easy for the child to misinterpret the illness being bad as meaning that he is somehow bad. This is particularly problematic at this age, since the child still sees himself as the cause of things, and thus may more firmly believe that he caused his own illness.

At this cognitive stage, the child may rigidly expand his notion of causality to events he associates with illness. Thus, he may believe that if he goes without a coat, he will get sick. These beliefs may develop into rituals to prevent the illness. When the child becomes ill despite the ritual, the child's sense of structure and order may be abolished. On the other hand, the child may identify his illness with only one symptom. He then fails to understand why restrictions or medications are necessary if the symptom is not present.

The child's heightened body awareness and concerns about body integrity can make medical procedures such as shots, blood drawing and operations particularly threatening to the preschool child. Preventive interventions which may be particularly useful with a preschool child include the following:

1) Encourage mastery in every area possible.

2) Arrange for social interactions with supportive adults. Be sure that the adults recognize the child's age (particularly if the illness causes growth delays) and abilities, so that the child is not infantilized or overprotected.

3) Arrange for supported peer interactions. Arrange for the "playdates" to center around activities where the ill child can succeed. Look for friends who enjoy the same things as the child to maximize the likelihood of a successful interaction. Be available to help guide the interaction should symptoms of the child's illness begin to have a detrimental effect on the interaction. However, give both children room to resolve their own problems as much as possible. If the child can manage preschool, encourage this type of social interaction as well. Here, teachers may need to be advised about whatever realistic restrictions should be placed on the child and should be discouraged from placing others.

4) Parents and health care providers must continually confront the child's idea that he is the cause of his illness. The child must be reassured that neither the illness nor its symptoms or treatment are punishments for bad behavior. Phrases such as "you are going to make yourself sick", "it is your own fault", or "if you don't behave, the doctor will give you a shot" should all be avoided. When specific behaviors

are required of the child to comply with medical treatment, the child should be advised that the behavior is required to help his body work better and that if he cannot do it by himself, an adult will help him do it. This takes the responsibility for success out ot the child's hands and places it with the adults who take care of him.

5) Do not label the child's illness as "bad". It may hurt, be uncomfortable or difficult, etc. But a bad illness is too likely to be misinterpreted as a bad child. Never label the child as "bad" because of the illness or behaviors related to the illness. Also, be aware of the child's likely interpretation that the illness is a form of punishment and assist the child in working through this issue. Assistance from a child mental health professional may be useful.

6) Help the child understand the cause of his illness and the symptoms associated with the illness. It will be important that all explanations be at a level understandable to a preschool child. Again, the help of a specialist in child development or a mental health professional may be useful.

7) Do as few invasive procedures as possible during this stage. If possible, do required surgeries before the age of three or after six. If procedures are unavoidable, it is important to prepare the child with careful, age appropriate explanations of what will be done and how it will feel. Providing information about the sensations the child will experience is as important as telling the child what will be done. Explanations should inform the child what to expect, step by step. Since the child will interpret this information quite literally, it is important that the procedure be done in the manner described to the child. Otherwise, the child will feel betrayed. It is often useful to give the child an opportunity to play through procedures on a doll in order to familiarize the child with the procedure and desensitize him to the equipment. It is important not to permit the child to practice painful procedures such as injection on real people. The child should never be allowed to physically hurt the parent or health care provider. Hurting the adult will likely be experienced by the child as loss of control of his own angry impulses, and he may expect that the adult will be angry and retaliate. In addition, the child is truly ambivalent, both loving the parent and being angry at the parent for not preventing the illness. The child needs for the adult to control the situation so that the child need not feel sorry or guilty about hurting a beloved adult.

8) Provide reassurance that no important part of the body will be removed, and provide bandaids for any holes in the skin.

School age child

This stage begins with entry into primary school and continues until puberty. Approximate ages for this stage are from 6 or 7 years to 12 or 13 years. Erikson called this the stage of Industry vs. Inferiority. During this stage, the major task is to master skills which will later be used on the job as a productive adult. Since Erikson described his stages in the early 1950s, the number of years of formal education experienced by most American children has lengthened considerably. However, this stage remains the period prior to the onset of adolescence when a child devotes himself to learning work related skills, usually in a setting where peers are learning the same skills. At this stage, the child feels that she *is* what she does and learns. For the first time she is aware of her peers in a comparative setting and evaluates her own worth by evaluating her achievements relative to theirs. She works hard to do well, and when she succeeds, she has a feeling of being industrious and accomplishing her goals. If she fails, she feels inferior to her peers.

Piaget describes this period as the beginning of logical thinking. During this stage, the child can reason about objects and events within her experience. As she develops these skills, she needs to handle materials to aid in developing her understanding of concepts. For this reason the stage is called the stage of concrete operations. During this stage the child develops an understanding of such concepts as number, volume, mass, and time by recognizing the conservation of these properties despite alterations of the salient perceptual cues. For example, the child learns that ten beads are still more than five beads even if the five beads are spread out so that they form a longer line than the ten beads. The reversibility of actions which change perceptual properties (ie. if you can stretch them out, you can push them back together) becomes obvious to the child during this stage. Many of the opportunities which children have to practice this kind of thinking arise in school settings.

During this stage, an illness may limit what the child can do. The illness may impede participation in athletics or acquisition of specific school or trade skills. Fatigue from the illness may prevent the child from concentrating as well or studying as much as peers. Illness and hospitalizations may take the child out of school repeatedly. The child may therefore lose time and instruction for mastering necessary skills, and fall progressively more behind. These problems can all lead to disappointment, and a negative self image.

Missing school because of illness also diminishes the opportunity to practice logical thinking, thus interfering with cognitive mastery. However, the development of logical thinking does help children with illnesses to understand their conditions better.

Children in this age group compare with peers, and want to fit in and be like them. This concern for peer acceptance is less intense than during adolescence, but it is an issue during this stage as well. A child with an illness often sees herself as different, and is seen by her peers as different. She does not fit in, and this feeling of isolation may lead to psychological distress.

During the school years, the following strategies are of particular importance:

1) Be sure that the child has whatever help is necessary to progress with school work. If the child must be hospitalized or confined to home for prolonged periods, most school systems will arrange for teaching at home or at the hospital. If the illness interferes with acquisition of specific school skills, special education techniques may be of value. Specialized testing for these services are available through the public school system as required by Public Law 94–142. Do not wait until the child is a year or more behind to begin help. If repeated absences are predictable, develop a program for maintaining academic levels immediately.

2) Determine what the child can master, and encourage her mastery in these areas.

This is especially true of any particular talents the child may have. Being excellent in one area can help offset a weakness in another. Physical activity which does not compromise the child's health and at which there is some possibility of success should be particularly encouraged.

3) Encourage peer interaction around activities at which the child excels and those with which the illness does not interfere. This will give the youngster an opportunity to experience themselves as performing among the best of the peer group and will provide the child's friends with an experience of the child as special in a very positive way.

4) Do not encourage the child to "pass as normal". This requires the child to pretend that she has no illness. She may come to believe that no one could like and accept her for who she is. However, it may be useful to help the child focus on ways in which she is no different than other children, so that she can continue to identify with them. Meanwhile, demonstrating how circumscribed the areas influenced by the illness are may also help.

Again, emphasizing any talents which make the child special in a positive way can be very supportive.

Adolescence

Today adolescence stretches from puberty (12 or 13 years) into the early twenties. During this period, which Erikson called Identity vs. Role Diffusion, the child has to integrate all of the tasks from the previous four stages into a coherent identity, and prepare to face the world as an independent adult. In addition to dealing with the changes in his body occasioned by the onset of puberty, the adolescent must compare and integrate how others see him with how he sees himself. In the process, he must separate parental values from his own values. There are a number of ways in which the teenager can do this. The adolescent often tries on the values of others by developing heroes. He fantasizes himself behaving like the hero and can thereby see how those behaviors might feel to him. The teenager forms very tight alliances with peers in order to identify with them and try on the group values. This approach becomes obvious through teenage fads where everyone must look and behave identically. This peer identification not only enables the adolescent to try on group values, but also provides him with a support system which will allow him to separate from his family sufficiently to rebel against parental values. Only after rejecting parental values can most teenagers avow those same values as their own.

The adolescent must also adjust to his budding sexuality. Changes in the body are brought on by puberty and include longitudinal growth, changes in body configuration, and emergence of sexual characteristics. The adolescent must alter his body image to accommodate for these changes. In addition, he must re-establish his motor coordination to accommodate for the changes in size and center of gravity of his body. When reaching for something, the teenager may find that his arm is now an inch longer than it was only several months ago. This type of change requires a reorientation of his spatial perception. Finally, the adolescent must adjust to the psychological effects of the hormone fluctuations which accompany puberty. The mood swings may be both surprising and uncomfortable for him. Throughout all of this, the teenager must also decide whether he will act on this emerging sexual abilities and, if so, how he will establish the relationship(s) in which he will do this.

During this phase, the adolescent must also connect roles and skills which he has learned with what he wants to be as an adult. Integrating these skills and desires with practical realities takes place through career planning.

Piaget calls this stage formal operations and describes it as mastering abstract thinking and hypothesizing about thoughts and ideas which are outside of the youngster's own experiences. These skills must be practiced until they are mastered, and most of this practice takes place in school settings. This type of thinking can be seen in history, literature and advanced math classes in high school, but really blooms in college where ideals, politics, and philosophy are often discussed for hours on end.

Physical illness can interfere with all of these developmental tasks. Children who are chronically ill often do not grow well and so may have concerns about their growth in comparison with peers. Ill children may also have some disfigurement from the illness or its treatment. Problems in either area can influence the adolescent's body image.

Children who are chronically ill often have delayed sexual maturation. This may present problems both because of concerns regarding ultimate sexual functioning as well as because of embarrassment as a consequence of being less developed than peers. In addition, if the youngster misses school frequently, he may lack the contact with peers necessary to develop relationships where sexual exploration is possible.

Illness interferes with the teenager's peer identification. The youngster may see himself as different, avoiding peers and becoming isolated and depressed. On the other hand, the teenager may deny his illness in order to be like his peers, and fail to comply with necessary medical treatments. The other teenagers are also likely to see the ill youngster as different. This is a particular problem in adolescence, since all adolescents need to see themselves as invulnerable in order to be able to separate from their families. An ill adolescent reminds his peers of their own vulnerability, and may consequently be ostracized.

Establishing independence from the family is also problematic for the adolescent with an illness. As noted above, the ill adolescent may not have a strong peer group to support him as he moves away from his family. Meanwhile, he may be truly dependent on his family because of needed medical care. Parents sometimes overrestrict ill adolescents in an effort to protect them. To assert his independence, the teenager may wildly reject all authority and stop following necessary medical regimes.

The ill adolescent may have difficulty finding appropriate role models with which to identify. Identification may be difficult if the teenager has restrictions which prohibit him from doing things which his hero does. This may limit available role models.

Ill adolescents often miss school frequently. As a consequence, they may not have the opportunity to develop skills which will be necessary for future careers. Missing school may also limit available opportunities for mastering abstract thinking. High school counselors are rarely trained to work with children with chronic illnesses, and thus, teenagers with such illnesses often receive inappropriate advice about career choices.

There are numerous ways to help adolescents with illnesses cope with their disorders. A few of them are listed below:

1) Counsel the youngster about growth retardation and delayed sexual maturation when appropriate. It is helpful if the teenager has realistic expectations about these issues. It is also important to reassure the adolescent appropriately about the eventual outcome of his growth and sexual maturation. Talking with a young adult with a similar illness can sometimes help the youngster see a brighter future.

2) Do whatever possible to ameliorate disfigurement. This is important at any age, but adolescents are more sensitive to physical differences than younger children are.

3) In school and other interactions with peers, help the teenager discover age appropriate, peer related activities at which the youngster can excel. These activities may include such things as music, computer games, board games, and make-up and hair styling. Encourage the adolescent to develop skills in these activities, especially any in which the youngster is talented.

4) Have the youngster take as much responsibility for his own treatment as early as possible. If the adolescent is already in control of his medical regimen by the time he reaches his teens, it is less likely that medical issues will become an arena for power struggles between parent and child.

5) Counsel parents about appropriate limits for the ill teenager, and help them to focus limit setting and power struggles on normal adolescent issues such as curfews, phone calls and dress, rather than on treatment issues.

6) Help the adolescent find a way to deal with his illness and its treatment with his friends. Honest, matter of fact explanations are usually best. Care should be taken that the youngster avoid flaunting his illness.

7) Be sure that someone familiar with the medical issues involved is actively discussing career goals with the adolescent. Encourage the youngster to explore the possibilities and to challenge himself.

8) When possible, adolescents should be hospitalized on an adolescent ward where their age-specific needs can be addressed. Teenagers can be permitted to wear street clothes which allows them to look normal rather than sick, to identify with peers, and to express their individuality. Having ward meetings gives the teenagers a voice in ward management and provides them with the opportunity to practice abstract thinking. Involving the youngster in decision making for medical management helps the teenager establish his independence and assume responsibility for his own medical care.

OTHER TREATMENT MODALITIES

Besides the more preventive approaches already described, there are a variety of other approaches to managing psychosocial problems in ill children. Many of these, such as behavioral therapy, cognitive therapy, individual dynamic psychotherapy, family therapy and group therapy, have already been discussed in this volume. There are two other treatment modalities which deserve special mention when developing treatment programs for children with physical illnesses.

Psychopharmacology

Over the last ten years, there has been increasing evidence that heterocyclic antidepressants, which have been very effective for treating depression in adults, may also be effective in prepubertal children. The data on this issue has already been summarized in Chapter 16. However, it is important to note that in all of the controlled, double blind, randomized trials conducted in children or adolescents, placebo has been as effective, if not more effective, than the heterocyclic medication tested (Puig-Antich *et al*, 1987: 81-89; Geller *et al*, 1989: 101-108; Kramer and Feiguine, 1981: 636-644). Meanwhile the heterocyclics antidepressants have potentially significant side effects. Mild increases in the PR and QRS intervals are common. Heart block and arrhythmias are less common, but there is evidence that children are more susceptible than adults to the cardiotoxic effects of these drugs (Ryan *et al*, 1987: 400-406). Elevation of heart rate to 120 beat/min is not unusual. Hypertension can be of clinical importance if there is a preexisting problem. Mild confusional states have been reported at higher plasma levels. There is a lowering of seizure threshold which can be important in children with neurological disorders or abnormal EEGS. Dry mouth and constipation are frequent side effects. Heterocyclic antidepressants can increase blood levels of cholesterol, transaminases, bilirubin, alkaline phosphatase, catecholamines and glucose. They can decrease the blood level of glucose, granulocytes and platelet. There are interactions with numerous drugs. Heterocyclic antidepressants can increase the effects of anticholinergic drugs, thyroid medications, seizure-potentiating drugs and phenytoin. They can decrease the effects of clonidine and guanethidine. The effects of heterocyclic antidepressants can be increased, even to toxic levels, by phenothiazines, methylphenidate and estrogen. Their effects can be decreased to ineffectiveness by barbiturates, chloral hydrate and smoking.

In view of the questionable effectiveness of the heterocyclic antidepressants in children and adolescents combined with numerous side effects and drug interactions which are potentially serious, particularly in a chronically ill population, great care should be exercised in the use of these drugs in depressed, chronically ill children. Thyroid disorders, cardiac problems, seizure disorders and possibly diabetes, have all been cited as relative contraindications to the use of these drugs (Ryan, 1990: 21-31).

Relaxation and mental imagery

Over the past twenty years, there has been increasing experience with and research on the use of relaxation and mental imagery (self-hypnosis) for control of certain symptoms of illness. Pain and chemotherapy related nausea and vomiting are the two most common physical problems for which hypnotic treatments have been used.

However, there is considerable evidence that self hypnosis can also be effective in the treatment of warts, and as adjunctive therapy in the treatment of asthma, hemophilia, sickle cell anemia, and hypertension. (For an excellent review of the research on self-hypnosis in children see Olness and Gardner, 1988). Children and adolescents are usually excellent hypnotic subjects and learn the skills needed to use self-hypnosis quickly and easily. In addition to the obvious advantages of decreasing illness related symptoms and, at times, decreasing the amounts of medication required for good illness control, self-hypnotic treatments have the additional advantages of having virtually no side effects and of providing the child with some measure of control over her own illness. Learning skills which permit the child to control physically distressing symptoms provides her with a sense of mastery and often engenders optimism about the future. Self-hypnosis increases independence and often permits the child to live a more normal life as disabling symptoms come under better control. All of these things should increase the psychological well-being of the ill child. For very young children, the parents can be trained to use hypnotic techniques with the child. This provides them with an important role in their child's medical care and may diminish any sense of helplessness.

While there has been increasing use of hypnosis as a treatment modality in medicine, it is still often difficult to find competent professionals who can teach these techniques. If self-hypnosis is to be used effectively with ill children, it is imperative that the health professional teaching these skills to the child be well trained in child development as well as in the use of hypnotic techniques. Listings of such professionals can be obtained from the American Society of Clinical Hypnosis or the Society for Clinical and Experimental Hypnosis.

This chapter has reviewed the research evidence which indicates that physical illness is a risk factor for psychological disturbance in children. Although there appears to be an increase in the prevalence of psychological problems, including depression, among children who are physically ill, it is still important to remember that the vast majority of ill children are psychologically normal. The chapter also reviewed how physical illness can be expected to interfere with normal emotional and cognitive development and what measures might be taken to prevent such disruption. The use of psychopharmacologic treatments for depression in ill children and of self-hypnosis was also discussed. It is a testament to the adaptational abilities of human beings that most children with illness and their families cope well in spite of the often overwhelming stresses imposed by chronic illness. It is a privilege for health care providers to aid children and families with this adaptational process.

[1] The fifteen case series without controls which did not use standardized instruments are: Amir *et al*, 1977: 744; Bernstein *et al*, 1969: 620–635; Boyle *et al*, 1976: 318; Bywater, 1981: 538; Dorner, 1975: 765; Gladston, 1972: 57–66; Heller *et al*, 1981: 459; Khan *et al*, 1971: 1194–1198; Long and Cope, 1961: 1121–1127; MacLean and Becker, 1979: 744; Minde *et al*, 1972: 1554–1560; Simonds, 1977: 500–516; Sullivan, 1979: 119; Wasserman *et al*, 1987: 626–631; and Woodward, 1955: 1009–1013.

[2] The twelve case series without controls which used standardized instruments are: Close *et al*, 1986: 337–340; Cowen *et al*, 1984: 363; Grey *et al*, 1980: 69; Harper, 1983: 859; Kashani *et al*, 1981: 123–134; O'Dougherty *et al*, 1983: 1129; O'Malley *et al*, 1979: 608; Richman *et al*, 1985: 93; Schowalter, 1977: 500–515; Smith *et al*, 1983: 230; Tavormina *et al*, 1976: 99; Teare, 1984: 237.

[3] The twenty-four case series with controls are: Billings *et al*, 1987: 343–359; Breslau, 1985: 87–94;

Cowen *et al*, 1985: 553; Drotar *et al*, 1981: 338; Evans *et al*, 1988: 127–130; Fitzpatrick, 1984; Froese *et al*, 1980: 469; Gath *et al*, 1980: 371; Gayton *et al*, 1977: 888; Gordon *et al*, 1982: 477; Hoare, 1984: 3; Kellerman *et al*, 1980: 126–131; Kumar *et al*, 1976: 859; Lavigne *et al*, 1982: 420; Lewis and Khaw, 1982: 636; McAnarney *et al*, 1974: 523-528; Meijer, 1980: 163; Simonds and Heimburger, 1978: 193; Steinhausen *et al*, 1977: 1; Steinhausen and Kies, 1982: 33; Steinhausen and Schindler, 1981: 74–77; Steinhausen *et al*, 1983: 559; Swift *et al*, 1967: 555-571; and Thompson, 1985: 37.

[4] The four prevalence studies are: Cadman *et al*, 1987: 805–813; Pless and Roghmann, 1971: 351-359; Rutter *et al*, 1970; and Walker *et al*, 1981.

[5] The eight cohort studies are: Ahnsjo *et al*, 1981: 321; Britten *et al*, 1984: 291; Densen *et al*, 1970: 981; Heller *et al*, 1985: 257-263; Kovacs *et al*, 1985: 827; Orr *et al*, 1984: 152; Peckham and Butler, 1978: 79; and Pless Roghmann, 1971: 352-359.

[6] Three intervention studies are: McGraw and Travis, 1973: 275; Pless and Satterwhite, 1975: 288-303; and Stein and Jessop, 1984: 845.

References

Achenbach, T.M., McConaughy, S.H. and Howell, C.T. (1987) Child/adolescent behavioral and emotional problems: implications of cross-informant correlations for situational specificity. *Psychological Bulletin*, **2**, 213–232.

Ahnsjo, S., Humble, K., Larsson, Y. *et al* (1981) Personality changes and social adjustment during the first three years of diabetes in children. *Acta Paediatrica Scandinavica*, **70**, 321.

American Psychiatric Association. (1987) Diagnostic and Statistical Manual of Mental Disorders—Revised, Washington, D.C.

Amir, S., Galatzer, A., Frish, M., Laron, Z. (1977) A sociological survey of 296 juvenile diabetics. *Pediatric and Adolescent Endocrinology*, **24**, 744.

Bernstein, N.R., Sanger, S. and Fras, I. (1969) The function of the child psychiatrist in the management of severely burned children. *Journal of the American Academy of Child Psychiatry*, **8**, 620–635.

Billings, A.G., Moos, R.H., Miller, J.J. and Gottlieb, J.E. (1987) Psychosocial adaptation in juvenile rheumatic disease: a controlled evaluation. *Health Psychology*, **6**, 343-359.

Boyle, I.R., di Sant'Agnese, P.A., Sack, S. *et al* (1976) Emotional adjustment of adolescents and young adults with cystic fibrosis. *Journal of Pediatrics*, **88**, 318.

Breslau, N. (1985) Psychiatric disorder in children with physical disabilities. *Journal of the American Academy of Child Psychiatry*, 24: 87.

Breslau, N. and Marshall, I.A. (1985) Psychological disturbance in children with physical disabilities: continuity and change in a 5-year follow-up. *Journal of Abnormal Child Psychology* **13**, 199–215.

Britten, N., Wadsworth, M.E.J. and Fenwick, P.B.C. (1984) Stigma in patients with early epilepsy: a national longitudinal study. *Journal of Epidemiology and Community Health*, **38**, 291.

Bywater, E.M. (1981) Adolescents with cystic fibrosis: Psychosocial adjustment. *Archives of Disease in Childhood*, **56**, 538.

Cadman, D., Boyle, M., Szatmari, P. and Offord, D.R. (1987) Chronic illness, disability, and mental and social well-being: findings of the Ontario Child Health Study. *Pediatrics*, **79**, 805–813.

Close, J., Davies, A.G., Price, D.A. and Goodyer, I.M. (1986) Emotional difficulties in diabetes mellitus. *Archives of Disease in Childhood*, **61**, 337-340.

Cowen, L., Corey, M., Keenan, N. *et al* (1985) Family adaptation and psychosocial adjustment to cystic fibrosis in the preschool child. *Social Science Medicine*, **20**, 553.

Cowen, L., Corey, M., Simmons, R. *et al* (1984) Growing older with cystic fibrosis: psychologic adjustment of patients more than 16 years old. *Psychosomatic Medicine*, **46**, 363.

Daniels, D., Moos, R.H., Billings, A.G. and Miller, J.J. (1987) Psychosocial risk and resistance factors among children with chronic illness, healthy siblings, and healthy controls. *Journal of Abnormal Child Psychology*, **15**, 295-308.

Densen, P.M., Ullman, D.B., Jones, E.W. *et al* (1970) Childhood characteristics as indicators of adult health status. *Public Health Report*, **85**, 981.

Dorner, S. (1975) The relationship of physical handicap to stress in families with an adolescent with spina bifida. *Developmental Medicine and Child Neurology*, **17**, 765.

Drotar, D. and Crawford, P. (1985) Psychological adaptation of siblings of chronically ill children: research and practice implications. *Journal of Developmental and Behavioral Pediatrics*, **6**, 355-362.

Drotar, D., Doershuk, C.F., Stern, R.C. *et al* (1981) Psychosocial functioning of children with cystic fibrosis. *Pediatrics*, **67**, 338.
Erikson, E.H. (1963) Childhood and Society, Second Edition. New York: W.W. Norton and Co., Inc., 247-274.
Evans, R.C., Burlew, A.K. and Oler, C.H. (1988) Children with sickle-cell anemia: parental relations, parent-child relations, and child behavior. *Social Work*, **35**, 127-130.
Fitzpatrick, C. (1984) Muscular dystrophy: emotional aspects, paper presented at ACPP.
Froese, A.P., Rose, V. and Allen, D.M. (1980) Emotional implications of primary familial hyperlipoproteinemia in childhood and adolescence. *Pediatrics*, **65**, 469.
Gath, A., Smith, M.A. and Baum, J.D. (1980) Emotional, behavioral, and educational disorders in diabetic children. *Archives of Disease in Childhood*, **55**, 371.
Gayton, W.F., Friedman, S.B., Tavormina, J.F. *et al* (1977) Children with cystic fibrosis. I. Psychological test findings of patients, siblings and parents. *Pediatrics*, **59**, 888.
Geller, B., Cooper, T.B., McCombs, H.G. *et al* (1989) Double-blind, placebo-controlled study of nortriptyline in depressed children using a fixed plasma level design. *Psychopharmacology Bulletin*, **25**, 101-108.
Gladston, R. (1972) The burning and the healing of children. *Psychiatry*, **35**, 57-66.
Gordon, M. Crouthamel, C., Post, E.M. *et al* (1982) Psychosocial aspects of constitutional short stature: social competence, behavior problems, self-esteem, and family functioning. *Journal of Pediatrics*, 101-477.
Grey, M.J., Genet, M. and Tamborlane, W.V. (1980) Psychological adjustment of latency age diabetics: determinants and relationship to control. *Pediatrics*, **65**, 69.
Harper, D. (1983) Personality correlates and degree of impairment in male adolescents with progressive and non-progressive physical disorders. *Journal of Clinical Psychology*, **39**, 859.
Heller, A., Rafman, S., Zvagulis, I. and Pless, I.B. (1985) Birth defects and psychosocial adjustment. *American Journal of Disease of Children*, **139**, 257.
Heller, A., Tidmarsh, W. and Pless, I.B. (1981) The psychological functioning of young adults born with cleft lip or palate. *Pediatrics*, **20**, 459.
Hoare, P. (1984) The development of psychiatric disorder among school children with epilepsy. *Developmental Medicine and Child Neurology*, **26**, 3.
Jessop, D.J. and Stein, R.E. (1985) Uncertainty and its relationship with psychological and social correlates of chronic illness in children. *Social Science Medicine*, **20**, 993.
Kashani, J.H., Barbero, G.J. and Bolander, F.D. (1981) Depression in hospitalized pediatric patients. *Journal of the American Academy of Child Psychiatry*, **20**, 123-134.
Kellerman, J., Zeltzer, L., Wallenberg, L. *et al* (1980) Psychological effects of illness in adolescence. I. Anxiety, self-esteem, and perception of control. *Journal of Pediatrics*, **97**, 126-131.
Khan, A.U., Herndon, C.H. and Ahmadian, S.Y. (1971) Social and emotional adaptations of children with transplanted kidneys and chronic hemodialysis. *American Journal of Psychiatry*, **127**, 1194-1198.
Kovacs, M., Feinberg, T.L., Paulauskas, S. *et al* (1985) Initial coping responses and psychosocial characteristics of children with insulin-dependent diabetes mellitus. *Journal of Pediatrics*, **106**, 827.
Kramer, A.D. and Feiguine, R.J. (1981) Clinical effects of amitriptyline in adolescent depression: A pilot study. *Journal of the American Academy of Child Psychiatry*, **20**, 636-644.
Kumar, S., Powars, D., Allen, J. *et al* (1976) Anxiety, self-concept, and personal and social adjustments in children with sickle cell anemia. *Journal of Pediatrics*, **88**, 859.
Lavigne, J.V., Traisman, H.S., Marr, T.J. *et al* (1982) Parental perceptions of the psychological adjustment of children with diabetes and their siblings. *Diabetes Care*, **5**, 420.
Lewis, B.L. and Khaw, K. (1982) Family functioning as a mediating variable affecting psychosocial adjustment of children with cystic fibrosis. *Journal of Pediatrics*, **101**, 636.
Long, R.T. and Cope, O. (1961) Emotional problems of burned children. *New England Journal of Medicine*, **264**, 1121-1127.
MacLean, G. and Becker, S. (1979) Studies of the psychological adjustment of the hearing-impaired. *Canadian Journal of Psychiatry*, **24**, 744.
McAnarney, E.R., Pless, I.B., Satterwhite, B. *et al* (1974) Psychological problems of children with chronic juvenile arthritis. *Pediatrics*, **53**, 523.
McGraw, R.K. and Travis, L.B. (1973) Psychological effects of a special summer camp on juvenile diabetics. *Diabetes*, **2**, 275.
Meijer, A. (1980) Psychiatric problems of hemophiliac boys and their families. *International Journal of Psychiatry in Medicine*, **10**, 163.

Minde, K.K., Hackett, J.D., Killou, D., and Silver, S. (1972) How they grow up: 41 physically handicapped children and their families. *American Journal of Psychiatry*, **128**, 11554-1560.
Nolan, T. and Pless, I.B. (1986) Emotional correlates and consequences of birth defects. *Journal of Pediatrics*, **109**, 201-216.
O'Dougherty, M., Wright, F.S., Garmezy, N. *et al* (1983) Later competence and adaptation in infants who survive severe heart defects. *Child Development*, **54**, 1129.
O'Malley, J.E., Koocher, G., Foster, D. and Slavin, L. (1979) Psychiatric sequelae of surviving childhood cancer. *American Journal of Orthopsychiatry*, **49**, 608.
Olness, K. and Gardner, G.G. (1988) Hypnosis and Hypnotherapy with Children, Second Edition. Philadelphia: Grune and Stratton.
Orr, D.P., Weller, S.C., Satterwhite, B. *et al* (1984) Psychosocial implications of chronic illness in adolescence. *Journal of Pediatrics*, **104**, 152.
Peckham, C. and Butler, N. (1978) A national study of asthma in childhood. *Journal of Epidemiology and Community Health*, **32**, 79.
Piaget, J. and Inhelder, B. (1969) The Psychology of the Child, New York: Basic Books, Inc.
Pless, I.B. and Roghmann, K.J. (1971) Chronic illness and its consequences: observations based on three epidemiologic surveys. *Journal of Pediatrics*, **79**, 351.
Pless, I.B. and Satterwhite, B. (1975) The family counselor, eds. Haggerty, R.J., Roghmann, K.J. and Pless, I.B., *Child Health and the Community*, New York: Wiley, 288-303.
Puig-Antich J., Perel, J.M., Lupatkin, W. *et al* (1987) Imipramine in prepubertal major depressive disorders. *Archives of General Psychiatry*, **44**, 81-89.
Quinton, D. and Rutter, M. (1976) Early hospital admissions and later disturbances of behavior: an attempted replication of Douglas' findings. *Developmental Medicine and Child Neurology*, **18**, 447-459.
Richman, L.C., Holmes, C.S. and Eliason, M.J. (1985) Adolescents with cleft lip and palate and behavior related to personality adjustment. *Cleft Palate Journal*, **22**, 93.
Rutter, M., Tizard, J. and Whitmore, K., eds. (1970) Education, Health and Behavior: Psychological and Medical Study of Childhood Development. New York: Wiley.
Ryan, N.D. (1990) Heterocyclic and antidepressants in children and adolescents. *Journal of Child and Adolescent Psychopharmacology*, **1**, 21-31.
Ryan, N.D., Puig-Antich, J., Cooper, T.B. *et al* (1987) Imipramine in adolescent major depression: plasma level and clinical response. *Acta Psychiatrica Scandinavica*, **73**, 275-288.
Schecter, N. (1989) The undertreatment of pain in children: An overview. Pediatric Clinics of North America, **36**, 781.
Schowalter, J.E. (1977) Psychological reaction to physical illness and hospitalization in adolescence: a survey. *Journal of the American Academy of Child Psychiatry*, **16**, 500-516.
Simonds, J.F. (1977) Psychiatric status of diabetic children in good and poor control. *International Journal of Psychiatry in Medicine*, 7, 133.
Simonds, J.F. and Heimburger, R.E. (1978) Psychiatric evaluation of youth with cleft lip-palate matched with a control group. *Cleft Palate Journal*, **15**, 193.
Smith, M.S., Treadwell, M. and O'Grady, L. (1983) Psychosocial functioning, life change, and clinical status in adolescents with cystic fibrosis. *Journal of Adolescent Health Care*, **4**, 230.
Stein, R.E., and Jessop, D.J. (1982) A noncategorical approach to chronic illness. *Public Health Reports*, 97, 354.
Stein, R.E. and Jessop, D. (1984) Does pediatric home care make a difference for children with chronic iliness? Findings from the Pediatric Ambulatory Care Treatment Study. *Pediatrics*, **73**, 845.
Steinhausen, H.C., Borner, S. and Koepp, P. (1977) The personality of juvenile diabetics. *Pediatric and Adolescent Endocrinology*, **3**, 1.
Steinhausen, H.C. and Kies, H. (1982) Comparative studies of ulcerative colitis and Crohn's disease in children and adolescents. *Journal of Child Psychology and Psychiatry*, **23**, 33.
Steinhausen, H.C. and Schindler, H.P. (1981) Psychosocial adaptation in children and adolescents with cystic fibrosis. *Journal of Developmental and Behavioral Pediatrics*, **2**, 74.
Steinhausen, H.C., Schindler, H.P. and Stephan, H. (1983) Correlates of psychopathology in sick children: an empirical model. *Journal of the American Academy of Child Psychiatry*, **22**, 559.
Sullivan, B.J. (1979) Adjustment in diabetic adolescent girls. I. Development of the diabetic adjustment scale. *Psychosomatic Medicine*, **41**, 119.
Swift, C.R., Seidman, F. and Stein, H. (1967) Adjustment problems in juvenile diabetes. *Psychosomatic Medicine*, **29**, 555-571.
Tavormina, J.B., Kastner, L.S., Slater, P.M. *et al* (1976) Chronically ill children: A psychologically and emotionally deviant population? *Journal of Abnormal Child Psychology*, **4**, 99.

Teare, J. F. (1984) Behavioral adjustment of children attending a residential school for the blind. *Journal of Developmental and Behavioral Pediatrics*, **5**, 237.

Thompson, R. J. (1985) Delineation of child behavior problems: a basis for assessment and intervention. *Journal of Developmental and Behavioral Pediatrics*, **6**, 37.

Walker, D. K., Gortmaker, S. L. and Weitzman, M. (1981) Chronic Illness and Psychosocial Problems among Children in Genesee County, Boston: Harvard School of Public Health.

Wasserman, A. L., Thompson, E. I., Wilimas, J. A. and Fairclough, D. L. (1987) The psychological status of survivors of childhood/adolescent Hodgkin's disease. *American Journal of Disease of Children*, **141**, 626–631.

Woodward, J. (1955) Emotional disturbance of burned children. *British Medical Journal*, **9**, 1009–1013.

7 Depression in Acutely Ill Children and Adolescents

Lois Lyon Neumann and David G. Inwood

Division of Child and Adolescent Psychiatry, State University of New York, Health Science Center at Brooklyn, 450 Clarkson Ave., Brooklyn, NY 11023, USA

DEPRESSION IN ACUTELY ILL CHILDREN AND ADOLESCENTS

Children who appear sad or withdrawn are a familiar sight on pediatric wards, and psychiatric consultants are frequently asked to evaluate such children for depression. In other instances, depression may be uncovered in the evaluation of hospitalized children who present with a variety of somatic complaints, anxiety symptoms, or behavior problems.

Reports of medically hospitalized adults have shown at least some degree of depression in 22% to 32% (Derogatis, 1989: 101–126). Kashani *et al* (1981: 123–134) studied one hundred pediatric inpatients, aged 7–12, and diagnosed depression in 7%, with dysphoric mood in an additional 38% of them. These figures include both acutely and chronically ill children.

Among pediatric patients, depression is probably more common in those who are chronically ill. These patients will be discussed in Dr. Erikson's chapter in this volume. This chapter will address depressive syndromes in children with acute illness or injury.

Etiology

In medically ill children and adolescents, depression may present in various ways. Some may suffer from a pre-existing depression which only comes to attention when treatment is sought for a medical condition. Depressive symptoms may occur as a psychological reaction to illness or injury. Alternatively, certain illnesses, as well as some medications, have been found to cause depression. Distinguishing among these possible causes of depression in a pediatric patient may be very difficult, but has important treatment implications.

A past history of affective disorder in the patient or family members may suggest the possibility that depression in the child is coincidental to the medical problem under treatment. One type of child in whom this possibility is easily overlooked is the victim of apparently accidental trauma. Occasionally, observation of depressive symptoms and careful interviewing lead to the disclosure that the injuries actually resulted from a suicide attempt, as, for example by the child's running in front of a car. Family history positive for depression may also suggest increased vulnerability to a depressive reaction to stresses such as illness. It is noteworthy that in Kashani's study of pediatric patients, there was a family history of depression in four of the seven depressed children (57%) but in only 14% of the families of the ninety-three non-depressed children (Kashani, 1981: 123–134).

Diagnosis

The occurrence and manifestations of mood disorders are influenced by developmental changes. Diagnosable major depression is uncommon before adolescence and rare in pre-school children. The criteria for diagnosing depressive disorders in children are now generally agreed to be the same as those used for adults (American Psychiatric Association, 1987; Carlson and Cantwell, 1981: 445–449). There are, however, some features of major depression which are more frequently seen in children than adults, such as irritable rather than depressed mood, hallucinations of an accusatory or threatening voice, and an association with anxiety disorders or phobias. Of particular concern to pediatricians is the frequency in depressed children of somatic complaints which raise differential diagnostic problems.

Alterations in mood and an appearance of sadness occur often in hospitalized children who cannot be diagnosed to have a mood disorder by strictly applied criteria. Nonetheless, their misery is manifest, and deserving of whatever can be done to give relief. Included in this group are infants and toddlers whose reactions to hospitalization may include a phase characterized as "despair" in which they are withdrawn and appear hopeless (Bowlby, 1960: 89–113). (Also see below).

Adjustment disorder

Probably the most frequently encountered affective disorder on pediatric wards is adjustment disorder with depressed mood (American Psychiatric Association, 1987), formerly called "reactive depression." By definition, this is a maladaptive reaction to an identifiable psychosocial stressor (such as illness or injury) that occurs within three months of the onset of the stressor and persists no longer than six months. The depressive symptoms do not meet the full criteria for major depression, but are in excess of the usual expectable reaction to that stressor. An example would be a ten-year-old boy in traction for a fractured femur who appears persistently sad and tearful much of the day but has no disturbance of sleep or appetite, nor other symptoms of major depression. The stressors include the accident, separation from family, pain, and immobilization. Adjustment disorders in children and adolescents frequently show mixed emotional features, such as anxiety and anger in addition to sadness. For example, this same ten-year-old boy may express anxiety that he couldn't get out if there were a fire in the hospital (this fear is particularly frequent among burned children) and curse angrily at nursing staff who dress his wounds.

Major depression

There are certain difficulties in diagnosing major depression in acutely ill children and adolescents. Criteria outlined in the American Psychiatric Association's "Diagnostic and Statistical Manual" (American Psychiatric Association, 1987) include an exclusion that "it cannot be established that an organic factor initiated and maintained the disturbance". If an organic factor is believed to be causative, the diagnosis of organic mood syndrome, rather than major depression, is used (see below). To make the diagnosis of major depression requires at least five of a list of nine symptoms to have been present for two weeks or more (American Psychiatric Association, 1987). Of these, it can be almost impossible to tell whether appetite disturbance and weight loss, sleep disturbance and fatigue or loss of energy are due to depression or to the illness itself. Cassem (1987: 227–260) discusses this problem in adult patients and suggests that certain symptoms (feelings of worthlessness, suicidal ideation, and markedly diminished interest in most activities) are more clearly associated with depression than with illness. He also recommends making the diagnosis of major depression if the requisite number of symptoms is present and this dilemma can't be resolved, as this may point to specific treatment.

Organic mood syndrome (depressed)

It is most important to consider whether symptoms of depression in a pediatric patient may be intrinsic to a medical illness itself or caused by a medication, in which case a diagnosis of organic mood syndrome is made (American Psychiatric Association, 1987).

Most of the literature about depression associated with illness is based on experience with adult patients. Hall (1980: 37–63) made an extensive review of the subject and listed 25 medical illnesses that frequently induce depression, 75 medical conditions presenting with depression and many others which may be associated with reactive depression, or cause dementia with depressive responses.

This sort of comprehensive catalogue is of limited help to the clinician and other authors have compiled shorter lists where the association with depression seems more clearly established. (Akiskal, 1986: 384–399; Cassem, 1987: 227–260; Derogatis, 1989: 101–126; Reus, 1986: 205–214). Table 1 is adapted from these sources, emphasizing categories of illness which have been most often reported as causing depression. It is not known whether the comparatively smaller number of reports in children with these illnesses reflects a truly lower incidence or the difficulty of recognizing depression in young patients.

Carek and Santos (1984: 108–111) reported thirteen cases, from six to sixteen years of age, referred for psychiatric evaluation of persisting unexplained physical symptoms following a variety of infections (flu-like illness, gastroenteritis, infectious mononucleosis, and viral hepatitis). They found objective evidence of dysphoric mood or blunted affect combined with a variety of signs of affective disorder (eg. sleep and appetite disturbance, loss of interest and energy, crying spells, etc.), as well as a peculiar inability of these children to recognize or acknowledge their own dysphoria. The authors suggest that these cases represent a post-infectious depressive equivalent. Abe (1988: 573–574) reported a unique case of a girl who had eleven episodes between ten and fourteen years of age, of depression, with mild hypersomnia, tearfulness and self-blame lasting about a week, following respiratory infections. During periods of prophylaxis with lithium she had four respiratory infections, none of them followed by depression. Although family history was negative for affective disorder, one wonders whether longer follow-up may reveal that this girl has a vulnerability to a cyclical affective disorder which manifested itself under the stress of these infections. White and Lewis (1987: 97–98) reported two cases of delusional depression after infectious mononucleosis, one of them in a sixteen year old boy. Electroconvulsive treatment was effective after no improvement was achieved with antidepressants.

Various neurologic disorders have been associated with depression (Table 7.1). Attempts to correlate affective symptoms with the location of brain lesions have led to somewhat confusing results. Studies of adult stroke victims, however, found that severity of depression was greatest with lesions of the left anterior hemisphere. With right hemisphere lesions, on the other hand, depression was more pronounced the more posterior the lesion (Robinson *et al*, 1984: 81–93).

Many drugs have been reported to be associated with depression in patients receiving them. Once again, the reports deal mostly with adult patients. The drug most clearly linked to depression is reserpine, a now rarely used antihypertensive, with as many at 15% of patients on the drug affected (Goodwin *et al*, 1972: 73–101).

Table 7.2 is adapted from various sources, listing drugs that have most often been reported as causing depression. It can be difficult in the individual patient to establish the link between depressive symptoms and an offending drug. Finding a relationship between the start or increased dose of a drug and the onset of depressive symptoms suggests the possibility of such a link. Trial withdrawal or change of a suspected drug may be necessary to see if symptoms will improve. Failure to improve promptly

Table 7.1 Illnesses which may cause depression*

Viral Infections
Influenza, infectious mononucleosis, infectious hepatitis, respiratory infection
Endocrine Disorders
Hypothyrodism, hypo- or hyperadrenocorticalism, hyperparathyroidism
Neurologic Disorders
Strokes, normal pressure hydrocephalus, multiple sclerosis, Parkinson's disease, brain tumors (temporal lobe), AIDS dementia
Cancer
Cancer of the pancreas
Metabolic or Nutritional
Hyponatremia, hypokalemia, hypercalcemia. Vitamin B_{12}, folate, or iron deficiency anemia.

* (Adapted from Akiskal 1986, Cassem 1987, Derogatis 1989, Reus 1986)

Table 7.2 Drugs associated with development of depression*

Reserpine, methyldopa, clonidine and other antihypertensives.
Propranolol
Corticosteroids, ACTH
Oral contraceptives
Cimetidine
Benzodiazepines
Barbiturates, other sedative hypnotics
Stimulant withdrawal
Anticancer chemotherapy

* (Adapted from Akiskal, 1986, Dietch and Zetin 1983, and Cassem 1987)

following withdrawal of a drug does not always rule out an etiologic role of that drug. Some drug-induced depressions require additional treatment.

Separation reactions

"Loneliness in infants" on hospital wards was reported by Bakwin (1942: 30). Others, notably Spitz (1946: 315–342) soon followed with descriptions of infants who appeared sad, listless, and failed to thrive under conditions of prolonged institutional care with little stimulation. Observations by Bowlby (1960: 89–113) emphasize the impact of separation from primary caretakers, which may be seen during the briefer admissions of acutely ill children. He describes three phases of these reactions:

1) *Protest*. The child cries loudly after the mother, clings to her, wildly protests her attempts to leave and may resist efforts of others to provide comfort.

2) *Despair*. The child becomes less active, more withdrawn, and appears to have given up hope. Crying may stop, or subside to quiet whimpering. The child accepts caretaking passively, with blunted social responsiveness.

3) *Detachment*. If separation is more prolonged, the child becomes more alert and responsive to alternate caretakers. These substitute attachments have a superficial, indiscriminate quality, however, and the child shows a reduced positive response to the mother when she appears.

The *despair* phase most resembles depression, but is probably more analagous to a grief reaction in the young child who perceives the separation as loss of the primary attachment figure. This type of reaction is most pronounced in children from six months to four years of age. Earlier than that, an infant may seem upset when removed from familiar circumstances, especially if little warm response is provided when he suffers discomfort or pain, but substitute caregivers are accepted fairly readily. When the older infant comes to recognize the mother as specific to his security, such substitution is no longer adequate to fend off feelings of abandonment in the absence of the mother.

TREATMENT

Concern about depression among pediatric patients should start with considerations of prevention. Since the early reports of the emotional effects of hospitalization on children (Bakwin, 1942: 30; Bowlby, 1960: 89–113; Robertson, 1970), there have been increasing efforts by pediatricians and others to reduce the associated stresses. Parents are encouraged to stay with their young children as much as possible. Child Life programs have been established to provide emotional support and preparation for children undergoing painful, frightening experiences (Gaynard *et al*, 1990). Primary nursing assignments increase the level of personalized care children receive. The American Academy of Pediatrics manual on "Hospital Care of Children and Youth" (Committee on Hospital Care, 1986) incorporates strong recommendations for these and related programs. These measures, where applied, have been effective in reducing the frequency of severe separation reactions, progressing to phases of despair and detachment, in infants and toddlers. They probably also reduce the frequency of depressive adjustment disorders in hospitalized children.

Pediatricians should be alert to children who are at particularly high risk for depression. These include children with a family history of depression, or who have suffered early separations and neglect, as well as those with a history of previous depression themselves. Conditions associated with a great deal of pain (e.g. burns) or losses of body integrity or function (e.g. spinal cord injuries, amputation, prolonged immobilization or isolation) increase the risk of depressive reactions. If a child appears to the pediatrician and other staff to be disproportionately dysphoric, and not responding to the usual efforts to relieve his unhappiness, consultation with a child psychiatrist may be indicated.

For most children with depressive syndromes in a pediatric setting, a flexible treatment approach is most appropriate, taking into account developmental level, social variables, psychiatric diagnosis, and specifics of the clinical condition. Organic contributing factors (Tables 1. and 2.) should be identified and, if possible, corrected. Adequate pain relief and ability to sleep should be assured.

A variety of verbal, behavioral and social interventions may be useful. For the younger child, the most important steps are usually those which enable the parents to spend more time with the child, or, failing that, to provide consistent alternative caretakers to give emotional interaction and comfort. In pre-school and younger school-age children, therapeutic play assumes great importance for expressing and mastering emotional disturbance. Ideally this will be carried out by a Child Life specialist or other skilled play therapist. Older children are more able to express their feelings verbally and can often be helped with some variety of supportive, behavioral or cognitive psychotherapy. Frequently, an important intervention is clarification of misperceptions or fantasies the youngster has about his condition and its treatment. This requires good communication between the primary physician and the psychiatric consultant to avoid ill-timed or mixed messages to the child.

Pharmacotherapy

Major depression is not commonly encountered in acutely ill children. When it is diagnosed, it is most likely to be in an adolescent or older school-age child. If criteria for major depression are met, the use of antidepressant medication should be considered. However, despite widespread use of tricyclic antidepressants by clinicians to treat depression in the pediatric age range, controlled studies have yet to demonstrate clear-cut superiority over placebo in pre-pubertal children or adolescents (Ryan, 1990: 21–31). Side effects of these drugs are of particular concern in medically ill patients. Most important are cardiovascular effects, especially slowing of conduction, to which children are more susceptible than adults. Prepubescent children may be particularly liable to toxic cardiac effects. Tachycardia and anticholinergic effects are common, but usually not serious. Variable effects on blood pressure or blood glucose and lowering of seizure threshold are infrequent, but may be significant in children with hypertension, diabetes, or neurologic abnormalities.

If tricyclic antidepressants are to be used, appropriate baseline screening and periodic monitoring should be carried out for conduction defects and electrolyte abnormalities. Such therapy will rarely be indicated in acutely ill children, and should be under the supervision of someone familiar with the use of this group of drugs. The antidepressants which have had the most use in children are imipramine, desipramine and nortriptyline. There is as yet too little experience with fluoxetine, reputed to have a low incidence of side effects, to make any recommendations about its use in children.

For some hospitalized children with depression, concomitant anxiety may be an equal or greater problem. Occasionally, judicious use of anxiolytics, along with supportive measures, may relieve the anxiety and secondarily the mood disturbance. Low doses of alprazolam have been used successfully for relief of anxiety in a group of children undergoing painful treatments for cancer (Pfefferbaum, 1987: 532–535). Alprazolam has been reported in adults to have antidepressant as well as anxiolytic effects (Dawson, 1984: 132–147).

CONCLUSION

The majority of acutely ill children who appear sad and upset do not merit a psychiatric diagnosis of depression. Most will respond to support from their families and a child-oriented hospital environment. Some, however, are disproportionately or persistently dysphoric and deserve evaluation for organic, social or psychological factors which may be causing a depressive reaction. Treatment, when indicated, will usually be some variety of supportive, play, behavioral or cognitive therapy, appropriate to the developmental level of the child. Antidepressant medication is rarely indicated for depression in acutely ill children and requires careful monitoring to avoid adverse side effects.

References

Abe, K. (1988) Depression after each respiratory infection in an adolescent girl. *Journal of Nervous and Mental Disorders*, **176**, 573-574.

Akiskal, H.S. (1986) Mood Disturbances, In *The Medical Basis of Psychiatry*, (eds. G. Winokur and P. Clayton). Philadelphia: W.B. Saunders Co., 384-399.

American Psychiatric Association (1987) *Diagnostic and Statistical Manual*, Third Edition, Revised. Washington, D.C., American Psychiatric Association.

Bakwin, H. (1942) Loneliness in infants. *American Journal of Diseases of Childhood*, **63**, 30.

Bowlby, J. (1960) Separation anxiety. *International Journal of Psychoanalysis*, **41**, 89-113.

Carek, D.J. and Santos, A.B. (1984) Atypical somatoform disorder following infection in children—a depressive equivalent. *Journal of Clinical Psychiatry*, **45**, 108-111.

Carlson, G. and Cantwell, D.P. (1980) Unmasking masked depression in children and adolescents. *American Journal of Psychiatry*, **137**, 445-449.

Cassem, N.H. (1987) Depression. Massachusetts General Hospital Handbook of General Hospital Psychiatry, 2nd ed., (eds. T.P. Hackett and N.H. Cassem). Littleton, Mass. Yearbook Publishing Co., 227-260.

Committee on Hosp. Care, American Academy of Pediatrics (1986) Hospital Care of Children and Youth., (eds. J.M. Garfunkel and H.E. Evans) Elk Grove, Ill., *American Academy of Pediatrics.*

Dawson, G.W. *et al* (1984) Alprazolam: a review of its pharmacodynamic properties and efficacy in the treatment of anxiety and depression. *Drugs*, **27**, 132-147.

Derogatis, L.R. and Wise, T.N. (1989) Anxiety and Depressive Disorders in the Medical Patient, Washington, D.C., American Psychiatric Press Inc., 101-126.

Dietch, J.T. and Zetin, M. (1983) Diagnosis of organic depressive disorders, *Psychosomatics*, **24**, 971-974.

Gaynard, L. *et al* (1990) Psychosocial Care of Children in Hospitals: Clinical practice manual from the ACCH Child Life research project. Washington, D.C., Association for the Care of Children's Health.

Goodwin, F.K. *et al* (1972) Mental effects of reserpine in man. In Psychiatric Complications of Medical Drugs, (ed. R.I. Shader). New York: Raven Press, 73-101.

Hall, R.C..W. (1980) Depression. In Psychiatric Presentations of Medical Illness, (ed. R.C.W. Hall), New York, S.P. Medical and Scientific Books, 37-63.

Kashani, J.H. *et al* (1981) Depression in hospitalized pediatric patients. *Journal of the American Academy of Child and Adolescent Psychiatry*, **20**, 123-134.

Pfefferbaum, B. *et al* (1987) Alprazolam in the treatment of anticipatory anxiety and acute situational anxiety in children with cancer. *Journal of the American Academy of Child and Adolescent Psychiatry*, **26**, 532-535.

Reus, V.I. (1986) Behavioral disturbances associated with endocrine disorders. *Annual Review of Medicine*, **37**, 205-214.

Robertson, J. (1970) Young Children in Hospital, 2nd ed. London: Tavistock Publications Ltd.

Robinson, R.G. *et al* (1984) Mood disorders in stroke patients; importance of location of lesion. *Brain*, **107**, 81-93.

Ryan, N.D. (1990) Heterocyclic antidepressants in children and adolescents. *Journal of Child and Adolescent Psychopharmacology*, **1**, 21-31.

Spitz, R.A. (1946) Anaclytic depression, *Psychoanalytic Study of the Child*, **2**, 315-342.

White, P.D. and Lewis, S.W. (1987) *British Medical Journal*, **295**, 97-98.

8 The Dying Child

Avron Kriechman

Division of Child and Adolescent Psychiatry, Schneider Children's Hospital of Long Island Jewish Medical Center, New Hyde Park, NY 11042, USA

Perhaps the most tragic of all life events is the death of a child. The very act of having children is, in itself, one of the most profound defenses against the inevitable permanency and irreversibility of death; a living legacy that, above all, survives. The death of a child thus confronts survivors with both the loss of a loved one and the symbolic loss of personal specialness and invulnerability that the child represents.

This chapter will review issues for parents and caregivers in the care of a dying child. An emphasis will be placed on a treatment approach which supports a sense of mastery in the face of seemingly interminable stress and uncertainty.

UNDERSTANDING THE DYING CHILD

In order to empower the dying child and his or her family, it is important for the caregiver to facilitate the provision of information. This requires an adequate understanding of concepts of illness, death and dying and the rationale for treatment particular to children of different ages and stages of development. As with any stage theory, the outline provided below offers a framework upon which to construct a richer and more complete understanding of the child in question.

Death and the preschool child

Those below the age five who fear death fear being separated from whose to whom they are closest.

For young children, death and separation from loved ones seems to be very much the same experience. Children this age tend to see death as reversible: the dead eat, sleep, see and move around. Death is also associated with darkness, thus the notion that the dead will revive at sunrise or awaken in terror once they discover they have (mistakenly) been buried alive. Toddlers may have almost no concept of death. While death is seen as an irrational and arbitrary accident for somewhat older children, for toddlers it is paradoxically connected to retribution for misbehavior (such as refusing or forgetting to obey one's parents). Children this age typically cannot even begin to envision their own death; death is something that happens only to others.

Case vignette

A three year old girl dying from cancer becomes increasingly frantic each night as darkness approaches. No one is able to soothe her. The consulting child psychiatrist, conducting his initial interview in the parent's presence, discovers that the girl suffers from recurring nightmares. These "bad dreams" involve the patient surrounded by the doctors and nurses of the ward who have become magically transformed into vampires, greedily sucking the helpless patient's blood. The patient's parents then emerge from the shadows, only to be overpowered by the vampires who then bite the necks of the parents in order to change them into fellow creatures of the night. The patient awakens in terror as the newly completed circle of monsters close in for the kill. When asked why this might be happening to her, the patient stated she was being "punished for being mean" to her older sister.

This horrifying dream neatly condenses the preschooler's vision of death: 1) the separation of the child from parents and loved ones; 2) images emblematic of darkness and reversibility (i.e., monsters who awaken at night and sleep during the day who threaten, kill or transform "normal" humans who do the opposite); and 3) punishment for inexplicable and dimly imagined wrongs.

Given the above, it is easy to understand the dying preschooler's intense fears of darkness (the setting for death) and separation (the equivalent of death). The child's defense against death as an experience unique to others is certainly congruent with the ideas of family and friends, who find the death of a small much more difficult to comprehend than that of someone more advanced in years.

It is also important to emphasize that treatment procedures are typically felt to be punitive in nature by the younger child, especially those ages five and six; the therapeutic aspect of such procedures is rarely understood. Given the dying child's association of his or her declining state with wrongdoing—especially wrongdoing in the eyes of authority figures such as parents and doctors—it is easy to see how the child might view venipunctures, the taking of vital signs in the middle of the night and the like as punishment for misbehavior. These procedures quickly become fertile ground for the child's expression of feelings of helplessness and rage over the unfair and arbitrary "punishment" of medical staff and parents. (Parents may seem to join this "conspiracy of torment" when they hold the child down for procedures.)

Restraining the dying preschooler is also problematic given the child's definition of life as almost anything that moves. For these children, especially children ages one to three, inactivity and/or restraint are all too powerful symbols, though most likely unconscious ones, of an approaching demise.

The child's belief that only *Other People* die is one of the two basic defenses against death. The counterpart of this belief in personal inviolability and specialness is the belief in an *Ultimate Rescuer* who protects one from personal devastation. For younger children, these beliefs are more basic: death can't happen to them and their parents will always protect them (thus the terror of abandonment and the bewilderment when parents restrain them). For older children, these defenses are exemplified in the child's efforts at isolating those traits which define one as special and exempt from those with the same diagnosis who have fallen ill or died (e.g., he had a different doctor, she forgot to take her medicine) and in the child's belief in the protection of a Supreme Being and the comfort of an afterlife.

The preschooler's concerns about changes in the body are more related to the judgments of peers than the judgments of the self. The relative lack of empathy and egocentricity characteristic for children of this age group accounts for the often harsh and negative response of other children to such alterations in the child's appearance as hair loss and obesity. The child fears of social ostracism combined with fears of being separated from parents and other loved ones may easily translate into school refusal and social isolation without appropriate intervention.

The school-age child and death

Grade school children (approximately ages six to nine) conceive of death as an external process involving physical harm rather than natural processes. Rather than separation, fear of death is more often connected to a fear of bodily mutilation. Death and illness are still connected with concerns about punishment for wrongdoing, although such misbehavior is less strongly linked to disobedience toward authority figures.

Case vignette

An eight year old boy tried to hang himself shortly after being diagnosed with bone cancer. While waiting in the clinic, he had become acquainted with a twelve year old who had suffered the amputation of a leg in order to save his life. The patient became preoccupied with the possibility of losing a limb – and losing his penis – in the hours prior to the suicide attempt. This patient was similarly panic-stricken in anticipating hair loss secondary to chemotherapy. Explanation and elaborate preparations concerning the selection and purchase of a wig were most helpful in preventing future self-endangering behavior.

These children begin to envision the possibility of a life after death at the same time that they are more secretive about magical thinking than younger children. Such covert beliefs are easily discernible, however, in the school-age child's anxiety to preserve the body's integrity tor survival beyond the grave.

Case vignette

A six year old child with cancer was frantic about venipunctures and insisted that each must be followed by a blood transfusion. This boy thought it was critical to "keep my blood inside of me", to "keep the blood where it belongs", else "I won't have a drop left and then I'll blow away like a dead leaf." (This same anxiety related to keeping the body intact is exemplified in the school age child's insistence on bandages for the slightest cut. As one child put it, "everything inside could come out through the hole and then you wouldn't be you anymore.")

A related phenomenon is the child's belief (approximately ages seven to ten) that almost all illness is caused by "germs". A youngster's concern with cleanliness, anxiety about the meaning of people who wear gowns and masks, desperation to close all wounds and wipe away secretions may relate to this premise.

Elementary school age children evidence an even more intense response to invasive procedures and bodily changes than their younger counterparts. These reactions, more common and overt in girls that in boys, related to an intensification of the need to conform to peer pressure as well as the beginning of the importance of body image and self-concept.

Control issues are also more apparent for this age group. These children are more often assertive of their needs, specifying the timing, body site, context, personnel and other conditions related to repeated and relatively predictable procedures (e.g., "Only Dr Adams can stick me, and he has only one chance to do it in my left arm while I'm watching TV.") Children this age begin to voice more "adult" concerns, such as questioning why they were singled out for such a calamity (the paradigmatic "why me?"). As the concept of time continues to develop, these older children express greater concerns about the future. School refusal and social isolation for this group more commonly relates to a perceived loss of status in the eyes of one's peers due to prolonged absences and shame over changes in one's appearance rather than separation anxiety.

While children under age seven or so characteristically believe that medical procedures are punishment for bad deeds, older children begin to appreciate that treatment is relatively well-intentioned. Although these children may understand that the doctors and nurses hope to get them better, they often complain that staff do not fully appreciate the extent of their pain (which may be the case). Thus, younger children may battle with medical staff over seemingly invasive and punitive procedures, while older children may rage that the staff doesn't fully understand their experience.

The dying adolescent

The older child and adolescent begins to conceive of death as an internal process involving the cessation of bodily functions. The understanding of death as a phenomenon which is permanent, irreversible, inevitable and universal begins for children at approximately age nine and continues to develop as the years pass. (It should be stated that the unusual and "unnatural" exposure of the terminally ill child to the frequent death and dying of other children during the course of prolonged hospitalizations may seem to accelerate the process of death understanding. This pseudomaturity may lull adults into assuming a corresponding maturity ir other areas of cognitive, emotional and social development.) These children begin to understand that illness, thus death, may have many causes, though they still harbor the feeling that death is mainly a condition of the old rather than the young.

The fear of death for these children is a fear of the loss of one's intimately personal and highly unique life's goals, although earlier fears of separation and/or mutilation and a more magical blending of fantasy and reality characteristically return as death approaches. Death is loss: not just the earlier losses of friends and family or the integrity of the body, but the devastating losses of independence and identity, of sexual prowess and sexuality, of ambitions and dreams.

A more mature understanding of the causality of illness and death is integrated within the context of more complex ideas concerning the nature of bodily processes. Unfortunately, this heightened awareness of the body also relates to a more acute knowledge of the body's deterioration. Both sexes feel strongly the lessening of physical attractiveness and athletic ability with the advance of illness and death. Contrary to gender stereotypes, adolescent boys may be extremely preoccupied with any alteration in appearance, often linking this directly to a decline in sexual attractiveness and ability. Assaults to the body may prove more alarming to these individuals than the threat of death itself (i.e., the "cure" seems worse than the disease.)

As illness progresses, the adolescent sense of autonomy is increasingly threatened due to the need to depend on parents, family, friends and health care workers for the provision of basic care and necessities. Having to rely on others in order to accomplish such simple tasks as eating, dressing, bathing, and eliminating may prove especially humiliating to the adolescent who prizes his or her burgeoning sense of independence above all. Faith in self-sufficiency is also a primary defense against fears of abandonment and rejection, a defense crippled by dependency needs which grow in direct correspondence to the body's deteriorations.

Case vignette

A young man with cancer became suicidal when he was unable to care for excruciatingly painful and embarrassing rectal fissures. He remarked that it was "disgusting enough to have to take care of it myself, but I can't even think about my mother or some nurse having to do something about it."

The adolescent's more mature understanding of death as universal and inevitable is paradoxically related to more complicated and difficult friendships between the dying adolescent and his or her peers, as each grapples with the implications of the patient's impending death for their own survival and well-being. similarly, as older children begin to understand the realistic purpose of treatment and become nore convinced of the ability of hospital staff to appreciate their feelings, they may withhold information from caregivers in order to protect them from the vicissitudes of death.

Case vignette

A teenage girl in the terminal stages of cancer became socially isolated in order to "protect my friends from thinking about their own death. It's too depressing for all of us. They don't know what to say and I don't know what to talk about." The patient's boyfriend, whom the patient met at a function for adolescents diagnosed with the same form of cancer, "can't even look at me. When he looks at me, it's like a mirror of himself and gets real scared. I don't blame him: I'd stay away from me, too."

Adolescents and other children express more concern than their younger counterparts about the condition of their fellow patients. This concern is but one expression of attempts at mastery of a complex and uncertain situation. Many children look for all sorts of reasons (as do parents and health professional) why some patients with the same diagnosis survive and others fail. At the same time that these patients seek some comfort in knowing more about the circumstances of others, they also project a profound sense of isolation: no one could possibly understand what they're going through.

Case vignette

One young woman with cancer was well-known by ward personnel and the parents of the other patients for a consuming and seemingly selfless interest in the welfare of others. The patient often assumed the role of nurse's assistant or co-therapist, comforting other patients during procedures, visiting patients in their homes. On the other hand, she was fiercely protective of her own privacy. She once stated to the psychiatrist who found her silently sobbing in a corner of the waiting area that "I'm the only one who can figure this out; no way would I ever tell anybody the kinds of things these kids and their parents tell me."

Concerns about protecting others from the grim facts of a terminal illness, shame regarding a deterioration in appearance and attractiveness, and a pervasive feeling that such a dreadful situation is inevitably personal and not to be shared account for social withdrawal and isolation characteristic of certain adolescents coping with death and dying.

Lifton (1983) describes the psychological transcendence of death—or a belief in immortality—as being achieved through the legacy of one's children (the biological mode); faith in a life after death (the theological mode); the symbolic mode of enduring creations (writings, teachings, works of art, etc.); a belief that nature itself survives; and the mode of experiential transcendence, ecstatic states in which restrictions of the senses, including the sense of mortality, no longer exist. For the dying child and adolescent, the ability to survive death may assume many guises. Patients may convert to another religion or recapture a previous faith. Adolescent girls may openly fantasize about having children. Most common is the utilization of the symbolic mode to create works that endure, such as letters, videotapes, diaries, poems, songs, audiotapes and the like.

Case vignette

A teenage girl in her final days insisted that all who had been close to her would gather at her bedside to pose for a series of photographs. She then created an album of pictures bordered by her drawings and poetry which she presented to her mother shortly before she expired. She told the consulting psychiatrist that "This is the only baby I can ever have and I want my mother to take care of it." In the months to come, the mother found great solace gazing at what she called her daughter's "album of love."

Reactions of caretakers and caregivers

Parents and other family members may undergo a similar process of anticipatory grief. In the final stages of this process, the inevitability of the child's death is recognized. Sorrow over the loss that is about to occur is followed by an acceptance of the fact of the child's demise. The family may then gradually withdraw their emotional investment in the child. As death approaches, parental fantasies of replacing the dying child may emerge. Family and friends may also begin to create an idealized image of the dying child, embellishing old stories and creating new ones.

Due to feelings of guilt or helplessness and the need to deny death, family members and hospital staff may find it difficult to communicate directly with the dying child. Doctors and nurses may find themselves treating the child as an interesting or troublesome clinical problem rather than a human being, finding themselves preoccupied with lab results and scans at the expense of connecting with and understanding the patient. Some may avoid the patient altogether, communicating with the patient through the intermediaries of family, nurses, or medical charts. The avoidance of others may be communicated subtly: averted eyes; a seeming prohibition on touching or coming close to the patient; talking about the patient to others inches from the child without ever addressing the patient or trying to ascertain the patient's response. Rage and disappointment at the failure of an imagined omnipotence may lead both parents and doctors to take their anger and feelings of inadequacy out on the dying child (e.g., she'd go into remission if she'd only try harder; he couldn't possibly have that much pain). Others may act out their rescue fantasies by failing to relinquish care of the patient to others (I'm the only one who gets her to take her medications, who understands him, who knows what to do.). This last reaction may create serious complications when the patient decompensates yet refuses to accept the necessary care because the ultimate rescuer is nowhere to be found.

HELPING THE DYING CHILD

Helping the child gain self-control

Although the tragedy of terminal illness lies in its inevitability, the trauma lies in the day-to-day uncertainty and unpredictability. Central to preserving the relative well-being of the dying child throughout the stages of childhood is a respect for the child's need to control the uncontrollable and maintain a sense of continuity and integrity in the face of inescapable disintegration.

Basic to the child's attempts at achieving mastery over an uncertain situation is the ability to anticipate problematic events and seek whatever information is necessary to meet each new stress as it occurs. The decision of caregivers and caretakers regarding how much to tell the dying patient should be grounded in the age-appropriate framework previously described and the understanding that open communication between all concerned – patient, parents, family and hospital staff – is more effective at diminishing stress, improving the child's attitude and helping the child gain self-control. It is especially important for the caregiver to examine his or her own feelings, beliefs and previous experiences before arriving at a decision about the nature of information disclosed to the dying child and when it is best disclosed.

Many adults feel that it is best to "protect" the child from seemingly deleterious information. It is the author's experience that dying children are anxious enough about the uncertainly of what lies ahead without having to be anxious about whether or not their loved ones are deceiving them. Even toddlers are sensitive to the parent whose eyes swell up whenever they are asked a question pertaining to the child's health or to the medical staff that murmurs in the corridors only to approach the bedside with stern or worried looks. An ongoing dialogue between all of the responsible adults as to what is in the best interests of the child concerning how much information to share is invariably helpful. It is also useful to make parents aware of research findings that strongly suggest both dying children and survivors appear to function best when communications are open and the appropriate information is provided rather than withheld.

In communicating with the dying child, it is always useful for the caregiver to let the patient take the lead in determining the pace and content of each conversation. Caregivers should always be open to the idea of discussing death and dying without forcing it on the patient. It is the author's experience that it is helpful for the caregiver to be free and more interactive with the dying patient than is customary; dying patients welcome what appears to be a more "vital" and intimate relationship with the providers of their care.

It is most important to distinguish between that which can be changed and that which must be endured. This principle is exemplified in the flexibility of the ward staff's efforts to help the child control his or her environment. This may be accomplished by encouraging the child to assist in procedures, select the site of an injection, determine the timing of a procedure or other such interventions. A similar concept is normalizing certain reactions to stress as unavoidable under the circumstances (needles may always prick, some medicines may always burn or have unpleasant tastes, etc.), Making the unpredictable predictable through the rehearsal of procedures in symbolic play or through more realistic and educational rehearsals and explanations is most helpful. (Given the younger child's propensity to live moment to moment, rehearsals should precede treatments by brief intervals.)

The paradox of stability amidst life-threatening change is demonstrated in attempts to provide security through an expectable environment. It is helpful to fill the patient's room with cherished and familiar items while restricting troublesome procedures and examinations to the treatment room, clarifying the boundary between the predictably safe and the predictably bothersome. It is also important to encourage the development of the patient's self-respect by protecting the child's privacy. (Adolescents are especially sensitive to being surprised when they are semi-clothed or having ward personnel pry into their personal phone calls and private diaries.) The patient's self-respect is also enhanced by encouraging the patient's participation in making decisions that effect them in correspondence to the patient's age and maturity. Hand in hand with including the patient in the decision-making process, of course, is an emphasis on open communication and accessibility.

Another principle in helping the child gain self-control is the clear delineation of behavioral boundaries. This is especially important for younger children. Setting limits on the dying child's behavior is respecting the child's normality. (As one overly indulged seven year old put it, "I must be sick really bad 'cause they're so afraid to tell me what to do, like I'll die or something if they just touch me: it's really scary.") Assisting the child in finding acceptable outlets for feelings is also most important, whether it be through play, through conversation, through work with a child life specialist or consultations with a mental health professional.

Freedom from pain

A fundamental right of the dying child is freedom from pain. Pain is a symptom, not a diagnosis. Proper assessment and treatment of physical pain is critical to the well-being of the terminal patient.

For a variety of reasons, pain is characteristically underdiagnosed, undertreated and too often labelled as psychological in origin. Pediatric staff often believe that children feel less pain than adults on a physiological as well as psychological basis. Children are undermedicated due to concerns about side effects and/or addiction. Undertreatment may also occur due to improper application of the available therapies and technologies. Many clinicians find children's verbal and nonverbal communications concerning pain difficult to interpret. Finally, both patients and staff may believe consciously or unconsciously that a modicum of pain establishes a boundary: between those who are ill and those who are not; between those who feel (and are able to communicate those feelings to others) and those who cannot.

Case vignette

A toddler with cancer was already being treated by a child psychiatrist when she began to complain of severe lower abdominal pain. The pain was alleviated somewhat when either parent stroked and soothed her. Given the latter, the hospital staff was convinced that the pain was purely psychological in origin and refused to give any medications for pain. They also overtly and repeatedly blamed the psychiatrist and parents for being unable to manage the child's behavior. While not denying the possibility of a psychological overlay, both the parents and the consulting psychiatrist disagreed, citing the child's awakening in intense pain from deep sleep, declining appetite and increasing complaints of nausea as indicative of a physical disorder. After a week-long battle between ward and family, the pediatric staff ordered a series of tests which revealed a disseminated fungal infection in the gastro-intestinal tract which could easily be connected to the symptoms at hand. The family never again trusted the pediatric staff in quite the same way after this episode.

Withdrawal, irritability, apathy and emotional lability are often related to delirium or other organic mental disorders in the dying child. Among the causes for delirium in the fatally ill patient are: infections of the central nervous system or those with secondary CNS effects; metabolic disorders; processes directly related to disease (such as CNS metastases and leukemic meningitis); sensory and sleep deprivation; cerebral hemorrhages; and drug-related effects. Terminally ill children often receive a multiplicity of pharmacological agents whose combination results in either unanticipated or exaggerated side effects. In particular, the psychological effects of such medications as corticosteroids, narcotic analgesics and chemotherapeutic agents have been well-established.

It is often difficult to differentiate between debility and depression. An emphasis on non-somatic symptoms of depression (e.g., changes in mood; hopeless, helpless and/or worthless feelings; overwhelming feelings of guilt; preoccupation with death) may be helpful in establishing guidelines for appropriate treatment.

Anxiety in the terminally ill may be situational (e.g., related to procedures or separations) and anticipatory in nature (e.g. awaiting impending surgery or the results of important tests); related to disease processes (e.g., drug withdrawal, delirium, drug intoxication, respiratory distress or poorly controlled pain); or be symptomatic of an anxiety disorder that preceded the onset of the terminal illness (e.g., phobias and panic attacks).

Many psychiatric symptoms may be alleviated through the careful adjustment of the existing drug regimen. Special attention should be paid to states of drug intoxication or withdrawal. As for psychopharmacological agents, antidepressants may be useful in the treatment of anxiety as well as depression. Stimulant medications may often prove to be the treatment of choice for depressed children with a debilitating physical illness. Anxiolytics or low dose antipsychotic medications may prove useful in the management of agitation in the child or adolescent with delirium. Anxiolytics are also useful in the treatment of separation anxiety and anxiety states related to procedures. Critical to the pharmacotherapeutic management of the dying child is the skillful use of narcotic and non-narcotic analgesics for pain management.

Psychosocial therapies are often useful either in tandem with psychoactive medications is or where such medications are contraindicated. Among those most commonly used in the treatment of the terminally ill child are: behavioral rehearsal, operant conditioning and other behavior therapies; cognitive coping strategies and congnitive therapy for anxiety and depression; relaxation therapy; biofeedback; self-hypnosis and hypnotherapy; acupuncture and acupressure; and visualization techniques.

The true incorporation of mental health professionals in the treatment team and the ability of the ward staff to lessen the stigma of mental health consultation for patients and their families are of great help in minimizing the patient's physical and psychological pain. The judicious use of psychopharmacological agents and psychosocial therapies in conjuction with consultation with experts in pain management and consultation-liaison child psychiatry and psychology is highly recommended.

HELPING THE CAREGIVING NETWORK

The profound effect of parental coping on child's adaptation has been well-documented. Health care workers should facilitate whatever closeness the child will allow between himself, family and health professional. The child's connections to his or her family and support system are facilitated by providing patient and family with the opportunity to talk about their concerns and receive information about their experiences. Clear information and guidance to the patient's social milieu should be provided concerning the patient's prognosis, abilities and limitations. It is critical for the hospital staff to strongly communicate the fact that they value the parents participation in the patient's care and then proceed to involve the family every step along the way.

Whenever possible, the child's participation in peer activities such as school and ward events should be encouraged. This may conflict with the parents' need to protect their child, so it is helpful to emphasize the importance of continued socialization and interpersonal contact in connection with the patient's ability to function and maintain some semblance of continuity and identity.

At the end, the presence of the family helps the child die more peacefully. After the child's death, the family needs support and an avenue for expressing the depression, guilt, grief and loss that is part and parcel of the mourning process.

The caregiving system must take care of itself in order to take care of patients and their families. The same principles concerning open communication and education about the process of death and dying outlined above are equally applicable to doctors, nurses,, social workers, child life specialists and the like. The ability of the hospital community to openly, candidly and reasonably address the issues connected to the treatment of the dying child provide a comfortable and secure model for the dying child and his or her support network. A unified and well-informed staff helps ease the passage of the family through this unfortunate and unforeseen phase of the family life cycle to the world that lies beyond the hospital doors.

References

Bracken, J.M. (1986) Children with Cancer: A Comprehensive Reference Guide for Parents, Oxford and New York: Oxford University Press.
Buckingham, R.W. (1983) A Special Kind of Love—Care of the Dying Child, New York: Continuum Press.
Easson, W.M. (1970) The Dying Child: The Management of the Child or Adolescent Who Is Dying, Springfield, IL: Charles C. Thomas.
Gyulay, J.E. (1978) The Dying Child, New York: McGraw-Hill.
Heiligenstein, E. and Jacobsen, P.B. (1988) Differentiating depression in medically ill children and adolescents. *Journal of the American Academy of Child and Adolescent Psychiatry*, **27**, 716-719.
Koocher, G.P. and O'Malley, J.E. (1981) The Damocles Syndrome: Psychosocial Consequences of Surviving Childhood Cancer,. New York: McGraw-Hill.
Kriechman, A. (1984) Illness in the therapist: the eye patch. *Psychiatry*, **47**, 378-386.
Kubler-Ross, E. (1983) On Children and Death, New York: Macmillan Publishing Company.
Lifton, R.J. (1983) The Life of the Self: Toward a New Psychology, New York: Basic Books.
Martinson, I.M. (1976) Home Care for the Dying Child: Professional and family perspectives, New York: Appleton-Century-Crofts.
Mellonie, B. and Ingpen, R. (1983) Lifetimes: The Beautiful Way to Explain Death to Children, Toronto and New York: Bantam Books.
Pattison, E.M. (1977) The Experience of Dying, Englewood Cliffs, NJ: Prentice-Hall.
Perry, S.W. (1984) The undermedication for pain. *Psychiatric Annals*, **14**, 808-811.
Ross, D.M. and Ross, S.A. (1988) Childhood Pain: Current Issues, Research, and Management, Baltimore: Urban and Schwartzenberg.
Sahler, O.J. (1978) The Child and Death. St. Louis: C.V. Mosby Co.

Talking to Children About Death. (1979) U.S. Department of Health, Education and Welfare, DHEW (ADM 79-878), Government Printing Office, 1979.
Wass, H. and Corr, C. A. (1984) Childhood and Death Washington, D.C.: Hemisphere.
Wass, H. and Corr, C. A. (1984) Helping Children Cope with Cancer: Guidelines and Resources, 2nd Edition Washington, D.C.: Hemisphere.
Yalom, I. (1980) Existential Psychtherapy, New York: Basic Books.

9 Depression and Anxiety

Greta Francis

Department of Psychiatry and Human Behavior, Brown University School of Medicine, Providence, RI 02915, USA

The goal of this chapter is to describe anxiety disorders seen in children and adolescents, discuss the overlap between anxiety and affective disorders, highlight normative data and common measures for assessing anxiety in youngsters, and provide relevant clinical case material.

ANXIETY DISORDERS SEEN IN CHILDREN AND ADOLESCENTS

The DSM-III-R delineates three anxiety disorders specific to children and adolescents: separation anxiety disorder, overanxious disorder, and avoidant disorder. In addition, children and adolescents may receive anxiety diagnoses which are not specific to children, including simple phobia, social phobia, panic disorder with or without agoraphobia, obsessive-compulsive disorder, and post traumatic stress disorder.

Separation anxiety disorder is characterized by marked distress related to the separation of the child from major attachment figures, usually parents, or the home. Children with separation anxiety disorder may be worried about their own or their parent's safety, reluctant to attend school or other activities away from parents, reluctant to sleep alone or away from home, clingy with parents, upset in anticipation of separation, complain of aches and pains at separation times, and show signs of distress (e.g., crying, diminished concentration, withdrawal) while separated from parents. According to the DSM-III-R, in order to receive a diagnosis of separation anxiety disorder, the child must evidence at least three of the above-mentioned nine symptoms for a period of at least two weeks.

Sam was a a ten year old male who presented with symptoms of Separation Anxiety Disorder. He was extremely reluctant to be away from his father, even for brief periods of time. Sam usually followed his father around the house and became tearful when father left for work. At separation times, Sam expressed fear that father would be in a car accident. If father failed to arrive home on time, Sam became quite panicky. When Sam went to school, he moved his desk so that it faced toward home.

He often complained of stomachaches on school days or when father left for business trips. Sam consistently turned down invitations to sleep over at friend's houses.

The hallmark of overanxious disorder is excessive or unrealistic worry. In contrast to the relatively circumscribed worries indicative of separation anxiety disorder, the worries of overanxious disorder children tend to be pervasive and may involve many social, athletic, and academic situations. The child with overanxious disorder may worry about past and future events, be overly concerned with his/her performance, express a variety of vague somatic complaints, evidence extreme self-consciousness, require excessive reassurance, and complain of tenseness or an inability to relax. According to the DSM-III-R, in order for a child to receive a diagnosis of overanxious disorder, he/she must evidence at least four of the above-mentioned seven symptoms for a period of at least six months.

Andrea was an eleven year old female who was referred for outpatient treatment because of excessive worrying and perfectionism. Although a superior student, Andrea worried almost constantly about her grades. She spent hours fretting over homework assignments and required much reassurance from her parents that her performance was adequate. Andrea also expressed many fears about past and future social behavior. She often became tearful in school when she perceived peers to be teasing her. Parents described Andrea as a tense and nervous child.

Children with avoidant disorder are said to show excessive shyness around unfamiliar people of sufficient severity so as to interfere with social functioning in peer relationships. The child with avoidant disorder typically avoids social situations in which he/she is exposed to unfamiliar peers. In order to receive a diagnosis of avoidant disorder, the child must value interpersonal involvement as evidenced by appropriate relationships with familiar people.

Kevin was a six year old male who presented as socially withdrawn and fearful. He demonstrated considerable anxiety when meeting new children and adults. Kevin reported that he wished he had more friends but was scared to ask children to play with him. His relationships with familiar adults generally were warm and satisfying. When Kevin's mother invited schoolmates over for Kevin's birthday party, he spent the majority of the time hiding in his room, too nervous to come out and join the party.

The diagnosis of phobia in children is identical to that in adults, and is subtyped according to the nature of the phobic object (social or simple). The phobic child shows persistent fear of a situation or object, avoids the feared object or endures contact with intense anxiety, recognizes that the fear is excessive or unreasonable, and evidences impairment in day-to-day functioning or is bothered by having the fear. Common simple phobias in children include fears of animals, dark places, and medical procedures. Common social phobias include public speaking, taking tests, and eating in public.

Gerry was a 15 year old male who sought treatment because of a phobia of needles. He was scheduled to undergo dental surgery in the near future and felt as though he needed to overcome this fear. He reported intense fear in response to being 10 feet away from a capped needle. Gerry's anxiety reached panic proportions when faced with an injection or blood draw. As such, prior to treatment, he had been unable to tolerate a blood test ordered by his physician or an injection of novocaine required for dental work.

Panic disorder with or without agoraphobia also may be diagnosed in children and adolescents using the adult criteria specified in the DSM-III-R. Panic disorder without agoraphobia is characterized by spontaneous anxiety attacks, consisting of multiple physiological symptoms (e.g., palpitations, sweating, dizziness), in the absence of significant avoidance behavior. In contrast, the diagnosis of panic disorder with agoraphobia requires both spontaneous anxiety attacks and significant avoidance (e.g., inability to enter situations outside the home). Agoraphobics are said to avoid situations because of fear of having panic attack or being incapacitated.

Jane was 17 year old female who came in for an evaluation because of an acute onset of anxiety attacks. During these attacks, she complained of difficulty breathing, palpitations, chest pain, dizziness, sweating, and fear that she was having a heart attack. Jane reported that these attacks came "out of the blue", particularly when she was in large crowded situations. As such, she had begun to avoid going to movies, shopping malls, and restaurants out of fear that she would panic and be unable to leave the situation.

Obsessive-compulsive disorder (OCD) in children and adolescents is virtually identical to that seen in adults. The hallmark of obsessive-compulsive disorder is persistent and repetitive disturbing thoughts and/or behavioral rituals. The interruption of these thoughts or rituals typically causes the person to become distressed. Common obsessions are thoughts of doubt or contamination. Common compulsions include washing, checking, touching, and counting rituals.

Roseanne was a 14 year old female who presented with pervasive OCD symptoms with an onset at age nine years. The majority of her compulsions involved elaborate rule-making and ordering. In fact, there appeared to be no aspect of her life that was not governed by these compulsions. Roseanne's day was organized according to a fixed hourly schedule. One of the more odd examples of the schedule was her daily 48 minute visits to five peers. If one of the peers was unable to visit, she went back home immediately to wait, with an alarm clock, for the next scheduled visit time. Roseanne also exhibited a complicated eating ritual which included the consumption of certain foods at certain times. Each meal began with one sip of beverage followed by a rigid cycle of three bites of meat, bread, vegetable, and dessert. She chewed her food for the amount of time required for her to sing a popular commercial jingle to herself.

Children and adolescents may present with symptoms indicative of post traumatic stress disorder (PTSD). The essential feature of PTSD is continued distress following an unusual, markedly distressing event (e.g., physical abuse, natural disaster). The continued distress is exhibited by reexperiencing of the traumatic event, avoidance of situations associated with the event, and persistent symptoms of increased arousal (e.g., hypervigilance).

Molly was a 13 year old female who was hospitalized one year after being sexually abused by an adult male neighbor. Her presenting complaints included extreme anxiety, particularly at night and when alone, recurrent nightmares of the abuse, and flashbacks of specifics of the assault. She had difficulty sleeping, was easily startled, and became very clingy with parents. Molly's fear had worsened over the two months prior to the anniversary of the abuse.

OVERLAP BETWEEN ANXIETY AND DEPRESSION

While the Diagnostic and Statistical Manual of Mental Disorders (American Psychiatric Association, 1987) delineates different types of anxiety and affective disorders, there is little empirical evidence available with which to make such distinctions. It often is difficult to distinguish among anxiety, depression, and social withdrawal in children. As such, it is not surprising that depressed children and adolescents frequently report significant anxiety symptoms and/or social withdrawal (Puig-Antich and Rabinovich, 1986). Bernstein and Garfinkel (1986: 235–241) investigated the relationship between anxiety and depressive symptoms in a group of 26 children and adolescents with school refusal. They reported that 69 percent of their sample received anxiety diagnoses, 62 percent received affective diagnoses, and 50 percent showed anxiety and depressive diagnoses concurrently. In particular, these children and adolescents received diagnoses including major depression, adjustment disorder with depressed mood, separation anxiety disorder, and overanxious disorder. They cautioned that the cause-effect relationship among school refusal, anxiety, and depression remains unclear. Anxiety and depression may bring on school refusal or chronic school refusal may lead to anxiety and depression. Information regarding the age of onset of anxiety and depressive disorders in children with school refusal would help to clarify this issue.

Kolvin, Berney, and Bhate (1984: 347–357) studied 51 children and adolescents between the ages of nine and 15 years who were markedly reluctant to attend school. They categorized 22 of these children as depressed using the following criteria: sad mood plus either tearful appearance or decreased energy or hopelessness. Thus, the depressed group included children with depressive *symptoms* rather than a DSM-III-R affective *disorder*. The authors reported that the depressed school refusers evidenced the following symptoms to a significantly greater degree than did the non-depressed school refusers: dysphoria, tearfulness, sense of emptiness/isolation, sense of being unloved, exaggerated illness behavior, loss of interest, loss of energy, initial insomnia, nocturnal restlessness, feeling that life was not worth living, and feeling of inappropriate familiarity or strangeness.

Hershberg and Carlson *et al* (1982: 358–361) evaluated the presence of anxiety and depressive symptoms in 28 depressed and 14 anxiety-disordered children. They found that while anxiety symptoms were present in the depressed youngsters and depressive symptoms were present in the anxiety-disordered youngsters, these comorbid symptoms rarely were of sufficient severity to warrant a diagnosis.

There also is significant overlap between anxiety and affective diagnoses. Kovacs and Feinberg (1984: 229–237) found that approximately one-third of their sample of 65 depressed youngsters (major depressive disorder and dysthymic disorder) had coexisting anxiety disorders (separation anxiety disorder, avoidant disorder, overanxious disorder, phobia).

Mitchell *et al* (1988) assessed the presence of anxiety symptoms and diagnoses in a clinic sample of children and adolescents with major depressive disorder. Compared to those without major depression, depressed youngsters had significantly higher rates of excessive worrying, somatic complaints, and social withdrawal. Moreover, 42 percent of the depressed children and 44 percent of the depressed adolescents presented with coexisting separation anxiety disorder. Those youngsters with both anxiety and affective disorders reported more severe depression than did youngsters with depression alone.

Strauss *et al* (1988: 57–68) studied the association between anxiety and depression in a sample of 106 children and adolescents with anxiety disorders. Twenty-eight percent of youngsters with anxiety disorders presented with coexisting major depressive disorder. These children were older, demonstrated higher rates of obsessive-compulsive disorder and agoraphobia, and reported more severe anxiety symptoms (i.e., generalized anxiety, state and trait anxiety, and fear) than did anxiety-disordered children without major depression. Interestingly, the two groups did not differ in their self-reports of depressive symptoms. Thus, the youngsters with comorbid anxiety and depressive disorders tended to be more anxious, but not more depressed, than the non-depressed anxiety-disordered youngsters.

There is evidence that affective disorders in children and adolescents frequently are superimposed on a background of longstanding anxiety symptoms. Kovacs *et al* (1989: 776–782) conducted a longitudinal study of depressed children with and without anxiety disorders. In about two-thirds of the cases of depressed/anxious youngsters, the onset of the anxiety disorder predated that of the depressive disorder. Moreover, the anxiety disorder often persisted after the depression had remitted.

In sum, anxiety and depression often coexist in children and adolescents, according to parent, teacher, clinician and self-report assessments. Depressed youngsters frequently present with anxiety symptoms and/or diagnoses. There also is evidence that depressed/anxious children display more severe pathology than children with depression or anxiety alone.

NORMATIVE AND DEVELOPMENTAL CONSIDERATIONS

In order to assess anxiety in youngsters it is important to consider a number of normative and developmental factors. There is empirical evidence to suggest that normal children evidence a relatively large number of fears (e.g., Agras, Sylvester and Oliveau, 1969; Jersild and Holmes, 1935; Lapouse and Monk, 1958; MacFarlane, Allen and Honzick, 1954). For example, in their classic epidemiologic study, Lapouse and Monk (1958: 1134–1144) discovered that 43 percent of children in the sample had seven or more fears, as reported by their mothers. No epidemiological information is available regarding the prevalence of other anxiety symptoms.

Studies of subclinical fears indicate a change in the type and number of fears over the course of childhood and adolescence (e.g., Graziano, DeGiovanni and Garcia, 1979; MacFarlane *et al*, 1954). For example, young children tend to evince more and different fears than do older children and adolescents. While there appears to be an age-related decrease in reported fears of imaginary creatures, the dark, and animals, there is an age-related increase in social-evaluative fears (e.g., Agras *et al*, 1969; Bauer, 1976; Mauer, 1965).

Generally, it has been found that girls tend to report more fear and anxiety than do boys (e.g., Abe and Masui, 1981; Anderson, Williams, McGee, and Silva, 1987; Lapouse and Monk, 1958; Richman, Stevenson, and Graham, 1975). However, as Graziano *et al* (1979: 804–830) aptly point out, it is unclear whether the higher rate of fears reported for girls reflects a greater prevalence of fearfulness in girls or a greater willingness by girls and their parents/teachers to report fears.

Children of varying socioeconomic status (SES) levels have been found to differ in the number and type of fears reported. Angelino *et al* (1956: 263–276) and Lapouse and Monk (1959: 803–813) found that children from lower SES levels reported more fears and worries than did children from higher SES levels. Moreover, low SES children were more likely to report fears of rats and drunks, while higher SES children were more likely to report fears of car accidents. Last *et al* (1987: 726–730) reported demographic differences in their sample of anxiety disordered children and adolescents as a function of diagnosis. They found that the majority of families of children with separation anxiety disorder received low socioeconomic status ratings, while the majority of families of children with a phobic disorder of school or overanxious disorder received middle-upper socioeconomic status ratings.

MEASURES OF ANXIETY IN CHILDREN AND ADOLESCENTS

A number of self-report measures of anxiety exist for children and adolescents. The most widely used include the Revised Children's Manifest Anxiety Scale (RCMAS; Reynolds and Richmond, 1978), State-Trait Anxiety Inventory for Children (STAIC; Spielberger, 1973), and the Fear Survey Schedule for Children-Revised (FSSCR; Ollendick, 1983).

Children's Manifest Anxiety Scale-Revised

The Children's Manifest Anxiety Scale-Revised (RCMAS: Reynolds and Richmond, 1978) is a 37-item questionnaire consisting of three anxiety subscales: physiological anxiety, worry-oversensitivity, and concentration anxiety. The RCMAS has been studied widely. Normative data are available, as well as data suggesting acceptable internal consistency and test-retest reliability (e.g. Reynolds, 1981; Reynolds and Paget, 1982; Reynolds and Richmond, 1978). According to Finch and Rogers (Finch and Rogers, 1984) less is known about the validity of the RCMAS.

State-Trait Anxiety Inventory for Children

The State-Trait Anxiety Inventory for Children (STAIC; Spielberger, 1973) contains two 20-item scales which are said to tap trait and state anxiety in school-aged children. On the trait scale, the child is asked to rate how he/she "usually feels", while on the state scale the child is asked to rate how he/she feels "right now, at this very moment." The distinction between state and trait anxiety, as measured by the STAIC, has been questioned, however. Contrary to expectations, the trait anxiety score has not been found to correlate more highly than the state anxiety score with other measures of trait anxiety such as the RCMAS (e.g., Finch and Nelson, 1974: 33–37; Montgomery and Finch, 1974: 293–298). However, as with the RCMAS, the STAIC has been used widely and found to possess adequate psychometric properties (Ollendick, 1983: 685–692).

Fear Survey Schedule for Children-Revised

The Fear Survey Schedule for Children-Revised (FSSCR; Ollendick, 1983: 685–692) is an 80-item questionnaire which instructs children to rate their level of fear on a 3-point scale ranging from "none" to "a lot." The FSSCR contains a meaningful five factor structure, including fear of the unknown, fear of failure and criticism, fear of danger and death, fear of minor injury and animals, and medical fears. In a recent study, Ollendick *et al* (in press) explored developmental and cultural differences in self-reported fear in a large group of children and adolescents from the United States and Australia. Consistent with earlier findings (Ollendick, 1983: 685–692; Ollendick *et al*, 1985 465–467), girls tended to have higher total fear and factor scores than did boys. Moreover, younger children tended to have higher total fear and factor scores than did older children and adolescents. The authors reported no significant differences between their American and Australian samples. Furthermore, there is empirical evidence that the FSSCR has clinical utility. Ollendick and Mayer (1984: 367–411) reported that the total fear score on the FSSCR discriminated between normal and school avoidant youngsters. Moreover, the FSSCR has been found to reliably differentiate the fears of blind and normally sighted children (Ollendick *et al*, 1985: 465–467). Finally, Last *et al* (1989: 137–141) reported that items on the FSSCR differentiated among separation-anxious, phobic, and overanxious outpatient youngsters.

Clinical case material

The following cases highlight the overlap between anxiety and depression that often is seen when youngsters present for outpatient or inpatient psychiatric treatment. The first study describes the outpatient treatment of a youngster with primary overanxious disorder coupled with depressive symptoms. The second study describes inpatient treatment of a youngster with equally severe depression and separation anxiety disorder.

Case study 1

Strauss (1989: 19–30) presented a case study of the treatment of overanxious disorder in an eleven year old girl (Ashley). Ashley worried excessively about most future and past events. She was perfectionistic and often sought reassurance as to the correctness of her academic and social behavior. She was extremely self-conscious and had difficulty relaxing. A multimethod assessment was conducted including self-report inventories and teacher rating scales. Ashley described herself as anxious, fearful, sad, and lonely. Her teachers characterized her as anxious, withdrawn, and socially neglected among her classmates.

Treatment consisted of a package based on interventions used successfully with generalized anxiety disorder in adults. The treatment package included relaxation techniques, cognitive restructuring, and assertiveness training. Ashley was seen for a total of 25 individual treatment sessions over a six month period. The initial phase of treatment consisted of deep muscle relaxation training. A reward system was added to encourage Ashley to practice relaxation exercises at home. She reported no reduction in anxiety or worrying following completion of the relaxation training. During this initial phase of treatment Ashley also self-monitored her cognitions and subjective anxiety. Cognitive rehearsal and cognitive restructuring were used to modify her maladaptive thoughts. She was taught to replace maladaptive thoughts with coping thoughts such "I know that I am as good as the other kids". In addition, Ashley was taught to modify faulty thinking by identifying and challenging cognitive errors such as catastrophizing thoughts. According to Strauss, progress in cognitive therapy was slow. However, once Ashley grasped the concept that her thinking impacted on her behavior, progress quickened. The final phase of treatment consisted of assertiveness training. Role-playing as used to increase assertive responding and initiations of social interactions. For example, Ashley practiced refusing unreasonable requests and calling peers on the telephone.

Strauss reported that this multicomponent treatment package was effective in modifying Ashley's overanxious symptomatology. At the end of treatment, Ashley no longer met DSM-III criteria for overanxious disorder. Her self-reported anxiety, fear, sadness, and loneliness also decreased. Three months after treatment, both Ashley and her parents reported that treatment gains had been maintained.

Case study 2

Francis and Hart (in press) reported the case of Douglas, a seven year old, white male who lived with his parents and younger sister. He attended school regularly and was in the second grade. Doug's mother was chronically depressed, and his father had a signficant alcohol problem. The family had experienced a number of recent losses including the deaths of Doug's paternal grandmother and maternal grandfather.

The first psychiatric contact for this youngster came after he attempted to choke himself at school while stating that he wanted to die. School personnel referred him for an emergency outpatient evaluation at a clinic specializing in the treatment of childhood depression. Doug was diagnosed with Major Depressive Disorder and placed on Imipramine. He and his mother attended weekly outpatient sessions focused on medication management and basic parent education. After nine months of outpatient treatment, Doug was referred for admission to the hospital because of a worsening of symptoms.

Upon admission, Doug and his parents were interviewed separately by a child psychiatrist and clinical child psychologist using a semistructured symptom oriented diagnostic interview. His teacher and outpatient therapist also provided information. It is important to note that initial assessment relied on reports from Doug's parents, school personnel, and outpatient therapist because Doug denied any and all problems. For example, he described himself as "mostly happy" even while tears were running down his face. On self-report measures of depression, anxiety, fear, self-esteem, and hopelessness, he also described himself as problem-free. The following symptoms were described by parents and significant others: pervasive sadness, extreme anhedonia, poor concentration, social withdrawal, decreased appetite with a nine pound weight loss over the previous nine months, difficulty falling asleep, and hypersensitivity to criticism. Moreover, Doug evidenced significant separation anxiety symptoms including frequent worry that his parents or sister would die, extreme distress when separated from the family, difficulty sleeping alone at night, and nightmares involving separation. Doug's separation anxiety was observed immediately upon his arrival on the unit. He cried on and off throughout the day and evidenced extreme distress once his parents left. Doug's mother also demonstrated extreme anxiety about having to leave, even though visiting had been arranged for the following day. There was no indication of disruptive behavior problems, psychosis, manic symptoms, or current suicidal ideation or intent.

During the first two weeks of hospitalization, a comprehensive assessment was completed. No medical problems were discovered, other than his recent weight loss. Doug was tapered gradually off his Imipramine. Intellectual and psychoeducational assessments revealed Doug to be a boy of above average intellectual ability with school performance at or above grade level. Doug was described best diagnostically as suffering from Major Depressive Disorder superimposed upon long-standing Separation Anxiety Disorder. His family was stressed both emotionally and financially. Unresolved issues included grief over the recent deaths of close family members, mother's chronic depression and separation anxiety, father's alcohol problems, and conflicting parenting styles between the mother and father.

Treatment was multifaceted and included activity increase strategies, graded exposure, and social skills training for Doug. In addition, the family was involved in treatment focused on uniting the parents around the issue of child management, encouraging parents to seek help for their individual problems, and resolving grief issues.

Activity increase strategies were implemented via the behavioral milieu management program. Doug was given a series of daily expectations including appropriate hygiene, attendance at school, participation in unit activities such as art, gym, and off-unit outings, adequate food intake at meals, and regular bedtime. In essence, Doug began to follow an activity-oriented daily schedule. He received tokens for appropriate participation in, and completion of, activities and tasks. Each day he traded in his tokens for preferred activities such as later bedtime, video game time, and one-to-one time with his primary nurse. Although reserved and inhibited at first, Doug was extremely compliant and met all expectations with ease. He clearly possessed the skills necessary to exhibit the prosocial behaviors. Once he mastered the minimal expectations, he was encouraged to demonstrate higher level skills like initiating activities and assuming a leadership role.

As an adjunct to the activity increase strategy, Doug participated in social skills training using a small group format. As noted above, although many of Doug's social behaviors were appropriate, he was hesitant to initiate interactions and often behaved in a rather passive manner. As such, the goals of social skills training were to teach and encourage Doug to initiate social interactions with peers and adults and to provide him with an opportunity to receive positive feedback for his attempts. Another important aspect of social skills treatment was teaching Doug to identify and express affect. Over the course of the hospitalization, Doug became an active participant in the group. He was able to engage in spontaneous interaction with group members and occasionally provided feedback to others regarding their performance. In addition, while initially Doug was hypersensitive to perceived negative feedback, he became better able to respond appropriately to constructive criticism. Finally, Doug made noticeable progress in his ability to label his emotions and let people know when he felt sad or scared.

Doug's concurrent separation anxiety was treated using graduated exposure. For approximately the first two weeks of hospitalization, his parents visited on a daily basis. Following this, they decreased their visiting frequency to four times per week. As expected, while Doug demonstrated initial nervousness with each change, eventually his anxiety diminished. Similarly Doug's phone calls to and from parents decreased from many times per day to once a day with a concurrent decrease in distress. One of Doug's major complaints was a fear of sleeping alone. Although Doug had a roommate during most of his hospital stay, he did practice sleeping alone a number of times. Finally, as Doug's discharge approached, he had a number of home visits which allowed him and his parents further opportunity to practice separating.

During the 6-week hospitalization, Doug demonstrated a number of positive changes. He gained back the weight he had lost and looked quite healthy. His activity level increased and his anxiety level began to decrease. Given these changes, it was felt that an additional trial of medication was not warranted. His parents utilized family therapy fairly well. They became more united in their approach to dealing with Doug, and mother's separation anxiety diminished. Both parents were hesitant to acknowledge their own problems. Mother reluctantly agreed to seek individual therapy while father refused. Upon discharge, referrals were made for individual therapy for Doug and mother, and for family therapy.

SUMMARY

It is clear that anxiety and depression frequently coexist in children and adolescents. As such, it is important for anyone coming in contact with depressed youngsters to evaluate the presence of anxiety symptoms and/or diagnoses. Such an evaluation can be facilitated by familiarity with anxiety disorders seen in children and adolescents, awareness of normative and developmental consideration, and knowledge of appropriate assessment instruments.

References

Abe, K. and Masui, T. (1981) Age-sex trends of phobic and anxiety symptoms in adolescents, *British Journal of Psychiatry*, **138**, 297-302.

Agras, S., Sylvester, D. and Oliveau, D. (1969) 'The epidemiology of common fears and phobias. *Comprehensive Psychiatry*, **10**, 151-126.

American Psychiatric Association (1987) Diagnostic and statistical manual of mental disorders. Washington, D.C.

Anderson, J.C., Williams, S., McGee, R. and Silva, P.A. (1987) DSM-III disorders in preadolescent children. *Archives of General Psychiatry*, **44**, 69-76.

Angelino, H., Dollins, J. and Mech, E.V. (1956) Trends in the fears and worries of school children as related to socioeconomic status and age. *The Journal of Genetic Psychology*, **89**, 263-276.

Bauer, D.H. (1976) An exploratory study of developmental changes in children's fears. *Journal of Child Psychology and Psychiatry*, **17**, 69-74.

Bernstein, G.A. and Garfinkel, B.D. (1986) School phobia: The overlap of affective and anxiety disorders. *Journal of the American Academy of Child Psychiatry*, **2**, 235-241.

Finch, A.J. and Nelson, W.M. (1974) Anxiety and locus-of-control in emotionally disturbed children. *Journal of Abnormal Child Psychology*, **2**, 33-37.

Finch, A.J. and Rogers, T.R. (1984) Self-report instruments, *Child Behavior Assessments: Principles and Procedures*, T.H. Ollendick and M. Hersen (eds. T.H. Ollendick and M. Herson). New York: Pergamon Press.

Francis, G. and Hart, K.J. (in press). Depression and suicide, *Inpatient Behavior Therapy for Children and Adolescents*, (eds. V.B. VanHasseh and D.J. Kolko). New York: Plenum Press.

Graziano, A., DeGiovanni, I.S. and Garcia, K. (1979) Behavioral treatment of children's fears: A review. *Psychological Bulletin*, **86**, 804-830.

Hershberg, S.G., Carlson, G.A., Cantwell, D.P. and Strober, M. (1982) Anxiety and depressive disorders in psychiatrically disturbed children. *Journal of Clinical Psychiatry*, **43**, 358-361.

Jersild, A.T. and Holmes, F.B. (1935) Children's fears, *Child Development (Monograph 20)*, New York: Teachers' College, Columbia University.

Kolvin, I., Berney, P. and Bhate, S.R. (1984) Classification and diagnosis of depression in school phobia. *British Journal of Psychiatry*, **145**, 347-357.

Kovacs, M., Feinberg, T.L., Crouse-Novak, M.A., Paulauskas, S.L. and Finkelstein, R. (1984) Depressive disorders in childhood: I. A longitudinal prospective study of characteristics and recovery. *Archives of General Psychiatry*, **41**, 229-237.

Kovacs, M., Gatsonis, C., Paulauskas, S.L. and Richards, C. (1989) Depressive disorders in childhood: IV. A longitudinal study of comorbidity with and risk for anxiety disorders. *Archives of General Psychiatry*, **46**, 776-782.

Lapouse, R. and Monk, M.A. (1958) An epidemiologic study of behavior characteristics in children. *American Journal of Public Health*, **48**, 1134-1144.

Lapouse, R. and Monk, M.A. (1959) Fears and worries in a representative sample of children. *American Journal of orthopsychiatry*, **29**, 803-818.

Last, C.G., Francis, G. and Strauss, C.C. (1989) Assessing fears in anxiety-disordered children with the revised Fear Survey Schedule for Children (FSSC-R). *Journal of Clinical Child Psychology*, **18**, 137-141.

Last, C.G., Strauss, C.C. and Francis, G. (1987) Comorbidity among childhood anxiety disorders. *Journal of Nervous and Mental Disease*, *175*, 726-730.

MacFarlane, J.N., Allen, L. and Honzik, M.P. (1954) *A Developmental Study of the Behavior Problems of Normal Children Between 21 Months and 14 Years*, Berkeley: University of California Press.

Mauer, A. (1965) What children fear. *Journal of Genetic Psychology*, **106**, 265-277.

Mitchell, J., McCauley, E., Burke, P.M. and Moss, S.J. (1988) Phenomenology of depression in children and adolescents. *Journal of the American Academy of Child and Adolescent Psychiatry*, **27**, 12-20.

Montgomery, L.E. and Finch, A.J. (1974) Validity of two measures of anxiety in children. *Journal of Abnormal Child Psychology*, **2**, 293-298.

Ollendick, T. H. (1983) Reliability and validity of the Revised Fear Survey Schedule for Children (FSSC-R). *Behavior Research and Therapy*, **21**, 685–692.
Ollendick, T. H., King, N. R. and Frary, P. (in press). Fears in children and adolescents in Australia and the United States. *Behaviour Research and Therapy*.
Ollendick, T. H., Matson, J. L. and Helsel, W. J. (1985) Fears in children and adolescents: Normative data. *Behavior Research and Therapy*, **4**, 465–467.
Ollendick, T. H. and Mayer, J. A. (1984) School phobia, *Behavioral treatment of anxiety disorders*, S. M. Turner (Ed.). New York: Plenum Publishing Corporation.
Puig-Antich, J. and Robinovich, H. (1986) Relationship between affective and anxiety disorders of childhood, *Anxiety disorders of childhood*, (ed. R. Gittelman). New York: The Guilford Press.
Reynolds, C. R. (1981): Long-term stability of scores on the Revised Children's Anxiety Scale. *Perceptual and Motor Skills*, **53**, 702.
Reynolds, C. R. and Paget, K. D. (1982) National normative and reliability data for the Revised Children's Manifest Anxiety Scale. Paper presented at the annual meeting of the National Association of School Psychologists, Toronto.
Reynolds, C. R. and Richmond, B. O. (1978) What I Think and Feel: A revised measure of children's manifest anxiety. *Journal of Abnormal Child Psychology*, **6**, 271–280.
Richman, N., Stevenson, J. E. and Graham, P. J. (1975) Prevalence of behavior problems in three-year-old children: An epidemiologic study in a London borough. *Journal of Child Psychology and Psychiatry*, **16**, 277–287.
Ross, A. O. (1980) Psychological disorders of children, *A behavioral approach to theory, research, and therapy*. New York: McGraw-Hill.
Spielberger, C. D. (1973) *Manual for the Stait-Trait Inventory for Children*. Palo Alto: Consulting Psychologists Press.
Strauss, C. C. (1989) Overanxious disorder, *Child behavior therapy casebook*, eds., M. Hersen and C. G. Last, New York: Plenum Press.
Strauss, C. C. and Francis, G. (1989) Phobic disorders, Chapter to appear in (eds. C. G. Last and M. Hersen), *Handbook of child psychiatric diagnosis* (170–190). New York: John Wiley.
Strauss, C. C., Last, C. G., Hersen, M. and Kazdin, A. E. (1988) Association between anxiety and depression in children and adolescents with anxiety disorders. *Journal of Abnormal Child Psychology*, **16**, 57–68.

10 Conduct Disorder and Depression

James T. McCracken, Dennis P. Cantwell and Gregory L. Hanna

Department of Psychiatry, UCLA School of Medicine, Los Angeles, CA 90024, USA

Conduct disorder and depression are disorders that often co-occur. This overlap carries important implications for the evaluation, treatment, and outcome of depressed youngsters. This chapter will review the various links between conduct disorder and depression, highlighting the clinical ramifications of these links for the pediatrician. As we will detail below, available data suggests that the combination of conduct disorder with depression is a dangerous mixture with respect to suicidal risk. With the awareness of the potential lethality of comorbid conduct disorder, the pediatrician may have the opportunity to intervene at an early stage with a depressed youngster to prevent a tragedy. For researchers interested in the phenomenology and etiology of depression in children and the determinants of outcome, data presented below suggest that the mixed conduct disorder/depressed group may require handling as a distinct subgroup of children within the spectrum of childhood affective disorders.

HISTORICAL VIEWPOINTS

Some of the oldest empirical research in child psychopathology suggested that within samples of delinquent youngsters, that is to say youngsters with histories of arrests or placement due to incorrigible behavior, there existed a subgroup of children described as "personality disordered", or "withdrawn" (Quay, 1972: 1–29). These children appeared to have many depressive features. In addition to their histories of antisocial behavior, these children rated highly on characteristics such as feelings of inferiority, anxiety, crying, chronic sadness, and social withdrawl. The validity of distinguishing these children as a separate subgroup was supported by the finding that these juveniles were found to be more responsive to treatment and less likely to commit repeat offenses than those delinquent subjects classified as "aggressive" (Quay, 1972: 1–29). Others argued (on less empirical grounds) that delinquents were comprised of three primary subgroups, one sociological, one characterological, and one neurotic. A frequent problem among the "neurotic" delinquents was believed to be underlying depressive symptoms (Weiner, 1975: 673). While these subgroups described delinquent children possessing a variety of emotional symptoms, including some of a depressive character, at that time depression per se was not highlighted as an co-existing disorder that deserved special treatment.

The possible role of underlying depression in the genesis of some cases of juvenile antisocial behavior was expanded upon by psychodynamic writers into the concept of "masked depression". In this formulation, due to the youngster's developmental immaturity intense affect was "acted out" in the service of reducing the pain and humiliation of the depressed state. Likewise, it was believed that the externalization of intolerable inner distress served to provide some sense of control for the child or adolescent. As a result, it was then argued that underlying depression could manifest itself as truancy, promiscuity, learning problems, somatic symptoms, encopresis, or hyperactivity (Glaser, 1967: 565–574). Not surprisingly, specific criteria for the determination of masked depression were not developed; subsequent studies revealed that adult symptom-based criteria for depression could identify a group of youngsters that appeared to have depressive syndromes equivalent to adults (Carlson and Cantwell, 1980: 445–449). Based on such studies, it appeared that the inability to diagnose depression in younger populations had more to do with the lack of a systematic review of depressive symptoms than with depression appearing in a "masked" form.

However, the notion of masked depression may have contained a grain of validity, at least with respect to the co-occurrence of a variety of problem behaviors with

Table 10.1 Diagnostic criteria for conduct disorder (DSM-III-R)

A. A disturbance of conduct lasting at least six months, during which at least three of the following have been present:
   (1) has stolen without confrontation of a victim on more than one occassion (including forgery)
   (2) has run away from home overnight at least twice while living in parental or parental surrogate home (or once without returning)
   (3) often lies (other than to avoid physical or sexual abuse)
   (4) has deliberately engaged in firesetting
   (5) is often truant from school (for older person, absent from work)
   (6) has broken into someone else's house, building or car
   (7) has deliberately destroyed other's property (other than by fire-setting)
   (8) has been physically cruel to animals
   (9) has forced someone into sexual activity with him or her
   (10) has used a weapon in more than one fight
   (11) often initiates physical fights
   (12) has stolen with confrontation of a victim (e.g., mugging, purse-snatching, extortion, armed robbery)
   (13) has been physically cruel to people

B. If 18 or older, does not meet criteria for Antisocial Personality Disorder

Reprinted with permission, American Psychiatric Association (1987) Diagnostic and Statistical manual of mental disorders, Third Edition-Revised, Washington, D.C.: APA, page 55.

syndromal depression, and subsequent studies have moved on to focus on the so-called co-morbid problems of depressed youth. These studies have now well established that depression in children and adolescents is commonly accompanied by other diagnoses, and of importance to this review, one group that appears with some frequency is a subgroup of juveniles with depression co-occurring with significant disturbances of conduct. In the discussion to follow, the use of conduct disorder refers to a pattern of persistent problem behaviors, present for at least six months, composed of at least three symptoms from the list of 13 displayed in Table 10.1 (American Psychiatric Association, 1987: 55).

RELATIONSHIP BETWEEN CONDUCT DISORDER AND DEPRESSIVE SYMPTOMS AND DIAGNOSES

Three types of studies have revealed the significant degree to which conduct disorder and depression accompany one another. These diagnostic and phenomenologic investigations have included assessment of depression in samples of delinquents, assessment of rates of conduct disorder in samples of children and adolescents with syndromal depression, and lastly, the extent to which children and adolescents evidence symptoms of both types of disorders. It is clear from these data that coexisting problems in both domains are not uncommon, but neither do they form the majority of all depressed or conduct disordered youth.

The studies of depressive disorders in delinquent youngsters have been largely restricted to adolescent samples, in spite of the common appearance of conduct disorder in prepuberty. The reported rates of current depressive disorders found in these youngsters presumably with severe antisocial histories consistently fall within the range of 15–25% (Table 10.2). In most of these studies depression was diagnosed by "adult" criteria, therefore it is not possible to assess whether the pattern of depressive symptoms differed in this clinical population. However, in at least one of the larger samples there did not appear to be noticeable divergence in symptoms from the adult pattern, in that depressed mood, appetite or weight disturbance, sleep disturbances, concentration problems, and loss of interest were evident in over 70% of the depressed delinquents (Kashani *et al*, 1980: 185–191). Another consistent finding across these samples of delinquents is that depression appeared more commonly in girls than boys. The only study that examined the effect of incarceration on rates of depressive diagnoses found that the frequency increased 4–5 fold after incarceration (Kashani *et al*, 1980). This increase highlights the need for closer monitoring in the early phases of confinement due to the associated increase in suicidal risk that would be expected to accompany the upsurge in depressive symptoms. The authors speculate that the effect of incarceration is likely multifactorial: separation from loved ones, the removal of acting out as a defense, and the stress and shame of the process of arrest and placement.

Not surprisingly, those studies that provided separate reports of the frequency of depressive symptoms in juvenile delinquents found them to be nearly twice as common as diagnoseable depressive disorders. For example, Kashani *et al*,

Table 10.2 Frequency of comorbid depression or conduct disorder in delinquent or depressed populations of children and adolescents.

Author	*(Number)*	*Major Depression (%)*	*Conduct Disorder Frequency (%)*
Delinquent Subjects			
Weinberg (1971)	(240)	15	
Chiles (1980)	(120)	23	
Kashani (1980)	(100)	18	
McManus (1984)	(71)	16	
Hyde (1986)	N/A	20	
Kutcher (1989)	(26)	19*	
Depressed Subjects			
Carlson (1980)	(28)		29
Puig-Antich (1982)	(43)		37
Geller (1985)	(59)		20**
Marriage (1986)	(44)		25
Ryan (1987)	(187)		14
Mitchell (1988)	(95)		15
Kutcher (1989)	(24)		15

* Sample of hospitalized conduct disorder patients: also 42% were diagnosed as having bipolar disorder
** Denotes antisocial behavior rather than conduct disorder per se

(1980: 185–191) reported that while 18% of their total incarcerated sample met criteria for the diagnosis of depression, 34% of the one hundred 11–17 year olds endorsed having persistent depressed mood or loss of pleasure. Similarly, 30% of a group of 71 incarcerated seriously delinquent adolescents were found to have active depressive symptoms (McManus *et al*, 1984: 602–615). Also, past histories of major depressions have appeared to be common in such youngsters. These data underscore the importance of carefully distinguishing between those antisocial youngsters who have dysphoric mood, perhaps in reaction to the consequences of their behavior, versus those with depressed mood accompanied by other persistent affective symptomatology. Systematic questioning regarding the full range of possible symptoms is a necessity.

Despite the relative consistency of the rates of depression in the above samples of conduct disordered children, it is not known how dependent these rates are on the particular population that is surveyed. The delinquent samples examined in the studies reported have been severe, incarcerated youth; given the finding that the "neurotic" emotionally disordered delinquent may have a less persistent delinquent pattern (Quay, 1972: 1–29), they may be underrepresented in such samples. By extension, the observed rates of depressive disorders in these severe samples could be underestimates for the much larger group of antisocial children and adolescents. Similarly, data are lacking on the frequency of depressive disorders among youngsters with oppositional defiant disorder, a less severe but more common disruptive behavior disorder characterized by provocativeness, irritability and argumentativeness, but without the more serious acting out behavior and violation of other's rights embodied by conduct disorder. Further studies of less severe antisocial samples may help to delineate the range in the frequency of depression in this population. Alternatively, studies of the rates of antisocial behavior and conduct disorder diagnoses in samples of youngsters referred for depression have approached this question from the opposite perspective, and results there agree there is an important overlap in some juveniles between affective disorders and disruptive behavior disorders.

Beginning with the first studies to employ systematic criteria for the diagnosis of depression in youngsters, a significant number of those children and adolescents diagnosed as having a major depressive episode were also found to have patterns of disruptive, antisocial behavior persistent and severe enough to warrant the coexisting diagnosis of conduct disorder (see Table 10.2). Presumably due to differences across samples with respect to age, inpatient status, and severity, the frequency of a conduct disorder coexisting with major depression or dysthymic disorder has varied in these reports from approximately 10–40%. In one of the largest studies to compare separate samples of depressed prepubertal children with adolescents, at least mild conduct problems were present in 38% of the children and in 25% of the adolescents (Ryan *et al*, 1987: 854–861). Judging by formal diagnostic criteria, the actual rate of conduct disorder was less than half of these percentages for both of the age groups, but the younger depressives continued to show a significantly higher rate of co-occuring conduct problems relative to the adolescents. Other studies have supported the observation that conduct problems associated with depressive disorders appear more commonly in younger children. While conduct disorder is not an uncommon comorbid disorder, it is clearly less prevalent than associated anxiety disorders, and possibly oppositional defiant disorder as well (Kashani *et al*, 1987: 931–934). This comorbidity does not appear to be an artifact of studying those depressed patients referred for treatment; depressed subjects from surveys of community samples also show similar proportions of conduct disorder diagnoses. One tentative, but potentially very important, additional diagnostic association between conduct disorder and affective illness was the high rate (42%) of the diagnosis of bipolar disorder among older adolescents with conduct disorder in one study (Kutcher *et al*, 1989: 526–529). The possible association between mixed depression/conduct disorder and bipolarity was also noted in a longitudinal follow-up study of depressed children (Kovacs *et al*, 1988: 205–217; see below).

The frequent coexistence of conduct disorder and depression that emerges from the diagnostic studies of delinquent and depressed populations is further supported by the significant relations between certain patterns of symptom reporting by youngsters with both disorders. For example, high positive correlations have been observed between self-ratings of depressive symptoms and dimensions of impulsivity and antisocial behaviors in adolescents (Martin *et al*, 1988: 123). Likewise, factor analysis of the symptomatology of the Ryan *et al* (1987: 854–861) sample of depressed children and adolescents produced an irritability-conduct problem factor among four other significant factors. However, closer analysis of the symptom reporting of conduct disordered versus depressed youth has suggested that there may be subtle differences in the types of depressive symptoms endorsed. Hospitalized children and adolescents with conduct disorder may tend to report more symptoms related to failure and generalized distress, while depressed youngsters may endorse more symptoms centering around sadness and loneliness (Politano *et al*, 1989:

431–438). It is less certain if such fine differences may be useful diagnostically in the clinical context of trying to ascertain the extent of depression in a child with a conduct disorder history. In fact, some comparative studies have found that conduct disordered youth report equal numbers of depressive symptoms as affective disordered subjects on standard self-report measures such as the Children's Depression Inventory (CDI). In some, but not all studies, the presence of a comorbid conduct disorder has been found to be associated with higher levels of symptom severity than depression alone, especially in adolescents with both disorders (Marriage *et al*, 1986: 687–691; Mitchell *et al*, 1988: 12–20). In spite of increasing the severity of symptom reporting, the presence of comorbid conduct disorder does not appear to alter the frequency of the depression being of the endogenous subtype; likewise those children with both diagnoses endorse similar patterns of core depressive symptoms as those with depression alone. So, we can again conclude from such data that conduct disorder youngsters are frequently dysphoric and many but not most have co-existing affective diagnoses. Conversely, associated disruptive behavior and conduct disorder diagnoses are relatively common among depressed youngsters. The significance of this co-occurrence is reflected in the inclusion of a separate diagnostic category of "depressive conduct disorder" in the forthcoming International Classification of Diseases, 10th edition (ICD–10), the major alternative classification system to DSM-III-R.

These cross-sectional studies raise many questions about the nature of the association between these two types of disorders. For example, is one disorder typically the primary disorder, with the other developing as a consequence? The suggestion that a comorbid conduct disorder may be be associated with greater symptom severity is also of interest. Does the presence of an associated conduct disorder have implications for the outcome or treatment response of depressed youth? Perhaps the most difficult issue broached by the co-occurrence of conduct disorder and depression relates to the classification of childhood psychopathology (Kovacs *et al*, 1988: 205–217). Most would consider these two disorders to represent independent types of behavior, one internalizing (depression) and the other externalizing (conduct/aggression problems). The comorbidity described above violates the presumption that such groupings reflect a natural division of psychopathology.

In fact, such symptom "overlap" between internalizing and externalizing problems has been noted in a variety of contexts. A study of 3–5 year olds observed high correlations between ratings of aggressive-destructive behavior and sadness, emotional insecurity, and anxiety (Rescorla, 1986: 162–169). In adults, violence and suicidal risk have long been associated, as well as links between depression, hostility, and suicide (Apter *et al*, 1990). So the finding of a mixed depressive/conduct disordered group from different populations is not surprising; we will next begin to address what is known about the interrelations between comorbid depression and conduct disorder in juveniles, particularly as it pertains to outcome.

LINKS BETWEEN DEPRESSION, CONDUCT DISORDER, AND OUTCOME

Studies of depressed youngsters suggest that when these disorders occur together, the depressive disorder usually is primary, and the disruptive behavior develops secondarily. Two studies that attempted to carefully delineate the time of onset of antisocial symptoms found that in almost all cases, the conduct disorder behaviors appeared concurrent to, or subsequent to the onset of the depressive symptoms (Puig-Antich, 1982: 118–128; Geller *et al*, 1985: 643–644). This was equally true for children and adolescents. Additionally, it was observed that in a small group of depressed children with comorbid conduct disorder, that the conduct problems tended to resolve in parallel with remission of the depression. Such a temporal relation between depression and onset of conduct disorder suggested that the presence of depression may serve as a risk factor for the development of conduct disorder. However, these studies were not longitudinal and reporting biases may have obscured a different pattern of development of disruptive behavior. Nevertheless, later studies did support the idea that depression serves to increase risk for subsequent conduct problems.

In a longitudinal study of depressed children by Kovacs *et al* (1988: 205–217), 16% were found to have co-existing conduct disorder at the time of first diagnosis of depression. In the majority of these cases, the conduct disorder symptoms had appeared to develop as a secondary consequence of the affective disorder. However, remission of the depression was not typically accompanied by the resolution of the conduct problems. In fact, over the course of the ten year follow-up period, the rate of conduct disorder increased to 23% by virtue of several children developing conduct disorder at some point after the remission of their depression. The estimated risk of these children developing a conduct disorder by age 19 was 36%. Also, about one-third of those depressed children who possessed comorbid conduct disorder at entry to the study showed a pattern of resolution of conduct problems followed by their later reappearance. Besides this unusual episodic pattern, the authors noted that several of these children who displayed resolution and relapse of conduct problems were also later diagnosed as having bipolar disorder. While depression acted as a risk factor for later conduct disorder, the presence of a comorbid conduct disorder did not increase the risk for relapse of depression or alter the length of the index episode of depression. Not surprisingly, the presence of a conduct disorder was associated with a greater likelihood of significant behavior problems occuring at any time during the follow-up period. These data add support to the notion that, when observed in cross-section, comorbid conduct disorder in children is more often a consequence of depression.

Comorbid conduct disorder also appears to increase risk for other adverse consequences. Several studies have well documented that among those adolescents who complete suicide, one of the largest groups is composed of adolescents with admixtures of impulsiveness, conduct problems, and emotional disorders, such as depression. In fact, this group would appear to outnumber those suicide completers with depression alone. Up to 71% of successful adolescent suicides in one study reportedly had histories of aggressiveness, truancy, stealing, and running away (Shaffer 1976: 275–291). Often the suicides occurred after personal disappointments or upsetting consequences of their misbehavior. Interestingly, one report found that adolescents with conduct disorder alone actually had higher ratings of suicidality than adolescents with affective disorders, although the absence of a comorbid group with mixed depression/conduct disorder makes these data difficult to interprete (Apter *et al*, 1988: 696–699). Assaultiveness, another dimension of conduct problems, has been noted to be a correlate of suicidal risk in hospitalized children (Pfeffer *et al*, 1989: 431–435). Impulsiveness and hostility are likely to be the linkages between these behaviors, as some have observed that conduct disorder and anger/irritability are highly correlated with ratings of suicidal ideation. Conduct problems have also been identified as indicators of increased risk for repeated suicide attempts. There may also be a non-specific increase in suicide risk conveyed by the simple presence of any comorbid diagnosis, including conduct disorder (Shafii *et al*, 1988: 227–233). Lastly, conduct disorder may also be linked to increased suicide risk through the strong association of alcohol and drug use with suicide in adolescents (Brent *et al*, 1987: 3369–3372). Clinically, the history of aggressiveness, alcohol or substance use, diagnoseable conduct disorder, or marked irritability in an adolescent should stand to significantly raise the estimation of their immediate and future suicidal risk.

In spite of the lack of influence in one study of the presence of conduct disorder on the length of time the child continued to meet criteria for depression, it has been suggested that comorbid conduct disorder is associated with a stormier course (Puig-Antich, 1982: 118–128; Kutcher *et al*, 1989: 526–529). This stands to reason, given the associated problems of such children and their families, including poor parental effectiveness, alcohol and substance use, poor peer relationships, and school failure. From this point of view, it is the conduct disorder and its correlates rather than the affective illness that is the more handicapping condition. Future studies are needed to better define what variables most influence the course of these disorders and their subtypes in youngsters.

POSSIBLE MECHANISMS OF ASSOCIATION BETWEEN CONDUCT DISORDER AND DEPRESSION

While the common overlap of depression and conduct disorder is clear, the underlying mechanisms that determine this comorbidity when it does occur are not well understood. However, some suggestions have emerged from the available data. These include the risk factor hypothesis discussed above, as well as possible shared environmental features, a common genetic vulnerability, and the influence of age on the lack of discreteness of psychopathology.

The association between family adversity, poor parent effectiveness and disruptive behavior is well known. Less widely appreciated however, are the suggestions that the parent-child interactions of depressed children and their mothers and fathers are characterized by significantly greater hostility and lack of involvement than other non-depressed psychiatric controls (Puig-Antich *et al*, 1985: 500–507). While no direct comparisions have been made between the family interactional styles of depressed children versus those with conduct disorder, such data raises the question of whether commonalities exist between these families. Of course, what then would determine the expression of externalizing versus internalizing symptoms is not clear. Alternatively, family factors may serve to influence the range and type of symptoms expressed during a depression. For example, it has been reported that family dysfunction is a greater determinant of suicidality than diagnosis per se in hospitalized children (Asarnow *et al*, 1987: 361–366). A possible link is suggested by an earlier study of the role performance of depressed mothers with their adolescent children. The depressed mothers were rated as having impaired involvement, greater friction, and less affection in their relationships, and their adolescent children were noted to have a greater number of serious behavior problems (Weissman and Siegel, 1972: 563–570). These adolescents would also be at high risk for affective disorders themselves based on the family studies reviewed below.

Two types of family studies have yielded interesting but somewhat divergent findings concerning links between depression and conduct disorder. A substantial number of high risk studies have examined the psychopathology of children of parents with histories of depression (Beardslee *et al*, 1983: 825–832). As described elsewhere in this volume, these studies have found children of depressed parents to be at increased risk for developing affective disorders. Somewhat surprisingly however, the majority of these studies have also reported higher rates of disruptive behavior disorders, including conduct disorder, oppositional disorder, and attention deficit disorder, in the offspring of depressives as compared to controls (Beardslee *et al*, 1988: 313–322). One possible interpretation of these findings is that a trait that increases vulnerability for psychopathology in a more non-specific fashion, perhaps poor self-regulation, is among what is inherited, rather than the predisposition for a specific disorder. Alternatively, the elevated rates of conduct and other disorders could reflect a shared family-environmental characteristic.

Family studies of children with major depression and children with conduct/oppositional disorder have yielded divergent findings, however when taken together tend to provide at least some support for a possible familial link between conduct disorder and depression. Families of children with conduct disorder may have significantly higher rates of depressive disorders than the families of youngsters with other psychiatric illnesses. One study reported that as many as 50% of the mothers of children with conduct disorder alone had histories of major depression (three times the rate in normal control mothers) (Lahey *et al*, 1988: 163–170), and an additional report noted that those children with attention deficit disorder who also had comorbid conduct disorder possessed elevated rates of major depressive disorder in their first-degree relatives versus families of normal controls (Biederman *et al*, 1987: 724–727). These data also raise the question of whether one linkage between conduct disorder and depression may be "through" attention deficit-hyperactivity disorder (ADHD), given the fact that most children with conduct disorder also have ADHD.

Of the two major family studies of juveniles with depression, data have been mixed as to whether conduct disorder/depression carries the same familial aggregation of psychopathology. While one found that the families of those depressed children and adolescents with comorbid conduct disorder were no different from the families of depressed children without conduct disorder in their likelihood of having higher rates of affective disorders (Mitchell *et al*, 1989: 352–357), the other study suggested that the families of children with comorbid conduct disorder differed significantly from the families of depressives without conduct disorder (Puig–Antich *et al*, 1989: 406–420). On the basis of these data, the authors went so far as to posit that the mixed conduct disorder/depressed subtype represents a phenocopy of the actual depressed genotype. It remains to be seen if the association between conduct disorder in the child and an apparent history of affective disorders in first degree relatives represents more of a pattern of high levels of family distress rather than the genetic transmission of an illness.

Lastly, the high rates of comorbidity in child psychopathology have been suggested to reflect a more general relation between age and the expression of symptoms. It is argued that the earlier the onset of disorder, the more likely it is that the child or adolescent will display a host of symptoms spanning more than one category of disorder, rather than a homogenous group of symptoms. This interaction with age is proposed to possibly reflect: (1) the negative cumulative impact of any early-onset disorder on overall adjustment, (2) the degree of combined social, cognitive, and emotional deficits frequently associated with early psychopathology, and (3) the relation between cognitive sophistication and symptom formation.

These possible mechanisms can only be considered speculative based on the available literature. However, numerous ongoing investigations of family psychopathology and family interactions are sure to add greater relief to these issues.

IMPLICATIONS FOR ASSESSMENT AND TREATMENT

The material presented above serves to underscore at least three important clinical points. First, the extent of comorbidity in childhood psychopathology should alert the clinician to pursue a comprehensive assessment. For the depressed child or adolescent, the need for a complete review with both child and parent of the range of conduct problems is obvious. Likewise, a historical review of symptoms of ADHD is indicated, especially in the presence of conduct disorder. Given the expected under-reporting of antisocial behavior by the youngster, parents should always be queried concerning past and present disruptive and antisocial behaviors. When antisocial behavior is reported, attempts should be made to ascertain as best as possible whether the antisocial behavior was antedated by depressive symptoms or not; the course of any conduct disorder problems should elicted, given the possible relation between a comorbid, episodic conduct disorder and bipolar outcome. Bipolar symptoms and family history of mood and conduct disorders should also be carefully reviewed, due to the potential impact these variables may have on outcome and treatment. More in-depth discussions of the assessment of conduct disorder are available elsewhere (Kazdin, 1987: 29–53).

Secondly, while suicide risk is always elevated to some degree with depressed children and adolescents, the past or present history of conduct/aggressive problems should indicate an even greater need to ascertain suicidality, and whether appropriate precautions should be instituted. Drug and alcohol use should be included as a portion of the review of conduct problems.

Lastly, it is reasonable to presume that those youngsters with comorbid conduct problems may require more aggressive and prolonged treatment. For example, in the case of the failure of medications to ameliorate depressive symptoms, a stronger indication exists for adding lithium therapy to ongoing antidepressant treatment, due to the significant number of subjects with both disorders that may evolve into bipolar disorder, as well as the studied effectiveness of lithium for treating explosive conduct/aggression problems in prepubertal children (Campbell *et al*, 1984: 650–656). A therapeutic trial with carbamazepine may be indicated in a small number of children with either suspected bipolarity or severe explosive and aggressive outbursts. Likewise, due to the possible greater risk for bipolar disorder, those depressed children with mixed disorders would be well served by providing longer monitoring and "maintenance" therapy. Psychosocial therapies, especially family therapy and parent mangement may be especially important in establishing effective limit setting, internalization of rules, and reduction in potentially self-destructive activities in youngsters with comorbid conduct disorder.

References

American Psychiatric Association (1987) Diagnostic and statistical manual of mental disorders, Third Edition-Revised, Washington, D.C., pp. 55.

Apter A. *et al* (1988) Suicidal behaviour, depression, and conduct disorder in hospitalized dolescents. *Journal of the American Academy of Child Psychiatry*, **27**, 696–699.

Apter, A. *et al* (1990) Interrelationships among anxiety, aggression, impulsivity, and mood: A serotoninergically linked cluster? *Psychiatry Research*, **32**, 191–199.

Asarnow, J.R. *et al* (1987) Coping strategies, self-perceptions, hopelessness, and perceived family environments in depressed and suicidal children. *Journal of Consulting and Clinical Psychology*, **55**, 361–366.

Beardslee, W.R. *et al* (1983) Children of parents with major affective disorder: A review, *American Journal of Psychiatry*, **140**, 825–832.

Beardslee, W.R. *et al* (1988) Psychiatric disorder in adolescent offspring of parents with affective disorder in a non-referred sample. *Journal of Affective Disorder*, **15**, 313–322.

Biederman, J. *et al* (1987) Conduct and oppositional disorder in clinically referred children with attention deficit disorder: A controlled family study. *Journal of the American Academy of Child Psychiatry*, **26**, 724–727.

Brent, D.A. *et al* (1987) Alcohol, firearms, and suicide among youth. *Journal of the American Medical Association*, **257**, 3369–3372.

Campbell, M. *et al* (1984) Behavioral efficacy of haloperidol and lithium carbonate: A comparison in hospitalized aggressive children with conduct disorder. *Archives of General Psychiatry*, **41**, 650–656.

Carlson, G. and Cantwell D.C. (1980) Unmasking masked depression in children and adolescents. *American Journal of Psychiatry*, **137**, 445–449.

Geller, B. *et al* (1985) Preliminary data on DSM-III associated features of major depressive disorder in children and adolescents. *American Journal of Psychiatry*, **142**, 643–644.

Glaser, K. (1967) Masked depression in children and adolescents. *American Journal of Psychotherapy*, **19**, 565–574.

Kashani, J.H. *et al* (1980) Depression among incarcerated delinquents. *Psychiatry Research*, **3**, 185–191.

Kashani, J.H. *et al* (1987) Depression, depressive symptoms, and depressed mood among a community sample of adolescents. *American Journal of Psychiatry*, **144**, 931–934.

Kazdin, A.E. (1987) Diagnosis and assessment, *Conduct Disorders in Childhood and Adolescence*, Volume 9, Newbury Park: Sage Publications, pp. 29–53.

Kovacs, M. *et al* (1988) Depressive disorders in childhood III. A longitudinal study of comorbidity with and risk for conduct disorders. *Journal of Affective Disorders*, **15**, 205–217.

Kutcher, S.P. *et al* (1989) Relationship between psychiatric illness and conduct disorder in adolescents. *Canadian Journal of Psychiatry*, **34**, 526–529.

Lahey, B.B. *et al* (1988) Psychopathology in the parents of children with conduct disorder and hyperactivity. *Journal of the American Academy of Child Psychiatry*, **27**, 163–170.

Marriage, K. *et al* (1986) Relationship between depression and conduct disorder in children and adolescents. *Journal of the American Academy of Child Psychiatry*, **25**, 687–691.

Martin, C.A. *et al* (1988) Investigation of affective state and impulsivity in adolescents with conduct

disorder, presented at the 141st annual meeting of the American Psychiatric Association, Montreal, NR249, pp. 123.
McManus, M. *et al* (1984) Psychiatric disturbance in serious delinquents. *Journal of the American Academy of Child Psychiatry*, **23**, 602–615.
Mitchell, J. *et al* (1988) Phenomenology of depression in children and adolescents. *Journal of the American Academy of Child and Adolescent Psychiatry*, **27**, 12–20.
Mitchell, J. *et al* (1989) Psychopathology in parents of depressed children and adolescents. *Journal of the American Academy of Child and Adolescent Psychiatry*, **28**, 352–357.
Pfeffer, C. R. *et al* (1989) Changes in suicidal behavior in child psychiatric impatients. *Acta Psychiatrica Scandinavica*, **79**, 431–435.
Politano, P. M. *et al* (1989) Comparisons of conduct and affective disordered youth: A psychometric investigation of responses to the children's depression inventory. *Journal of Child Psychology and Psychiatry*, **30**, 431–438.
Puig-Antich, J. (1982) Major depression and conduct disorder in prepuberty. *Journal of the American Academy of Child Psychiatry*, **21**, 118–128.
Puig-Antich, J. *et al* (1985) Psychosocial functioning in prepubertal major depressive disorders. *Archives of General Psychiatry*, **42**, 500–507.
Puig-Antich, J. *et al* (1989) A controlled family history study of prepubertal major depressive disorder. *Archives of General Psychiatry*, **46**, 406–420.
Quay, H. C. (1972) Patterns of aggression, withdrawl, and immaturity, *Psychopathological Disorders of Childhood*, ed. H. C. Quay and J. S. Werry, New York: John Wiley and Sons, pp. 1–29.
Rescorla, L. A. (1986) Preschool psychiatric disorders: Diagnostic classification and symptom patterns. *Journal of the American Academy of Child Psychiatry*, **25**, 162–169.
Ryan, N. D. *et al* (1987) The clinical picture of major depression in children and adolescents. *Archives of General Psychiatry*, **44**, 854–861.
Shaffer, D. (1974) Suicide in childhood and early adolescence. *Journal of Child Psychology and Psychiatry*, **15**, 275–291.
Shafii, M. *et al* (1988) Comorbidity of mental disorders in the post-mortem diagnosis of completed suicide in children and adolescents. *Journal of Affective Disorders*, **15**, 227–233.
Weinberg, J. and Van Den Dungen, M. (1971) Depression and delinquency in adolescence, *Depressive States in Childhood and Adolescence*, ed. Almquist and Wiksell, Stockholm, pp. 296.
Weiner, I. B. (1975) Juvenile delinquency, *Pediatric Clinics of North America*, pp. 673.
Weissman, M. M. and Siegel, R. (1972) The depressed woman and her rebellious adolescent, *Social Casework*, Nov., pp. 563–70.

11 Substance Abuse in Depressed Adolescents

John Piacentini* and Caroly Pataki**

Division of Child and Adolescent Psychiatry, College of Physicians and Surgeons of Columbia University, New York, NY 10032, USA
Division of Child and Adolescent Psychiatry, New York University School of Medicine, New York, NY 10016, USA

Substance abuse in children and adolescents has rapidly become one of the most critical problems facing health care and mental health care workers dealing with this age group today. According to the American Academy of Pediatrics, alcohol-related motor vehicle accidents are the leading cause of death among 15–24 year olds (American Academy of Pediatrics 1987). Moreover, the association between illicit substance use and other high-risk behaviors such as trouble with the law, promiscuity, truancy, and suicide place the drug-using adolescent at even greater risk for a negative, and potentially lethal, outcome. Depression, which is a potent risk factor for the development of substance abuse, can likewise seriously impair normal development in affected youth, especially those in which the disorder goes unrecognized and/or untreated. Both depression and substance abuse have been associated with significantly increased rates of suicidal behavior. Given the high social and physical cost of both adolescent drug use and depression, it is critical that pediatricians and other front line professionals working with adolescents become aware of both the nature of the relationship between the two disorders and issues related to the identification and treatment of these "dual-diagnosis" individuals. Pediatricians seeing adolescents who have a suspected or confirmed depression, should as a matter of course conduct an evaluation for substance abuse problems as well. Conversely, any evaluation of a child for drug or alcohol problems should also routinely include probes for depression. Disturbances in sleep, appetite, or concentration, increased social isolation, apathy, or school absence, loss of interest in usual activities, and/or acute deterioration in academic or occupational performance are all symptoms associated with both adolescent depression and substance use and should alert the pediatrician that one or both of these disorders may be present.

While it has long been noted that depression and substance abuse often co-occur, it has only been in the last several years that advances in diagnostic classification and

*Address all correspondance to the author at the New York State Psychiatric Institute, 722 West 168th Street, Unit 78, New York, New York 10032, USA

assessment have allowed researchers and clinicians to critically examine the relationship between these two disorders. Although substantial progress has been made in our understanding of substance abuse and depression in adolescence, much of what is known has been derived from studies with adult populations. This chapter will examine the association between adolescent depression and substance abuse through a review of a number of relevant topics, including the rates of co-occurrence among the two disorders and their developmental course. Issues related to the clinical presentation, assessment, and treatment of these dual-diagnosed youngsters will also be discussed. First, however, information regarding the prevalence and classification of substance abuse in adolescents will be presented.

PREVALENCE OF ADOLESCENT SUBSTANCE USE

The most recent prevalence data suggests that drug abuse is widespread among adolescents. According to "Monitoring the Future," the National Institute of Drug Abuse (NIDA) annual survey of high school seniors (Johnston *et al*, 1989), 54% of high school seniors surveyed in 1988, reported illicit drug use at some time in their lives. The most commonly used substance, other than alcohol, was marijuana with 47% of seniors having used this drug at some time in their lives, 33% reporting use in the past year, and 18% reporting use in the past month. One-third of high school seniors (60% of those using drugs) reported using an illicit drug other than marijuana at some time, while 21% of the sample (40% of those using drugs) reported using only marijuana. The survey also revealed that alcohol use was nearly universal with 92% of seniors reporting lifetime use, 85% reporting use in the past year, and 64% reporting use in the past month. The use of specific drugs other than marijuana was also relatively common, as the 1988 NIDA survey found 20% of high-school seniors reporting lifetime use of stimulants, 18% had used inhalants, 12% had used cocaine or crack, 9% had used hallucinogens, and over 9% had used heroin or other opiates. Lifetime, past year, and past month use prevalence for 13 types of drugs are presented in Figure 11.1

While the above findings appear to indicate that drug use is rampant among American youth, recent evidence suggests, that after two decades of steady increase, the percentage of adolescents using drugs may be decreasing. For example, the 54% prevalence rate for any time drug use reported in the 1988 NIDA survey was over 14% lower than the 63% rate reported in the 1983 survey, just five years earlier (Johnston *et al*, 1984). While rates for marijuana use and other illicit drug use showed similar declines of almost 18%, alcohol use remained relatively constant (93% vs. 92%) over this five year interval. Although recent indications of a decrease in the rates of adolescent substance use are encouraging, future survey results are needed to determine whether or not this downward trend is a stable phenomenon or just a temporary drop. Moreover, given the adverse consequences of drug use for most users, their families, and society in general, it is certain that adolescent substance use will remain a major concern of health care professionals for many years to come.

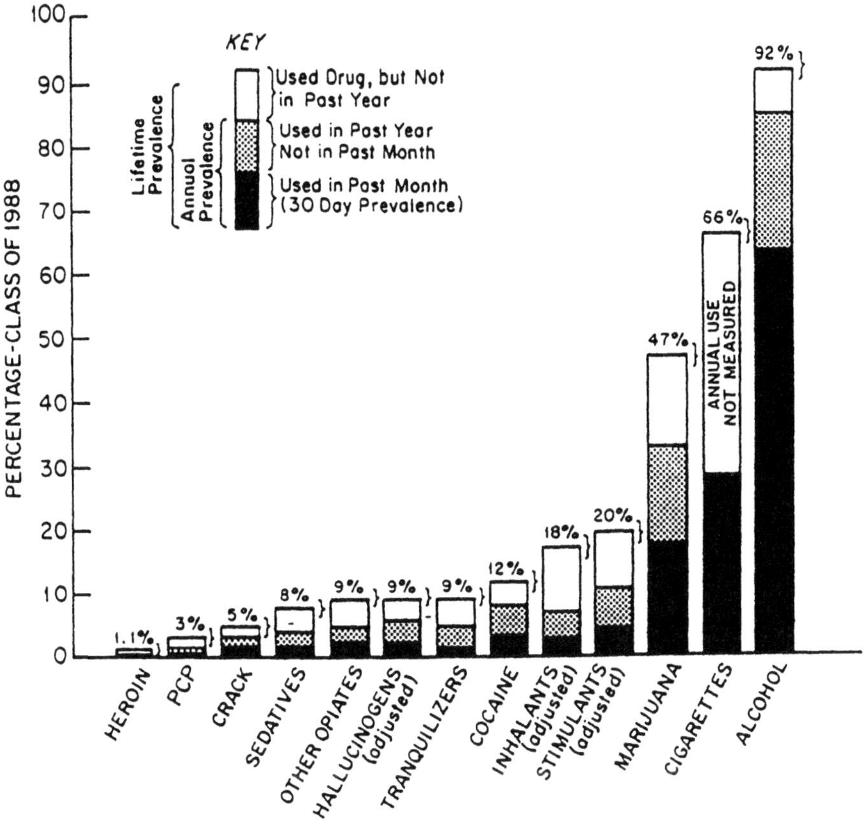

Figure 11.1. Prevalence and recency of use of 13 types of drugs, Class of 1988. NOTE: The bracket near the top of a bar indicated the lower and upper limits of the 95% confidence interval. (Source: Johnston *et al*, 1989: Reproduced through the courtesy of NIDA).

CLASSIFICATION OF SUBSTANCE USE DISORDERS

One of the primary problems hampering research in adolescent substance abuse has been the lack of an agreed upon definition of what constitutes abuse. While some definitions utilize frequency or intensity of use, for example, requiring the child to have been drunk six or more times in past year, a diagnosis of abuse usually requires evidence that use of the substance continues even in light of adverse consequences associated with its use. Bailey (1989: 151–162) lists several alternative definitions of drug abuse, including those outlined by the World Health Organization (WHO, 1964):

A physical or psychic state resulting from the interaction of a person and a drug characterized by behavioral and other responses that always include a compulsive desire or need to use the drug on a continuous basis in order to experience its effect and/or avoid the discomfort of its absence (p. 159).

and Johnston *et al* (1981):

> Use of a mind-altering substance in a way that differs from generally approved medical or social practices (p. 159).

DSM system

DSM-III

DSM-III (American Psychiatric Association 1980) provided diagnostic categories for both Substance Abuse and Substance Dependence. In order to be given a diagnosis of Substance Abuse, one had to evidence a pattern of pathological use sufficient to cause impairment in social or occupational functioning. The pattern of abuse had to be of at least one month duration. Substance Dependence, however, required physiologic dependence as evidenced by either tolerance (significantly larger amounts of the substance are required to achieve the same effect, or use at the same dose results in a markedly effect) or withdrawal. In addition, alcohol and cannabis dependence required evidence of social or occupational impairment. Substance-specific signs of pathological use, tolerance, and withdrawal were provided for the several classes of substances (e.g., alcohol, marijuana, opioids, cocaine, etc.) covered. Three classes of drugs in DSM-III, cocaine, phencyclidine (PCP), and hallucinogens, were associated with abuse only, since physiologic dependence for these substances had not been demonstrated.

DSM-III-R

According to DSM-III-R (American Psychiatric Association, 1987), psychoactive substance use disorders are characterized by symptoms and maladaptive behavioral changes which are associated with frequent to regular use of psychoactive substances affecting the central nervous system and which would be viewed as undesirable in almost all cultures. As opposed to DSM-III, DSM-III-R provides criteria for both dependence and abuse which are applicable to all classes of psychoactive substances (i.e., alcohol, cannabis, cocaine, amphetamines or similarly acting sympathomimetics, hallucinogens, opioids, sedatives, inhalants, phencyclidine or similarly acting arylcyclohexylamines, and nicotine). Psychoactive Substance Dependence is characterized by a cluster of cognitive, behavioral, and physiological symptoms which indicate that the individual has impaired control of his or her substance use and continues to use the substance despite negative consequences associated with that use. DSM-III-R criteria for psychoactive Substance Dependence are presented in Table 11.1. As can be seen, the inclusion of impairment criteria and the fact that symptoms of tolerance and withdrawal no longer need to be present in order for the diagnosis to be given have considerable expanded the scope of the diagnosis from DSM-III.

According to DSM-III-R, Psychoactive Substance Abuse is a residual category for describing patterns of substance use which do not meet the criteria for dependence but, which nevertheless, would still be regarded as maladaptive. Individuals meeting criteria for this diagnosis must either continue to use the substance in spite of known

Table 11.1 DSM-III-R diagnostic criteria for psychoactive substance dependence disorder

A. At least three of the following:
  1. substance often taken in larger amounts or over a longer period than the person intended
  2. persistent desire or one or more unsuccessful efforts to cut down or control substance abuse
  3. a great deal of time spent in activities necessary to get the substance (e.g., theft), taking the substance (e.g., chain smoking), or recovering from its effects
  4. frequent intoxication or withdrawal symptoms when expected to fulfill major role obligations at work, school, or home (e.g., does not go to work because hung over, go to school or work "high", intoxicated while taking care of his or her children), or when substance use is physically hazardous (e.g., drives while intoxicated)
  5. important social, occupational, or recreational activities given up or reduced because of substance use
  6. continued use despite knowledge of having a persistent or recurrent social, psychological, or physical problem that is caused by or exacerbated by use of the substance (e.g., keeps using heroin despite family arguments about it, cocaine-induced depression, or having an ulcer made worse by drinking)
  7. marked tolerance: need for markedly increased amounts of the substance (i.e., at least a 50% increase) in order to achieve intoxication or desired effect, or markedly diminished effect with continued use of same amount
  8. characteristic withdrawal symptoms*
  9. substance often taken to relieve or avoid withdrawal symptoms*

B. Some symptoms of the disturbance have persisted for at least one month, or have occurred repeatedly over a longer period of time.

* these items may not apply to cannabis, hallucinogens, or phencyclidine (PCP)
Reprinted with permission, American Psychiatric Association (1987) Diagnostic and Statistical Manual of Mental Disorders, Third Edition-Revised, Washington, D.C.: APA, page 167.

persistent or recurrent physical, social, or occupational problems caused by use of the substance or must repeatedly use the substance in situations in which use is physically hazardous. Similar to Substance Dependence, at least some symptoms of the disorder have persisted for at least one month or have occurred repeatedly over a longer period of time. The criteria for DSM-III-R Psychoactive Substance Abuse are presented in Table 11.2.

While the DSM-III-R diagnostic criteria were written to apply to both adolescents and adults equally, there are some problems in applying these criteria to adolescents in that not all of them may be age appropriate for younger individuals. For example, there is no evidence that tolerance and withdrawal occur to any significant degree

Table 11.2 DSM-III-R diagnostic criteria for psychoactive substance abuse disorder

A. A maladaptive pattern of psychoactive substance use indicated by at least one of the following:
  1. continued use despite knowledge of having a persistent or recurrent social, occupational, psychological, or physical problem that is caused by or exacerbated by use of the psychoactive substance
  2. recurrent use in situations in which use is physically hazardous (e.g., driving while intoxicated)

B. Some symptoms of the disturbance have persisted for at least one month, or have occurred repeatedly over a longer period of time.

C. Never met the criteria for Psychoactive Substance Dependence for this substance

Reprinted with permission, American Psychiatric Association, Diagnostic and Statistical Manual of Mental Disorders, Third Edition-Revised, Washington, D.C.: APA, page 169.

in adolescent drug abusers (Halikas, 1990: 210–234) as these symptoms typically develop in response to long periods of chronic substance use. Similarly, while it is possible that some physical symptoms may develop after only a short period of heavy substance use, most physical problems become manifest only after years of abuse. Another problem with the current diagnostic system is that younger adolescents may not have the opportunity to meet certain criteria because of their age. For example, the repeated use of drugs in situations in which use is physically hazardous most often refers to driving while intoxicated or using drugs in a potential dangerous work environment, such as around heavy machinery. Given that youngsters under the age of sixteen are not allowed to drive alone and are seriously limited in the types of jobs they may hold, they are much less likely than older teens or adults to meet this criterion.

According to DSM-III-R, a key feature in making a diagnosis of substance use disorder is impairment in social, psychological, or occupational functioning related to use of the substance. This can be a difficult distinction to make in drug abusing adolescents with comorbid major depression or other psychiatric disturbance because of the difficulty in determining which psychopathology (depression or substance abuse) is the primary cause of impairment. While depressed substance users whose impairment is solely or primarily attributable to drug use would qualify for a substance use disorder diagnosis, those whose impairment is solely or primarily a consequence of their depression would not.

Alternate diagnostic approaches

In response to the above criticisms, alternative diagnostic systems incorporating age-appropriate criteria have been developed for adolescent substance abuse. One such system, originally developed to define adolescent alcoholism but recently refined to include criteria for drug abuse as well (Blum, 1987: 523–537; Halikas *et al*, 1984: 581–585), eliminated criteria calling for tolerance, withdrawal, dependence, and lack of control of substance use, and instead placed a greater emphasis on the presence of age-appropriate adverse consequences directly related to substance use and which occur in multiple life areas, including at home, at school, or with friends. Criteria are grouped into three adolescent life areas: 1) psychosocial (e.g., "drinking patterns cause family fights or arguments"), 2) biomedical (e.g., "behavior changes due to alcohol"), and 3) school (e.g., drinking on school grounds) with at least one positive criterion from each of the three domains required to make the diagnosis. According to Halikas (Halikas, 1990: 210–234) this diagnostic system is able to significantly differentiate between adolescent substance abusers and recreational drug users in terms of both characteristics of substance use and associated life problems.

OVERLAP OF ADOLESCENT DEPRESSION AND SUBSTANCE ABUSE

Prevalence

Clinic studies

As described earlier, relatively few studies have examined the relationship between depression and substance abuse in adolescents, and much of the early work examining the comorbidity of these two disorders was conducted with adults (Dorus and Senay, 1980: 699–704; Keeler *et al*, 1979: 586–588; Rounsaville *et al*, 1982: 151–166; 1983: 257–289, Schuckit, 1983: 122–126; Weissman and Myers, 1980: 372–273). These studies reported prevalence rates for depression ranging from 3% to 98% in samples of adult alcoholics (Keeler *et al*, 1979: 586–588) and from 17% to 63%, depending on the severity and treatment status, for adult opiate addicts (Mirin and Weiss, 1986: 503–514). Conversely, 33% to 50% of adult psychiatric inpatients have been found to have serious drug and/or alcohol problems (Mirin and Weiss, 1986).

In one of the first studies of comorbidity in adolescents, Kashani (Kashani *et al*, 1985: 153–157) found 34 out of 100 teenaged substance users from a youth drop-in counseling center to meet DSM-III criteria for either major depression (n = 13), dysthymia (n = 5), or both (n = 16). Demilio (Demilio, 1989: 1212–1214) reported that 53% of 57 consecutive admissions (mean age 16 years) to one of two inpatient substance abuse treatment facilities met criteria for major depression at admission. However, only 20 subjects (35% of the total) remained depressed two weeks later; suggesting that many of the depressive symptoms reported at admission were sequelae of drug use or detoxification as opposed to a true affective disorder. Halikas (1990: 210–234) found 11% of males and 36% of females in a group of 95 abusing adolescents, screened from a total sample of 1185 involved with an urban country court system in the midwest, to have had a major depressive episode at some point in their lives. Reichler (1983: 338–339) found 17% of the adolescents seen for psychiatric evaluation in a general hospital emergency room to have elevated blood alcohol levels, and of these, almost one-half had one or more psychiatric diagnosis, most commonly depression. However, subject diagnoses were based on a retrospective chart review, thus limiting their validity.

Even less is known about the rates of substance abuse in clinically depressed adolescents, due perhaps to the fact that many psychiatric treatment facilities do not treat youngsters with significant drug problems and when these problems are discovered, during either initial evaluation or treatment, the patients are often referred elsewhere for more specialized treatment. In one of the few studies addressing this issue, 75 inner city adolescents, ranging in age from 11 to 17 years old, were interviewed with a structured diagnostic interview, the Revised Diagnostic Interview for Children (Shaffer *et al*, 1988b) either during their initial evaluation or shortly after they had entered treatment at a child and adolescent psychiatric clinic (Piacentini, 1990). While none of the subjects met DSM-III-R criteria for a substance abuse or dependence disorder, significantly more subjects with major depression reported using drugs and alcohol than did their nondepressed counterparts. Over 55% of the depressed adolescents had used marijuana in the six months preceding the evaluation, as compared to 7% of the nondepressed adolescents, while 43% of the depressed youngsters reported using alcohol at least once a month or more versus 9% of the nondepressed youngsters. Lifetime rates of illicit drug usage other than marijuana were 67% and 8% for the depressed and nondepressed youth, respectively.

Community studies

Given the fact that the above findings were based on clinic samples and that patients with multiple disorders are more likely to receive treatment than those with only one, it is possible that the studies described above have overstated the association between substance abuse and depression, at least as they occur in the general population. This does not appear to be the case, however, as several epidemiologic studies have shown a relationship between substance abuse and depressed mood or psychological distress in community samples of adolescents (Paton and Kandel, 1978: 595–598; Paton *et al*, 1977: 267–289; Schuckit, 1982: 1431–1436). Deykin (Deykin *et al*, 1987: 178–182) has provided one of the only reports utilizing standardized diagnostic criteria to directly examine the overlap of major depressive disorder and substance abuse in this age range. They interviewed 424 college students (94% of whom were between the ages of 18 and 19) using the Diagnostic Interview Schedule, a structured psychiatric interview based on DSM-III criteria, and found lifetime prevalences of 6.8% for major depression, 8.2% for alcohol abuse, and 9.4% for substance abuse. Subjects with major depression were three times as likely as those without depression to have met criteria for either a substance abuse or alcohol abuse disorder. Twenty-three percent (8/35) of the adolescents with major depression met criteria for substance abuse versus only 8% (32/389) of nondepressed subjects. The rates of overlap for major depression and alcohol abuse were strikingly similar (23% versus 7%).

Temporal relationship

There are at least three potential pathways describing the development of depression and substance abuse in adolescents: 1) substance abuse may develop in response to pre-existing depression, 2) substance abuse may play an etiologic role in the development of future depression, or 3) both substance abuse and depression may develop concurrently. It should be noted, however, that investigation of the temporal relationship of these two disorders is complicated by the fact that many of the defining symptoms of major depression, such as appetite or sleep disturbance, trouble concentrating, and fatigue or lack of energy, are commonly associated with drug and alcohol use as well. It is important, therefore, that studies of comorbidity use operationalized diagnostic criteria, carefully define the onset of symptoms, and time the assessments to ensure that subjects are not intoxicated or experiencing acute withdrawal symptoms at the time of assessment.

Depression as a precursor to substance abuse

The traditional adult psychiatry literature has long presumed that psychopathology plays an etiologically significant role in the development of substance abuse (Meyer, 1986; Schuster *et al*, 1979: 1–19). Along these lines, Khantzian (Khantzian, 1985: 1259–1264) has described a "self-medication" hypothesis of addiction which states that drug addiction develops from individuals' attempts to self medicate painful affective states and related psychiatric disturbance. There is some evidence to support the self-medication hypothesis. Several longitudinal epidemiological studies have indicated that adolescent drug use may develop in response to various forms of psychological distress including low self-esteem and depressed mood. Kaplan (1977a: 86–101; 1977b: 77–85; 1980) reported that decreasing self-esteem over time predicted initiation into drug use and continuation of use led to subsequent improvement in self-esteem, while others (Kandel, 1982: 328–347; Paton *et al*, 1977: 267–289) have found that depressed mood predicted initiation of marijuana use by nonusers and initiation of illicit drug use by marijuana users, and that continued illicit drug use was associated with decreased levels of self-reported depression over time. Newcomb (1986: 525–531) reported that elevated scores on a depression rating scale predicted, in conjunction with several other factors, later drug use in an adolescent sample. It also has been shown that among multiple drug users, depressed adolescents tend to show a stable pattern of use versus a more experimental use pattern for their non-depressed counterparts, and that future illicit users are more likely to have used marijuana to cope with depression (Paton *et al*, 1977: 267–289). In one diagnostic survey, major depressive disorder preceded the diagnosis of alcohol abuse in six out of the eight (75%) subjects who received both diagnoses (Deykin *et al*, 1987: 178–182). The temporal relationship between depression and substance abuse was identical to that for the alcohol abusers in that the depressive disorder either preceded or occurred concurrently with substance abuse in six of the eight subjects comorbid for these disorders. On average, the onset of major depression occurred 1.7 years prior to the onset of substance abuse and 4.5 years prior to the onset of alcohol abuse. The results of the NIMH Epidemiologic Catchment Area Program (Christie *et al*, 1988: 971–975), an adult epidemiologic survey of five communities revealed that the presence of an early onset (i.e., onset in late adolescence or young adulthood) DSM-III depressive or anxiety disorder was a significant risk factor for a future drug abuse disorder. By contrast, however, the presence of early onset major depression or an anxiety disorder did not predict later alcohol abuse.

Substance abuse as a precursor to depression

While it appears that pre-existing depression plays a potent etiological role in the development of substance abuse for many adolescents, there is a growing body of evidence suggesting that in some cases the converse is true; namely, that depression develops in response to drug and/or alcohol use. One of the acute responses to the ingestion of alcohol, for example, is euphoric mood. Over time, however, the euphoria changes to dysphoria and irritability. On a larger scale, there is evidence that chronic alcohol use often leads to a more persistent depression (Bukstein *et al*, 1989: 1131–1141). One study of depressed, substance abusing adolescents, diagnosed according to DSM-III-R criteria, found that the onset of the substance use disorder preceded or was concurrent to the onset of depression in 78% of the cases (Piacentini *et al*, 1990a: 69). In addition, the dual diagnosis group was found to more closely resemble a substance-abusing, non-depressed control group, but not a group of non-substance-abusing, depressives, in that the former two groups had significantly higher rates of conduct disorder (56% and 73%, respectively) than the latter (8%). Although these results were based on a small pilot sample (n = 34), and await further replication, similar results have been reported by Shaffer (1990) who conducted psychological autopsies, which included the assessment of lifetime psychiatric disorders, in a consecutive series of all completed suicides of individuals aged nineteen and under in the Metropolitan New York area over a two-year period. The most common developmental progression of psychiatric disturbance in the successful suicides was one in which major depression appeared following the onset of substance abuse. Moreover, the appearance of substance abuse was closely related to the presence of conduct disorder in these youths. The fact that conduct disorder often precedes or closely parallels the development of substance abuse in both depressed and non-depressed adolescents is consistent with the findings of other longitudinal studies, such as the one by Gittelman (1985: 937–947) who found a strong relationship between the development of conduct disorder and substance abuse in hyperactive children followed into late adolescence and young adulthood and reported that in no case did the onset of substance abuse precede that of conduct disorder.

Other pathways

A large body of evidence has accumulated over the last several years which suggests a genetic transmission for both substance and alcohol abuse (e.g., Goodwin, 1985: 171–174; Shuckit, 1983: 439–443) and affective illness (e.g., Weissman *et al*, 1982: 1397–1403). Attempts to demonstrate familial links across these two disorders, however, have been less successful (see Bukstein *et al*, 1989: 1131–1141 for a review). In summary, Merikangas (1985: 367–372) reported that the co-occurrence of depression and substance abuse may be due to the clustering in families of the social risk factors associated with the development of these disorders.

CLINICAL PICTURE

Little work has been done examining the impact of concurrent substance abuse on the clinical characteristics of depression in adolescents. In fact, not one study comparing the symptom picture of depressed adolescents with and without concurrent substance abuse could be found. There is some limited data, however, examining this issue from a different perspective. In his study of double depression in the attendees of an adolescent substance abuse treatment program, Kashani (1985: 153–157) compared those youngsters with double-depression to those without (although 14% of this group had either depression or dysthymia but not both) and, not surprisingly, found significantly higher rates of almost all depressive symptoms in the double-depression group. What is of interest is the high rate of depressive symptoms reported by subjects in the non-double-depressed group. These symptoms (and their prevalence rates) included: trouble concentrating (61%), sleep disturbance (59%), irritability (46%), guilt (39%), appetite disturbance (37%), fatigue (37%), school refusal (36%), and psychomotor agitation or retardation (33%). While 25% of this group described themselves as dysphoric, only 4% reported significant anhedonia.

Symptom-substance specificity

The self-medication hypothesis (Khantzian, 1985: 1259–1264) described earlier also specifies that the type of substance abuse is determined by the nature of the underlying psychopathology that the individual is "self-medicating". According to this hypothesis, depressives should show a preference for mood elevating substances, such as cocaine and stimulants, anxious individuals would prefer alcohol and other anxiolytics, and those with impulse-control disorders would favor the calming effects of opiates. While the findings regarding a substance-symptom match are not conclusive, there is some evidence that choice of drug is not random for at least some individuals. Mirin (1984: 57–78) examined drug of preference and DSM-III psychiatric diagnosis in 160 adult admissions to an inpatient drug dependence treatment unit and found that unipolar depression was significantly more common among stimulant abusers (31%) than opiate and depressant drug abusers (17.6% and 18.2%, respectively). Rates for bipolar disorder were lower than for unipolar depression, but showed a similar distribution across substance categories (22%, 3%, and 6% for stimulant abusers, opiate abusers, and depressant drug abusers, respectively). Similarly, Kashani (1985: 153–157) reported that adolescents with coexisting major depression and dysthymia exhibited more frequent amphetamine use than those with either major depression or dysthymia alone.

Substance abuse and suicide

Several investigators have reported sharply increased rates of suicidal behavior in substance abusers. Fowler (1986: 962–965) found that 53% of 133 consecutive successful suicides between the ages of 20 and 29 had a principal psychiatric diagnosis of substance abuse, while Shaffer (1988a: 675–687) found that 37% of a consecutive series of completed male suicides aged 19 or younger met criteria for substance abuse. Levy and Deykin (1989: 1462–1467) studied a non-referred population of 424 college students and found major depression and substance abuse to be independent and interactive risk factors for both suicidal ideation and suicide attempts. In general, substance abuse was a significantly higher risk factor for males than for females. A desire to be dead was reported by over 70% of the male substance abusers as opposed to only 6 of the non-abusers. Male substance abusers reported similar high rates for thoughts of death (71%) and thoughts of suicide (65%) and 12% had made an actual suicide attempt. Corresponding rates for the above behaviors in the non-abusing males were 40%, 18%, and 0%, respectively. Female substance abusers showed slightly lower rates of suicidal behavior than non-abusers, but 43% reported suicidal ideation and almost 9% had made a suicide attempt. According to Shaffer (1988a: 675–687) suicide does not occur randomly but rather strikes those individuals who are experiencing an extreme emotional state, such as fear or rage, often as the result of some stressful event. In these predisposed individuals, intoxication associated with substance abuse may augment the induction of extreme emotion and/or cloud the individual's judgment thus increasing the likelihood of a successful attempt.

TREATMENT

One of the most important reasons for conducting a comprehensive assessment and recognizing all comorbidity in dual-diagnosis individuals is the finding that increased levels of psychiatric disturbance including depression have been found to negatively affect treatment outcome and continued abstinence in substance abusers. Conversely, co-existing substance abuse can also impair treatment outcome for targeted psychiatric disorders such as depression (McLellan, 1986; McLellan *et al*, 1983: 620–625; Rounsaville *et al*, 1982: 151–166; 1984: 133–151).

The broadening of the diagnostic criteria for psychoactive substance abuse and dependence from DSM-III to DSM-III-R has had an important impact on the attainment of services since many treatment and reimbursement programs require that a formal diagnosis of substance dependence or abuse be present in order to be eligible for treatment. These changes have also modified certain implications for treatment. For example, since symptoms of either tolerance or withdrawal were required by DSM-III, detoxification was a requisite first step in the treatment of these individuals. Under the broader DSM-III-R criteria, however, many adolescents do not need to undergo this procedure.

The initial approach to treatment is naturally dependent upon the circumstances under which the problem comes to attention. Situations of medical or psychiatric emergency, such as drug overdose or suicidal behavior, warrant an immediate evaluation and often result in inpatient assessment. The emergence of less catastrophic symptoms, either in the course of psychological services or in the context of school or at home, may be dealt with on an outpatient basis provided that the motivation and abilities of both the individual and the family to participate in treatment are sufficiently developed. The ability of the family to be supportive yet firm participants in treatment is likely to influence the level of additional external supervision necessary to insure abstinence and treatment of associated problems.

Once an adolescent is identified by a mental health worker as having a problem with drug use, some professionals advocate the use of an "intervention" in order to facilitate the beginning of treatment. This type of meeting which should be conducted by a trained professional, involves bringing together significant people in the adolescent's life, such as family members and friends, in order to identify to him or her in a non-judgmental way the need for immediate treatment (Niven, 1983: 596–607). During the intervention session, participants confront the substance abuser with specific examples of how his or her drug use has negatively impacted his or her life and the lives of others around them and inform the adolescent of the consequences they will take if he or she does not consent to treatment. While such an interaction is often seen, at least initially, as confrontative by the adolescent, its primary purpose is to provide a supportive and concerned forum in which to mobilize the individual to seek appropriate treatment.

In cases where parents are resistant either to acknowledging their child's drug problem or to seeking treatment, the chances of a successful outpatient treatment are diminished. In extreme situations in which the families of adolescents in need of treatment either are unable to acknowledge the necessity of treatment or refuse to allow the adolescent to participate in treatment, a report of medical neglect by the mental healthworker to a child protective service agency may be justified (Niven, 1983: 596–607).

In cases where it is determined that a short term inpatient program would best serve the needs of the individual, factors including the severity of the psychiatric and substance problem as well as the responsivity of the family and the ability of the adolescent to cooperate with the rules of the proposed program are taken into consideration before the adolescent is admitted. Since many programs have strict guidelines regarding disruptive behavior and maintenance of abstinence, the adolescent must fully understand the expectations before entering into such a program. Nevertheless, for adolescents who are unlikely to be able to maintain abstinence on an outpatient basis, a controlled well supervised drug-free structured environment is indicated to begin the treatment process (Hendren, 1986).

As described previously, the dual-diagnosis adolescent most commonly presents with a myriad of associated problems in addition to substance abuse and depression, including family discord, academic dysfunction, and impaired peer relationship skills. Regardless of the setting , if treatment is to be successful, all of these areas must be addressed. Unfortunately, many of the available treatment programs for adolescents are based on, or simply downward extensions of, adult programs. While the specific modalities provided by these programs, which include many detoxification centers and residential or day programs staffed primarily by ex-addicts, may be important components of the adolescent's treatment experience, they are lacking many important services, such as school, peer counseling, and family therapy, which must be present to address in a comprehensive manner the specific needs of the adolescent (Semlitz and Gold, 1986: 455–474).

While there are still relatively few inpatient programs specifically designed to treat adolescents with coexisting substance abuse and psychiatric disorder, those that do exist often advocate a multidimensional approach based upon a biopsychosocial model which emphasizes the premise that both substance abuse and psychiatric illness derive from a common constitutional basis (Chatlos, 1989: 189–201). These programs most commonly utilize a multimodal treatment approach that includes a comprehensive psychiatric evaluation, a structured behavioral milieu, individual and family psychotherapy, and, when necessary, psychopharmacologic intervention. The long term goals of treatment are permanent abstinence and the maintenance of the necessary changes in lifestyle to maintain this drug-free state. Most treatment programs emphasize the commitment to abstinence through the use of a structured step-by-step guideline, such as the 12-step program of Alcoholic's Anonymous (AA) or Narcotics Anonymous (NA) (Wheeler and Malmquist, 1987: 437–447) since it is believed that the high degree of structure characteristic of this and similar approaches are critical if the adolescent is to maintain his or her commitment to abstinence and recovery. If psychopharmacologic interventions are being considered, a two-to three-week drug-free washout period is necessary prior to starting medication,unless the psychiatric diagnosis has been firmly established on the basis of past history, in order to differentiate between actual psychiatric symptoms and sequelae of substance use or withdrawal (Semlitz and Gold, 1986: 455–473).

Aftercare, in the form of day-treatment or outpatient therapy, is an essential component of the treatment process once the adolescent has completed an inpatient stay since the greatest threats to the maintenance of abstinence occur following discharge when the individual is allowed to return to his home environment (Wheeler and Malmquist, 1987: 437–447). Aftercare is almost always associated with continued affiliation with a step-program, such as AA or NA (Bailey, 1989: 151–162).

SUMMARY

Substance abuse and depression can seriously impair normal development in affected adolescents and are among the leading causes of morbidity and mortality in these youth today (Joshi and Scott 1988: 1349–1364). The presence of either disorder places the teenager at significant risk for the development of the other, and both disorders are associated with increased risk of suicide. Dual-diagnosis adolescents, or those with comorbid substance abuse and depression, are a heterogenous group in terms of the developmental course of these disorders. In many cases, substance abuse arises out of attempts to cope with, or self-medicate, pre-existing affective illness. In other cases, however, depression develops or intensifies only after the substance abuse disorder has become established and may be the result of environmental factors, i.e., academic, occupational, legal, social, or familial problems, associated with the adolescent's drug or alcohol problem. Conduct disorder is common in these latter individuals and usually predates both depression and substance abuse.

Given the serious nature of, and high degree of overlap between, these two disorders, it is imperative that pediatricians and other health care professionals working with adolescents conduct an evaluation for the other disorder when the presence of either depression or substance abuse is suspected or confirmed. Since many of the symptoms of depression and substance abuse are similar, for example, sleep and appetite disturbance, apathy, agitation, and trouble concentrating, the physician must ascertain the age of onset and pattern of occurrence for each symptom in order to differentiate between those symptoms associated with a true affective disorder and those occurring only in the context of substance intoxication and/or withdrawal.

References

American Academy of Pediatrics, Committee on Adolescence (1987) Alcohol use and abuse: A pediatric concern. *Pediatrics*, **79**, 450–453.

American Psychiatric Association (1980) Diagnostic and statistical mannual of mental disorders (3rd ed.), Washington, D.C.: Author.

American Psychiatric Association (1987) Diagnostic and statistical manual of mental disorders (3rd ed.-revised), Washington, D.C.: Author.

Bailey, G. W. (1989) Current perspectives on substance abuse in youth. *Journal of the American Academy of Child and Adolescent Psychiatry*, **28**, 151–162.

Blum, R.W. (1987) Adolescent substance abuse. *Pediatric Clinics of North America*, **34**, 523–537.

Bukstein, O.G., Brent, D.A. and Kaminer, Y. (1989) Comorbidity of substance abuse and other psychiatric disorders in adolescents. *American Journal of Psychiatry*, **146**, 1131–1141.

Chatlos, J.C. (1989) Adolescent dual diagnosis: A 12-step transformational model. *Journal of Psychoactive Drugs*, **21**, 189–201.

Christie, K.A., Burke, J.D., Regier, D.A., Rae, D.S., Boyd, J.H. and Locke, B.Z. (1988) Epidemiologic evidence for early onset of mental disorders and higher risk of drug abuse in young adults. *American Journal of Psychiatry*, **145**, 971–975.

Demilio, L. (1989) Psychiatric symptoms in adolescent substance abusers. *American Journal of Psychiatry*, **146**, 1212–1214.

Deykin, E.Y., Levy, J.C. and Wells, V. (1987) Adolescent depression, alcohol and drug abuse. *American Journal of Public Health*, **77**, 178–182.

Dorus, W. and Senay, E.C. (1980) Depression, demography, dimension, and drug abuse. *American Journal of Psychiatry*, **137**, 699–704.

Fowler, R.C., Rich, C.L. and Young, D. (1986) San Diego suicide study: II. Substance abuse in young cases. *Archives of General Psychiatry*, **43**, 962–965.

Gittelman, R., Mannuzza, S., Shenker, R. and Bonagura, N. (1985) Hyperactive boys almost grown up: I. Psychiatric status. *Archives of General Psychiatry*, **42**, 937–947.

Goodwin, D.W. (1985) Alcoholism and genetics. *Archives of General Psychiatry*, **42**, 171–174.

Halikas, J., Lyttle, M., Morse, C. *et al* (1984) Proposed criteria for the diagnosis of alcohol abuse in adolescence. *Comprehensive Psychiatry*, **25**, 581–585.

Halikas, J. (1990) Substance abuse in children and adolescents, Psychiatric Disorders in Children and Adolescents, (eds. B, Garfinkle, G. Carlson and B. Weller). Philadelphia: W.B. Saunders.

Hendren, R.E. (1986) Adolescent alcoholism and substance abuse. *Annual Review of Psychiatry*, 5.

Johnston, L.D., Bachman, J.G. and O'Malley, P.M. (1981) Drugs and the nations high school students, Drug Abuse in the Modern World, (eds. G. Nahas and H. Frick). New York: Pergamon.

Johnston, L.D., O'Malley, P.M. and Bachman, J.G. (1984) Highlights from drugs and American high school students 1975–1983. National Institute on Drug Abuse Monograph. DHHS Pub. No. (ADM) 84–1317. Washington, D.C.: Superintendent of Documents, U.S. Government Printing Office.

Johnston, L.D., O'Malley, P.M. and Bachman, J.G. (1989) Drug use, Drinking and Smoking: National Survey Results for High School, Collegeand Young Adults: 1975–1988. National Institute on Drug Abuse Monograph. DHHS Pub. No. (ADM) 89–1638. Washington, D.C.: Superintendent of Documents, U.S. Government Printing Office.

Kandel, D.B. (1982) Epidemiological and psychosocial perspectives on adolescent drug use. *Journal of the American Academy of Child Psychiatry*, **21**, 328–347.

Kaplan, H.B. (1977a) Antecedents of deviant responses; predicting from a general theory of deviant behavior. *Journal of Youth and Adolescence*, **6**, 86–101.

Kaplan, H.B. (1977b) Increase in self-rejection and continuing/discontinuing deviant response. *Journal of Youth and Adolescence*, **6**, 77–85.

Kaplan, H.B. (1980) Deviant behavior in defense of self. New York: Academic Press.

Kashani, J.H., Keller, M.B., Solomon, N. Reid, J.C.and Mazzola, D. (1985) Double depression in adolescent substance abusers. *Journal of Affective Disorders*, **8**, 153–157.

Keeler, M.H., Taylor, C.I. and Miller, W.C. (1979) Are all recently detoxified alcoholics depressed?. *American Journal of Psychiatry*, **136**, 586–588.

Khantzian, E.J. (1985) The self medication hypothesis of addictive disorders: Focus on heroin and cocaine. *American Journal of Psychiatry*, **142**, 1259–1264.

Levy, J.C. and Deykin, E.Y. (1989) Suicidality, depression and substance abuse in adolescence. *American Journal of Psychiatry*, **146**, 1462–1467.

McLellan, A.T. (1986) Psychiatric severity as a predictor of outcome from substance abuse treatments, Psychopathology and addictive disorders, (ed., R. Meyer). New York: Guilford.

McLellan, A.T., Luborsky, L., Woody, G.E., Druley, K.A.and O'Brien, C.P. (1983) Predicting response to drug and alcohol treatments: Role of psychiatric severity. *Archives of General Psychiatry*, **40**, 620–625.

Merikangas, K.R., Leckman, J.F. and Prusoff, B.A. (1985) Familial transmission of depression and alcoholism. *Archives of General Psychiary*, **42**, 367–372.

Meyer, R.E. (Ed.) (1986) Psychopathology and addictive disorders. New York: Guilford.

Mirin, S.M. and Weiss, R.D. (1986) Affective illness in substance abusers. *Psychiatric Clinics of North America*, **9**, 503–514.

Mirin, S.M. Weiss, R.D., Sollogub, A. and Michael, J. (1984) Affective illness in substance abusers, Substance Abuse and Psychopathology, (ed., S. Mirin). Washington: American Psychiatric Press.

Newcomb, M.D., Maddahian, E. and Bentler, P.M. (1986) Risk factors for drug use among adolescents: Concurrent and longitudinal analyses. *American Journal of Public Health*, **76**, 525–531.

Niven, R.G. (1983) Adolescent drug abuse. *Hospital and Community Psychiatry*, **37**, 596–607.

Paton, S. and Kandel, D. (1978) Psychological factors and adolescent illicit drug use. Ethnicity and sex differences. *Adolescence*, **13**, 595–598.

Paton, S. Kessler, R. and Kandel, D. (1977) Depressive mood and illegal drug use: a longitudinal analysis. *Journal of Genetic Psychology*, **131**, 267–289.

Piacentini, J.C. (1990) Psychiatric co-morbidity in substance abusing adolescents. Presented at the Medical Scientific Conference of the American Society of Addiction Medicine, Phoenix, AZ.

Piacentini, J.C., Klein, R.C., Koplewicz, H., Dicker, R., Amann, K., Morrissey, R. and Willheim, E. (1990a) Comorbidity of depression and substance abuse in adolescents. *Scientific Proceedings of the Annual Meeting of the American Academy of Child and Adolescent Psychiatry*, **6**, 69.

Reichler, B.D., Clement, M.S.W. and Dunner, D.L. (1983) Chart review of alcohol problems in adolescent psychiatry patients in an emergency room. *Journal of Clinical Psychiatry*, **44**, 338–339.

Rounsaville, B.J. and Kleber, H.D. (1984) Psychiatric disorders and the course of opiate addictions: Preliminary findings on predictive significance and diagnostic stability. Substance Abuse and Psychopathology, (ed., S. Mirin). Washington, D.C.: American Psychiatric Press.

Rounsaville, B.J., Weissman, M.M. and Kleber, H.D. (1983) An evaluation of depression in opiate addicts. *Research in Community and Mental Health*, **3**, 257–289.

Rounsaville, B.J., Weissman, M.M., Wilber, C.H., Crits-Cristoph, K. and Kleber, H.D. (1982) Diagnosis and symptoms of depression in opiate addicts: Course and relationship to treatment outcome. *Archives of General Psychiatry*, **39**, 151–166.

Schuckit, M.A. (1982) Prevalence of affective disorders in a sample of young men. *American Journal of Psychiatry*, **139**, 1431–1436.

Schuckit, M.A. (1983) Alcoholism and other psychiatric disorders. *Hospital and Community Psychiatry*, **34**, 1022–1026.

Schuster, C.R., Renault, P.F. and Blaine, J. (1979) An analysis of the relationship of psychopathology to non-drug medical drug use. Psychiatric factors in drug abuse, (eds., R. Pickens and L. Heston). New York: Grune and Stratton.

Semlitz, L.S. and Gold, M. (1986). Adolescent drug abuse: Diagnosis, treatment, and prevention. *Psychiatric Clinics of North America*, **9**, pp. 455–474.

Shaffer, D. (1990, April). *The relationship between substance abuse and teenage suicide*. Presented at the Medical Scientific Conference of the American Society of Addiction Medicine, Phoenix, AZ.

Shaffer, D., Garland, A., Gould, M., Fisher, P., and Trautman, P. (1988a). Preventing teenage suicide: A critical review: *Journal of the American Academy of Child Psychiatry*, **27**, pp. 675–687.

Shaffer, D., Schwab-Stone, M., Fisher, P. Davies, M., Piacentini, J., and Gioia, P. (1988b). *A revised version of the Diagnostic Interview Schedule for Children (DISC-R): Results of a field trial and proposals for a new instrument (DISC-2)*. Washington, DC: National Institute of Mental Health.

Shuckit, M.A. (1983). Alcoholic men with no alcoholic first-degree relatives. *American Journal of Psychiatry*, **140**, pp. 439–443.

Weissman, M.M. and Myers, J.K. (1980). Clinical depression in alcoholism. *American Journal of Psychiatry*, **137**, pp. 372–373.

Weissman, M.M., Kidd, K.K., and Prusoff, B.A. (1982). Variability in the rates of affective disorders in the relatives of severe and mild major nonbipolar depressives and normals. *Archives of General Psychiatry*, **44**, pp. 1397–1403.

Wheeler, K. and Malmquist, J. (1987). Treatment approaches in adolescent chemical dependency. *Pediatric Clinics of North America*, **34**, pp. 437–447.

WHO Expert Committee on Addiction-Producing Drugs. (1964). Thirteenth Report publication 273, Geneva: Who Technical Report Series.

12 Depression and Eating Disorders

Lynne Hoffman and Katherine A. Halmi

Department of Psychiatry, The New York Hospital-Cornell Medical Center, 21 Bloomingdale Road, White Plains, NY 10605, USA

INTRODUCTION

The eating disorders, anorexia nervosa and bulimia nervosa are well-recognized clinical syndromes in psychiatry. The diagnostic criteria for the two illnesses are listed below, as defined by the DSM-III-R, the diagnostic manual of the American Psychiatric Association (1987).[1]

Anorexia Nervosa:

a) Refusal to maintain body weight over a minimal normal weight for age and height, eg., weight loss leading to maintenance of body weight 15% below that expected; or failure to make expected weight gain during period of growth, leading to body weight 15% below that expected.

b) Intense fear of gaining weight or becoming fat even though underweight.

c) Disturbance in the way in which one's body weight, size or shape is experienced, eg., the person claims to "feel fat" even when emaciated, believes that one area of the body is "too fat" even when obviously underweight.

d) In females, absence of at least three consecutive menstrual cycles when otherwise expected to occur (primary or secondary amenorrhea). (A woman is considered to have amenorrhea if her periods occur only following hormones, eg., estrogen administration.)

Bulimia Nervosa:

a) Recurrent episodes of binge eating (rapid consumption of a large amount of food in a discrete period of time).

b) A feeling of lack of control over eating behavior during the eating binges.

c) The person regularly engages in either self-induced vomiting, use of laxatives, or diuretics, strict dieting or fasting, or vigorous exercise in order to prevent weight gain.

d) A minimum average of two binge eating episodes a week for at least three months.

e) Persistent over-concern with body shape and weight.

In both anorexia and bulimia the onset frequently occurs in adolescence (Halmi *et al*, 1979: 209–215). These patients often initially present to their pediatrician with one of the many medical complications which can arise from starvation, vomiting or diuretic and laxative abuse. At other times, they are brought in by worried parents

[1]Reprinted with permission, American Psychiatric Association (1987) Diagnostic and Statistical manual of mental disorders, Third Edition-Revised, Washington D.C.: APA, pps. 67 and 68.

who have noticed the weight loss or a change in eating behavior. Amongst the most common associated psychological and behavioral changes seen in patients with eating disorders are signs and symptoms of depression.

The fact that anorexia and bulimia are often associated with depression has long been recognized in the clinical literature (Kay and Leigh, 1954: 411–432; Halmi, 1974: 18–24; Russell, 1979: 429–448). It has also been long appreciated that the state of starvation itself can cause psychological changes that closely resemble those seen in depression. The controlled data for this observation came from "The Minnesota Experiment" (Keys *et al*, 1950: 63–81, 819–921). In 1944, 36 volunteers who were conscientious objectors took part in an 11 month experiment designed to obtain data on the physiological and psychological effects of semi-starvation and subsequent dietary rehabilitation. These men lost a mean of 24% (range of 19–28%) of their initial body weight. Fatigue, loss of libido, irritability, loss of sociability, decreased concentration, and a depressed mood were amongst the behavioral manifestations observed in the course of the experiment. These are commonly seen in depressive states and anorexia nervosa. Thus, the condition of being underweight and malnourished can produce signs and symptoms indistinguishable from those frequently observed in depression.

However, emaciation does not explain the high rate of depression seen in bulimia nervosa in which the patients are generally near normal weight. Nor does it explain the observation that depression in anorexia can occur subsequent to weight restoration or prior to emaciation. (Reviewed in detail later in this chapter.) The debate in the psychiatric literature surrounding the nature of the association between the eating disorders ahd depression has been heated and still continues. (For reviews see Hatsukami *et al*, 1984: 349–365; Levy *et al*, 1989: 162–169; Halmi, 1985: 667–680.)

Some authors have gone so far as to suggest that the eating disorders may be just a variant of an affective disorder (Cantwell *et al*, 1977: 1087–1093; Hudson *et al*, 1982: 685–687). Others believe that the mood disturbance is secondary to the eating disorder itself. For example, in anorexia it is often stated that depression is due to the gross physiological and psychological distortions that characterize this disorder. Similarly, it has been suggested that in bulimia depression results from the loss of control over eating. Another viewpoint suggests that patients with an eating disorder are a heterogenous group, and that certain subsets may also be afflicted with an underlying affective disorder (reviewed by Swift *et al*, 1986: 290–299).

In this chapter the data from epidemiological and biological studies, and medication trials establishing a link between depression and eating disorders will be reviewed. At this time, the nature and extent of the relationship between these disorders is speculative. The current available evidence does not permit the conclusion that the eating disorders are merely a variant of affective disorders.

Prevalence studies: depression and anorexia nervosa

The observation that anorexia nervosa and depression are associated with each other has been present in the psychiatric literature for several decades. As early as 1954 Kay and Leigh (1954: 411–432) noted symptoms in their 38 anorectics, such as tiredness, irritability, depression, attempted suicide, insomnia, loss of interest, and inertia.

However, it is only in the last two decades that a number of investigators have examined the co-incidence of these two disorders in a systematic and controlled manner. Their collective results, presented in this section, clearly illustrate the relatively high frequency in which both depression and anorexia nervosa co-exist and the need for clinicians to approach eating disordered patients of all ages, with a very high index of suspicion for the presence of concommitant depression.

These prevalence studies fall into two major categories. In the first group, the incidence of depression was calculated at the time the patient presented for treatment for anorexia. These studies are somewhat difficult to interpret as many of the side-effects of starvation and emaciation can mimic the signs and symptoms of depression, and are alleviated by refeeding. This was clearly shown in a 1981 study (Eckert *et al*, 1981: 1–8) which used a variety of psychiatric scales and questionnaires to look at depression during the course of a six week inpatient treatment program for anorectics. They found that most of their patients started treatment with a mild to moderate level of depression, and that the initial depression generally correlated with the extent of emaciation. As the patients gained weight there was a decrease in their depression, (on all scales used, both by objective and subjective measures), that clearly correlated with the amount of weight they had gained. In order to overcome the confusion over the influence emaciation has in the evaluation of depression, several researchers have focused on doing follow-up studies when at least some of the patients are no longer symptomatically anorectic. In reading through these results and thinking about the data, it is necessary to remember that these studies span almost two decades. During that period, diagnostic criteria and psychiatric research instruments underwent considerable change and refinement. This tends to make comparisons amongst the studies difficult, so wherever possible the methodology used will be clearly stated. The diagnostic criteria are those of DSM-III (Diagnostic and Statistical Manual-III, adopted by the APA in 1980) unless otherwise indicated.

One of the earliest systematic studies of anorexia nervosa and depression was done by Hendren (1983: 59–62). He reviewed the charts of 84 patients with a diagnosis of anorexia nervosa with special emphasis on their MMPI scores (Minnesota Multiphasic Personality Inventory), the clinical evaluation, and reports of depressive symptomatology. He found that 56% of this population met Research Diagnostic Criteria (RDC) for a major depressive episode at the time of hospitalization. He acknowledged that some of these depressed patients were still quite emaciated at the time of evaluation, but stated that the results are probably valid given that the severity of the depression did not correlate with the extent of weight loss. His paper did not divide the anorectics into those who were purely restrictors and those who also had bulimic symptomatology.

In 1983, Hudson *et al* (1983: 345–354) obtained data on 16 patients with a past or present history of anorexia and 25 patients who had met criteria for both anorexia and bulimia at some point in their lives (not necessarily simultaneously or currently). Using the Diagnostic Interview Schedule (DIS), they reported that 63%

of their population had been depressed at some time in their lives and that this rate was independent of the presence of eating disorder symptoms. At the time of their interviews, approximately 70% of their patients had an active eating disorder, so most of them were not in remission.

Shortly thereafter, Herzog (1984: 1594–1597) published his data on 27 anorectics. Unlike the patients in Hendren's study, this group was presenting for outpatient evaluation and had not ever been hospitalized, suggesting that they may not have been as sick a group. Nevertheless, 40% of these patients were moderately to severely depressed when they were administered the Hamilton Depression Rating Scale (HDRS), and up to 74% were depressed on the basis of a clinical interview. He also found that the presence of some bulimic symptoms in his group did not affect the prevalence of depression.

Somewhat later, Piran *et al* (1985: 395–400) published their results on the prevalence of current depression in a symptomatic group of anorectics awaiting hospitalization, and found 42.8% of their sample met criteria for a major depression. This was based on a number of psychiatric scales including the MMPI, Beck Depressive Inventory (BDI), and Hopkins Symptoms Checklist-90-R (HSCL-90-R). Unfortunately, they had a rather small sample size of only 14 patients.

Finally in 1987, Laessle (1987: 785–789) reported on a German population in which 13 had a lifetime history of anorexia and another 13 had, at some time, met criteria for both anorexia and bulimia. Their results differed from those reported thus far in that only 15% of their anorectic restrictor group had ever been depressed, but 46% of the group that had carried a diagnosis of both bulimia and anorexia also reported depression at some time.

The next group of studies are those that looked at depression as part of a follow-up study to avoid, if possible, the confounding variable of emaciation. One of the earliest attempts to do this was carried out by Moyan and Russell (1975: 355–371). This was a follow-up study of 41 anorectics (including three males) four to ten years after the initial presentation, and relied on a personal interview for data collection. At follow-up 55% of their patients were eating normally and maintaining their weight, 20% remained anorectic, and the rest had some difficulty with food. However, the rate of depression remained constant—42% at presentation and 45% at follow-up.

Similarly, Cantwell (1977: 1087–1093) looked at 26 out of 33 adolescents diagnosed as anorectic by Feighner criteria (which are stricter than DSM-III), an average of 4.9 years after discharge. He found only one adolescent was fully anorectic, although a majority continued to show signs of an eating disorder behaviorally or had developed obesity. Approximately 45% of this group were depressed at follow-up on the basis of interviews with either the patient, their parents, or both. In 1988, Toner *et al* (1988: 357–364) published one of the few follow-up studies that included a control population of 26 females matched for age, weight, and socio-economic status. At follow-up (five and 14 years after initial treatment) 32% of the patients were symptomatic, 28% were improved, and 40% asymptomatic with respect to their eating disorder. Forty percent of the anorectic patients had a lifetime history of depression, compared to only 12% of the controls. The lifetime rate of depression, or even the occurrence of depression in the last year, was nôt correlated with the outcome of the anorexia. Unfortunately, this well-controlled study is seriously flawed by a very high failure-to-trace rate, (i.e. only one-third of their original 149 patients were located and evaluated).

Finally, and most recently, Halmi *et al* (1991: 712–718) presented the results of a ten year follow-up study that included 62 out of 71 original anorectic patients, and a control group matched for age, sex and socio-economic status. At the time of follow up, 8% remained anorectic and 27.4% had no eating disorder at all. The remainder were either bulimic or symptomatic without meeting criteria for either diagnosis. They found a lifetime history of depression in the 62 patients of 68% compared to 21% of controls. The *lifetime* prevalence of depression did not correlate with the outcome of the anorexia; however, those who were *currently* depressed tended to be normal weight bulimics at the time of follow-up. This latter finding differs from that of Toner *et al* (1988: 357–364). In comparing these latter two studies, it is most likely that the discrepancies between their results reflect differences in the original populations, or in those who were found and agreed to participate in the follow-up study.

In summary, these studies allow the following general conclusions to be made: 1. Approximately 40% of anorectics at presentation will have sufficient symptomatology to warrant a diagnosis of major depression. It is not clear from these studies how often the diagnosis of depression will remain once refeeding has been accomplished. 2. The lifetime prevalence of major depression in those with a diagnosis of anorexia is at least 40% and may be as high as 68%. This is in contrast to the accepted lifetime prevalence rate of depression of approximately 25% in the general female population (Weissman and Myers, 1978: 1304–1311; Vernon and Roberts, 1982: 47–52). 3. In general, (although this was not a unanimous finding), the lifetime incidence of depression was not correlated with the outcome of the anorexia or whether or not bulimic symptomatology had also been present.

Prevalence studies – bulimia and depression

Bulimia nervosa has been recognized as a distinct disease entity for a much shorter time than anorexia nervosa. Despite this, the association between depression and bulimia has been well documented. Since most bulimics are at normal weight, estimates of the incidence of major depression at the time of presentation for bulimia are not confounded by the psychological effects of emaciation. Most of the studies looked at depression and bulimia together at the time of the initial presentation, largely because bulimia has only been recognized as separate and distinct from anorexia for a decade, so very few follow-up studies of any type exist. The studies summarized below focus on patients diagnosed with only bulimia, not bulimia and anorexia.

In one of the earliest papers fully describing the syndrome of bulimia, Russell (1979: 429–448) noted severe signs of depression in 43% of his group of 30 female bulimics. In his landmark description of the psychopathology of this group, he stated that "next to the preoccupations directly concerned with eating and weight, depressive symptoms were the most prominent feature of the patients' mental state".

In 1983 Hudson *et al* (1983: 345–354) reported on 49 females who had met DSM-III criteria for bulimia at some point in their lives. Using a semi-structured interview, they found 59% had a lifetime history of major depression. This rate was much higher (two to five times) than that of two control populations composed of relatives of schizophrenic or bipolar patients. A few years later, the same authors (Hudson *et al*, 1987: 1283–1287) published results on a second group of 70 bulimic women of whom 51 were actively bulimic and 19 were in remission. The two sub-groups were very similar and had a lifetime rate of depression of 55%. The rate of depression in their non-psychiatric controls was only one half as high.

In 1984 Hatsukami (1984a: 701–704) published her data on 108 bulimics, the largest study presented here. She found that 24.1% of her group had either a current (11.1%) or past (13.0%) history of major depression on the basis of a clinical interview. Using the Beck Depression Inventory (BDI), 45% were moderately to severely depressed at the time of presentation. Although this study had a very large sample size, the findings are limited by the absence of a suitable control population. In another study (Herzog, 1984: 1594–1596) of 51 bulimics, 24% were depressed (at the time of evaluation in an outpatient clinic) as measured using the Hamilton Rating Scale vs. 49% who met criteria for major depression on the basis of a clinical interview. The discrepant results between the clinical interview and psychiatric rating scales points to difficulties in the measurement of depression.

Despite the many differences in approaches, there are now several other studies which confirm a very high lifetime rate of major depression in bulimia ranging from 36% to 70% (all using either DSM-III criteria or RDC) (Piran *et al*, 1985: 395–400; Lee *et al*, 1985: 231–238; Walsh *et al*, 1985: 123–131; Laessle *et al*, 1987: 785–789).

In the only study of its sort, Swift *et al*, (Swift *et al*, 1985: 111–122) looked at the incidence of depression in a group of 30 normal weight bulimics at two to five years following their hospitalization. At the time of follow-up, 87% still met DSM-III criteria for bulimia (suggesting this can certainly be a chronic illness) although their symptoms were generally much attenuated in both frequency and intensity compared to their admission. Despite the low remission rate for the bulimia, their population showed almost no depression at follow-up (only 6.6% had Beck scores in the moderate to severe range). At admission 40% had moderate to severe depression as determined using the same or similar instruments. This certainly suggests that recovery from concurrent bulimia and depression need not occur at the same pace.

Like anorexia nervosa, depression seems to be strongly associated with bulimia, allowing the following generalizations to be made: 1) At presentation, roughly one-third to one-half of bulimics will meet DSM-III criteria for major depression. As bulimics are generally at normal weight, these estimates do not need to be interpreted cautiously because of the possible confusion caused by weight loss present in anorexia. 2) Roughly one-half to two-third of bulimics will ultimately develop a major depression.

Temporal relationship between the onset of depression and eating disorders

In studies of depression and anorexia or bulimia, it has repeatedly been shown that depressive symptomatology can precede, appear simultaneously with, or follow, the onset of the eating disorder (Herzog, 1984: 1594–1597; Lee *et al*, 1985: 231–238; Hudson *et al*, 1983: 345–354; Toner *et al*, 1988: 357–364). This variability in the relative onset of these illnesses strongly suggests that neither is simply a secondary phenomenon of the other. The clinician treating any individual with either anorexia or bulimia has the additional burden placed on him of being sensitive to the emergence of depressive symptomatology as it can appear at any time during the course of the eating disorder.

Eating disorders and suicidal behaviors

Patients with eating disorders will frequently express suicidal ideation and many will make suicide gestures. This is of particular concern as the eating disorders largely arise in adolescence and young adulthood, groups whose potential for suicide has recently been well recognized. An early report noted the high incidence of death wishes and suicidal ideation in an anorectic population (Cantwell *et al*, 1977: 1087–1093). Dally and Gomez (1979: 140) stated that 11% of their anorectic population in the 15–18 year age group, and 20% of the group over 19 had made at least one suicide gesture.

Similarly, the finding of suicidiality is frequently present in the literature on bulimia. In Russell's original group of 30 bulimics (Russell, 1979: 429–448), 11 had made at least one suicide attempt, of which five were serious and one successful. Very similar findings were reported by Hudson's group (1983: 345–354) who found that one-third of 90 eating disordered patients had made at least one suicide attempt, primarily in the bulimic subgroups. Finally, Hatsukami (1984a: 701–704) reported suicide attempts in 16% of 108 bulimic females. Given these findings, clinicians evaluating this group must be vigilant in checking for the presence of suicidal ideation when treating this population.

Family history – anorexia nervosa

Further evidence for a strong association between depression and anorexia nervosa has come from family history studies. Many of the early studies from the 1950's through the 70's (reviewed in Swift *et al*, 1986: 290–299) were based on patient's reports, lacked structured diagnostic criteria, and related contradictory results. Interpretation was made even more difficult by the lack of a control or reference group. However, as will be discussed, more recent studies with improved methodologies, have found a very high prevalence of affective disorders among the relatives of anorectics.

In the earliest study to interview family members, Cantwell (1977: 1087–1093) found a high incidence of major affective disorder in the first degree relatives of anorectics. Of the 26 anorectic probands studied, 15 mothers, two fathers and six siblings were given a diagnosis of an affective disorder, and four of the mothers had made suicide attempts. The results are difficult to interpret, however, as no control group exists and it is unclear from the description given exactly what is included as a major affective disorder.

Several more recent studies had both appropriate controls and well-defined diagnostic criteria. In 1980 Winokur *et al* (1980: 695–698) published data on the family histories of 25 anorectics and 25 normal controls using Research Diagnostic Criteria. The patient and at least one relative were extensively interviewed to obtain information about grandparents, parents, and siblings over the age of 18. They found 17.7% of 192 relatives of anorectics had a diagnosis of major depression vs. 9.0% of 177 relatives of controls. A family history of depression in the relatives of probands did not predict the likelihood of depression in the patients.

Shortly thereafter, Gershon *et al* (1984: 1419–1422) published their results on the family histories of 24 anorectics and 43 normal controls. Their study used a primarily blind diagnostic assessment, a structured interview and direct interviews of 54% of 394 first degree relatives of patients and controls. Although they found that 13.3% of the relatives of the anorectics had major depression vs. only 5.8% of the controls' relatives, this difference was not statistically significant. The presence of affective disorder in the patients (50% of the anorectics met criteria for major depression) did not predict the presence of affective disorder in the relatives.

However, at around the same time, another team of researchers published data which resulted in somewhat different conclusions (Rivinus *et al*, 1984: 1414–1418; Biederman *et al*, 1985: 1495–1497). Both reports utizilzed data from the same studies of 40 anorectics and 23 normal controls. Parents of all subjects were interviewed with a structured interview and the data from the interview used to formulate the diagnoses according to the Research Diagnostic Criteria. Again they found a much higher incidence of affective disorders in the relatives of anorectics (9.9%) vs. those of controls (2.4%), although the percentages in both groups were much lower than in other comparable studies. However, they then re-analyzed their data by dividing their anorectics into the group that was depressed compared to the non-depressed group. They then found that the observed familial aggregation of depression in anorectic probands was entirely attributable to the high rate of depression in the relatives of depressed probands. The relatives of non-depressed anorectics had rates of depression the same as the relatives of controls. Thus in this study, depression in patients did predict depression in family members.

This debate has continued with two more large scale, well-controlled studies recently concluded. Strober's group looked at family histories in 97 anorectics, 66 patients with primary affective disorders (including bipolars) and 117 mixed disorder controls, all between the ages of 13 and 18 (Strober *et al*, 1990: 239–253). They used DSM-III-R criteria (the only study to do so thus far), a structured interview, and directly interviewed 79.3% of 1125 relatives (all consenting first degree relatives over the age of 12). They also divided their anorectic group into those who were depressed and those who were not. Like Biederman *et al* (1985: 1495–1497), they found high rates of affective disorders in the relatives of depressed anorectics (18.0%) but not in the families of non-depressed anorectics (5.1%). In fact, the rate of affective disorders in the families of depressed anorectics was as high as in the families of patients with a major affective disorder (19.7%). This effect was particularly notable in mothers, who were four times more likely to have a diagnosis of major affective disorder if depression was present in the anorectic proband. The results obtained from the analysis of their data did not support the hypothesis that depression and eating disorders represent divergent manifestations of the same underlying disturbance. Another recent large study failed to show this difference in family histories of depressed and non-depressed anorectics. As part of a ten year follow-up study, Halmi *et al* (1991: 712–718) did a family history study of 62 anorectics and matched controls using a structured interview, the DIS (different from that employed by Strober *et al*), and DSM-III criteria. They were able to directly interview 57 mothers and 49 fathers of the anorectics, and matched them to the same number of control parents. The remainder of the family history information came from the mothers and the subjects. First of all, they found no significant difference in the rates of major depression in the families of anorectics (4.9%) compared to controls (4.0%), although there was a non-significant trend towards more recurrent depression in the anorectic relatives (4.5%) compared with control relatives (2.0%). This study also concluded that the presence of affective disorder in the anorectic patient did not predict affective illness in the relatives.

To summarize, the data from family history studies in anorexia confirm, but in no way define or even clarify, the strong association between depression and eating disorders. Whether or not this familial aggregation of affective disorders in the relatives of eating disorder probands is explained by the presence of co-existing depression in a subset of anorectic probands remains uncertain; large scale studies by independent investigators continue to produce conflicting data. The only conclusion which the literature allows at this time is that there exists an increased prevalence of major affective disorder in the families of anorectics compared to the families of controls.

Family history – bulimia nervosa

Several studies now exist which look at family histories of depression in bulimic patients. Although the results are interesting and provocative, the true prevalence of family depression in bulimics is difficult to interpret as the overwhelming majority of these reports lack stringent diagnostic criteria, an appropriate control group or diagnostic interviews by investigators who were blind to the diagnosis of the proband.

In the earliest report to comment on the prevalence of depression in the families of bulimics, Pyle *et al* (1981: 60–64) noted that 16/33 probands had a least one first degree relative with a history of depression. However, the report relied strictly on the patients' report and lacked any control group. The diagnostic criteria were also unclear. Shortly thereafter, Hudson *et al* (1982: 685–687) found that six out of ten bulimic probands had at least one relative with major affective disorder, and that 15% of these family members had a probable or possible major depression. The morbid risk for depression in these families was significantly greater than for the families of a group of schizophrenics or patients with borderline personality disorder, and similar to that seen in relatives of those with bipolar illness. This study was limited by its small sample size and the fact that the interviewers were not blind to the diagnosis of the proband. Similar data were later presented by the same group (Hudson *et al*, 1983a: 133–138) using a large sample size (n = 55), standard diagnostic criteria, and a combined family interview and history method. The results remain difficult to interpret however, as the interviewers were, again, not blind to the diagnosis of the proband, and no non-psychiatric control group was used.

Lee *et al* (1985: 231–238) analyzed self-reports and interviews from 56 bulimic women and found that 58.9% of them reported a history of affective disorder in at least one first degree relative, and that in at least two-thirds of those cases, the family member had been ill enough to seek professional care. Again, this study is flawed by the lack of any control group and the fact that none of the family members were directly interviewed.

At this point, there has only been one study of the family history of depression in bulimia which had a suitable control group, used well-established research diagnostic criteria, and in which the family interview was done by individuals blind to the diagnoses of the proband (Stern *et al*, 1984: 1224–1227). This group studied 27 bulimics and 27 matched controls without a diagnosis of an eating disorder, and directly interviewed at least one parent of every participant. (In more than 95% of the cases the mother was interviewed.) They found no difference in the prevalence of affective disorder in the relatives of the bulimic probands compared to the controls. In both groups the rate was about 10 percent. There was still no difference when male relatives were compared separately from female relatives, or even when just the mothers were examined.

As noted earlier, the data on the familial incidence of depression in bulimic patients is not at all clear at this point. The vast majority of the literature could lead one to conclude that there is an increased incidence of major affective disorder in the families of bulimics. However, most of these reports have major methodological flaws. In the one well-controlled study published to date, no difference in rates of depression were found in control families compared to bulimic families.

It is possible that a family history of depression is related to certain characteristics of bulimics. For example, Lee *et al* (1985: 231–238) found that a family history of depression correlated with an earlier onset of bulimia in the proband. Similarly, it has been reported (Mitchell *et al*, 1986: 215–219) that bulimic patients with a family history of depression were more likely to have been treated for depression and to attribute their binge eating to dysphoric symptoms.

BIOLOGICAL STUDIES

In both the eating disorders and depression, many abnormal biological variables, especially of neuroendocrine and neurotransmitter function, have been described (for reviews see Halmi, 1985: 667–680; Fava *et al*, 1989: 963–971, Ettigi and Brown, 1977: 493–501; Walsh B.T., 1982: 85–91). In the following section these studies will be reviewed and summarized with an emphasis on differences and similarities in biological markers between eating disorders and depression.

Neuroendocrine function: Hypothalamic-pituitary-adrenocortical axis

Adrenocortical function has been well studied in depression. Approximately 50% of patients with a major depressive illness exhibit elevated levels of plasma cortisol which is largely due to an increased rate of secretion by the adrenal glands, coupled with a normal degradation rate (Sachar *et al*, 1973: 19–24; Sachar *et al*, 1970: 289–298). In patients with anorexia nervosa, there is also an increase in the 24-hour mean plasma levels of cortisol, but in anorectics this is due to both an increased rate of cortisol secretion relative to body size and a decrease in the breakdown rate (Walsh *et al*, 1978: 499–506; Boyar *et al*, 1977: 190–193). Women with bulimia have been found to have normal 24-hour secretions of cortisol (Walsh *et al*, 1987: 131–140).

Thus, cortisol levels in anorexia and depression share some common abnormal features and differ in others. However, any interpretation must bear in mind that patients with other forms of serious malnutrition have elevated levels of plasma cortisol and diminished rates of cortisol metabolism; these findings are not pathognomonic of either depression or anorexia (Smith *et al*, 1975: 43–52; Rao *et al*, 1968: 365–367).

The Dexamethasone Suppression Test (DST) has also been studied in all of these disorders. In this test, the synthetic steroid dexamethasone is given at 11 pm. In normal individuals, this suppresses adrenal activity so that the level of plasma cortisol remains low for the next 24 hours. In a significant proportion of patients with either depression, anorexia or bulimia, the effects of dexamethasone are neither as potent nor as long-lasting (Carroll *et al*, 1981: 15–22; Walsh *et al*, 1978: 499–506; Lindy *et al*, 1985: 1375–1376).

The results of the DST might initially suggest a strong connection between affective and eating disorders. However, it is well-established that weight loss and emaciation alone will cause an abnormal DST which may entirely explain the results seen in anorexia nervosa (Carroll *et al*, 1981: 15–22; Smith *et al*, 1975: 43–52). Although bulimics are usually within normal weight range, they can often show dramatic weight fluctuations which could possibly influence the test. Moreover, in the studies of bulimics, many of the patients also had a concurrent affective disorder, making the test interpretation even more difficult (Gwirtsman *et al*, 1983: 559–563; Lindy *et al*, 1985: 1375–1376). Finally, abnormalities in the DST are by no means limited to depression and eating disorders, but have been reported in a wide number of apparently unrelated disorders, including Alzheimer's disease and obsessive-compulsive disorder (Schwartz and Dunner, 1982: 1309–1312; Insel *et al*, 1982: 153–160; Spar and Gerner, 1982: 238–247).

In summary, the eating disorders and depression do share the common feature of a frequently abnormal DST, a non-specific finding in many illnesses and one that is very sensitive to fluctuations in weight. This finding does not imply that depression and eating disorders are forms of the same illness.

Hypothalamic – pituitary-thyroid axis

In depression, basal levels of the thyroid hormones thyroxine (T_4) and triiodothyronine (T_3) are normal. However, for a decade it has been recognized that the pituitary's release of thyroid stimulating hormone (TSH) in response to an infusion of thyrotropin-releasing hormone (TRH) was diminished in approximately 25% of depressed subjects (Hollister *et al*, 1976: 106–113; Prange *et al*, 1972: 999–1002).

Patients with anorexia nervosa in the emaciated state exhibit many of the signs and symptoms of hypothyroidism, such as bradycardia, cold intolerance, low basal metabolic rates, and delayed relaxation of deep tendon reflexes (Garfinkel *et al*, 1975: 739–744). Plasma levels of T_4 are generally normal, but there is a striking decrease in the plasma level of T_3 which probably results from a reduction in the rate of conversion of T_4 to T_3. TSH levels are generally normal (Moshang *et al*, 1975: 470–473; Miayi *et al*, 1975: 334–338). TSH response to TRH in anorexia nervosa tends to be delayed, but not blunted, in about 70% of the cases studied in the emaciated state (Gold *et al*, 1981: 51–57; Casper and Frohman, 1982: 59–68). Thus in comparing thyroid function in depression and anorexia, one finds more differences than similarities.

In bulimia, basal levels of T_3, T_4, and TSH are generally normal. Early uncontrolled studies of the TSH response to TRH produced conflicting results with some finding a blunted response in most bulimics (Gwirtsman *et al*, 1983: 559–563), and others reporting little or no diminution in response (Mitchell and Bantle, 1983: 355–365; Kiriike *et al*, 1987: 167–176). Controlled studies have been more consistent and generally show no differences between bulimic subjects and normal controls in the response of TSH to TRH (Norris *et al*, 1985: 215–219; Levy *et al*, 1988: 476–484). However, several investigators have found that the TSH response to TRH is delayed up to 50% of the time in bulimics (Gwirtsman *et al*, 1983: 559–563; Witschy *et al*, 1984: 321–331; Mitchell and Bantle, 1983: 355–365). Although these studies are generally small, this pattern clearly contrasts with that described in depression, in which the TSH response to TRH is characteristically blunted, but rarely delayed.

Hypothalamic-pituitary-ovarian axis

The major endocrine abnormality in anorexia nervosa is present in the hypothalamic-pituitary-ovarian axis and presents clinically as amenorrhea, which often occurs before weight loss is significant and frequently lags behind the return to normal weight. Basal levels of LH, FSH and estrogen are decreased and the 24-hour secretion pattern of LH is abnormal (reviewed by Weiner, 1983: 109–116). In bulimia there has been a report of low basal LH and FSH levels and a greater response to LH-RH than in controls. (Levy *et al*, 1989a: 425–427). Although this area of endocrine function has not been extensively studied in depressive illness, there is evidence that the hypothalamic pituitary-ovarian axis is normal, and certainly amenorrhea is *not* a feature of depression (Amsterdam *et al*, 1981: 367–380). Thus, in this area of endocrine function, there is a major difference in depressive illness and the eating disorders.

Growth hormone

In depression, basal levels of growth hormone (GH) are generally normal. The GH response to insulin-induced hypoglycemia, clonidine, and L-dopa is blunted. Additionally, TRH induces an increase in GH in some studies of depressed patients, which is not observed in normal subjects (reviewed by Ettigi and Brown, 1977: 493–501, and Brambilla, 1986: 191–202).

In anorexia, serum basal GH levels are elevated in about one-third of emaciated patients which may be entirely due to their state of starvation (Garfinkel *et al*, 1975: 739–744), and is clearly different from the situation in depression. An impaired GH response to perturbation tests, such as L-dopa and insulin is observed in anorexia, similar to that seen in depression (Halmi and Sherman, 1977: 63–65; Brauman and Gregoire, 1975: 289–295). Thus there are some changes in GH regulation seen in anorexia nervosa comparable to depression, but also some differences.

Several studies of GH in bulimia now exist. In a controlled study it was reported that normal weight bulimic patients had a significantly greater mean basal GH level and a greater GH response to TRH than did control subjects (Levy *et al*, 1988: 476–484) which is somewhat different than the profile seen in depression. A further distinction between bulimia and depression lies in the GH response to clonidine which has been reported to be normal in bulimic patients (Kaplan *et al*, 1986), but blunted in depression as described earlier. Several differences distinguish GH metabolism in bulimia from that seen in depression.

Neurotransmitter studies

The catecholamine hypothesis of affective disorder proposes that some, if not all depressions, are associated with an absolute or relative deficiency of catecholamines., particularly norepinephrine, at functionally important noradrenergic synapses in the brain. Similarly, diminished activity of serotonin has also been implicated in the etiology of depression. Although neither hypothesis explains all of the findings in depression, there is considerable support in the literature for abnormally low catecholamine and serotonin levels in at least certain subsets of depressed individuals. Evidence comes from studies of the concentration of neurotransmitter metabolites in both CSF and urine, and indirectly, from the putative effects of many antidepressants which are known to increase the effects of these neurotransmitters. (For reviews see Ettigi and Brown, 1977: 493–501; Schildkraut, 1965: 509–522; Coppen *et al*, 1972: 474–478.) There is no suggestion of a dopamine regulation disturbance in major depression.

Low CSF and urinary levels of 3-methoxy-4-hydroxyphenylglycol (MHPG), a metabolite of norepinephrine occurs in anorexia nervosa (Biederman *et al*, 1984: 149–160; Halmi *et al*, 1978: 458–460) and normalizes with weight recovery. CSF norepinephrine levels have been found to be low in underweight anorectics and also normalize after nutritional rehabilitation (Gerner *et al*, 1984: 1441–1444, Kaye *et al*, 1984: 350–355). However, lower CSF norepinephrine levels may persist in some apparently weight recovered anorectics—if confirmed, this finding may indicate impaired norepinephrine metabolism in anorexia nervosa.

Also seen in anorexia nervosa are low levels of 5-hydroxyindole acetic acid (5-HIAA—a metabolite of serotonin), in the CSF of underweight anorectics, particularly bulimic anorectics. The CSF 5-HIAA levels increase with partial weight restoration (Kaye *et al*, 1988: 102–105). This may indicate a deficit of serotonin functioning in the brains of some anorectics. CSF levels of the dopamine metabolite homovanillic acid have been found to be either low, or not different from normals. (Reviewed by Fava, 1989: 963–971). Other studies have shown an impaired growth hormone response to L-dopa (Halmi and Sherman, 1979: 609–614) and impaired prolactin response to chlorpromazine (Owen *et al*, 1983: 578–581) suggesting a disturbance in dopaminergic regulation, possibly at the post-synaptic receptor site.

In one study, CSF opioid activity was increased in the emaciated state and normalized with weight recovery (Kaye *et al*, 1982: 643–645). In another study B-endorphin immuno-reactivity was normal in underweight anorectics (Gerner and Sharp, 1982: 244–247). At this point it is impossible to interpret these results. However, it does seem that although anorexia nervosa may, like depression, share features of diminished indoleamine and catecholamine activity, other neurotransmitter abnormalities are likely to exist in anorectics which are not characteristic of depression.

Some studies suggest alterations in noradrenergic function in bulimia nervosa, although few have examined central function. During the first week after hospital admission, some bulimics were reported to have a blunted rise in plasma norepinephrine concentration on standing (Pirke *et al*, 1985: 33–39). Another group reported significantly lower resting plasma levels of norepinephrine after three weeks of inpatient treatment (Kaye *et al*, 1986). Bulimia patients have been reported to have a higher number of platelet alpha-2 adrenergic receptors (Heufelder *et al*, 1985: 1053–1060).

There is also some evidence of diminished serotonin release in the central nervous system in bulimia. In one study weight-restored anorectics with bulimia had smaller probenecid-induced increases in CSF levels of 5-HIAA than weight-restored anorectics without bulimia (Kaye *et al*, 1984a: 1598–1601). Recovered bulimics, but not those still symptomatic, had an increase in their L-tryptophan to large amino acid ratio which is considered the most important factor determining transport of tryptophan (the serotonin precursor) from the plasma to the CSF. Since greater levels of L-tryptophan increase serotonin synthesis, these data could suggest that bulimic symptomatology may be associated with diminished serotonin in the central nervous system (Kaye *et al*, 1988a: 31–43).

Most studies of the opioid system in bulimia have focused on peripheral activity, and have been quite contradictory. Baseline plasma B-endorphin immunore-activity in bulimic patients was found to be significantly lower than in control subjects (Waller *et al*, 1986: 20–23) and was inversely correlated with the severity of the bulimic symptoms. Conversely, a second smaller study showed exact opposite results, with B-endorphin concentrations higher than in control subjects (Fullerton *et al*, 1986: 20–23). Further studies of all the neurotransmitters, focusing on central functions, are needed before any meaningful conclusions can be formulated about their role in bulimia nervosa.

Sleep studies

Characteristic sleep abnormalities have been reported in depression in both adults and adolescents. These include shortened rapid eye movement (REM) latency (considered by many a hallmark of depression), increased REM density, and an increase in total REM sleep (Kupfer and Foster, 1972: 684–686; Feinberg *et al*, 1982: 305–316; Lahmeyer *et al*, 1983: 1150–1153).

In a pilot study, Foster and associates (Foster *et al*, 1976: 143) compared the sleep patterns of five anorectic subjects before and after refeeding, and five control subjects. Although not reaching statistical significance, they found a longer REM latency period and lower REM density in both the underweight and refed anorectic group. These findings are the opposite to those generally seen in major depressive episodes. More recently, in a study of 54 anorectics, a shorter REM latency was reported for the anorectics with normal waking EEGs (Nell *et al*, 1980: 9–15). Katz *et al* examined 20 women who reported anorexia nervosa at some time in their lives (only four subjects were within 15% of their ideal weight at the time of the study), and in some cases, bulimia as well. They found a significantly shortened REM latency in the anorectics compared with the controls. However, on close examination of the data, only six of the anorectics values were so short as not to overlap with those of the control group, and all six of these patients had scores on the Hamilton Rating Scale for Depression of over 30, indicating moderate to severe depression (Katz *et al*, 1984: 753–759). There is no consistent evidence that sleep changes in anorexia nervosa mirror those seen in depression.

Studies of bulimics indicate that there are no significant differences between their polysomnograms and those of age matched controls. Walsh *et al* (1985a: 947–956) investigated the sleep EEG of 16 bulimic females and found REM latencies and densities comparable to those of normal controls. There was a trend (that did not reach statistical significance) for the depressed group of bulimics to have shorter REM latencies than the non-depressed group. Levy *et al* (1988a: 99–101) examined the sleep patterns of nine bulimic women and ten controls. None of their sample had concurrent endogenous major depression, and there were no differences in the sleep architecture of the two groups. Thus in the absence of depression, bulimic subjects do not have sleep abnormalities similar to those seen in patients with major depression.

Although some similarities exist in the results of biological studies of depression and eating disorders, there appears to be more features which distinguish the two types of disorders. These data do not support the conclusion that eating disorders and affective disorders are different forms of the same disease entity.

ANTIDEPRESSANT TRIALS IN THE TREATMENT OF EATING DISORDERS

Given the strong association between eating disorders and depression, it is not surprising that many investigators have studied the efficacy of a wide variety of antidepressants in the treatment of anorexia and bulimia. In this section, these reports will be summarized, first for anorexia and then for bulimia. Only antidepressant medications will be dealt with here. Drugs in other classes, such as neuroleptics or those used primarily in the treatment of manic-depressive illness, will not be included. There are however, several reviews which include the literature on those medications (Johnson *et al*, 1983: 524–534; Gwirtsman *et al*, 1984: 863–878; Bond *et al*, 1986: 659–665).

Surprisingly, the literature on the use of anti-depressant medications in anorexia nervosa is relatively small and generally discouraging in terms of the results.

The effects of clomipramine, a tricyclic anti-depressant also known to be effective in the treatment of obsessive-compulsive disorder, has been studied in the treatment of anorexia (Lacey and Crisp, 1980: 79–85; Crisp *et al*, 1987: 355–358). Their research utilized a double-blind, controlled design, using patients hospitalized for treatment of anorexia. Those on clomipramine showed no difference from those on placebo in weight gained during the refeeding time, or in the time taken to reach their target weight, although initially the clomipramine group reported more hunger and an increased appetite. At four year follow-up there was no difference between the two groups in terms of weight (as a percentage of target), sexual adjustment scores, and social adjustment scores. Although these data are disappointing, their interpretation is clouded by the small size of the study (eight women in each group), and the low dose of medication (50 mg) used in the study (up to 250 mg is recommended for the treatment of depression and obsessive-compulsive disorder).

A couple of controlled studies have used amitriptyline to treat anorexia. In one study (Biederman *et al*, 1985a: 10–16) patients were divided into three groups with 11 on active drug, 14 receiving placebo, and 18 receiving a psychosocial intervention. Up to 175 mg of medication was used and the study was carried out for five weeks, double-blind. In this study no group showed much improvement, and there were no statistically significant differences favoring amitriptyline in any outcome variable, including weight gain, symptoms of disturbed eating behavior, and scores on ratings of depression, anxiety and obsessive-compulsive symptoms. Additionally, there were large numbers of side-effects reported in the drug group, including diaphoresis, drowsiness, and various anti-cholinergic manifestations (dry mouth, constipation, blurred vision and urinary retention). Blood levels of the medication averaged 131 ng/ml, which is somewhat lower than that recommended in the treatment of depression. These results are in contrast to encouraging results reported earlier (Needleman and Weber, 1977: 357–362) in a small sample of anorexia nervosa patients treated openly with amitriptyline at doses similar to this study, but are supported by the data of Halmi *et al* (1986: 177–181). They examined the effects of amitriptyline on anorectics as part of a drug treatment study and compared 24 patients receiving the medication to an equal number of controls using a double-blind design. They used up to 160 mg of amitriptyline, if tolerated. In their study amitriptyline-treated patients showed a trend towards reaching their target weights sooner than the control group. Other variables were not statistically different from controls. Given the mediocre results obtained from amitriptyline in most studies, and its significant side-effect profile, there is little data to support the use of this medication in the treatment of anorexia.

Surprising and encouraging results have been obtained using cyproheptadine, an antihistamine with serotonin antagonist action and a chemical structure related to tricyclic antidepressants. Double-blind, controlled studies with anorectics have shown that cyproheptadine can be effective not only in inducing weight gain, but also as an antidepressant, as seen by a significant decrease in scores on both the Beck Depression Inventory and the Hamilton Depression Rating Scale (Halmi *et al*, 1983: 103–105; Halmi *et al*, 1986: 177–181). Given the lack of anticholinergic, cardiotoxic and other side-effects seen with this medication, it is particularly appealing for the anorectic population which often presents with medical complications. Of particular interest was the finding that cyproheptadine was effective only for the non-bulimic anorectics; it significantly impaired treatment efficiency for the bulimic patients when compared to both amitriptyline and placebo-treated groups (Halmi *et al*, 1986: 177–181). Although there is no data on long-term effects, the authors conclude that cyproheptadine can be useful for increasing the rate of weight gain and reducing depressed mood in non-bulimic anorectics, and may be a useful therapeutic adjunct to a structured milieu and psychotherapy treatment program for hospitalized anorectics.

The available data does not in any way support the routine use of antidepressants in the treatment of anorexia nervosa. Cyproheptadine may be useful as an adjunct treatment in the weight gaining stage of treatment, but has not been shown to be efficacious in long term weight maintenance, or in changing anorectic attitudes. In fact, there is a clear lack of research evaluating the possible usefulness of any antidepressant medication in the long-term treatment of anorexia, and these studies need to be undertaken in the future.

The role of antidepressants in the treatment of bulimia is far more optimistic. A variety of different classes of medications have been evaluated in well-controlled studies, and several comprehensive reviews of these data are available (Hudson and Pope, 1987: 52–57; Pope *et al*, 1983: 274–281; Pope and Hudson, 1987: 123–129).

Following the reports of good outcome for bulimics treated with monoamine oxidase inhibitors (MAOI) in several open trials with a small sample size (Walsh *et al*, 1982: 1629–1630; Stewart *et al*, 1984: 217–219; Hardy *et al*, 1985: 39–42), a number of controlled studies appeared in the literature. In a long-term study, Walsh *et al* (1988: 471–475) examined the efficacy of phenelzine, an MAOI in the treatment of bulimia. Fifty women completed their study which used a double-blind, placebo-controlled format. Patients on medication received 60–90 mg/day, which is the equivalent of an antidepressant dose. On almost all measures of eating behavior, the phenelzine treated group was superior to placebo, including the number of binges/wk (5.4 vs. 8.4), the number of patients in remission (eight vs. one), and scores on the Eating Attitudes Test. In the phenelzine-treated group there was a 64%

reduction in binge frequency from randomization to termination, versus only a 5% change in the placebo treated group. Moreover, their analysis showed that the effect of phenelzine on binge reduction was not significantly related to whether or not the patients were classified as depressed.

A similar outcome was reported in another study using a different MAOI, isocarboxazid (Kennedy *et al*, 1988: 391- 396). In this report, 18 women completed a double-blind, placebo-controlled, crossover study utilizing 60 mg of drug, the usual antidepressant dose. The degree of monoamine oxidase inhibition averaged 85% as assessed by platelet MAOI activity. They report a significant reduction in vomiting episodes, binge episodes, and pathological eating attitudes and behaviors as measured by the Eating Attitudes Test. A comparison between patients with and without major depression indicated no significant differences in reduction of binge eating and vomiting. Thus data from two large, well-controlled studies suggests that MAOI's are effective in controlling bulimic behavior and possibly, changing attitudes towards food in general. It should be remembered that the patients who participated in this study were highly selected for compliance to the study. An MAO inhibitor in most circumstances would not be the first choice to give to bulimic patients (see discussion on pg. 169).

Results from studies using tricyclic antidepressants have also generally been encouraging, although not exclusively so. Two double-blind, placebo-controlled studies of the efficacy of imipramine in the treatment of bulimia have been completed. In the first of these (Pope *et al*, 1983a: 554–558) 22 patients were randomized into a medication group (receiving up to 200 mg/day of drug) and a placebo group for a six-week study. The treatment group had significantly fewer bingeing episodes by the end of the study compared to the placebo group. At termination, the number of binges/wk in the imipramine treated group had declined by a mean of 7.49, compared with a decline of .18/wk in the control group. Of the nine subjects receiving imipramine, four reported more than 75% reduction in binges, four had a more than 50% reduction, and one was unchanged. In the control group, one reported a decrease of 50% or more, and the remainder were unchanged or worse. In a second study (Agras *et al*, 1987: 29–38) 20 patients were randomized into placebo and medication groups for a 16-week study of imipramine at a dosage of up to 300 mg. By design, no other therapeutic interventions were included. They reported a significant reduction in the frequency of purging in the drug group compared to placebo. Again, baseline depression scores were unrelated to outcome.

Reports of the usefulness of desipramine (a tricyclic antidepressant which is the major metabolite of imipramine) are also encouraging. In one study (Hughes *et al*, 1986: 182–186) 22 female, non-depressed patients were given placebo or up to 200 mg of desipramine in a six-week study. No other treatment was offered. They found a 91% reduction in bingeing in the medication group compared to an actual worsening of the placebo-treated group. Later, they gave the placebo group a trial with the drug; overall 15 out of 22 patients completely stopped bingeing. Encouraging results, although not as dramatic as those above, were also seen in another trial with desipramine using a double-blind, placebo-controlled crossover design which lasted a total of 15 weeks. Of the 47 normal weight bulimics originally enrolled in the study,

25 completed all 15 weeks. Desipramine was significantly more effective than placebo in reducing the frequency of both vomiting and bingeing. Ultimately 11 patients showed a greater than 50% reduction in binges, and three improved more than 80%. Although these results are modest compared to the previous trial of desipramine, this may be explained by the high dropout rate in the trial, the relatively low dosage of desipramine (150 mg maximum) used, and the low plasma drug levels which resulted (Barlow *et al*, 1988: 129–133).

There is one placebo-controlled, double-blind study of amitriptyline (Mitchell and Groat, 1984: 186–193). In this study 32 female bulimic outpatients received either placebo or up to 150 mg of medication. In addition, all patients received a minimal behavioral treatment program. Surprisingly, both groups showed significant improvement. The medication group improved more on all the parameters studied (including the number of binges and the number of vomiting episodes each week), but not to a statistically significant extent. Also in this group, the depressed patients improved less in terms of their bulimia than the non-depressed group. It is possible that the results would have been more impressive if higher serum drug levels had been achieved, but the authors note that there was no relationship between serum levels and the percentage of improvement on eating parameters. Given these results and a report that amitriptyline may produce carbohydrate craving as a side-effect (Paykel *et al*, 1973: 501–507), which would be very distressing to the bulimic population, amitriptyline is probably not the antidepressant treatment of choice for bulimics. Also, of note, are the relatively impressive results obtained with a minimal behavioral intervention in the control group suggesting that other approaches may be equally efficacious in treating some bulimic women.

In addition to the trials of traditional antidepressants already reported, studies of the utility of some new antidepressants in treating bulimia have appeared in the literature. Amongst the most promising of these newer drugs is fluoxetine, a potent inhibitor of serotonin reuptake which has also been shown to have a mild anorectic effect in both animals and humans. This feature makes it very appealing to the bulimic population which is so distressed by the small weight gain that can accompany other medications (Goudie *et al*, 1976: 318–320; Ferguson, 1986: 1496). Following several small or uncontrolled reports suggesting that fluoxetine could be useful in treating bulimic patients (Freeman and Hampson, 1987: 171–177; Freeman *et al*, 1988; Wilson, 1990: 81–82), a large multi-center study of the drug was undertaken and recently completed (Levine *et al* Submitted for publication). In this eight week trial, there were three cells—128 patients received 20 mg/day of drug, 127 received 60 mg/day, and 127 received placebo. Fluoxetine at 60 mg/day proved significantly better than placebo in decreasing binge eating (p .004) and vomiting ($p < .001$). Patients showing a greater than 50% reduction in bulimic behavior in the first eight weeks were allowed to continue at 60 mg/day in a 44 week extension, during which time the response was maintained. Fluoxetine at 20 mg/day was significantly inferior to 60 mg/day at reducing vomiting and bingeing, but was superior to placebo for reducing vomiting. The drug was generally well-tolerated and appears to be a promising treatment for bulimia. The major precaution with fluoxetine centers around recent reports that the medication may induce intense suicidal preoccupation in a very small, but unpredictable subset of depressed patients treated with it, a possibility that clinicians need to be aware of and vigilant in searching out (Teicher *et al*, 1990: 207–210).

Several other newer antidepressants have been found effective in the treatment of bulimia, but for various reasons are not recommended at this time. Nomifensine, an antidepressant with dopaminergic amphetamine-like effects, and largely free of anticholinergic and sedative effects, was found to be highly effective in controlling bulimic behavior in two small, uncontrolled, open trials (Nasser, 1986: 373–374; Pope *et al*, 1986: 371–373). However, it has been withdrawn from the world market due to its documented potential to cause hemolytic amenia.

Similarly, bupropion, a heterocyclic antidepressant, has been shown to significantly reduce binges and purging in two studies, one of which was a large, controlled, double-blind study (Horne, 1984; Horne *et al*, 1988: 262–266). However, bupropion is associated with a significantly higher rate of grand mal seizures than is seen with other antidepressants and this rate is even higher in bulimics, for unknown reasons. This finding has prompted the manufacturer to issue a contraindication for the use of the drug in patients with a history of an eating disorder.

Trazodone has also shown promise in the treatment of bulimia with significant decreases in vomiting and binge eating episodes reported at doses used in depression (250- 600 mg/daily) (Solyom, 1989: 287–290). An earlier report however, noted the occurrence of delirium in three patients with bulimia treated with trazodone which was not explained by a medical event (Damlouji and Ferguson, 1984: 434–435). Until these reports are explained, trazodone should probably not be considered a first line pharmacological treatment for bulimia.

In fact, the only antidepressant not found superior to placebo in a controlled study of pharmacological treatments for bulimia is mianserin, a tetracyclic piperazino-azepine (Sabine, 1983: 195s–202s). Although this medication was not superior to placebo in that study, it may have been due to the low dosage used (60 mg/day, compared to 150 mg in treating depression). Further studies with this medication at higher doses are needed before valid conclusions can be drawn about its effectiveness in bulimia.

Most of the studies described here are short-term in duration, lasting several weeks. In one report (Pope, 1985: 320–327), 20 patients on a variety of medications were followed for up to two years. Ninety-five percent had achieved a partial remission of their bulimic symptomatology, and 50% were completely abstinent. Many of these patients had required multiple drug trials until the right medication for them was determined. Although there was no control group, the findings suggest that antidepressants may well be useful in the long-term treatment of bulimia in some patients.

It appears that most classes of antidepressants are effective in the treatment of bulimia. It is notable that antidepressants seem to be effective in treating bulimia even in the absence of current symptoms of major depression. In the major study that specifically excluded depressed bulimic subjects, the results with medication were still very impressive (Hughes *et al*, 1986: 182–186). Thus it seems reasonable that antidepressant drugs need not be reserved only for those with overt depressive symptomatology in addition to their bulimia. It may be necessary to try more than one class of medication to obtain a good outcome.

These data should not be interpreted ds evidence that the first line of treatment for bulimia should necessarily be antidepressant medications. Tricyclic antidepressants have many side-effects that can be both annoying (i.e., constipation, blurred vision, dry mouth) and potentially dangerous (cardiotoxicity, orthostatic hypotension, overdose fatalities). The role of these drugs in the pediatric population has not been well established. Monoamine oxidase inhibitors also have many side-effects, but moreover, require strict adherence to a tyramine-free diet to avoid a hypertensive crisis, a restriction which many bulimics find very difficult to tolerate. The risk benefit ratio needs to be carefully considered before starting an antidepressant in any patient.

There is evidence that both individual and group psychotherapies may be as useful in the treatment of bulimia as antidepressants (Mitchell and Groat, 1984: 186- 193; Freeman and Munro, 1988: 647-660) without carrying any of their risks. Clearly further studies comparing different therapeutic modalities are required to clarify the exact role antidepressants should play in the treatment of bulimia.

Although antidepressants are useful in treating bulimia, this finding does not lead to the conclusion that bulimia is merely a form of an affective disorder. Response to a medication alone is not an adequate basis for inclusion in one diagnostic class or another. For example, propranalol, a beta-blocker, is widely used in the treatment of illnesses as diverse as coronary artery disease, hypertension, social phobia, and neuroleptic-induced akathisia. Similarly, antidepressants are effective, not only for depression and bulimia, but also for enuresis, panic attacks, and attention deficit disorder. It is highly unlikely that all these disorders are simply variant manifestations of a single underlying disturbance.

SUMMARY

In this chapter the association between eating disorders and depression has been examined by reviewing epidemiological, biological and treatment studies connecting the disorders, as well as illustrating differences. The data supports the view that eating disorders and depression are separate clinical entities associated with each other in a manner that has not yet been determined.

Clinicians treating the adolescent population medically are often the first professionals to see patients with an eating disorder. They need to be aware of the high co-incidence of depression with both anorexia nervosa and bulimia nervosa in order to provide the safest, most effective treatment for this group.

References

Agras, W. S. *et al* (1987) Imipramine in the treatment of bulimia: a double-blind controlled study. *International Journal of Eating Disorders*, **6**(1), 29–38.

American Psychiatric Association (1987) Diagnostic and Statistical Manual of Mental Disorders, Third Edition, Revised. Washington, D.C.

Amsterdam, J. D. *et al* (1981) Gonadotropin release after administration of GH-RH in depressed patients and healthy volunteers, *Journal of Affective Disorders*, **3**, 367–380.

Barlow, J. *et al* (1988) Treatment of bulimia with desipramine: a double-blind crossover study. *Canadian Journal of Psychiatry*, **33**, 129–133.
Biederman, J. *et al* (1984) Urinary MHPG in anorexia nervosa patients with and without a concomitant major depression disorder. *Journal of Psychiatric Research*, **18**, 149–160.
Biederman, J. *et al* (1985) Depressive disorders in relatives of anorexia nervosa patients and and without a current episode of non-bipolar major depression. *American Journal of Psychiatry*, **142**, 1495–1497.
Biederman, J. *et al* (1985a) Amitriptyline in the treatment of anorexia nervosa: a double-blind placebo controlled study. *Journal of Clinical Psychopharmacology*, **5**(1), 10–16.
Bond, W.S. *et al* (1986) Pharmacotherapy of eating disorders: a critical review. *Drug Intelligence and Clinical Pharmacy*, **20**, 659–665.
Boyar, R.M. *et al* (1977) Cortisol secretion and metabolism in anorexia nervosa. *New England Journal of Medicine*, **296**, 190– 193.
Brambilla, F. (1986) Anorexia nervosa and depression: A common biochemical pathogenesis?. *Functional Neurology*, **1**:(2), 191– 202.
Brauman, H. and Gregoire, F. (1975) The growth hormone response to insulin induced hypoglycemia in anorexia nervosa and control underweight of normal subjects. *European Journal of Clinical Invesgitation*, **5**, 289–295.
Cantwell, D.P. *et al* (1987) Anorexia nervosa: an affective disorder?. *Archives of General Psychiatry*, **34**, 1087–1093.
Carroll, B.J. *et al* (1981) A specific laboratory test for the diagnosis of melancholia: Standardization, validation and clinical utility. *Archives of General Psychiatry*, **38**, 15–22.
Casper, R.C. and Frohman, L.A. (1982) Delayed TSH release in anorexia nervosa following injection of thyrotropin-releasing hormone (TRH). *Psychoneuroendocrinology*, **7**, 59–68.
Coopen, A. *et al* (1972) Abnormalities of indolamines in affective disorders. *Archives of General Psychiatry*, **26**, 474– 478.
Crisp, A.H. *et al* (1987) Clomipramine and 'drive' in people with anorexia nervosa: A inpatient study. *British Journal of Psychiatry*, **150**, 355–358.
Dally, P. and Gomez, J. (1979) Anorexia Nervosa. London: William Heinemann Medical Books Ltd., p. 140.
Damlouji, N.F. and Ferguson, J.M. (1984) Trazodone induced delirium in bulimic patients. *American Journal of Psychiatry*, **141**, 434–435.
Eckert, E.D. *et al* (1981) Depression in anorexia nervosa. *Psychological Medicine*, **11**, 1–8.
Ettigi, P.G. and Brown, G.M. (1977) Psychoneuroendocrinology of affective disorder: An overview. *American Journal of Psychiatry*, **134**(5), 493–501.
Fava, M. *et al* (1989) Neurochemical abnormalities of anorexia nervosa and bulimia nervosa. *American Journal of Psychiatry*, **146**, 963–971.
Feinberg, M. *et al* (1982) EEG studies of sleep in the diagnosis of depression. *Biological Psychiatry*, **17**, 305–316.
Ferguson, J.M. (1986) Fluoxetine induced weight loss in overweight non-depressed subjects. *American Journal of Psychiatry*, **143**, 1496.
Foster, F.D. *et al* (1976) EEG sleep in anorexia nervosa, in Sleep Research. (abstract) ed. M.H. Chase. Brain Information Institute, Los Angeles, California, p. 143.
Freeman, C.P. and Hampson, C.P.C. (1987) Fluoxetine as a treatment for bulimia nervosa. *International Journal of Obesity*, **11** (Suppl.), 171–177.
Freeman, C.P. *et al* (1988) A double-blind, controlled trial of fluoxetine vs. placebo for bulimia nervosa. Presented at the Third International Conference on Eating Disorders, New York.
Fullerton, D.T. *et al* (1986) Plasma Immunoreactive beta-endorphin in bulimics. *Psychological Medicine*, **16**, 59–63.
Garfinkel, P. *et al* (1975) Hypothalamic-pituitary function in anorexia nervosa. *Archives of General Psychiatry*, **32**, 739–744.
Gerner, R.H. and Sharp, B. (1982) SFC beta-endorphin-immunoreactivity in normal, schizophrenic, depressed, manic and anorexic subjects. *Brain Research*, **237**, 244–247.
Gerner, R.H. *et al* (1984) CSF neurochemistry of women with anorexia nervosa and normal women. *American Journal of Psychiatry*, **141**, 1441–1444.
Gershon, E.S. *et al* (1983) Anorexia nervosa and major affective disorders associated in families: A preliminary report, Child Psychopathology and Development, (ed. S.B. Guze). New York: Raven Press, pp. 279–284.
Gershon, E.S. *et al* (1984) Clinical findings in patients with anorexia nervosa and affective illness in their relatives, *American Journal of Psychiatry*, **141**, 1419–1422.

Gold, M.S. *et al* (1981) TSH and GH responses to TRH in anorexia nervosa. *International Journal of Psychiatry in Medicine*, **10**, 51-57.
Goudie, A.J. *et al* (1976) Effects of Lilly 110 140 a specific inhibitor of 5-hydroxytryptamine uptake on food intake and on 5-hydroxytryptophan induced anorexia—evidence of serotonergic inhibition of feeding. *Journal of Pharmacology*, **28**, 318-320.
Gwirtsman, H.E. *et al* (1983) Neuroendocrine abnormalities in bulimia. *American Journal of Psychiatry*, **140**, 559-563.
Gwirtsman, E.E. *et al* (1984) Pharmacologic treatment of eating disorders. *Psychiatric Clinics of North America*, **7**(4), 863- 878.
Halmi, K.A. (1974) Anorexia nervosa: Demograpic and clinical features in 94 cases. *Psychosomatic Medicine*, **36**, 18-24.
Halmi, K.A. (1985) Relationship of the eating disorders to depression: biological similarities and differences. *International Journal of Eating Disorders*, **4**(4), 667-680.
Halmi, K.A. and Sherman, B. (1977) Dopaminergic and serotonergic regulation of growth hormone secretion in anorexia nervosa. *Psychopharmacology Bulletin*, **13**(1), 63-65.
Halmi, K.A. and Sherman, B. (1979) Prediction of treatment in response in anorexia nervosa. Biological Psychiatry Today, ed. J. Obiols and E. Ballus, Elsevier/North. Hall and Biomedical Press, New York, pp. 609-614.
Halmi, K.A. *et al* (1978) Catecholamine metabolism in anorexia nervosa. *Archives of General Psychiatry*, **35**, 458-460.
Halmi, K.A. *et al* (1979) Unique features associated with age of onset of anorexia nervosa. *Psychiatric Research*, **1**, 209-215.
Halmi, K.A. *et al* (1983) Cyproheptadine, an antidepressant and weight-inducing drug for anorexia nervosa. *Psychopharmacology Bulletin*, **19**(1), 1-3-105.
Halmi, K.A. *et al* (1986) Anorexia nervosa: Treatment efficacy of cyproheptadine and amitriptyline. *Archives of General Psychiatry*, **43**, 177-181.
Halmi, K.A. *et al* (1991) Comorbidity of psychiatric diagnoses in anorexia nervosa. *Archives of General Psychiatry*, **48**, 712-718.
Hardy, B.W. *et al* (1985) Bulimia and monoamine oxidase inhibitors: A predictor study, Texas Medicine, **89**, 39-42.
Hatsukami, D.K. *et al* (1984) Eating disorders: A variant of mood disorders? *Psychiatric Clinics of North America*, **7**(2), 349-365.
Hatsukami, D.K. *et al* (1984a) Affective disorder and substance abuse in women with bulimia. *Psychological Medicine*, **14**, 701- 704.
Hendren, R.L. (1983) Depression in anorexia nervosa. *Journal of the American Academy of Child Psychiatry*, **22**(1), 59-62.
Herzog, D.B. (1984) Are anorexic and bulimic patients depressed? *American Journal of Psychiatry*, **141**(2), 1594-1597.
Heufelder, A. *et al* (1985) Platelet alpha-2-adrenoceptor and adenylate cyclase in patients with anorexia nervosa and bulimia. *Journal of Clinical Endocrinology and Metabolism*, **61**, 1053-1060.
Hollister, L.E. *et al* (1976) Pituitary response to thyrotropin releasing hormone in depression. *Archives of General Psychiatry*, **38**, 106-113.
Horne, R.L. (1984) Bupropion in the treatment of bulimia. Presented at the First International Conference on Eating Disorders, New York.
Horne, R.L. *et al* (1988) Treatment of bulimia with bupropion-a multi-center controlled trial. *Journal of Clinical Psychiatry*, **49**, 262-266.
Hudson, J.I. and Pope, H.G. (1982) Bulimia related to affective disorder by family history and response to the Dexamethasone Suppression Test. *American Journal of Psychiatry*, **139**(5), 685- 687.
Hudson, J.I. and Pope, H.G. (1987) Newer antidepressants in the treatment of bulimia nervosa. *Psychopharmacology Bulletin*, **23**(1), 52-57.
Hudson, J.I. *et al* (1982) Bulimia related to affective disorder by family history and response to the Dexamethasone Suppression Test. *American Journal of Psychiatry*, **139**(5), 685- 687.
Hudson, J.I. *et al* (1983) Phenomenologic relationship of eating disorders to major affective disorder. *Psychiatric Research*, **9**, 345-354.
Hudson, J.I. *et al* (1983a) Family history study of anorexia nervosa and bulimia. *British Journal of Psychiatry*, **142**, 133- 138.
Hudson, J.I. *et al* (1987) A controlled study of lifetime prevalence of affective and other psychiatric disorders in bulimic outpatients. *American Journal of Psychiatry*, **144**, 1283-1287.
Hughes, P.L. *et al* (1986) Treatment of bulimia with desipramine: a double-blind placebo controlled study. *Archives of General Psychiatry*, **43**, 182-186.

Insel, T.R. *et al* (1982) The Dexamethasone Suppression Test in patients with primary obsessive-compulsive disorder. *Psychiatric Research*, **6**, 153-160.
Johnson, C. *et al* (1983) Psychopharmacological treatment of Anorexia and Bulimia: Review and Synthesis. *Journal of Nervous and Mental Disorders*, **171**(9), 524-534.
Kaplan, A.S. *et al* (1986) Clonidine Challenge Test in bulimia. In: *New Research Abstracts*, 139th Annual Meeting of the American Psychiatric Association.
Katz, J.L. *et al* (1984) Is there a relationship between eating disorder and affective disorder? New evidence from sleep recordings. *American Journal of Psychiatry*, **141**, 753-759.
Kay, D.W.K. and Leigh, D. (1954) The natural history, treatment, and prognosis of anorexia nervosa, based on a study of 38 patients. *Journal of Mental Science*, **100**, 411-432.
Kaye, W.H. *et al* (1982) Cerebrospinal fluid opioid activity in anorexia nervosa. *American Journal of Psychiatry*, **139**, 643-645.
Kaye, W.H. *et al* (1984a) Differences in brain serotonergic metabolism between non-bulimic and bulimic patients with anorexia nervosa. American Journal of Psychiatry, **141**, 1598: 1601.
Kaye, W.H. *et al* (1984) Abnormalities in CNS monoamine metabolism in anorexia nervosa. Archives of General Psychiatry, **41**, 350-355.
Kaye, W.H. *et al* (1986) Noradrenergic disturbance in normal weight bulimia. In: *CME Syllabus and Scientific Proceedings in Summary Form*, 139th Annual meeting of the American Psychiatric Association.
Kaye, W.H. *et al* (1988) CSF-5-HIAA Concentration in anorexia nervosa: Reduced values in underweight subjects normalized after weight gain. *Biological Psychiatry*, **23**, 102-105.
Kaye, W.H. *et al* (1988a) Bingeing behavior and plasma amino acids: A possible involvement of brain serotonin in bulimia nervosa, *Psychiatric Research*, **23**, 31-43.
Kennedy, S.H. *et al* (1988) A trial of isocarboxazid in the treatment of bulimia nervosa, *Journal of Clinical Psychopharmacology*, **8**(6), 391-396.
Keys, A. *et al* (1950) The Biology of Human Starvation. Vol. I and II. Mineapolis, the University of Minnesota Press, pp. 63-81, 819-921.
Kiriike, N. *et al* (1987) Thyrotropin, prolactin and growth hormone responses to thyrotropin-releasing hormone in anorexia nervosa nad bulimia, *Biological Psychiatry*, **22**, 167-176.
Kupfer, D.J. and Foster, F.D. (1972) Interval between onset of sleep and rapid eye movement sleep as an indicator of depression, *Lancet*, **2**, 684-686.
Lacey, J.H. and Crisp, A.H. (1980) Hunger, food intake, and weight: The impact of clomipramine on a refeeding anorexia nervosa population, *Postgraduate Medical Journal*, **56** (Suppl.1), 79-85.
Laessle, R.G. *et al* (1987) Major affective disorder in anorexia nervosa and bulimia—a descriptive diagnostic study. *British Journal of Psychiatry*, **151**, 785-789.
Lahmeyer H.W. *et al* (1983) EEG sleep in depressed adolescents. *American Journal of Psychiatry*, **140**, 1150-1153.
Lee, N.F. *et al* (1985) Bulimia and depression. *Journal of Affective Disorders*, **9**, 231-238.
Levine, L.R. *et al* (1990) Fluoxetine in the treatment of bulimia nervosa: A multi-center, placebo-controlled double-blind study. Submitted for publication.
Levy, A.B. *et al* (1988a) Sleep architecture in anorexia nervosa and bulimia. *Biological Psychiatry*, **23**, 99-101.
Levy, A.B. *et al* (1988) Pituitary response to TRH in bulimia. *Biological Psychiatry*, **22**, 476-162-169.
Levy, A.B. *et al* (1989a) Gonadotropin response to LRH in anorexia nervosa and bulimia. *Bilogical Psychiatry*, **26**, 425- 427.
Lindy, D.C. *et al* (1985) The dexamethasone suppression test in bulimia. *American Journal of Psychiatry*, **142**, 1375-1376.
Miayi, K. *et al* (1975) Serum thyroid hormones and thyrotropin in anorexia nervosa. *Journal of Clinical Endocrinology and Metabolism*, **40**, 334-338.
Mitchell, J.E. and Bantle, J.P. (1983) Metabolic and endocrine investigations in women of normal weight with the bulimia syndrome. *Biological Psychiatry*, **18**(3), 355-365.
Mitchell, J.E. and Groat, R. (1984) A placebo-controlled, double-blind trial of amitriptyline in bulimia. *Journal of Clinical Psychopharmacology*, **4**(4), 186-193.
Mitchell, J.E. *et al* (1986) Bulimia with and without a family history of depressive illness. *Comprehensive Psychiatry*, **27**, 215-219.
Morgan, H.G. and Russell, G.F.M. (1975) Value of family background and clinical features as predictors of long term outcome in anorexia nervosa: Four year follow-up of 41 patients. *Psychiatric Medicine*, **5**, 355-371.
Moshang, T. *et al* (1975) Low serum triiodothyronine in patients with anorexia nervosa. *Journal of Clinical Endocrinology and Metabolism*, **40**, 470-473.

Nasser, D. G. (1986) Successful treatment of bulimia with nomifensine. American Journal of Psychiatry, **143**, 373–374.

Needleman, H. L. and Weber, D. (1977) The use of amitriptyline in anorexia nervosa, ed. R. A. Vigersky, Anorexia Nervosa. Raven Press. New York. pp. 357–362.

Nell, J. F. *et al* (1980) Walking and all-night sleep EEG's in anorexia nervosa. *Clinical Electroencephalography*, **11**, 9–15.

Norris, P. D. *et al* (1985) The TRH Test in bulimia and anorexia nervosa: A controlled test. *Journal of Psychiatric Research*, **19**, 215–219.

Owen, W. P. *et al* (1983) Dopamine regulation in anorexia nervosa. *Psychopharmacology Bulletin*, **19**, 578–581.

Paykel, E. S. *et al* (1973) Amitriptyline, weight gain and carbohydrate craving: A side-effect. *British Journal of Psychiatry*, **123**, 501–507.

Piran, N. *et al* (1985) Affective disturbance in eating disorders. *Journal of Nervous and Mental Disorders*, **173**(7), 395–400.

Pirke, K. M. *et al* (1985) Metabolic and endocrine indices of starvation in bulimia: A comparison with anorexia nervosa. *Psychiatric Research*, **15**, 33–39.

Pope, H. G. and Hudson, J. I. (1987) Antidepressant medication in the treatment of bulimia nervosa. *Psychopathology* **20**(Suppl. 1), 123–129.

Pope, H. D. *et al* (1983) Antidepressant treatment of bulimia: Preliminary experience and practical recommendations. *Journal of Clinical Psychopharmacology*, **3**(5), 274–281.

Pope, H. G. *et al* (1983a) Bulimia treated with Imipramine: A placebo-controlled, double-blind study. *American Journal of Psychiatry*, **140**, 554–558.

Pope, H. G. *et al* (1985) Antidepressant treatment of bulimia: A two year follow-up study. *Journal of Clinical Psychopharmacology*, **5**(6), 320–327.

Pope, H. G. *et al* (1986) Treatment of bulimia with nomifensine. *American Journal of Psychiatry*, **143**, 371–373.

Prange, A. J. *et al.* (1972) Effects of TRH in depression. *Lancet*, **2**, 999–1002.

Pyle, R. L. *et al.* (1981) Bulimia: A report of 34 cases. *Journal of Clinical Psychiatry*, **42**, 60–64.

Rao, K. S. J. *et al* (1968) Plasma cortisol levels in protein calorie malnutrition. *Archives of Disease in Childhood*, **43**, 365–367.

Rivinus, T. M. *et al* (1984) Anorexia nervosa and affective disorders: A controlled family history study. *American Journal of psychiatry*, **141**, 1414–1418.

Russell, G. F. M. (1979) Bulimia nervosa: An ominous variant of anorexia nervosa. *Psychological Medicine*, **9**, 429–448.

Sabine, E. J. *et al.* (1983) Bulimia nervosa: A placebo-controlled, double-blind therapeutic trial of mianserin. *British Journal of Clinical Pharmacology*, **15**, 195.S–202.S.

Sachar, E.J. *et al* (1970) Cortisol production in depressive illness. *Archives of General Psychiatry*, **23**, 289–298.

Sachar, E. J. *et al* (1973) Disrupted 24-hour patterns of cortisol secretion in psychotic depression. *Archives of General Psychiatry*, **28**, 19–24.

Schidkraut, J. J. (1965) The catecholamine hypothesis of affective disorders: A review of supporting evidence. *American Journal of Psychiatry*, **122**, 509–522.

Schwartz, C. M. and Dunner, F. J. (1982) Dexamethasone suppression testing of alcoholics. *Archives of General Psychiatry*, **39**, 1309–1312.

Smith, S. R. *et al* (1975) Cortisol metabolism and the pituitary adrenal axis in adults with protein calorie malnutrition. *Journal of Clinical Endocrinology and Metabolism*, **40**, 43–52.

Solyom, L. *et al* (1989) Trazodone treatment of bulimia nervosa. *Journal of Clinical Psychophar-mapology*, **9**, 287–290.

Spar, G. E. and Gerner, R. (1982) Does the Dexamonethasone Suppression Test distinguish dementia from depression? *American Journal of Psychiatry*, **139**, 238–247.

Stern, S. L. *et al* (1984) Affective disorder in the families of women with normal weight bulimia. *American Journal of Psychiatry*, **141**, 1224–1227.

Stewart, J. W. *et al* (1984) An open trial of MAO inhibitors in bulimia. *Journal of Clinical Psychiatry*, **45**, 217–219.

Strober, M. *et al* (1990) A controlled family study of anorexia nervosa: Evidence of familial aggregation and lack of shared transmission with affective disorders. *International Journal of Eating Disorders*, **9**(3), 239–253.

Swift, W. J. *et al* (1985) Depression in bulimia at 2–5 year follow-up. *Psychiatric Research*, **16**, 111–122.

Swift, W. J. *et al* (1986) The relationship between affective disorder and eating disorders: A review of the literature. *American Journal of Psychiatry*, **143**, 290–299.

Teicher, M.H. *et al* (1990) Emergence of intense suicidal preoccupation during fluoxetine treatment. *American Journal of Psychiatry*, **147**, 207–210.

Toner, B.B. *et al* (1988) Affective and anxiety disorders in the long-term follow-up of anorexia nervosa. *International Journal of Psychiatry in Medicine*, **18**(4), 357–364.

Vernon, S.W. and Roberts, R.E. (1982) Use of the Schedule for Affective Disorders and Schizophrenia – Research Diagnostic Criteria in a tri-ethnic community survey. *Archives of General Psychiatry*, **39**, 47–52.

Waller, D.A. *et al* (1986) Eating behavior and plasma beta-endorphin in bulimia. *American Journal of Clinical Nutrition*, **44**, 20–23.

Walsh, B.T. (1982) Endocrine disturbances in anorexia nervosa and depression. *Psychosomatic Medicine*, **44**(1), 85–91.

Walsh, B.T. *et al* (1978) Adrenal activity in anorexia nervosa. *Psychosomatic Medicine*, **40**, 499–506.

Walsh, B.T. *et al* (1982) Treatment of bulimia with monamine oxidase inhibitors. *American Journal of Psychiatry*, **139**(12), 1629–1630.

Walsh, B.T. *et al* (1985) Bulimia and depression. *Psychosomatic Medicine*, **47**(2), 123–131.

Walsh, B.T. *et al* (1985a) EEG-monitored sleep in anorexia nervosa and bulimia. *Biological Psychiatry*, **20**, 947–956.

Walsh, B.T. *et al* (1987) Hypothalamic-pituitary-adrenal-cortisol activity in anorexia nervosa and bulimia. *Psychoneuroendocrinology*, **12**, 131–140.

Walsh, B.T. *et al* (1988) Phenelzine vs. placebo in 50 patients with bulimia. *Archives of General Psychiatry*, **45**, 471–475.

Weissman, M.J. and Myers, J.K. (1978) Affective disorders in a United States urban community: The use of Research Diagnostic Criteria in an epidemiological survey. *Archives of General Psychiatry*, **35**, 1304–1311.

Wiener, H. (1983) Hypothalamic-Pituitary-Ovarian axis in anorexia nervosa and bulimia nervosa. *International Journal of Eating Disorders*, **2**, 109–116.

Wilson, J. (1990) Fluoxetine and bulimia. *Journal of Psychoactive Drugs*, **22**, 81–82.

Winokour, A. *et al* (1980) Primary affective disorder in relatives of patients with anorexia nervosa. *American Journal of Psychiatry*, **137**, 695–698.

Witschy, J.K. *et al* (1984) TRH-induced prolactin release is blunted in females with endogenous unipolar depression. *Psychiatric Research*, **12**, 321–331.

13 Psychotherapy of Depression in Childhood and Adolescence

Clarice J. Kestenbaum and Ian A. Canino

Division of Child and Adolescent Psychiatry, Columbia University College of Physicians and Surgeons, New York, NY 10032, USA.

INTRODUCTION

Depression has long been one of the neglected syndromes of the psychopathology of childhood. Full depressive disorders as in adults were rarely thought to occur in children partly due to the belief that children lacked the necessary intrapsychic, maturity for depression to occur (Rie, 1966) and partly, if it did occur, it took a "masked" form. Toolan (1962), for example, discussing the interaction of developmental levels and the manifestation of depressive feelings, coined the term "depressive equivalents" including temper tantrums, disobedience, and accident proneness. Other authors (i.e. Wolfenstein, 1966) contended that even normal mourning could not occur until mid-adolescence when certain developmental tasks had been completed.

The past decade, however, has brought in its wake a renewed interest in depressive reactions in children, and there has been a marked change in the psychiatric view of affective disorders of early life. Depressive conditions meeting adult criteria have now been shown to occur in childhood.

DEPRESSION IN EARLY CHILDHOOD

One definition of depression as compared to sadness, grief and mourning in the psychoanalytic literature is "an experience of loss that triggers rage and hostile responses directed at the self . . . and transformed consequentially to a mood state" (Milrod, 1988). Themes of childhood sadness and grief reactions date back to the writings of Anna Freud and Dorothy Burlingham (1944) who described the responses of infants and children to the loss of parental affection and need gratification caused by death, foster care placement, illness and divorce. Rene Spitz in 1945 designated the term "hospitalism" to specify the destructive effects of institutional care on infants. He coined the term "anaclitic depression" for the syndrome occuring in children over six months of age as a result of separation from their mothers after the mother-child tie had been established. In the emotionally deprived children he studied he encountered severe withdrawal, apathy, and regression. In a two-year follow-up study of these children in a foundling home, Spitz (1946: 113–117) found them to be severely delayed in their gross motor development, capacity to handle materials, toilet training, language development, and social relations. Their height and weight fell below the normal ranges and he postulated that their resistance to physical illness had been severely impaired. This clinical picture was to later become the "failure to thrive" syndrome often seen in many pediatric wards.

John Bowlby (1973), in his work with hospitalized children, stated that there is a causal relationship between loss of maternal care in early life and disturbed personality development. The pathogenic factor, he believes, is loss of the mother (or primary caretaker) during the period between six months and three years, the period considered optimal for the establishment of object permanence (6 to 18 months) in the Piagetian sense of cognitive stages of development and object constancy (6 to 36 months) when the internal representation of a familiar person is complete. The child becomes closely attached to the mother and is distressed by her absence. Most children do not suffer disruption of the primary attachment in the early years, but if the mother should die or if a series of short term caretakers are employed as substitutes in the total absence of the mother, or if the child is hospitalized for long periods of time, a clinical picture resembling adult mourning may indeed result. Bowlby (1973) through observations of hospitalized children described a series of specific stages the child underwent after maternal loss and mentioned the time limits beyond which lost object restoration would not reverse the reaction. He described the children as undergoing three stages: protest, despair, and detachment. He postulated that protest may result in subsequent separation anxiety, that despair could lead to grief and mourning, and that detachment was a defensive maneuver which protected the child from emotional pain.

Despite the findings of Spitz and Bowlby there is still controversy about the existence of depression in children under five. Kovacs and Beck (1977) contend that depression is rare and difficult to diagnose before age seven when communication skills become fully developed. Poznanski and Zrull (1970) disagree and have described children as young as three who displayed lack of appetite, failure to gain weight, withdrawal and lack of attachment to the caretaker. Depression in the mother has been implicated, along with separation and loss, as highly significant risk factors (Weissman 1972). A depressed mother who is unable to meet the needs of an infant or young child does not provide a healthy emotionally stable environment. In order to fulfill the developmental tasks of the preschool age—separation and individuation according to Margaret Mahler (1952), a firm attachment bond to the primary caretaker must be established first.

O'Brien (1983) observes "Maternal depression disrupts the mutual activation and regulation that characterizes a healthy mother-child relationship . . . preschool children of depressed mothers have a high incidence of behavioral disorders, difficulty in eating, difficulty in obtaining bladder control and a high accident rate"

DEPRESSION IN MIDDLE CHILDHOOD

As previously noted, the psychoanalytic literature underscores the importance of development in determining the timing of particular symptoms (Bemporad and Won Lee, 1986). Developmental tasks of middle childhood include acquisition of new motor skills, such as bike riding and language skills. Cognitive development proceeds by leaps and bounds. In terms of socialization the child develops a number of peer relationships, frequently a best friend and participates actively in groups. Self-esteem is dependent in most part on a feeling of success academically and socially. The middle years are also the period for conscience development and a deepening sense of values. Behavioral problems as the child matures frequently indicate underlying depressive feelings. Children may appear sullen, complain of fatigue and behave in a provocative, negativistic or bored manner. Just as loss of the mothering figure may lead to depressive reactions in infancy, losses of loved ones or friends by separation and divorce can lead to overt or covert depressive symptoms. Some children experiencing a loss might defend against the feelings engendered by the loss by fighting or refusing to conform to academic requirements in school.

Anthony (1967) noted that the difference between child and adult depression stems from "the child's inability to verbalize his affective state, the incomplete development of the superego (i.e. conscience) and the absence of a consistent self representation." His studies of depressed children describe weepiness, flattened affect, fear of death, irritability, somatic complaints, loss of appetite, difficulties in school and hostility directed toward the parents. Some of these children, Anthony felt, had a constitutional predisposition to depression and often came from families with a history of depression or manic-depressive illness.

Sandler and Joffee (1965) observed that the children they studied did not display the psychomotor retardation of adult depressives but did display sad affect, withdrawal, feelings of rejection, passivity and insomnia. They contend that depression can be the "result of the loss of a prior state of well-being rather than solely as the deprivation of a love object."

Poznanski and Zrull (1970) focused on the negative self-image or loss of self esteem as being of primary importance in understanding the psychopathology of childhood depression. Glaser (1967) utilized the phrase "masked depression" as did Cytryn and McKnew (1972).

Bemporad (1988) concentrated his work on children and adolescents and defines depression somewhat more generally as the "deprivation of some aspect of psychic life that was necessary to the individuals' sense of esteem or worth." He describes the individuals' vulnerability to severe dysphoria as due to (a) the individual's inordinate need for nurturance or affirmation from others in order to secure a sense of self-esteem and/or (b) the individuals' inability to substitute or create new sources of worth subsequent to such a loss. He states that the possible precipitant of depression are experiences that can influence negatively the self-concept in relation to important others and/or the loss of relationships, achievements, or ideas that have been utilized to support a needed self-regard.

DEPRESSION IN ADOLESCENCE

Adolescence is a period of physiological and psychological change. According to Blos (1968) character formation will proceed optimally only if the following conditions are met:

1) *Loosening of Parental Ties*: Adolescents must increasingly seek new models for themselves in teachers, counselors, friends, and heroes of sport, television, and films, with whom they can identify, and by whose example they shape their own efforts at individuation and independence.

2) *Resolution of Earlier Traumas*: Adolescents must come to terms with certain traumatic childhood events. These may involve only early disappointment with one or both parents, who are seen to have human frailties, or something as severe as the death of a parent.

3) *Establishment of Continuity*: Adolescents seek to establish a sense of continuity with respect to their previous feelings, remembered experiences, and their own family history. One cannot have a future without having a past.

4) *Solidification of Sexual Identity*: Early adolescence is characterized by a growing capacity to make a sexual object choice and to solidify one's sense of gender identity, an aspect of self-awareness that had begun in infancy. Most often the goal of the mature individual is to find an intimate relationship with a partner of the opposite sex. Failure to complete these developmental tasks may lead to subsequent depression.

Mood swings in adolescence are common manifestations of this developmental period. Usually these are transient and related to such events as dissolution of a friendship, disappointment with performance in grades or sports, or parental discipline. Bemporad (1988) observes that adolescence is a vulnerable period and notes that depressive responses in adolescence range from normative to pathological. Adolescents sense of worth often comes from relationships and achievements that are outside the family nucleus and is highly determined by the adolescents' ability to convince themselves as well as others that they are no longer children. Feelings of inadequacy, disappointment, or shame are dependent on socially-related activities especially those related to heterosexual coupling. At a cognitive level, the adolescent develops self-consciousness, a sense of consequences of his or her behavior, and a more realistic grasp of their abilities and liabilities both intellectual as well as physical. They must relinquish their childhood fantasies and thus deal with their feelings of loss and resignation.

Bemporad furthermore describes two types of depression in adolescence—anaclitic and introjective. Anaclitic depression is that occurring in adolescents who have not emancipated themselves from their familial role (being too gratified or protected): thus, they cannot form a separate satisfactory sense of worth. It also includes those coming from dysfunctional families in which the adolescents assume pseudoparental roles, therefore having difficulty forming allegiances and relationships outside the household. Introjective depression, Bemporad believes, is observed in adolescents who are more individualized but have unrealistic demands and expectations internalized from familial relationships. They feel they must live out some parental aspiration and this precludes feelings of pleasure and/or freedom. Serious depressive symptoms in adolescence include school refusal, avoidance of former friends, lack of interest in sports or hobbies, or reckless behavior, alcoholic or drug abuse. Self reproach, expressions of worthlessness and of course, suicidal preoccupation are all important warning signs that should not be ignored.

Clearly, there is a wide spectrum of what may be considered depression; from normal sadness to depressive feelings secondary to grief reactions, physical illness, and psychosocial stress to the full syndrome of major depression.

In each case of childhood or adolescent depression, strengths, vulnerabilities, and the developmental level must be considered. The child's ability to report, express, and experience depressive feelings has to be understood within the context of the family and of the environment. The strengths and vulnerabilities, self-image, defensive style, as well as temperamental traits and genetic predisposition will certainly effect symptom expression and resolution as well as level of dysfunctionality and prognosis.

PSYCHOTHERAPEUTIC INTERVENTIONS FOR PRESCHOOL CHILDREN WITH DEPRESSIVE REACTIONS

It is obvious from the foregoing discussion that depression in childhood and adolescence has multiple determinants and that a psychiatric evaluation should be done in order to choose the best kind of therapeutic intervention. If a seven year old is dysthymic and cannot learn to read dynamic psychotherapy would not be the first line of intervention, even if the child is able to discuss his frustration with an understanding adult. He would need a special class placement, and language and learning therapy; only if the mood disorder persisted after appropriate academic help was instituted should the consultant consider a course of psychotherapy. Psychosocial distress due to poverty, homelessness or family turmoil needs environmental manipulation, social service intervention or family therapy in addition to individual counselling or psychotherapy.

PSYCHIATRIC CONSULTATION AND BRIEF INTERVENTION

The sine qua non of the psychiatric consultation is the evaluation. Brief therapeutic intervention is sometimes enough to allow the depressed child to get back on the path of normal development.

Case I – Maria, age 4

Maria was referred for a psychiatric consultation by her preschool principal because of apathy and withdrawal. The teacher had tried to engage her in a variety of activities without success. Maria's mother, Mrs. S., a sad young woman from the Dominican Republic, told the consultant that Maria did not love her any more; she described Maria as having been happy and outgoing as an infant. When she was two years old, Mrs. S. who was pregnant again, sent Maria to live with her grandmother in Santo Domingo. She felt the grandmother would be better able to care for Maria during her confinement as life was very difficult in New York City, and she did not want to leave her little girl with strangers.

The first few days in a strange land were hard for Maria. At first she cried bitterly, then she refused to eat, but soon she was "her old self" and became attached to the grandmother. Unfortunately, the grandmother became ill several months later, and Maria was sent to live with an aunt in a nearby town. Again the traumatic scene of grieving and resignation repeated itself. At age $3\frac{1}{2}$ Maria returned to her mother in New York "but she didn't know me anymore," Mrs. S. reported weeping. "She didn't cry, but nothing I could do made her happy and she just ignored me." The consultant explained that Maria's reaction to the repeated separation was typical. She behaved, as every mother will testify after a vacation, with a "who needs you?" attitude. It is as if she said "I trusted you and you abandoned me. I'll never allow myself to get close to you – or anyone – again." It was Mrs. S's own feeling of rejection and her own subsequent depression which prevented her from reaching out to Maria despite the little girl's aloofness.

The consultant recommended counselling for Mrs. S. and several conjoint sessions with Mrs. S. and Maria. Mrs. S. responded well to the help offered by the social worker. She gained understanding about Maria's life experiences and developed better ways to cope with her daughter's seeming detachment. Discussing her concerns about her competence as a mother, her guilt about anger and feelings of frustration led to amelioration of her depression. Within a few months Maria was responding to her mother's attempts to reach out to her and she once again became a happy, well adjusted child both at home and at school.

In the case of Maria, depression in the mother in addition to multiple separations resulted in depressive symptoms in the child. The treatment strategy selected by the consultant was to address the mother's depression, heighten the awareness of school personnel and recommend several family sessions to help the mother-daughter pair reestablish communication. In most instances, however, individual psychotherapy as well as parental counselling is the treatment of choice for depressive reactions which do not respond to environmental manipulation or conjoint therapy.

PLAY THERAPY

Play therapy is the treatment modality most suited for young children. Just as dreams are considered to be the royal road to the unconscious for the adult, so play and imagination (which is mental play) are considered to be the pathways toward the understanding of repressed wishes and unconscious fantasies of the child.

The healthy child plays out universal fantasies giving full vent to his rich imagination; the neurotic child plays out personal fantasies in an attempt to resolve unconscious conflicts and master an earlier psychic trauma. "It is often difficult for psychiatrists who deal with adults (and whose 'sock in trade' is verbal interpretation) to understand how children can play out fantasies and work through areas of conflict without much more than a hint from the therapist. When a child pummels a father doll unmercifully or smashes a clay ball with a mallet, the result is more than merely a release of tension. Fantasies are being enacted, games won, villains conquered in the safety of the familiar office with an understanding adult nearby" (Kestenbaum, 1985). The observing therapist may note in the repetitive play and stories of children the repetition of psychic trauma, an effort for mastery. Neurotic symptoms of the school age child such as obsessional behavior and phobias, may have origins in experiences completely inaccessible through verbal mediation. Inventive child therapists have found that a different therapeutic approach is necessary, whether through doll play (M. Klein, 1948), painting, wood work, puppet play, squiggles, (Winnicott, 1965) or mutual storytelling, a technique suggested by R. Gardner (Gardner, 1971). What is more important than the medium selected for working with children is the degree to which both child and therapist feel comfortable with the choice.

Case 2 – Melanie

Melanie was seen in the pediatric emergency room after her mother found that she had swallowed an undetermined amount of her aspirin tablets. The child psychiatrist was called to evaluate this highly verbal child because she was saying she wanted to die and did not like herself. During the evaluation interview the child stated she was ugly, unloved, felt she was bad, and wanted to die. In her play, mommy and daughter puppets were constantly engaged with each other but frequently were upset, scared and lonely. This information triggered the child psychiatrist consultant to obtain a more detailed family history. The child's mother then confessed that for the last year or so she had been feeling quite dejected and depressed after the loss of her boyfriend. She and Melanie were very close and resembled each other both physically and emotionally. Since Melanie was so verbal and alert, her mother considered her to be her best friend and shared with her all her problems. When she was happy Melanie was happy. When she was sad Melanie either became her only solace or became sad as well. There was no extended family and due to her boyfriend's departure, they had become increasingly close and isolated. As the session evolved the mother burst out into tears and confessed she had been contemplating suicide herself.

The over identification of Melanie with her mother was clearly evident. Melanie, in a way, reflected her mother's mood states, low self-esteem, and most inner wishes. She had acted out her mother's "unspoken" suicidal episodes and consequentially brought them both to treatment.

A dynamically oriented approach was successfully implemented with this dyad.

Themes of separation, individuality and identification were addressed through play with the child and through dyadic interventions with the mother, who was also advised to seek individual treatment. In order to complement, facilitate, and expedite the treatment, an excellent preschool nursery was identified for Melanie and the mother was urged to go back to school and find an "adult" support network.

In many instances depressive reactions in children are related to other developmentive problems. While it is important to address the emotional disturbance, it is crucial to assess the concomitant problem and offer appropriate intervention for the disability. The following case is illustrative.

Case 3 – Gregory, age 5

Gregory was referred for psychotherapy by a speech pathologist with whom he was in treatment for an articulation problem. Gregory's I.Q. was in the superior range; neurological findings, apart from his inability to pronounce most consonants, were negative. Gregory was extremely shy with adults and children alike. He would cling to his mother's skirt refusing to separate from her.

Mrs. T. was Gregory's constant companion who interpreted his needs to the world. She remained with him for the first ten psychotherapy sessions, not only because Gregory would not allow her to leave, but also because the child psychiatrist could not understand him. "Ii ee aa ook" he said, for example, pointing to a Dr. Seuss story. "Gregory wants you to give him that book", his mother translated. Gregory was furious when he was not understood or when anyone, including children, asked him to repeat himself. He would either become sullen and petulant or would fling himself onto the floor in spasms of rage. He said he hated himself and was no good.

The speech therapist worked patiently with him and in a few months Gregory progressed to the point where he was almost always understood. Nevertheless, he would not allow his mother to give up her role as interpreter, however, and became furious when she tried to spend more time with his younger brother.

Gregory's psychotherapy sessions utilized doll play extensively. He was an imaginative child who invented a kingdom where Prince No-No ruled supreme, never allowing anyone to oppose his most simple request. In fact, No-No did not have to ask to have his wishes obeyed. His omnipotence was such that whatever he wished for simply happened, without his having to speak at all. Gregory was both separation-anxious and depressed. He needed help for his basic speech problem but also for his emotional reaction to being different, unable to express himself as others did.

It is impossible to know whether or not those very factors which produced the speech pathology to begin with also played a role in Gregory's more than ordinary fear of new situations, in the degree of his rage outbursts, his separation anxiety and in the lability of his mood. Nonetheless, Gregory's distress from not being able to communicate created such a problem with his developing self-concept, such as lowered self-esteem, that psychotherapeutic intervention was necessary. He was later able to achieve a sense of mastery over his handicap and continue on the path of normal development.

Case 4 – Charles, age $5\frac{1}{2}$

Charles A was referred for psychotherapeutic evaluation by the kindergarten principal because of immaturity, antisocial classroom behavior, and for "being a really sad kid." The psychiatrist found him to be an attractive, well developed child whose occasional grimaces detracted from his overall appearance. He appeared to be clumsy, bumping into furniture, dropping toys and walking with an awkward stride. He was, however, skillful at throwing and catching a ball, balancing, and riding a bike. His fine motor movement was difficult to judge because he refused to hold a pencil or even attempt to draw. He spoke in a high-pitched voice and seemed immature in the development of both articulation (W for L) and diction ("me go there"). When away from his mother, however, these infantilisms for the most part disappeared. He had an extremely short attention span, running to the toy cars one minute, to the puppets the next, and finally to the blocks. When asked to build with lego blocks, his usual response was "No! I won't! I can't!" His overall expression was mournful and anxious.

Mr. A. was a successful professional man who came from a deeply troubled family. His own mother had been hospitalized nine times for manic-depressive disorder before lithium carbonate was prescribed. Two of Mr. A's siblings suffered from depressions but had never been hospitalized. Mr. A was deeply concerned about mental illness in his family but at the same time denied that there was anything wrong with Charles. He quoted the family pediatrician, "Charles is just like a bull around a bunch of sheep – he may be a little overactive but he'll outgrow it."

Mrs. A. was an only child of a wealthy industrialist. A brilliant student, she worked for a prestigious law firm. She had never wanted children and was depressed about Charles' nursery school report, being highly perfectionistic and judgmental herself. She abused alcohol but denied being an alcoholic.

Reportedly, Charles lacked confidence since age three, made no attempt to do new things, and was easily frustrated. Mrs. A. recalled that he had been hypersensitive to noise as an infant and fearful in the presence of strangers. Until age three, moreover, he sucked his fingers continually, and would not leave the house without his favorite pillow. He was teased by his classmates for crying, and for having tantrums; his teacher reported he occasionally lost control and struck children and even adults.

A psychological test had been performed prior to the consultation. The full scale I.Q. was 112 with much scatter; the Bender-Gestalt was poor. Impulsivity was evident; the T.A.T. responses were full of punitive and retaliatory comments. "In this picture the boy is killed and that's all, because Jesus killed him and you know why? Because he didn't say grace after lunch."

The psychiatrist considered the child developmentally immature, very depressed with low self-esteem, and thought of him as someone who "gave up" in the face of perfectionistic parental demands. She felt that his inhibition of curiosity would result in a future learning disability without psychiatric intervention. She recommended psychotherapy, a low-pressured, structured first grade with small classes and sensitive teachers, and weekly parental counselling. The mother, however, failed to come to the family sessions except on rare occasions, so the father became the actively involved parent. There were frequent teacher-therapist contacts, usually by telephone which helped coordinate the therapeutic goals.

In his first therapy session Charles acted out a story with hand puppets, a scene which appeared and reappeared on numerous occasions. A baby tiger, five years old, ran away from his forest cave "because his daddy spanks him and his mother leaves him with the baby sitter. He hates school and wants to hide in his own cave and never come out. He has no friends. He is always scared." The play sessions which followed dealt with similar themes. Charles spent many hours preoccupied with Lego blocks, constructing castles that were safe "with a very strong base." Occasionally he agreed to draw but would give up after one or two attempts, tearing up the paper and sulking. Eventually he would copy the therapist's drawing of a face with simple features or a house with a tree in the yard stroke by stroke. He complained frequently about boys who hate him and frequently called the therapist "stupid, dumb-dumb and idiot."After several months of therapy Charles' school reports from first grade were better. His teacher, nurturing yet firm, was able to set limits from the onset. Charles was soon able to join a group; he began to participate in activities and to read with comprehension and pleasure.

Charles began playing more age-appropriate games, and for the first time, had several friends. By the end of the first grade Charles had reportedly developed more curiosity and was less inhibited in trying new things; he was doing very well scholastically but was still socially very immature, unable to share, to "lose gracefully" or to play happily with others. He still had great difficulty in not "being perfect." Once he attempted to make a clay kangaroo like the one in a picture book. When he couldn't succeed, he threw down the clay, fell to the floor, and cried in a high pitched whining voice. The therapist asked him why he felt he had to be perfect. "It is perfect! I am perfect," he screamed. "But if I'm not perfect, then you won't like me anymore. The kids don't like me . . . I hate everything I do!", he sobbed. The therapist assured him that no one was perfect—not the parents, not the teachers and not her. He reluctantly accepted her statement.

Charles soon began speaking of his troubles with friends and of his concerns about abandonment. The school report at the end of the year was excellent. Charles was reading, spelling and doing math on a second or third grade level. He was more self-reliant and less clinging. He was retested and his I.Q. was now in the superior range (Stanford-Binet, 122). The Bender Test was mature, and his achievement scores in reading and math were consistently several grade levels above second grade. In school Charles displayed an ability to plan an event and did not seem to need the immediate gratification previously required to complete a task. His play became more age appropriate. After two years of therapy, Charles was no longer depressed or anxious—he was an outgoing bright child, competent and on par with his peers both academically and socially.

Charles' case presents several concurrent therapeutic problems. He has a family history of manic depressive illness, and therefore was at risk for developing an affective disturbance. By age three Charles was displaying problems of low self-esteem, mood disturbance and a sense of hopelessness about succeeding in age appropriate tasks such as drawing, reading or playing with other children. In addition, his mother was critical, rejecting, and unwilling to involve herself in Charles' treatment.

The psychodynamic treatment, besides involving the school and the father, consisted of helping Charles become motivated, chiefly through identification with the psychiatrist, try new things in a safe, non-judgmental atmosphere and develop feelings of competence and heightened self-worth.

PSYCHOTHERAPEUTIC INTERVENTIONS WITH SCHOOL AGE DEPRESSED CHILDREN

Psychotherapy with disturbed school age children according to Escalona (Escalona, 1964) has taken two directions: expressive and suppressive. The latter therapy "would be directed at discouraging the expression and acting out of fantasies and providing as much realistic pursuits and strengthening reality testing by all possible means." In treating non-psychotic depressed children of average or above intelligence, expressive therapy is usually the treatment of choice. This type of therapy is derived from concepts inherent in the psychoanalysis of neurotic individuals (i.e. those driven by inner conflicts), and permits the expression of previously unconscious material (i.e. inaccessible to conscious thoughts or memories).

Escalona notes that "fantasies are seen as meaningful and interpreted in the context of the child's reality experience and the relationship between affects (i.e. emotions) and their source, as well as between symptoms and their deeper meaning." While adolescents and adults can deal with their fantasies and dreams by accepting the analyst's interpretations of their deeper meanings and as attempts to solve problems, children are usually unable to draw such conclusions when direct interpretations are made concerning their play and frequently become upset when confronted by their own feelings. How, then, does the child psychotherapist produce change?

The answer lies in the development phase of latency (school age) children, according to Sarnoff (Sarnoff, 1977). Sarnoff views latency as a time of cognitive maturation, in Piagetian terms, and acquisition of new skills and defensive operations. These, in turn, he believes, serve to protect the child from the sexual and aggressive drives so prevalent in the Oedipal phase (preschool). There is a persistence of magical thinking in many neurotic children which interferes with verbalization of certain thoughts and feelings.

It is all right for such a child to "code" his feelings in stories or even write forbidden words on paper to hand to the therapist, but very upsetting to say the words aloud. As one child told her therapist many months after a premature interpretation on his part, "Do you remember that session when I became so angry with you I ran from the room when you said the witch in my story reminded me of mother? Well, you were right, but I couldn't admit it. Somehow hearing you say it made it true, and I couldn't bear thinking that she was really like that. After all, she's the only mother I have."

Since most children are unaware of the origins of their problems, treatment modalities such as the story telling technique is often the most successful method of bringing to the surface hitherto hidden feelings so that they can be dealt with in the therapeutic setting.

In Kestenbaum's modification of the Gardner technique (Kestenbaum, 1985), the young child dictates a story to the therapist so that spontaneity and flow will not be hampered by the rules of spelling or grammar. She recommends that the therapist keep a loose-leaf notebook for each child who wants to "write a book" with plenty of space for illustrations (that can be made when the child becomes "too tired to talk"). The therapist asks many questions about the characters, their backgrounds and their motives which she records in a separate notebook for future reference. Thus a dual purpose is served: the child has a store of information to include in the book at a later date and the therapist has meaningful material that can help him or her plan the direction of the treatment.

Case 5 – Susan, age 7*

Susan was a charming child, a motivated student, but socially isolated, and considered to be a loner by her teachers. Having recently moved from another state she seemed to be in mourning for her best friend, Carol. Her grandfather had died a year earlier. Since that time she had become listless and appeared sad much of the time. Susan eagerly took to her twice weekly sessions with enthusiasm – she delighted in drawing and painting, and illustrated the following story in graphic detail.

Once there was a little girl named Mary. She loved flowers. There was a special hill where Mary planted her seeds. One day she noticed that at the top of the plant there was a bud. Everyday she went back to see if it opened yet. One morning it finally opened up. Inside was a little lady!

"What is your name? My name is Lena," she said.

"You have three wishes, Lena."

"My first wish is that I would want you to play with me – when I am alone, at night time."

"That wish is granted," the little lady said.

"For my second wish I want to go where no one can see me."

The bud closed up. From inside the bud a little voice called "Mary, repeat my name three times and kiss the petals."

Out came a little woman. "Whenever you call, even in your dreams, just call my name three times, kiss the bud, and I will appear."

Mary was happy; she wished for ten more wishes. Her first wish was that if anyone got sick, she would wish them well again. Mary's mother was very upset when Mary went upstairs, thought very hard of the bud and called:

'Lena, Lena, Lena."

Suddenly the little lady appeared.

"What is the trouble?"

"I'm afraid my uncle will die."

"Go to sleep, and don't worry. I'll take care of it."

* Cases 5 and 6 are abstrated from Kestenbaum (1985) "The Creative Process in Child Psychotherapy"

Lena flew to the hospital.

"Uncle Bill, Mary needs you—you can't die; you will get better."

The next day Mary's mother called upstairs:

"Uncle Bill is better. His temperature is normal."

Mary jumped out of bed and raced up the hill, saw her special flower, and kissed it:

"Oh thank you so much for helping." "If it weren't for you, Mary, if you hadn't planted me, I wouldn't be here either."

Susan's subsequent stories continued to contain similar thematic material—prevention of death and loneliness through wish-fulfilling fantasies. Each new tale contained a wish.

One day Mary called upon Lena and said:

"For my tenth wish I want to be as small as you."

"Think of tiny things," Lena told her.

Mary counted to ten and soon became as small as Lena. She stepped on a butterfly and gently sailed up to the flower. It was closed. A bee flew by and opened it for her.

"Now I can live anywhere, whether I'm big or small. Now I am queen of the fairies and I can visit anyone in the world and never be lonely again."

Case 6—William, age 9

William was brought to psychiatric evaluation because of disobedience at school and continual fighting with his younger brother, Tim, aged seven. William was angry and sullen most of the time, and chose to spend most of his free time alone in his room. He was extremely jealous of Tim who, the parents agreed, "knew just how to get his goat". After several initial silent sessions (he was brought to treatment under duress) William agreed to dictate original radio plays into a tape recorder which the therapist then transcribed for the permanent radio script. Often the therapist and the patient acted the various parts aloud using the script written the previous session.

The central characters were two best friends who happened to be cats named Pogo and Chris. Pogo lived with the Wilson family in a small town in the midwest.

One day Mr. and Mrs. Wilson walked into the house with big smiles on their faces. Pogo was sitting on the window still watching the birds.

"Oh how delicious that black one would be for Sunday dinner," he thought.

"Pogo, we have a surprise for you," said Mrs. Wilson. "Look at what we have here."

She pointed to a cage covered by a cotton cloth. Pogo lifted the cloth and looked inside; he jumped back, his tail extended straight up in the air, his eyes as big as saucers. There in the cage was a beautiful colorful parrot. The bird tried to poke her head out of the cage.

"Who are you, anyway?" it squawked. "They didn't tell me there was a stupid cat living here."

"Never mind," said Mrs. Wilson. "You two have to become good friends if you're going to live in the same house."

"I'd rather be dead than make friends with him," Pogo muttered under her breath.

"We're going now," said Mr. Wilson, "So you two be good."

"Well dumb head," Peter said after they had gone. "What's there to do around here for entertainment?"

"I don't know," Pogo answered. "But I'm sure as hell not going to entertain for you."

"If you don't do exactly what I say," Peter croaked, "I'm going to tell the Wilsons that you put ant poison in my bird seed. Then you'll get it. So go entertain me right now. Be quick about it!"

Poor Pogo was so bewildered he didn't know what to do. He didn't want to get the Wilsons angry but he hated Peter, an intruder in his life, and a very obnoxious intruder at that. At first Pogo did everything Peter commanded:

"Play that tuba a little faster, will you dumb head?" Peter ordered, "And hurry up with that pizza. I'm starving. I'm getting hungry for that."

Pogo was still getting sick and tired of being a servant for that stranger. She decided she would think of something to do!

"I have an idea. I'll call Chris over. He'll probably have some good ideas."

She went to the telephone and dialed Chris's number:

"Hello Chris, can you come over here right away?" "I need some help with a new problem—I mean—parrot-we have got."

"OK Pogo. I'll be there in two shakes," Chris answered.

Chris started over. He walked slowly, planning his strategy. By the time he got to the Wilsons, he had decided what to do.

Chris arrived at the Wilsons: "Hi Pogo—what's happening?"

"Oh Chris, the most upsetting thing. This dumb parrot has come to live in our house, and he is driving me crazy."

"Don't worry," said Chris. "I figured out a plan on the way over here. I'll hypnotize the bird, and of course the Wilsons will want him to talk once in a while, and under hypnotic suggestion he won't be able to say anything."

"Gee Chris, that is a terrific idea."

"Well what other genius would think of it?" said Chris modestly. "Well, we're not going to get anywhere just standing here. Come on. Let's get to it."

The two friends went into the living room where Peter was talking up a storm:

"Hi dumb head! I see you have an even dumber friend with you. Is he as stupid as you? Ha, ha!" he crackled.

"Oh shut up," said Pogo, "Stay in your cage and look at the watch that Chris has."

Peter saw a shiny gold watch that Chris was slowly swinging back and forth from a golden chain.

"What are you doing with that watch?" he asked. "Did you steal it?"

"Maybe I did and maybe I didn't. Why don't you look at it for a minute and see if you can tell where it comes from."

"Looks like a watch I've seen before. Help! My eyes are closing and I don't seem to be able to help it," said Peter.

"Keep your eyes on the watch," Chris said slowly in a deep voice. When the clock strikes twelve, you will forget how to speak and you will not be able to speak even one word for twenty-four hours."

The clock started to strike twelve times. "Bong, bong, bong" it goes. At that moment the Wilsons returned from their shopping trip:

"Hello you two. Hello Chris. I've hoped by now you're good friends. Here are some toys and some bird seeds for Peter. How are you Peter?"

The cats stood quietly in silence.

"Peter, I asked you a question. How are you dear?"

Peter felt blank!

"I think the store cheated us. He isn't saying a word. And all the money we spent! What's the use of having a parrot if he can't even say anything?"

"You're right. Let's take him back to the store at once, and get our money back."

Just as they left, Chris spoke. "It worked. We won't have any trouble with jerks like that again, at least not from that pet store."

"It really pays to have a friend like you," Pogo said. "I guess two heads are better than one—you are right!"

William thoroughly enjoyed Pogo's solution to the problem of the unwelcomed intruder. His subsequent stories on themes of sibling rivalry were based on Pogo's attempts to share, to cooperate, to allow the presence of "The New Cat in Town"—the title of his third story—to co-exist with him and Chris.

At no time during the one year treatment was William able to discuss his problem, but there was a remarkable change in behavior at school and at home. His depressive symptoms abated. His school work improved, and he became popular with peers and established a lasting truce with his brother.

DISCUSSION

The two cases presented of school age depressed children demonstrated in part how some child patients who have been unable to master psychic trauma or conflict can make dramatic improvement without directly addressing their own problems or consciously expressed insight.

Susan needed to express her deep sadness and loss in the presence of an understanding adult. William found an interesting way of solving his problem, at first eliminating the brother from his life in the guise of Peter, the parrot, in the first story. He was eventually able to settle for peaceful co-existence.

In both reported cases the parents were seen for counselling at frequent intervals. Without parental involvement and cooperation therapeutic progress is most instances cannot occur. The parents have to be able to entrust the therapist with their children, weather the shifts in behavior and emotions that may occur in their children as a consequence of the therapeutic process, and be willing to understand their own areas of conflict with their children in order to facilitate the effectiveness of the therapeutic interventions.

PSYCHOTHERAPY OF DEPRESSED ADOLESCENTS

The psychotherapeutic modalities that are used in the treatment of depressed adolescents range from those techniques described previously for the treatment of children to those more traditionally employed with adults. The choice of treatment depends upon the maturational level and motivation of the adolescent. In addition to individual psychotherapy, parental counseling, group therapy and family therapy may be required, as well as the use of antidepressant medication. Pharmacotherapy is almost always the treatment of choice for major depressive disorder but it is not helpful unless interpersonal, social and academic problems are dealt with concomitantly by psychotherapeutic intervention (Kestenbaum and Kron, 1987).

The type of psychotherapy is often decided by the consulting psychiatrist. A psychoanalyst will usually recommend a psychoanalytically oriented psychotherapy; a cognitive psychologist will recommend behavior therapy. Both types of treatments have been used successfully as adjunctive to antidepressant medication.

Case 7 – Barbara, age 14

Barbara was an attractive girl, tall and blond who seemed to be completely unaware of her physical beauty. She walked slumped over, her long hair covering her face, her eyes downcast. Her pediatrician recommended a psychiatric evaluation because of poor school performance, especially in history and science. Barbara had lost 12 pounds in two months. She was obviously depressed, but since she refused to speak to the pediatrician or to her parents, she reluctantly agreed to see a psychiatrist.

The family was in the midst of tumultuous change. The parents were living under one roof for financial and legal reasons, but they were actually going through a divorce. The mother had a long history of major depressive disorder (post partum psychosis which the patient had heard about) and had been hospitalized twice for three weeks, once when Barbara was three and again when she was seven. The father, a respected attorney was depressed as well (he was never actually treated for depression). There were two younger siblings, extremely gifted musically as well as academically. The father spent a great deal of time with the boys.

Barbara's first session set the tone for the first weeks of treatment. She barely looked at the interviewer, made little eye contact, and finally said "I'm not going to tell you anything."

The psychiatrist decided that a trial of antidepressant medication (Imipramine) should be given and waited three or four weeks for the medication to have an effect. Barbara soon became more responsive and interested in the treatment process. She used the time to discuss school projects, writing stories, bringing in homework but did not reveal very much in terms of what actually troubled her.

One Sunday afternoon Barbara telephoned the therapist and asked for "talking time." She was sobbing, obviously distraught. Her parents had been fighting when suddenly her father packed his bag and left home, slamming doors and hurling epithets. The psychiatrist asked Barbara to come over on the spot. She talked nonstop for an hour. Memories poured forth about the time when her mother was taken to the hospital in a coma, how frightened she was along in her room at night, how she could not think about homework or friends or anything but her fear of being alone and abandoned. When the therapist saw her the next day Barbara behaved as though nothing had happened. "It seems that displaying emotion must be a punishable crime," the therapist noted. From that time on Barbara was more spontaneous, more revealing of her inner world. She accepted clarifications of feelings and explanations without protest—how she felt insecure and unattractive, ashamed of her natural desires and human emotions.

It soon became clear that emotions in Barbara's home were truly kept under tight control until they exploded in incidents such as the father's sudden leaving. He returned home several nights later, of course, but the scene repeated itself many times during the ensuing months.

Barbara, because of a positive therapeutic alliance, became adept at sharing her feelings with her therapist (her anger towards her parents, her indignation for being subjected to "surprise" traumatic events). She kept a record (she carried a small diary with her) of daily events and recorded her own responses which she shared with the therapist. She was soon able to find more adaptive ways of handling her distressing emotions.

Six months after treatment had begun Barbara's school reports were considerably better. She had won a creative writing award at school, was going out with friends more frequently and her depressive symptoms had disappeared.

Barbara was discharged from treatment after one year. It was difficult to sort out the various factors which had led to Barbara's depression—her own genetic predisposition, her parents' divorce, her early life experiences with a psychotic, depressed mother, but with treatment Barbara became an outgoing and engaging young woman.

A reality-oriented therapeutic approach helped Barbara cope with her difficult family situation and her own sense of worthlessness. She was subsequently able to find more adaptive ways of solving problems.

Case 8—Joshua, age 14

Joshua was referred to treatment due to poor academic performance and irritable behavior. He had low self esteem, a poor self image, and had undergone depressive mood swings that had merited an unsuccessful trial of anti-depressant medication. On closer inspection Joshua was a frail, sensitive young man with an artistic bent who had never been fully accepted by his tougher male peer group even though he had excellent relationships with the adults who surrounded him. He had exhibited many depressive features but did not meet sufficient criteria to place him in a major depressive disorder or dysthymia category. The new therapist wanted Joshua to participate in a process that would be more exploratory and insight-oriented. Themes about close and suffocating parental ties, sexual identity doubts, and early memories of always having to be a good and sensitive boy or "love would be withdrawn" evolved. These themes were explored as the therapist underlined Joshua's unusual and special talents. At the therapy evolved Joshua rediscovered his true self, allowed himself to be more assertive with his family and consequentially with his peer group and his irritable behavior diminished markedly. As he felt happier he felt more secure and accepted by his peers and his grades improved significantly.

Case 9–Naomi, age 16

Naomi was referred by a neurologist for psychiatric evaluation after a comprehensive workshop for headache and vomiting revealed no physical cause for her symptoms. A brilliant high school student, she had become withdrawn and depressed; she was often tearful and had trouble falling asleep. She had begun to express concerns about leaving home for college in another city.

Naomi was the only child of two university professors. The family history was negative for psychiatric disorder. She had been born with a congenital club foot and wore leg braces from six months until age two. She was, therefore, unusually dependent upon her mother, and separation anxiety persisted until after the age of eight. At that time she was evaluated by a child psychiatrist who felt she was not only separation-anxious but depressed as well. She expressed negative feelings about herself, stating she was ugly and stupid. The therapist recommended psychotherapy which involved doll play and story telling. Her doll play revealed a shy, insecure and depressed girl who felt she couldn't compete with other children who could run faster, ice skate better, and "have play dates" with other children. The symptoms disappeared after six months of therapy and the parents decided to discontinue treatment. Naomi did extremely well at school and had several close friends but was still anxious in new environments.

The only time Naomi left home was to attend a summer camp at age 12 but she remained only three days before insisting her parents bring her home. As a teenager Naomi was still shy and reserved; her friends described her as puritanical and prudish. During the initial diagnostic interview the psychiatrist explained that she believed Naomi's preoccupation with bodily complaints and concern about physical illness was a way of not focusing on her real concern–her apprehension about leaving her mother. The consultant recommended psychoanalytically oriented therapy on a twice-weekly basis.

Naomi was a very pretty teenager who looked sad and she seemed unaware of her physical attractiveness. Early sessions were spent describing her headaches, her insomnia and her feelings of ugliness. Despite her high marks she was not concentrating in school and had little interest in her work. She felt basically stupid–"only boys are smart," she insisted. She described her life as "utterly miserable" but she didn't know why.

Naomi believed her parents were "perfect in every way," especially her mother who, despite her own academic work, had always been available to her for correcting homework, criticizing her compositions, shopping for her and "running my life." The idea of life in a dorm with other girls filled her with dread. She was totally unaware of any negative feelings toward her mother. Therefore the first dream was revealing.

Dream: "I'm climbing up a huge, ice-covered hill. I see a woman with a baby trapped by an avalanche. A lady in a toll booth says she has had training as a life saver and will help, but only for money. The mother of the child looks threatening–as if she really wants the baby to die.

The therapist pointed out the obvious association between the lady in the toll booth and her own role as a "paid helper" – and Naomi was able to accept the interpretation. Negative aspects of the mother-child relationship were not discussed at that point.

Within several months Naomi's relationship with the therapist became more secure. She began to express faintly critical feelings about her mother's intrusiveness. "I would really like to choose my own clothes – mother and I have completely different taste. I might hurt her feelings. Then I'd feel guilty." Any attempt the analyst made to suggest that she might be angry with mother at times, that no one could be as perfect as the mother she described, was met by resistance and denial. "You weren't there. You don't understand everything." Naomi began to be more assertive with the therapist and became angry on several occasions, who pointed out that Naomi had a right to all of her feelings, and the therapist didn't seem to be demolished by them, as she feared.

Six months into the treatment Naomi began to speak critically about one of her friends – Barbara. "She is so pushy – so sure her ideas are right – I got so mad at her I finally blew up and told her what I think." To her amazement Barbara didn't "collapse," didn't abandon her, and if anything, the friendship became stronger. Shortly after this episode Naomi revealed a fantasy with which she had been preoccupied for years.

"I am a teen-age thief forced to work for a female version of Fagin who is so evil, so vicious, so corrupt that she sends all her daughters on the street to steal or sell their bodies so she can live in luxury.

The fantasies were elaborate and full of graphic detail. These revelations led to a discussion of Naomi's real-life, how she felt trapped at home, afraid to ask for anything for herself or even attend school parties. Her mother would be disapproving of any dating, she believed. Naomi was deeply afraid of her mother's criticism. Naomi's association led to her perceived difference in her parents' attitudes about social life with peers compared to those of her friends' parents.

Several weeks later, a gradual change in Naomi's social behavior became evident. She began to have "sleep-overs" at girlfriends' homes, went on a shopping spree with a friend, and had a momentous battle over a new short skirt she bought by herself.

During the next few weeks torrents of rage emerged, chiefly directed toward the mother (detailed recollections of prohibitions and subtle "put-downs"). "She always made me feel I was too stupid to get anything right by myself," she complained. Naomi seemed to forget all the positive aspects of the relationship she had described in the past when mother had stayed home from work to care for her when she was ill and when she had carefully worked with her to overcome her orthopedic handicap in early life.

After several months, however, Naomi's view of her mother became more realistic and more integrated. She also began to see herself as separate from her mother with her own personality, her own needs, her own special attributes. The analyst frequently commented on the positive comments Naomi's friends and teachers made about her appearance, intellect, special attributes as a way of helping her change her negative view of herself. By now her depressive symptoms had, for the most part, disappeared. There were no more physical complaints.

The analysis was shortened by necessity; Naomi left for college after 13 months of analysis. Follow-up semi-annual visits revealed that Naomi made successful adaptation to college life, was popular with girls and boys, and had her first intimate relationship with a fellow pre-law student. She remained on excellent terms with both parents and experienced none of the symptoms which had so troubled her in high school. The initial analytic work with Naomi had centered around her inability to integrate the good-mother, bad-mother fantansies into a whole person (in psychoanalytic terminology "splitting").

Once Naomi could view her mother in a more realistic light, she could go through the "transference plus real" therapeutic relationship and allow herself to separate from her mother. Fearful of her sexual and aggressive drives, Naomi had remained dependent on her mother in order to avoid facing her own secret wishes. "Mother wouldn't want me to date, to be sexual," she had rationalized. As long as mother was an external law-enforcer, Naomi did not have to deal with her own specific feelings. She learned through the analytic therapy that she herself could control these feelings and was able to regulate her own life, make choices about dates and burgeoning sexual relationships and feel she could handle her own life as an individual separate from her parents.

Naomi's treatment illustrates some of the issues confronting the therapist working with depression in adolescence. An understanding of those regressive forces which kept the child as toddler and later as teenager, from the push toward independence and mastery, is, of course, crucial in this case. The therapist as "transference object plus," is important in maintaining equilibrium, and helping the adolescent establish their own set of values as different but not too different as to be ego alien from the family's values (Kestenbaum, 1981).

After psychotherapeutic intervention the Naomi with heightened self-esteem was able to make independent decisions about her future. She was able to establish new intimate relationships outside the family while still maintaining a loving relationship with the primary family.

This vignette illustrates traditional psychoanalytic therapy with a depressed adolescent. Such therapy differs from a cognitive approach in that neurotic conflicts are resolved by the use of transference (i.e., as traits of past relationships projected on to the analyst), interpretation of childhood experiences as well as of current day to day activities and interpersonal involvements (Kestenbaum, 1980).

CONCLUSION

As exemplified by all these vignettes, depression in children and adolescents can span a variety of presentations. The intensity and style of the symptom expression will depend on the individual's genetic loading, cognitive and developmental level, and family and peer environment. The severity and variety of depressive features can include a range of diagnostic categories; from Major Depressive Disorders, to Dysthymia, to Adjustment Disorders with depressive features, to brief depressive reactions. certainly several depressions cause a high level of dysfunctionality and frequently consist of many vegetative signs, require pharmacotherapy and occasionally hospitalization. Those that are secondary to specific traumatic events, psychosocial stressors, or separations may require more focused interventions. Those that are mainly the product of conflict, inner turmoil, and/or misunderstandings based on previous experiences often require more individualized approaches. In all, nevertheless, depression has an impact on the child or the adolescent as well as on their families. How the individual feels about the depression, how it effects him, and how he copes with it in view of his previous experiences has to be also addressed.

Certainly treatment efficacy and specificity with children and adolescents has to be yet further explored. This is an area fraught with methodological problems and still not sufficiently researched. In terms of psychoanalytically-oriented approaches, there has been much revision and many questions posed in terms of adequate research methodology. While we wait for further knowledge, we still depend on the somewhat controversial research literature and still depend highly on the clinical and theoretical basis of our knowledge.

Psychoanalytic approaches with children and adolescents must include their ongoing maturational growth as well as the strong influence of parental figures in their conflict development and resolution. As a consequence, but frequently as an adjunctive approach to the primary individually oriented therapy, environmental manipulation and family intervention is necessary. The individual child or adolescent in the "neutrality" of the office will hopefully be able to express without inhibitions his or her innermost feelings, develop and strengthen better coping styles, and have the chance to re-experience the conflicts with therapist. It is not an approach that works for all children and there are many who do well, others who remain the same, and still others who would benefit more from other approaches.

Through play therapy, story telling and dream recanting, the fantasy world of the individual and the complex process of his inner world is both understood and facilitated. The child can often be released of his tension and indirectly allowed to develop new and more mature coping mechanisms. Issues of self-esteem and self-image can be addressed within the supportive and safe "laboratory" of the therapeutic setting. In many cases as the child re-experiences, releases, and better understands his conflicts, he feels empowered and his depressive affect is diminished. As this occurs his understanding of his parents becomes more realistic and the behavior secondary to his maladaptive depression is often no longer necessary. This process is certainly catalyzed by the concomitant cooperation of the child's family and important others and certainly requires well trained, empathic, and creative therapists well immersed in child and adolescent developmental theory.

References

Anthony, E. J. (1975) Two contrasting types of adolescent depression and their treatment in *Depression and Human Existence*, ed. E. J. Anthony and T. Benedek, Boston: Little Brown.

Arieti, S. (1967) *The Intrapsychic Self*, New York: Basic Books.

Arieti, S. (1970) The structural and psychodynamic role of of cognition in the human psyche, in *The World Biennial of Psychiatry and Psychotherapy*, Vol. I, ed. S. Arieti, New York: Basic Books.

Beck, A. (1976) *Cognitive Therapy and Emotional Disorders*, New York International Universities Press.

Bemporad, J. (1982) Depression in childhood and adolescence in *Handbook of Affective Disorders*, ed. E.S. Paykel, Edinburgh: Churchill Livingstone.
Bemporad, J., Won Lee, K. (1984) Developmental and psychodynamic aspects of childhood depression. *Child Psychiatry and Human Development*, **24**(3), 145–157.
Blos, P. (1968) Character formation in adolescence, *Psychoanalytic Study of the Child*, 23: New York: International Universities Press, pp. 245–265.
Bowlby, J. (1973) *Separation: Attachment and Loss*, Vol. 2, New York: Basic Books.
Bowlby, J. (1980) *Attachment and Loss III: Loss, Sadness, and Depression*. New York: Basic Books.
Bowlby, J. (1988) Psychodynamic treatment of depressed adolescents. *Journal of Clinical Psychiatry*, **49**(9), 26–31.
Carlson, G.A., Cantwell, D.P. (1980) Unmasking masked depression in children and adolescents. *American Journal of Psychiatry*, **137**, 445–449.
Cytryn, L., McKrew, A. H. (1972) Proposed classification of childhood depression. *American Journal of Psychiatry*, **129**, 149–155.
Escalona, S. (1964) Some considerations regarding psychotherapy with psychotic children in *Child Psychiatry*, ed. R. Haworth, New York: Basic Books, pp. 50–58.
Freud, A., Burlingham, D. (1944) *Infants Without Families*, New York: International Universities Press.
Gardner, R. (1971) *Therapeutic Communications with Children: The Mutual Story Telling Technique*, New York: Jason Aronson.
Glaser, K. (1967) Masked depression in children and adolescents. *American Journal of Psychotherapy*, **21**, pp. 565–574.
Harter, S. (1983) Developmental perspectives on the self-system in socialization, personality, and social development, *Mussen's Handbook of Child Psychology*, 4th Edition, ed. E.M. Hetherington, New York: Wiley Press.
Kestenbaum, C.J. (1979) Children at risk for manic-depressive illness. *The American Journal of Psychiatry*, **156**, 1206–1207.
Kestenbaum, C.J. (1981) Aspects of the therapeutic relation in child analysis in *Changing Concepts in Psychoanalysis*, ed. S.E.O. Klebanow, New York: Gardner Press.
Kestenbaum, C.J. (1985) The creative process in child psychotherapy. *American Journal of Psychotherapy*, **39**(4), 479–489.
Kestenbaum, C.J., Kron, L. (1987) Psychoanalytic intervention with children and adolescents: A combined treatment approach. *Journal of the Academy of Psychoanalysis*, **15**(2), 155–174.
Klein, M. (1948) *Contributions To Psychoanalysis*, 1921–1945, London: Hogarth Press.
Kovacs, M., Beck A.T. (1977) An empirical-clinical approach towards a definition of childhood depression, *Depression in Childhood: Diagnosis, Treatment and Conceptual Models*, J.G. Schulterbrandt, A. Rosten (eds) New York: Raven Press.
Kovacs, M. (1986) A developmental perspective on methods and measures in the assessment of depressive disorders, *The Clinical Interview in Depression in Young People: Developmental and Clinical Perspectives*, ed. Rutter, M, Izard, C, *et al.* New York: Guilford Press.
Mahler, M.S. (1952) On child psychosis and schizophrenia – autistic and symbiotic infantile psychoses. *Psychoanalytic Study of the Child*, **7**, 286–305.
McConville, B.J., Boag, L.C. *et al* (1973) Three types of childhood depression. *Canadian Psychiatric Association Journal*, **18**, 244–138.
Milrod, D. (1988) A current view of the psychoanalytic theory of depression with notes on the role of identification, orality, and anxiety. *Psychoanalytic Study of the Child*, **2**, 113–117.
O'Brien, J.D. (1983) *Intervention and Prevention Strategies for Children and Depressed Mothers*, ed. T.A. Petti, New York: Hayworth Press.
Pozanski, E., Zrull, J. (1970) Childhood depression: clinical characteristics of overtly depressed children. *Archives of General Psychiatry*, **23**, 8–15.
Rholes, W.S., Blackwell, J. *et al* (1980) A developmental study of learned helplessness. *Developmental Psychology*, **16**, 616–624.
Rie, H.E. (1966) Depression in childhood: A survey of some pertinent contributions. *Journal of the American Academy of Child Psychiatry*, **5**, 653–683.
Rutter, M. (1986) The developmental psychopathology of depression: issues and perspectives in depression in young people. *Developmental and Clinical Perspectives*, ed. Rutter, M. Irsard, C., *et. al* New York: Guilford Press.
Sandler, J., Joffe, W.G. (1965) Notes on childhood depression. *International Journal of Psychoanalysis*, **46**, 88–106.
Sarnoff, O. (1977) *Latency*, New York: Jason Aronson.

Spitz, R. (1945) An inquiry into the genesis of psychiatric conditions in early childhood. *Psychoanalytic Study of the Child* **1**, 53–74.

Spitz, R. (1946) Hospitalism: A follow-up report on investigation described in Volume I, 1945. *Psychoanalytic Study of the Child*, **2**, 113–117.

Toolan, J.M. (1962) Depression in children and adolescents. *American Journal of Orthopsychiatry*, **32**, 404–414.

Winnicott, D.W. (1965) *The maturational process and the facilitating environment*, New York: New York University Press.

14 Pragmatic Approaches to the Treatment of Prepubescent Depression

Emily Klass and Richard Gallagher

Division of Child and Adolescent Psychiatry, Schneider Children's Hospital of Long Island Jewish Medical Center, New Hyde Park, NY 11042, USA

PEDIATRICIAN AS GATE-KEEPER

From the late 1970s, groups of researchers have investigated the rate of presentation of psychiatric illness in pediatric settings. These studies were designed to examine the role of the pediatrician in the assessment and treatment of childhood disorders. Although rates vary with each study, researchers indicate that 50% of persons with a mental disorder were treated in primary care settings rather than by mental health specialists. According to one study, 20% of children with mental disorders receive specialist treatment while the rest are cared for by pediatricians and or receive no treatment (Regier *et al*, 1978: 685). This and other finding suggest that the pediatrician should play a vital role in the care of the mental health needs of children. In the case of depressive disorders, although rates are low in the pediatric population, emphasis should be placed on making the diagnosis since it is a chronic and debilitating condition that can be underdiagnosed.

Epidemiological studies highlight the high rates of psychiatric disorders found in the general population. For example, data from a survey of Monroe County, New York (Goldberg *et al*, 1984: 285) indicate a point prevalence of 5.1% for emotional problems among children seen by pediatricians. Pediatricians pinpointed more boys having emotional problems than girls and found that the prevalence increases with age with the peak in children of 10 to 14 years. Specific review by demographic characteristics pointed to a higher rate of problems for African-American patients, and a greater prevalence for patients who qualified for Medicaid. Children from single-parent families had twice the rate of problems of 2-parent families. Diagnoses made for all children were predominantly "adaptation" reactions, specific developmental disorders, hyperactivity and conduct disorder with half evaluated as having at least a moderate degree of functional impairment. Fifty percent of the patients found to have had a mental illness or mental problem were referred for psychological care. Goldberg's findings were comparable with other researchers who report rates of 9% (Bailey *et al*, 1978: 621) or 5–15% (Starfield *et al*, 1980: 163) with the higher rates present in children of low socioeconomic status.

Costello (1986: 1048) discusses the accuracy of pediatricians' diagnoses of psychopathology by comparing their rates of diagnoses with the rates of corresponding diagnoses from community based surveys. The comparison suggests that pediatricians underdiagnose psychiatric problems by as much as one half. Costello raises several hypotheses for this situation: (1) parents may not present pediatricians with their concerns; (2) pediatricians do not identify these problems; or, (3) pediatricians do not want to attach labels to children. Interviews indicate that pediatricians believe that "they do not have the time and/or training to treat" (Costello, 1986: 1048). Pediatricians may be asking important questions but may not question specifics which would uncover psychiatric difficulties.

These studies indicate that pediatricians could serve as the initial contact for mental health services for a significant portion of the population of youth with mental health disorders. However, to serve in that role, primary care givers need to be familiar with the characteristics of mental disorders and learn practical methods for their treatment. For depressive disorders, evaluation and treatment methods are different for prepubscent and adolescent patients. This chapter discusses the differences between prepubescent and adolescent disorders and details evaluation and treatment methods for the younger group.

CLINICAL CHARACTERISTICS OF PREPUBERTAL DEPRESSION

Depression can be a debilitating experience for adults, adolescents and young children. Researchers have been focusing on the manifestations of depression in childhood and adolescence and are beginning to make strides in treatment. Although it had been thought that many syndromes in childhood were "masks" for depression, it has become clear that children and adolescents can express depression either verbally or nonverbally. It is still believed to be rare to see chronic depression, but long episodes of major depressive disorder, repetitive unhappy episodes in dysthymia, and adjustment reactions with depressed mood are present and hinder functioning in early childhood.

Asking salient questions to diagnose depression and treating the condition are complex tasks which require attention to methods of obtaining information and decisions about from whom information should be obtained. Direct questioning of children is often fruitless as they might not want information known or they do not know how to tell what is wrong.

Many observable behaviors associated with depression in children provide clues for its detection. *Depressed mood* is the cornerstone of the clinical diagnosis of depression. Investigating signs of depressed mood in children, especially in preschool children, requires attention to non-verbal signs which can include a persistent look of sadness, downcast eyes, saggy lips, a distinct look of unhappiness or even a "bland" or "frozen" expression. The last two signs are most difficult to identify and are easily overlooked. For children, reliance on non-verbal signs is important for it is difficult for them to label their mood. Usually, this changes in adolescence as the capacity for self-reflection increases.

A second sign of depression concerns interest level and capacity to experience pleasure. A chief attribute of childhood is the ability to experience joy. It is said that children's baseline mood is one of happiness whereas adults usually experience a more neutral mood. A striking characteristic of depression in children and adolescents is *anhedonia*. Children or adolescents who look bored or apathetic or who do not seem to enjoy or be interested in anything may be expressing sadness. Children, but particularly adolescents, are apt to say they are bored rather than feeling unhappy. In a comprehensive study of the clinical signs of depression in children and adolescents, researchers found that anhedonia or lack of interest was experienced by 88% of the children in the sample (Ryan *et al*, 1987: 854–861).

Another significant symptom of depression is impairment in *concentration*. Abrupt decline in children's school work may indicate the onset of depression. A slow decline in school work may be due to a depression with an insidious onset. Poor school performance may be due to lack of interest or difficulty in concentration. Of course, it may indicate other difficulties as well. School and family make up much of a child's experiences in the world, so a decline in functioning in either one of these areas is quite significant. Therefore, it is always important to question school performance, interest and changes in ability to concentrate. In the study cited earlier, 86% of children and adolescents with a major depression exhibited decreased concentration. By itself, however, school performance should not be used because strong students who are depressed can continue to perform well academically.

Although not commonly associated with adult depression, *irritability and anger* are quite common in depressed adolescents, and somewhat common in children. Indeed, according to the latest American Psychiatric Association Diagnostic and Statistical Manual of Mental Disorders (American Psychiatric Association, 1987: 222), depression in teenagers and adolescents can be suspected by either the presence of persistent depressed *or* irritable mood.

Fatigue, a behavior which is also at odds with normal expectations of the behavior of youth, should serve as a warning signal. Children who take naps after school and teenagers who remain in bed even when not sleeping may be demonstrating physiological signs. Children with this problem often present in the pediatric setting on repeated occassions.

Feelings of *worthlessness* and lack of self-esteem are common in children and adolescents who are depressed. Younger children can talk about concrete concerns, how they look, if their friends like them or whether they would like to change things about themselves, but they often do not have the language or cognitive ability to talk about feelings of self-worth.

Forms of insomnia (initial, middle or terminal) or *hypersomnia* are fairly frequent symptoms associated with depression as well. Some children lie awake at night waiting to fall asleep—some worrying, others simply watching TV. Often associated in parents' minds with medical illnesses, sleep and eating disturbances are usually brought first to the pediatrician.

Social withdrawal is frequently seen in children and adolescents who are depressed although it may be a sign of other difficulties the child is experiencing as well. It also may be long standing, or have abrupt onset. Difficulty making friends is extremely troubling to children. Children or teenagers who have been depressed for a long time will often have poor social skills from lack of interest and experience. Often children or adolescents who are depressed feel unworthy of having friends and will give up trying. Sometimes, children and adolescents turn to animals for comfort and will become extremely attached to them. One 10 year old girl we saw had become socially withdrawn from parents and friends, but took extremely good care of her pet rabbit.

Other symptoms of depression include extreme lethargy or restlessness, hyperphagia or anorexia, feelings of helplessness or guilt, conduct problems, and suicidal thoughts or actions. Suicidal thoughts, gestures and attempts are rare in childhood, but become more prevalent in adolescence. Physiological changes may explain why this transition occurs or it may be that adolescents have greater ability to look ahead and plan. When combined with a negative depressed approach to the world, the future may be seen as too bleak to face. Adolescents who have a Major Depressive Disorder are at an increased risk for attempting suicide, particularly if there are co-occuring conditions of conduct problems, impulsivity and substance abuse.

When comparing the symptom picture of depressed children with that of depressed adolescents, it appears that prepubertal children display more depressed appearance, have more somatic complaints, experience agitation, and have more depressive hallucinations than adolescents. Hopelessness, oversleeping, weight loss and weight gain seem to occur more often in adolescents than in prepubertal children (Ryan *et al*, 1987: 860).

Case report

Jennifer's parents brought their 11 year old daughter to the pediatrician because of a panoply of symptoms. She was complaining of shooting pains in her arms and legs, and frequent headaches, eye blinking and urination. The weekend before the visit to the pediatrician, Jennifer told her father that it would be easier to go to sleep and never wake up. Symptoms were very similar to those of Jennifer's older sister who had them a few years prior when she was 13 years of age so her parents had a feeling that "there might be something more" to her condition than met the eye.

Jennifer was a tall, lanky, brown haired girl, who walked and sat in a stooped position. When asked about school, she reported that she had begun having trouble completing her work and did not care whether it was done as well as her parents expected. Mother, a teacher, reported that Jennifer frequently forgot to bring her assignments home and, although she had always been disorganized, this trait was now interfering markedly with performance. Within the last year, tension was building at home, a divorce was planned although parents continued to live under the same roof. Mother stated that Jennifer "is wilting before their eyes". Her pediatrician asked Jennifer why she thought she may be having difficulties and she said that her first cousin was killed in a car accident 4 years ago and that lately she had been "thinking about him a lot". She also stated that her maternal grandmother died 2 years ago and that when she thinks about her, she begins to cry. She reported difficulty falling asleep at night because of such thoughts. When told of these concerns, parents were surprised that their daughter was still giving any thoughts to these experiences. Her doctor asked if she still enjoyed usual activities and Jennifer reported that she did, but not nearly as much as she had in the past. When asked to address what she thought would happen, she said she felt that she was going to become a cripple and maybe die, go to heaven and meet up with her cousin and grandmother.

Jennifer presented with compelling physical symptoms but because she was questioned adroitly, clear symptoms of depression emerged as well – initial insomnia, anorexia, disinterest, fatigue, passive suicidal thoughts. Family stress and a model for the presentation of physical symptoms complete the picture of a child with a depressive disorder.

Differential diagnosis

Other chapters in this volume review co-morbidity, questions of differential diagnosis and theories of etiology of depression in childhood. Presented here is a brief compilation of key problems associated with the presentation of symptoms of depression in children.

1) *Physical or emotional treatment*: As discussed comprehensively in Dr. Green's chapter, neglect and physical or sexual maltreatment can often result in symptoms of depression, particularly dysphoria and difficulties with sleeping and eating, guilt, low self-esteem, and suicidal thoughts and actions. Indeed, the relationship between depression and abuse and neglect is so compelling in its frequency that whenever symptoms of depression are present, the assessment of physical and emotional neglect is recommended.

2) *Chronic Physical Illness*: The impact of chronic physical disorder on children is discussed extensively in Dr. Erickson's chapter. Chronic illnesses function as a risk factor for depression. Although most children with physical illnesses remain psychologically healthy, there is an increase in the prevalence of depression in this population and an increase in the rate of psychological distress in siblings of the chronically ill.

3) *Divorce*: Attending to family functioning when there is a question of depression is vital. As outlined in Dr. Weisman's chapter, there is a strong familial relationship in depression, particularly in early childhood. A nearly universal response to divorce appears to be a reaction of fear and anger which can lead to an anxious or depressed state (Hetherington *et al*, 1985: 525). Depending on the age of the child and the circumstances of the divorce, the nature of the difficulties will vary. Wallerstein (1985: 550) found that the predominant response of younger children (6–8) was an open and pervasive sadness. They felt grief that was overwhelming and it was not possible to allay their anxiety. Most of their sadness was connected with a longing for an absent father.

If these symptoms are present independent of the associated features of depression, then this would be a considered a more usual response to divorce in this age group. Just as with a bereaved child, it is important for the primary care practitioner to evaluate the child to make certain of an effective adjustment.

4) School Difficulties: The relationship between depression and learning disabilities is clear. Demoralization can accompany undiagnosed learning disabilities. Loss of self-esteem and feelings of guilt may also be present when children do not believe that they are performing as they should. Years of feeling frustrated, confused, stupid or impaired naturally take their toll and create a situation of "learned helplessness" which may be generalized outside of the school situation.

5) *Acute Illness*: Depressive disorders can be present in children with other illnesses because of a pre-existing depression, a psychological reaction to the illness or as a manifestation of the illness or medications used to treat it. (Dr. Neumann's chapter in this volume reviews the possibilities.)

ASSESSMENT METHODS

The previous section delineates areas that require review when depression is suspected. This section discusses the practical steps for accomplishing the evaluation. The recommended procedures rely on multiple methods and multiple sources of information. The approach is redundant to make certain that cases of depression in mild and severe forms are not missed.

Several aspects of childhood depression support the need for a multi-method, multi-source evaluation. Since, as noted, depressed children's moods may be markedly more variable than those found in depressed adults, reliance on observation at one particular time is not valid. Second, children have a difficult time discussing their feelings in general and sadness in particular so reliance on self-report is dangerous. Children below puberty are not able to view themselves objectively and may not report their feelings accurately. When they do report, their evaluations are often highly inaccurate. Children under 5 years of age have a strong tendency to deny the occurrence of sad events even after they were witnessed to respond with extended crying to those events (cf. Digdon and Gotlib, 1985: 169). Older children up to the age of 9 or so are unstable in their reports on feelings often shifting from one interview to another. Parental reports by themselves are not sufficient because parents can be effective reporters on their children's behavior, but often miss indications of depressive and anxiety disorders. Additionally, in the pediatric setting, parental report or lack of report of problems cannot be considered to be perfectly useful because parents do not always perceive pediatricians as interested in mental health problems and do not discuss them even when they are worried (Costello, 1986: 1046). Finally, observation of a child in the typical office encounter cannot be utilized alone because this method fails to detect known cases of psychiatric disturbance in children (Costello, 1986: 1047).

Given the problems with detection, it is recommended that evaluation be based on a combination of: (1) parental report, (2) self-report, (3) teacher report, and, (4) where feasible, observations by others including the physician, siblings, and peers.

Parental report measures and teacher report measures

The initial step in assessment requires a broad review of behavioral and emotional adjustment to pinpoint children at risk. Several instruments are available that help determine which children are likely to have problems. These instruments are most often completed by parents, but teacher versions are also available so that two perspectives can be gained. They require little professional time for administration. When provided on a consistent basis to all patients encountered in well-child and sick visits, they have utility in finding the children at risk and sensitizing parents to the idea that the practitioner is concerned about behavioral and emotional development. When provided only for children in which a suspicion of problems is present, the measures help place the child in comparison to others of the same age and gender, so that the seriousness of the complaints can be determined. Two instruments with particular utility in a pediatric setting are the Child Behavior Checklist (CBCL, Achenbach and Edelbrock, 1983) and the Pediatric Symptom Checklist (PSC, Jellinek and Murphy, 1990: 273–278).

The CBCL is an 108-item measure that asks parents to determine whether certain descriptions are either "very true", "mostly true", or "not at all true" of the child of concern. Items sample a broad range of behavioral and emotional problems including inattention, opposition to authority, nervousness, limited happiness, and expressions of self-hate. The instrument has received extensive attention during its 15-year development so that standards and norms have been set for clusters of items representing different forms of psychopathology. For the purposes of screening, the clusters of concern are the collection of items reflecting "internalizing" and "externalizing" problems. Internalizing disorders include depression, anxiety, social withdrawal, and retreat from challenges. Aggressive behaviors, noncompliance, and hyperactivity are subsumed in the externalizing disorders. A child's score on either dimension can be compared with a nationally representative set of norms to determine if he or she falls in the range suggestive of maladjustment. For the purposes of assessing depression, any child with an elevated internalizing score should be targeted for further review.

The Pediatric Symptom Checklist can be used in a similar way. It is less well-developed as a diagnostic instrument, but has the advantage of short administration time and fewer items. Thirty-two problematic behaviors or reactions are presented and the rating person, a parent or teacher, indicates the frequency with which the items are observed in a particular child. In well-care settings, it has been used to accurately select children at risk for mental health disorders. For depression, it is expected to be useful if pinpointing children in need of further review if relevant items such as "spends more time alone", are marked as frequently observed.

Self-rating scales and diagnostic interviews

The second step in assessment requires focusing attention on children indicated to be at risk by the broad measures completed. Neither of the suggested measures for broad screening provides a specific review for depression. To attain a detailed determination of a child's problems, two further steps are suggested. First, children should be provided with questionnaires specifically designed for depression. Second, parents and children should be interviewed about the child's behavior for symptoms that reflect the diagnostic criteria for the range of depressive disorders from adjustment disorder to dysthymic disorder to major depressive disorder.

In the first step, two brief questionnaires have been found effective. The Depression Self-Rating Scale (DSRS, Birelson, 1981: 73–88) is recommended for use with young children because it has a simple format and questions are presented in easily understood language. Children are asked to acknowledge whether they recently experienced symptoms of depression including sadness, loneliness, and physical symptoms such as frequent stomach aches. This measure, available in the original article reporting on its development, has been shown to pinpoint the vast majority of children with depressive disorders in psychiatric samples (Asarnow and Carlson, 1986: 496). The Children's Depression Inventory (CDI; Kovacs, 1985: 995–998), is a 27-item measure that can be read by the child or to the child that reviews symptoms of depression which may be experienced by the child. For example, a child indicates whether he or she is "sad all of the time", "sad sometimes", or "not sad at all". Using established norms obtained from several studies (Finch *et al*, 1985: 424; Kovacs, 1983:; Smucker *et al*, 1986: 25–40), the CDI can be effective in detecting levels of depression. Scores of 16 or higher reflect unusual levels of sadness, limited energy, and low self-esteem.

Detailed interviewing provides the next set of data. The responses of the child to the DRS or CDI can be used as a starting point for the interview. The pediatrician can discuss the frequency and length of time that a child has demonstrated the behavior of concern or experienced the reaction highlighted by items. For example, if a child indicates that she or he has been "feeling like crying most of the time", this can be explored through sensitive questioning which reviews the frequency with which the child experiences this sensation and the estimated time period in which such a sensation has been present. All aspects of depression can be reviewed in such a way using the diagnostic criteria spelled out in DSM-III-R. Thus, physical aspects (e.g. sleep patterns, eating habits), emotional aspects (e.g. level of excitement, frequency of crying, anhedonia) , and psychological aspects (e.g. tolerance for disappointment, level of esteem, suicical thoughts) are to be reviewed in detail. Parental observation of the same symptoms should also be questioned in detail. Guidelines for conducting such an interview can be found through review of structured diagnostic interviews such as the Kiddie SADS (Puig-Antich and Ryan (1986) and the Diagnostic Interview for Children and Adolescents (Herjanic and Campbell, 1977).

Child observers

If time and resources permit, a final area for review is the child's relationships with siblings and peers. Often direct questioning of children who spend a great amount of time with the child provides data that neither the child him/herself nor adult observers are able to gather. Classmates have proven to be useful in pinpointing members of their class who show signs of depression (Lefkowitz and Tesiny, 1980: 47). A practical version of peer review could be obtained by discussing the target child's behavior with a best friend. Of course, using this method will require appropriate consent from the parents of the best friend as well as the child's parents. Another version of peer review could occur through discussion with siblings. Siblings may be aware of the child's energy level in play, may be able to discuss frustration tolerance and emotional reactivity, and could describe situations in which the child expressed hopelessness or intense discouragement. The advantage of questioning siblings results from their ability to report on situations and reactions of the child that occurred outside of their parents' awareness.

TREATMENT IN PREPUBESCENT CHILDREN

Once depression is strongly suspected, the pediatrician's choice is to refer the case to appropriate mental health personnel or to continue primary care of the case. In a survey of the treatment provided to children with emotional disorders by primary care physicians, Goldberg *et al* (1984: 285) found that supportive therapy and counseling were provided to 81% of the cases. Environmental changes were recommended in 45% of the cases and 11% were prescribed medication. Although pediatricians are providing much care (only 49% are referred out of practices) , the ethical and responsible course for treatment is that it is guided by a mental health professional through frequent consultation by the treating physician or through direct referral. Consultation or direct referral is essential because treatment for depression in prepubertal children is not clear cut. Inappropriately treated depression can have lasting effects on the child's health, academic status, psychological growth, and, in some cases, safety.

It is suggested that the approaches discussed below be used by the pediatrician as long as several conditions are met. First, the child is not suicidal. Second, the child is free from physiological symptoms of major depression such as major alterations in sleep or eating habits. Third, there is no evidence of abuse or major parent-child problems such as significant neglect or frequent derogation of the child by the parent. Fourth, the parents or caretakers are willing to change their actions and a collaborative relationship with the child's caretakers can be established because much of the effort required for treatment will come from the caretakers. If these conditions cannot be met, it is recommended that the child be referred to a child mental health professional for evaluation.

Definitive guidelines for treatment are not available because necessary research studies are yet to be conducted. Several small scale studies of careful design provide suggestions on treatment methods that have utility, but no specific protocol can be pinpointed as more effective or efficient than others. Therefore, the information provided should be considered as suggestive and in need of modification as further data are gathered.

Two factors guide selection of treatment methods. The first is the developmental status of the child and the second is the complexity of children's lives. A child's experience is composed of many components including activities, family life, social life, emotional responses, intellectual processing, and physiological status. Depression can be present because of problems in one or several of these components.

Developmental considerations

For children 8 years and younger, psychotherapeutic attention is most fruitfully directed toward their environments, while older children benefit from attention to their environment and to discussions of their experience. Counseling or psychotherapy in the traditional sense is of limited utility with younger children for they are poor at reflecting on their own experiences and cannot use advice on altering such abstract internal states as their feelings or thoughts. Play therapy and its variants could be considered, but no well-designed studies have indicated that they have utility with childhood depression.

Ages eight and younger

It is likely that children 8 years and younger experience depression as a consequence of decreases in two facets of life: (1) pleasurable events and (2) reinforcement of efforts expended. Although it could be assumed that these facets refer to "fun" activities and praise in a simple sense, broader definitions are intended. Pleasurable experiences could include simple things such as trips to the zoo or having play dates, but may also include frequent contact with a busy parent, security-providing hugs, and dinner times together with the child's favorite foods. Reinforcers could include praise for efforts at school and at home, but can also include repeated exposure to statements from adults that indicate that the child's ideas are respected or that his/her actions are useful. Treatment is designed to arrange that pleasurable events and reinforcers for efforts occur frequently so that the child experiences more positive emotions.

Several methods are available to assist in building the number of pleasurable and reinforcing experiences that a child has. A method that children find supportive and rewarding is adopted from programs for noncompliant children. Referred to as the "Child's Game" (Barkley, 1987: 73), parents are asked to set aside 20 minutes of time to play with the child each day for several weeks. The child selects an activity and the parent plays with the child in a nondirective, supportive fashion. The parent frequently comments neutrally or positively about the child's behaviors as a sportscaster describes an athletic contest. By engaging in this activity, the parent provides high amounts of attention which are free of criticism or tension. Children experience this as a highly enjoyable activity which fosters a strong relationship between a parent and child. Additionally, it provides the opportunity for the child to experience her/himself uncritically.

Often the sources of depression are problems that the child cannot solve or are insoluable. If parents are not highly attentive, children may not reveal these problems, or, children may be worried that they cannot raise complaints about problems with other family members. If "Family Meetings" or "Problem Solving Councils" are set once a week, children can have the opportunity to raise their concerns and get the assistance of other family members in resolving difficulties with school, peers, projects, or other family members.

The Problem Solving Council should be conducted in a relaxed atmosphere, but follow a consistent pattern. An agenda for the meeting is set by asking each member to discuss any problems that she/he is having. In turn, each problem is reviewed and potential solutions are generated. The positive and negative outcomes possible with each solution are reviewed. Then, a solution is selected and a plan for following that strategy is developed. Many of the concerns of a depressed, discouraged child could be resolved within this context. As a result, fewer negative experiences are encountered. With persistent use, the Councils could counter a sense of hopelessness that a child is experiencing. The Councils may help build rapport between parents and children in families in which limited communication is the pattern. They may decrease a child's sense of isolation when confronting problems. Finally, by demonstrating how problems can be discussed rationally and solved through careful thinking, children may learn methods for resolving dilemmas that they encounter when alone.

In treating depressed children the development of an Activity Schedule (Beck *et al*, 1979: 77) is recommended. Often, the depressed child has retreated from activities that had previously been rewarding. To improve mood, it is helpful to make certain that a child participate in activities that are enjoyable even if that pleasure is not as high as would have occurred in a different affective state. The Activity Schedule involves setting a plan of activities for each day in order to increase the number of

Table 14.1 Methods of helping young depressed children

1. The child's game
   - 20 minutes of time/day
   - Child selects activity
   - Parent verbally tracks behavior
   - Parent is nondirective
   - Positive behaviors are praised often
2. Problem solving councils
   - Held weekly or as needed
   - Set agenda
   - Clarify problems
   - Generate potential solutions
   - Consider consequences
   - Select an alternative
   - Review previous efforts
3. Activity schedule
   - Plan pleasurable events
   - Plan mastery experiences
4. Social skills training
   - Directive lessons
   - Designated to help increase contacts
   - Requires role-playing and practice
5. Behavior modification
   - Provide rewards and praise for non-depressed behaviors
   - Used to decrease "benefits" of sympathy-seeking responses
   - Use judiciously

activities in which the child experiences pleasure and experiences a sense of mastery or accomplishment. In an interview process, the child and caretakers provide information on activities which are enjoyable to the child and in which the child performs well. The schedule is then arranged to include one of several pleasurable and mastery activities per day. A reasonable set of activities should be set as the goal for each day. It must be made clear that a series of trips and movies will not lead to a cure, but that persistence at a mild increase of intensity is needed. In some cases in which adult-child contact is limited, the caretakers' participation in planning a child's schedule may have a healing effect alone as it provides predictable interaction on a daily basis.

For many depressed children, "Social Skills Training" is key. Evidence suggests that depressed children may not be effective at obtaining social rewards because they are not skilled in interacting with adults or peers. Direct training to build conversational skills, assertiveness, and the capacity to seek out and initiate contact with others may open an array of positive experiences for a child. As the treating person, the pediatrician can teach the child these skills through structured lessons. Many protocols are available including *Skillstreaming the Elementary School Child* (McGinnis and Goldstein, 1984) and *Getting Along with Others* (Jackson *et al*, 1983).

The use of behavior modification to alter depressive reactions to events is helpful since dysphoria and complaints of boredom may become habitual especially in family situations where other initiatives for attention are ignored. In this method, specific alternative responses to stress and frustration are monitored and rewarded. For example, the child receives points that count toward prizes whenever a smile is observed or when he/she indicates that a negative event was "not that bad". This technique can be used with children who are overly reliant on sympathy and who have adopted an excessively pessimistic response style (Frame *et al*, 1982).

Ages nine to thirteen

All of the methods described for younger children can be used for this age group. In addition, more psychotherapeutic efforts designed to alter the child's inner experience through discussion and specific exercises are helpful. The approaches that have been shown to be effective are based upon theories of depression proposed by Beck (1963), Ellis (1977), and Rehm (1977). Beck, Ellis, and Rehm share the broad idea that the way in which a person thinks about events and thinks about her/himself influences the emotions that are experienced. All three writers believe that depressed persons experience more dysphoria because they focus on negative aspects of events, predict pessimistic outcomes, and consider themselves to be inadequate. Studies with adults, adolescents, and children support the idea that a person's thinking style and belief system influences the level of depression.

More specifically, children who are prone to depressed moods have a tendency to concentrate on negative events and remember their failings with greater accuracy than their accomplishments. Additionally, children at risk for depressive reactions explain events to themselves in different, destructive ways. First, depressed children are likely to believe that they, as opposed to situational factors, are the cause of negative outcomes while, on the other hand, they believe that positive outcomes are due to factors outside of themselves. For example, a child who is prone to depression may believe that she failed a test because she was stupid while thinking that she was praised for an art project because the teacher was "just being nice". Second, they are likely to consider that the characteristics that they have which contribute to failure and rejection are global characteristics. For example, a child may believe that he does poorly in math because he is stupid, when a more accurate picture indicates that he has simply not learned multiplication well and his performance in other subjects is average. Third, depressed children are likely to believe that the negative events are never going to change nor are their characteristics going to change. As a result, they believe that there is little that they can do to change outcomes because they lack positive influence. Another common problem with beliefs and thinking style in depressed children is "black or white" thinking. This form of thinking leads children to review their efforts on a scale which allows for no gradation of performance. They have either met a high standard of accomplishment or they have failed. In effect, they are not pleased when efforts include any mistake or bumps along the road to meeting a goal.

Treatment is focused on changing the way children think about present events or just-prior events and varies from previous forms of psychotherapy in emphasizing the present more than the past. Treatment also varies from more traditional forms of psychotherapy in being directive with an the therapist taking an active position. The task for therapy is to help alter the style of thinking and change the beliefs through methods of discussion and practice of exercises. Details on the application of these methods are provided in other readings (Bedrosian, 1981: 68–83; DiGiuseppi, 1981: 50–67; Stark *et al*, 1987: 91–113). Some of the methods are, briefly considered.

Diary of events

Having children keep records of events that have occurred in their lives for several days provides information for discussion which can alter their view of the world. As noted above, a child prone to depression will probably remember only negative events. This selective memory can lead to conclusions that his/her life is full of unhappiness. Having the child maintain an unbiased record can help change this perception. Once gently shown the misperception, many children begin to change their beliefs and take notice of the pleasurable events. By itself this method is not likely to lead to dramatic change, but it can begin a process of change by demonstrating to the child that his/her thinking is not correct.

In those cases in which the diary accurately reflects the occurrence of numerous and persistent negative events, the pediatrician can also use the information constructively. The diary can pinpoint the sources of the events. The child can be directed to avoid those situations or, when appropriate, can be provided with problem-solving advice on how to respond differently to those situations. The information can also be given to parents so that the situations can be part of the agenda in Problem Solving Councils at home.

Table 14.2 Cognitive therapy methods for use with older depressed children

1. Diary of events
   - Child records events
   - Several days at a time
   - Review for positive and negative events
2. Self-monitoring
   - Child records emotional reactions to events
   - Keep track of situations that lead to depressed moods
   - Plan new responses
3. Self-reward
   - Child learns to give self rewards for effors
4. Attribution retraining
   - Review child's explanations about the causes of outcomes
   - Help develop more accurate and healthy explanations
5. Changing thinking style and beliefs
   - Review events and notice patterns of those that lead to depression
   - Look for errors of thinking which contribute to depressed mood (e.g. inappropriate self-blame, minimization of achievements)
   - Look for negative philosophy of life (e.g. I must be perfect in order to feel happy)
   - Challenge negative beliefs and replace with functional philosophy

Self-monitoring

Once children have been taught to record the occurrence of significant events, it is useful to have them indicate their emotional reactions to the events. As would be expected, depressed children will respond with fewer pleasant emotions, but their moods are likely to vary, a fact that they are not likely to recognize. Very often depressed children will indicate that they experienced no pleasure or satisfaction. A child should be instructed in how to rate his/her reactions to events. A simple 5-point scale is suggested. Have the child indicate whether an experience resulted in: great sadness (1), great pleasure (5) or a level of pleasure in between these extremes (2–4). To train the child in using such ratings, hypothetical situations can be used and the child can be asked what his/her reaction to them would be.

The data collected from self-monitoring is useful in two ways. First, it helps dispute the child's perception that she/he never experiences happiness. As with the use of the diary, recognition of the fact that some pleasure has been experienced even if it is only at low levels helps the child alter her/his thinking style and can begin to crack rigidly pessimistic thinking. Secondly, information collected during self-monitoring can be used to construct Activity Schedules. The child, pediatrician, and parents can learn what events and experiences lead to pleasure. Subsequently, more of those events can be scheduled into the child's life.

Self-rewards

It is important to make certain that the child is providing himself/herself with praise and appropriate rewards for efforts and accomplishments. The depressed child often deprives himself/herself of pleasant activities, self-praise, and other rewards including enjoyable foods or contact with friends and family. It is recommended that the child be advised to practice self-reward. This is done by reviewing the child's schedule and helping him/her plan time periods in which rewards can be placed. The child should be instructed in using words of encouragement and praise for efforts expended in school and play and learn to engage in rewarding activities after putting in time to meet a goal. Self-reward can be an adjunct for the Activity Schedule so that the child uses enjoyable motivators after engaging in the activities selected. Parents can be encouraged to model the use of self-reward to make certain that it becomes an acceptable practice. For example, a father could make certain to indicate that he states that he has decided to relax by watching television after cleaning the bathroom and doing the laundry.

Attribution retraining

Depressed children can often benefit from efforts to alter their thinking about the causes of events. Since the depressed child will blame himself/herself for most errors and negative outcomes and view his/her shortcomings as reflections of a comprehensive inadequacy, it is helpful to review with a child his/her understanding of negative events and his/her understanding of how they developed.

As a first step to understanding the child's style, Pope *et al* (1988: 63) suggest that the child be asked to complete a series of incomplete sentences. These stems can include: "When I make a mistake I think. . . ."; "When my friends are mad at me I say to myself . . ."; "When I get a bad grade I think . . ."; and, "When I try and can't do something other kids can, I think . . ." (Pope *et al*, 1988, p. 63). The depressed child thinks that mistakes result because she/he is "stupid", that she/he always does something wrong to "make friends made at me", and that limited accomplishments result because she's/he's "no good". Carefully reviewing alternative explanations may help the child change to a more useful style of attribution. Consider the child who thinks that mistakes result from global stupidity. The pediatrician can help the child by pointing out that mistakes could result from poor concentration for the moment or reflect the fact that a child was not feeling well at the time. Or, the pediatrician can help by pointing out that a child may not do well at something that others demonstrate effectively because she/he has only practiced the skill once and the other kids have been using that skill for a long time. Specific characteristics such as talent in a particular skill and situational factors such as the mood of others are often more accurate possibilities than the internally-based, globally-defined reasons provided by the pessimistic, depressed child. The pediatrician can help to crack rigid pessimistic thinking by offering alternative explanations to the child.

The next step in changing the child's thinking style relies upon the diary of experiences recorded by the child. Relying upon the diary, the negative events recorded can be discussed. The child should be asked to describe what he/she thinks caused the events. When alternative explanations are possible, they should be provided. This procedure helps the child see how alternative explanations can be provided for real life events. Use of this procedure over several weeks' time is often a powerful practice that can shake a child free of pessimism and inappropriate self-criticism.

Changing thinking style and disputing negative beliefs

A child prone to frequent episodes of low mood may not only possess an attributional style that is pessimistic, but make errors in processing events and have a philosophy of life filled with negative beliefs that should be challenged. The child's thinking style and ideas will become apparent as the events that lead to low mood are reviewed. The events are usually repetitious. For some children, they will occur primarily at school, for others, they may result from interactions with peers. For example, a child may believe that he/she does not deserve pleasure because he/she is not a good student. In any event, most children will show a consistent pattern that becomes known after several weeks reviewing situations. Once the pattern is revealed, it is possible to speculate about the thinking style of the child and beliefs that the child holds which makes the episodes so disturbing.

To challenge the beliefs that are suspected to be held by the child, the therapist must first discuss them with the child. The discussion should be presented as a review of the ideas with the therapist asking the child whether or not he/she holds the suspected beliefs. Children generally acknowledge their ideas when reviewed in this fashion. Once acknowledged, the therapist can then discuss and challenge the veracity of the ideas. Examples of experiences that run counter to the beliefs can be provided to help challenge their abosolute truth. For example, if a child believes that he/she has no capacity to change outcomes, he/she might be presented with situations in which that was clearly untrue. Reports when the child cooperated with a pediatric exam which resulted in a pleasant interaction or times when the child made an effort on a test and had a good result, for instance, could be used to dispute the truth of the belief. A persistent, supportive review of these beliefs helps the child develop a more functional philosophy which can prevent future depressive episodes.

Components of children's lives

The methods discussed can be used to effect change in 6 arenas.

1) Activities: If children are participating in activities that are distinctly unpleasant or unfulfilling, the recommended course of action should include the use of the Activity Schedule.

2) Family life: Although there are many details which could be discussed, the scope of the presentation only allows the indication that family life may not contain enough emotional support or it may be too stressful. Methods that help build support include the use of The Child's Game and the use of Problem-Solving Councils. When family life contains too much stress, the pediatrician needs to forthrightly discuss methods to reduce tension. In many cases tension will be due to marital discord or unresolved separations or divorces. Referral for couple's therapy or divorce counseling is appropriate for these situaitons. Other sources of tension may include harsh disciplinary style, blatant or inadvertent pressure on children to perform in school or other activities, and subtle or blatant negative feelings for a child. When the latter conditions are present, family therapy is advised.

3) Social life: The depressed child is often neglected by peers because the child is unskilled in social behavior. These children can experience relief following social skills training. When too few social contacts are the problem the use of the Activity Schedule and problem-solving discussions to help the child increase contacts can be useful. Problem-solving councils at home can also be used if peer conflict is present to help build effective methods for avoiding and resolving conflicts.

4) Emotional responses: Frequently the child who is depressed experiences a low mood because of emotional sensitivity and reactivity to events that are not distressing to most other children. In these situations, the diary of experiences, stress innoculation or training in stress management could be useful for children.

In stress innoculation children are exposed to planned "doses" of stress in order to build their capacity to respond calmly and effectively. For a particular child, the pediatrician could determine through interview what situations are most distressing. Plans could be made to have the child participate in similar situations for short periods of time or with assistance. For example, if a child is discouraged or stressed by teasing from peers, role play situations of brief duration in which the child is asked to listen to taunts may build tolerance for these situations. Similarly, another child stressed by mathematics may be guided in completing problems for increasingly longer periods of time.

Stress management methods may also be important. For some children, management may require scheduling of tasks to be accomplished in chunks as opposed to all at once. This may mean helping a child plan school work so that it is not done at the last minute, helping children take on chores one part at a time or helping children learn new, challenging skills over extended periods of time. Training a child in active relaxation techniques such as deep muscle relaxation may be useful to alleviate tension that accompanies depressed moods. However, this method needs to be used cautiously with children with severe or moderate depressions.

5) Intellectual processing: When the thoughts associated with events and misperceptions of events contribute to depression, the methods discussed for use with children above the age of 9 provide techniques for understanding and altering children's thinking.

Independent of these cognitive methods, other factors of intellectual processing may need to be addressed. If a major depressive disorder is present, children may experience intellectual changes including slowness of thinking, difficulties generating alternative ideas for problems, decreases in concentration, and problems with memory access and storage. When a child is evaluated to have a major depressive disorder, it is usually necessary to help the child by decreasing intellectual demands. For most children, the school schedule should be altered until their thinking returns to normal. Schooling will not need to be stopped, but assignments may need to be reduced in number and size.

6) Physiological status: Children suffering from a major depressive disorder experience most of the changes that are experienced by adults with this disorder. When this is the case, consideration of methods to alter the physiological state need to be considered. The chapter on psychopharmacology by Koplewicz discusses medication use and its effectiveness in detail.

INTEGRATED TREATMENT

The most effective treatment for any child will require a careful application of the procedures discussed. No child will be served if the techniques reviewed are haphazardly utilized. Instead each child's characteristics, situation, and the nature of the depressive disorder being experienced must be considered so that methods are applied systematically. It is recommended that the techniques described be utilized in a step-by-step fashion. Most of the procedures require that instruction be provided to the parents and/or the child so that only a small number of them can be used simultaneously. Parents and children facing a serious mental health disorder are not likely to be capable of changing a broad range of behaviors at one time. They will need guided instruction in applying most of the techniques discussed. Therefore, treatment planning needs to be conducted to determine which methods should receive first priority and to determine the order in which other techniques are introduced.

For young children, a good start would include the application of Activity Schedules in combination with use of the Child's Game. Once these procedures have been administered correctly by the child and the parents, Problem-Solving Councils can be implemented. By the time these are working effectively, the family and child have made major changes in their routines and styles of interaction. If depressive reactions persist, use of behavior modification could be helpful in further altering the child's responses to stress and discouragement. Discussions with the child can continue as the entire package is utilized so that external support and encouragement is provided while the depressive disorder dissipates.

Older children would also be treated with the application of procedures in a logical progression. If the child is severely depressed as manifested by decreased activity and withdrawal from others, the Activity Schedule and a mature version of the Child's Game would serve as the initial intervention to elevate mood and increase support and external reward. With disorders at a lower level of virulence, application of the cognitive techniques may be able to be initiated right away. Having the child collect information through the Diary of Events and monitoring reactions to those events through Self-Monitoring are effective starting points. Discussions of these events provide the data about the child's attributions, thinking style, and beliefs. Recurrent attributions, persistent errors in thinking style, and persistent negative beliefs will be unveiled after several sessions reviewing the child's reactions to negative events. Finally, training in Self-Reward usually needs to occur only after some cognitive changes can be documented. It is difficult for a child to implement self-praise and self-rewards before holding the belief that such bonuses are deserved, a belief that is accepted by the typical depressed child only after negative beliefs are disputed.

Treatment by the therapist is often enhanced by activating other resources. Consultation with other sources of help should also be considered. Members of the child's school system often prove invaluable as increased attention and training on child and adolescent depression have been provided to school mental health and guidance personnel and detailed programs for building children's self-esteem are available (cf. Pope *et al*, 1988). Consultation with school mental health personnel or guidance professionals can unveil resources that could be available to the child. For example, if sessions in the primary care setting are focused on building a child's activity schedule and improving social contact, a school psychologist could encourage the child to initiate contacts with children at recess and support the child's efforts to build activities. In the same vein, a teacher or guidance counselor could help a child challenge overly negative self-evaluations by reviewing a child's mood and thinking immediately after he/she receives a test grade. Other potential sources include clergy, youth leaders such as Boy and Girl Scout leaders, supportive tutors, and recreational or instructional programs that can broaden a child's pleasure and sense of accomplishment such as gymnastics, karate, team sports, or sports instruction.

CONCLUSION

The treatment of prepubertal depressive disorders should be approached with caution, but should not be avoided as there are many steps that can be taken by the primary care physician. Of course treatment requires more direct patient contact and time than treatments for physical disorders, but intervention by the pediatrician can prove effective for the child and rewarding for the practitioner. Our goal in discussing methods for assessing and treating childhood depression is to expand the resources available to children when they encounter significant psychological distress. The pragmatic approach provided is expected to facilitate a step-by-step intervention that addresses many of the concerns believed to be important in detecting depressive disorders and alleviating their impact. Although many of the procedures may prove inappropriate when research efforts improve our understanding of childhood depression, it is hoped that adherence to suggestions will assist in the care of youth confronted by a serious mental health problem.

References

Achenbach, T. M. and Edelbrock, C. S. (1983) *Manual for the Child Behavior Checklist and Revised Child Behavior Profile*. Burlington: University of Vermont, Department of Psychiatry.

Asarnow, J. R. and Carlson, G. A. (1985) Depression self-rating scale: Utility with child pscyhiatric inpatients. *Journal of Clinical and Consulting Psychology*, **53**, 491–499.

Bailey, V. *et al* (1978) How much child psychiatry does a general practitioner do? *Journal of the Royal College of General Practioners*, **28**.

Barkley, R. A. (1987) *Defiant Children: A Clinician's Guide for Parent Training*, New York: The Guilford Press, pp. 73–82.

Beck, A. *et al* (1979) *Cognitive Therapy of Depression*. New York: The Guilford Press.

Bedrosian, R. C. (1983) The application of cognitive therapy techniques with adolescents. In G. Emery, S. D. Hollon, and R. C. Bedrosian (Eds.) *New Directions in Cognitive Therapy*. New York: Guilford, 68–83.

Birelson, P. (1981) The validity of depressive disorders and the development of a self-rating scale: A research report. *Journal of Child Psychology and Psychiatry*, **22**, 73–88.

Costello, E. J. (1986) Primary care pediatrics and child psychopathology: A review of diagnostic, treatment and referral practices. *Pediatrics*, **78**, 1044–1051.

Costello, E. J. *et al* (1988) Psychopathology in pediatric primary care: the new hidden morbidity. *Pediatrics*, **82**, 415–424.

Digdon, N. and Gotlib, I. H. (1985) Developmental considerations in the study of childhood depression. *Developmental Review*, **5**, 162–199.

DiGuiseppe, R. (1983) Cognitive therapy with children. In G. Emery, S.D. Hollon, and R.C. Bedrosian *New Directions in Cognitive Therapy*. New York: Guilford.

Ellis, A. (1977) *Humanistic Psychotherapy*. New York: McGraw-Hill.

Finch, A.J. *et al* (1985) Children's depression inventory: Sex and grades norms for normal children. *Journal of Consulting and Clinical Psychology*, **53**, 424–425.

Frame, C.L. *et al* (1982) Behavioral treatment of depression in a prepubertal child. *Journal of Behavior Therapy and Experimental Psychiatry*, **3**, 239–243.

Giel, R. *et al* (1981) Childhood mental disorders in primary health care: Results of observations in four developing countries. *Pediatrics*, **68**.

Goldberg, I.D. *et al* (1984) Mental health problems among children seen in pediatric practice: Prevalence and management. *Pediatrics*, **73**, 278–293.

Herjanic B. and Campbell, W. (1977) Differentiating psychiatrically disturbed children on the basis of a structured interview. *Journal of Abnormal Child Psychology*, **51**, 127–154.

Hetherington, E.M. *et al* (1985) Long-term effects of divorce and remarriage on the adjustment of children. *Journal of Child Psychiatry*, **24**, 518–530.

Ivens, C. and Rehm, L. (1988) Assessment of childhood depression: Correspondence between reports by child, mother, and father. *Journal of the American Academy of Child and Adolescent Psychiatry*, **27**, 738–741.

Jackson, N.F. *et al* (1983) *Getting Along with Others: Teaching Social Effectiveness to Children*. Champaign, Ill.: Research Press.

Jellinek, M.S. and Murphy, J.M. (1990) The recognition of psychosocial disorders in pediatric office practice: the current status of the Pediatric Symptom Checklist. *Developmental and Behavioral Pediatrics*, **11**, 273–278.

Kazdin, A. (1987) Assessment of childhood depression: Current issues and strategies. *Behavioral Assessment*, **9**, 291–319.

Kovacs, M. (1983) The Children's Depression Inventory: A self-rated depression scale for school-aged youngsters. University of Pittsburgh School of Medicine, Unpublished manuscript.

Lefkowitz, M.M. and Tesiny, E.P. (1980) Assessment of childhood depression. *Journal of Consulting and Clinical Psychology*, **48**, 43–50.

Matson, J. (1989) *Treating Depression in Children and Adolescents*. New York: Pergamon Press.

McGuiness, E. and Goldstein, A.P. (1984) *Skill-Streaming the Elementary School Child: A Guide for Teaching Prosocial Skills*. Champaign, Ill.: Research Press.

Pope, A.W. *et al* (1988) *Self-Esteem Enhancement with Children and Adolescents*. New York: Pergamon Press.

Puig-Antich, J. and Ryan, N. (1986) *Schedule for Affective Disorders and Schizophrenia for School-Age Children (6–18 years) -Kiddie SADS*. Unpublished manuscript. Pittsburgh: Western Psychiatric Institute and Clinic.

Regier, D.A. *et al* (1978) The de facto mental health services system. *Archives of General Psychiatry*, **25**, 685–692.

Rehm, L. (1977) A self-control model of depression. *Behavior Therapy*, **8**, 787–804.

Ryan, N.D. *et al* (1987) The clinical picture of major depression in children and adolescents. *Archives of General Psychiatry*, **44**, 854–861.

Smucker, M. *et al* (1986) Normative and reliability data for the Children's Depression Inventory. *Journal of Abnormal Child Psychology*, **14**, 25–40.

Starfield, B.S. *et al* (1980) Psychosocial and psychosomatic diagnoses and care of children. *Pediatrics*, **66**, 159–167.

Stark, K.D. *et al* (1987) A comparison of the relative efficacy of self-control therapy and a behavior problem-solving therapy for depression in children. *Journal of Abnormal Child Psychology*, **15**, 91–113.

Wallerstein, J.S. (1985) Children of divorce: Preliminary report of a ten-year follow-up of older children and adolescents. *Journal of the American Academy of Child and Adolescent Psychiatry*, **24**, 545–553.

15 Pragmatic Approaches to the Treatment of Depressed Adolescents

G. Randolph Schrodt Jr., Cyrus E. Adams and Anthony J. Siegel

Department of Psychiatry and Behavioral Sciences, University of Louisville School of Medicine, Norton Psychiatric Clinic, 200 East Chestnut Street, Louisville, KY 40232, USA

INTRODUCTION

Recent studies suggest that adolescent depression is increasing in frequency and constitutes a significant public health problem (Klerman and Weissman, 1989: 2229–2235). Suicide accounts for one in eight teenage deaths, second only to accidents (Pfeffer, 1988: 652–656). Depression is a significant predictive factor for later substance abuse, although early recognition and treatment might mitigate the risk (Christie *et al*, 1988: 971–975). Kandel and Davies (1986: 255–262) found that depressive symptoms during teenage years predicted dysphoria and social and interpersonal maladjustment in young adulthood.

Major depressive disorder is underdiagnosed in adults, and few patients receive treatment that would meet contemporary psychiatric standards (Keller *et al*, 1982: 1848–1855). There is little evidence that the situation is better with depressed adolescents. In fact, Offer's data (1987: 3407–3408) suggests that the majority of the 3.4 million psychiatrically disturbed adolescents do not receive adequate treatment.

Primary care physicians can play a significant role in the detection and treatment of depressed teenagers. This chapter will review practical aspects of the establishment of a working relationship, evaluation, and treatment.

THERAPEUTIC ALLIANCE ISSUES

One of the most important variables in the treatment of depressed adolescents is the degree of cooperation and collaboration that is achieved between the physician and teenager. There are many potential obstacles to establishing a good working relationship.

Cognitive factors

Adolescents vary considerably in their level of maturity and ability to understand the treatment process (Schrodt and Fitzgerald, 1987: 402–408). Teenagers do not typically initiate requests for treatment and are unlikely to approach the situation with enthusiasm. They commonly expect an adversarial relationship and are hypersensitive to "criticism". Although many adolescents are well organized and responsible, depressed adolescents may have difficulty in keeping appointments and completing self-help assignments. Depressed adolescents characteristically believe that they have little control over their environment, which may lead to a general feeling of helplessness and hopelessness. Cognitive limitations commonly include the inability to consider alternatives, overgeneralization of problems, and misattributions of blame and responsibility. A general distrust or suspiciousness of adults is often encountered, and most adolescents have overt or covert suspicions regarding the motives and intentions of the physician. Issues regarding autonomy and control are to be expected.

Physician attitudes

A number of physician characteristics have been described which appear to foster a good therapeutic alliance with adolescents (Meeks, 1980). A general openness and honesty is critical, as teenagers exhibit an uncanny ability to detect deceit and manipulation. Depressed teenagers and their families frequently present in crisis situations which require a consistently patient, nonjudgmental, and predictable approach by the physician. Although the behavior of certain adolescents can trigger strong emotional reactions in their doctors, a warm and respectful attitude must be maintained. A relaxed sense of humor can be especially therapeutic as long as the teenager does not perceive it as sarcastic or insulting.

Age of consent and confidentiality

Medical, legal, and ethical issues concerning consent and confidentiality with teenagers are complex and change over time (Holder, 1987: 3400–3402). In general, younger teenagers, especially those who show less maturity and poor decision making, require the consent of their parents for medical treatment. Mature teenagers who demonstrate the capacity to assume responsibility for their decisions are treated more as adults. Although few states have statutes that specifically define emancipated minors, it is generally accepted that minors who are in college, in the service, or living independently from their family are considered emancipated. Special consideration is also given to teenagers who themselves are parents.

The ability to give consent can be significantly influenced by the nature of the problem for which they are seeking medical treatment. For instance, teenagers who present with a medical or psychiatric emergency, such as suicidal behavior, can generally be treated without immediate parental consent. Most states have legally defined circumstances in which an adolescent can receive treatment without parental consent, including venereal disease, the prescription of contraception and the treatment of substance abuse. The legal status of an adolescent seeking an abortion without parental consent or notification is currently being debated at the Supreme Court level.

The American Psychiatric Association Committee on Confidentiality (1987: 1522–1526) concluded: "although the rights of adolescent patients to confidentiality may be limited, the need for confidentiality in their treatment parallels that of adults. Withholding of information from the parents is often a necessary condition for therapy except when risk to life or other major danger justifies a breech of confidentiality. In most situations, adolescent patients should be encouraged to inform their parents themselves about matters the parents need to know. No matter how tedious and complex, confidentiality considerations exert a powerful influence on treatment outcome in teenage patients."

However, complete confidentiality cannot be truthfully promised to any adolescent. For instance, there are clear legal requirements for a physician to report physical, emotional or sexual abuse or neglect, as well as a duty to warn or protect potential victims from a dangerous patient of any age. Furthermore, some adolescents may resort to using "protection of privacy" as a means of denial of a problem such as an eating disorder or substance abuse. If serious concerns for the safety and welfare of a teenager arise, it is best for the physician and teenager to discuss the issue and inform the parents together.

An adolescent's right to refuse treatment probably exceeds their right to consent to treatment. However, in life-threatening or seriously self-destructive situations, treatment or hospitalization may need to be initiated on an involuntary basis. Legal criteria for involuntary hospitalization vary from state to state, but most commonly allow a teenager under the age of 16 to be admitted to a hospital with parental consent alone. Most states approach the hospitalization of teenagers 16 years and older as they would for an adult. This includes the ability to voluntarily sign themselves into the hospital as well as legal procedures to protect again involuntary hospitalization. In general, any adolescent who demonstrates signs and symptoms of a mental illness, represents a significant risk of danger to self or others, and who can be expected to benefit from treatment, can be admitted to the hospital if no less restrictive alternative is available (Kalogerakis, 1986: 497–513).

Role of the family

There is no simple formula for the establishment of a good therapeutic alliance with the family of a depressed adolescent. Nevertheless, their cooperation and involvement may be critical to successful treatment. Although some families appear to have little difficulty in working with their teenager and physician, typical emotional reactions include anxiety and feelings of guilt. Family members often have serious misunderstandings of the basic concept of depression as an illness that can be treated. Parents may have selectively focused on particular behaviors that are difficult to understand or accept, such as school failure and oppositional attitude. In other situations, the family may have difficulty in believing that there is an "emotional problem" involved.

These common reactions are generally overcome by adequate explanation, answering questions and providing reading materials on depression and its treatment.

However, some parents have extreme attitudes that may undermine effective treatment. For instance, some parents have an implicit or explicit expectation that their teenager be "fixed" or changed into some particular mold or model. They may inadvertently reinforce negative labels such as "lazy", "worthless" or "hopeless". Some parents have dysfunctional beliefs about depression as a type of personal weakness, and may have significant fear of the opinions of other family members, neighbors, or friends. Parents may share their adolescent's mistrust of professionals and perceive therapy as an intrusion of invasion into "family business". Some families fail to set age appropriate limits or, in contrast, have repressive rules and expectations.

Not uncommonly, other family members exhibit serious psychopathology. Studies suggest an increased incidence of depression in the mothers of depressed adolescents (Keller *et al*, 1986: 930–937). Alcoholism, substance abuse, and other psychiatric disorders may also be observed. There is growing appreciation of the frequency of physical or sexual abuse within the families of depressed and suicidal teenagers (Deykin *et al*, 1985: 1299–1303).

Generally, a cordial professional attitude toward the family is advised. The physician will usually find that availability and responsiveness to parents' questions and concerns is a good investment of time. Clear expectations regarding issues such as payment, regularity of appointments, confidentiality, family therapy and self-help assignments should be spelled out at the onset of treatment.

Specific therapeutic goals

A good therapeutic alliance is grounded in a mutual understanding of the problems and therapeutic objectives. As can be expected, it is not uncommon for parents to have different expectations than their teenagers. In many circumstances, these concerns and objectives are complimentary. In other cases, they are conflicting or impossible to achieve. Failure to identify clear expectations for treatment outcome can result in resistance to treatment and dropout. In some cases, the family's commitment of time, energy and money decreases significantly after the acute crisis resolves. In some situations, parents do not like the changes they observe. For instance, some teenagers significantly increase their social activities and become more assertive when they become less depressed.

Short-term therapeutic objectives include the evaluation of biological, psychological, and social factors which contribute to the depressive disorder. Target symptoms such as hopelessness, suicidal ideation, insomnia, and inactivity can generally be reduced within the first weeks of treatment. Although antidepressants medications may lead to immediate improvement in certain symptoms such as insomnia, two to six weeks are generally necessary to observe full clinical response. Supportive and cognitive behavioral approaches can also produce rapid improvement in hopelessness, suicidal ideation, inactivity, and depressed mood.

Longer term objectives might include the modification of lifestyle through stress management. An adolescent with a good self-esteem and the ability to communicate and solve problems effectively appears to be more resilient to life stress and it is reasonable to expect that their rate of a recurrence of depression is decreased. These more ambitious goals generally require individual, group, or family therapies and are a gradual developmental process.

EVALUATION OF THE DEPRESSED TEENAGER

Structure of the interview

With most outpatient evaluations, the adolescent is initially interviewed alone. The physician may begin by sharing information that has been given by the family in the initial phone intake. It is useful to inquire about the teenager's reaction to seeing a physician and to gauge the degree of participation and willingness to seek help.

In general, the first interview begins with a more open-ended discussion of current problems and their development and shifts into a more semi-structured, symptom-oriented interview. At the completion of the first interview, the parent(s) is (are) asked to join the physician and teenager. It is during this time that the medical opinion is given, recommendations are made and questions are answered. This also provides an opportunity to discuss issues of confidentiality and follow-up.

Chief complaint

Depressed adolescents present with a variety of chief complaints. Most presenting problems can be described as disorders of mood, biology, cognition or behavior. Parents will typically focus on behavioral features such as school failure, family conflicts or suicide attempts. Physical complaints such as sleep disturbances or appetite problems may represent a symptom of depression. Presenting complaints may also represent a symptom of another coexisting psychiatric disorder such as substance abuse, conduct disorder, eating disorder, or a psychophysiological or anxiety disorder.

History of the present illness

The history of the present illness should include a chronology of the development of current problems and establish the relationship to stressful life events. Once again, parents and their adolescents may differ considerably in their descriptions of how problems develop. Many clinicians employ an intake information form for parents which asks questions such as: 1) "For what specific problem is your son/daughter seeking help?" 2) "How long have these problems existed?" 3) "How often do they occur?" 4) "Please describe how these problems have developed?" 5) "What kinds of things has your family done in the past that have helped to cope with these problems?" 6) "Why are you seeking treatment at this time?" and 7) "What expectations do you have for treatment?"

Mental status examination

1) General appearance – Many depressed adolescents do not "look depressed". However, decreased attention to personal appearance, a style of dress which is intended to alienate peers or adults, or the presence of lacerations or burns may suggest an underlying affective disturbance.

2) Affect/mood – Although most depressed teenagers describe a sad, tearful mood, the intense dysphoria may be transient and responsive to environmental changes. Many adolescents with major depressive disorder report a pervasive feeling of boredom, apathy, and anhedonia. Increased irritability is commonly observed. The lack of interest and enthusiasm contributes to a withdrawal from previous activities, family, and peers.

3) Cognition – Depressed adolescents demonstrate a distinct negative bias in their thinking and report more depressive, distorted thoughts than nondepressed controls (Haley *et al*, 1985: 535–537). Poor body image, low personal esteem and self-concept, and a low estimate of self-efficacy have been observed in depressed teenagers (Koenig, 1988: 111–126; McCauley *et al*, 1988: 903–908; Schrodt *et al* [unpublished data]). Depressed adolescents also have a negative outlook on their environment, and frequently report negative family relations, poor impulse control, and low sense of mastery of the external world (Teri, 1982: 101–106). Hospitalized depressed adolescents express great concern about peer relations, sexual acceptance, social tolerance, family rapport, and academic confidence (Schrodt *et al.* [unpublished data]). Depressed adolescents typically view the future in a pessimistic, hopeless fashion (Rotherman-Borus and Trautman, 1988: 700–704; McCauley *et al*, 1988: 903–908; Schrodt *et al* [unpublished data]). These findings have significant implications for treatment. Worthlessness, helplessness, and hopelessness can lead to diminished motivation for change and a lack of persistence when confronted with obstacles (Schrodt, 1992: 197–217). An adolescent's resistance to completing self-help assignments or initiating behavioral changes may be a reflection of this negative, distorted, cognitive set.

4) Vegetative disturbances – A variety of sleep disturbances including onset and middle insomnia, early morning awakening, day-night reversal, and hypersomnia are reported by most depressed teenagers (Goetz *et al*, 1987: 61–68). Changes in appetite and weight, decreased energy, impaired concentration, and somatic complaints are also common (Ryan *et al*, 1987: 854–861). Disturbances in neurobiologic function can lead to behavioral changes which may be incorrectly attributed to "laziness" or "irresponsibility", such as difficulty in getting up in the morning and diminished school performance.

5) Self-report measures – The clinical assessment of the severity of depression can be enhanced by the office administration of brief self-report measures such as the Children's Depression Inventory (CDI) (Kovacs, 1983). The CDI is a 27-item multiple choice questionnaire which evaluates the affective, cognitive, vegetative, and behavioral symptoms of depression. In general, the CDI shows good internal consistency and reliability, although elevated scores can be observed in adolescents with

disorders other than depression (Kendall *et al*, 1989: 109–146). The utility of this instrument is dependent on the adolescent's candor in choosing their responses, but in most cases it can provide a "depression thermometer" which can be used to evaluate response to treatment.

Evaluation of suicide risk

1) Sociodemographic factors – In spite of the fact that suicide is the second leading cause of death in this age group, Hodgman and Roberts (1982: 118–123) found that few pediatricians routinely asked about suicidal thoughts. Friedman and her colleagues (Friedman *et al*, 1987: 1203–1206) found that over 60% of high school students reported having suicidal thoughts. Their study also revealed a surprisingly high rate of students who had attempted suicide (9%), with half reporting at least two attempts. Although females attempt suicide more frequently, white males are the most likely to complete suicide. Most adolescents who commit suicide have had a previous attempt (Shafii *et al*, 1985: 1061–1064). The availability of firearms (which were used in over half of adolescent suicides), combined with increased alcohol and drug abuse, appear to be major factors in the rising teenage suicide rate (Brent *et al*, 1987: 3369–3372; Levy and Deykin, 1989: 1462–1467).

2) Precipitating stress and predisposing factors – Most adolescents can identify an event or series of events which triggered their suicide attempt. Common stressful life events include the disruption of significant relationships (e.g., conflicts with parents, break up of a relationship) or a significant personal failure or disappointment (e.g., school suspension, legal problems). In some cases, the precipitating stress is transient, and active suicidal ideation and intent will quickly abate. As a result, the teenager and their family may underestimate the potential seriousness of a suicide attempt. Nevertheless, a suicide attempt is a cardinal symptom of serious psychopathology, and a thorough diagnostic assessment and exploration of predisposing risk factors is indicated (Crumley, 1982: 158–165).

a) Biological factors: Although there has been relatively little research on biological factors in adolescent suicide, adult studies suggest that genetic predisposition and neurochemical abnormalities may be involved (Brown *et al*, 1982: 741–746; Egeland and Sussex, 1985: 915–918).

b) Psychological factors: A pattern of poor impulse control (previous attempts, substance abuse, aggressiveness, antisocial behavior) is commonly observed in adolescents who attempt and commit suicide (Shafii *et al*, 1985: 1061–1064; Pfeffer, 1988: 652–656). Difficulties in emotional stability, problem solving, and communication can lead to a pervasive feeling of hopelessness, a significant risk factor for suicidal behavior (Rotherman-Borus and Trautman, 1988-700–704; Pfeffer, 1988: 652–656).

c) Social factors: Teenagers who attempt suicide frequently report histories of sexual or physical abuse (Deykin *et al*, 1985: 1299–1303). A family history of suicide, or exposure to the suicide of peers of acquaintances, is often found in the background of teenagers who commit suicide (Shafii *et al*, 1985: 1061–1064). Family turmoil, alienation from peers, and academic or legal problems increase suicide risk.

Differential diagnosis and comorbidity

1) Organic mood disorder – A diagnosis of organic mood disorder is suspected when depressive symptoms can be attributed to an underlying medical illness or the concurrent use of prescribed or illicit drugs. Various endocrinopathies, autoimmune disorders, and infectious diseases may present as a primary affective disorder. Steroids, antihypertensives, and drugs of abuse such as cocaine and amphetamines, can produce symptoms indistinguishable from depressive and manic states.

2) Bipolar disorder – Strober and Carlson (1982: 549–555) found that 20% of adolescents hospitalized for depression had a subsequent manic episode at three to five year follow-up. Adolescents with bipolar disorder often demonstrate rapid cycling, with marked affective instability, intermittent impulsivity, and an increased use and abuse of alcohol and drugs (Akiskal *et al*, 1985: 996–1003). These factors contribute to the high risk of suicide by bipolar adolescents (Brent *et al*, 1988: 581–588). Irritability, decreased need for sleep, restless hyperactivity, pressured speech, and hypersexuality are frequently observed in the manic phase (Carlson and Strober, 1979: 511–526). The depressed phase is characterized by psychomotor retardation, hypersomnia, anhedonia, and mood-congruent delusions and hallucinations (Strober and Carlson, 1982: 549–555). A family history of bipolar disorder or multigenerational depressive disorders significantly increases the risk of bipolar disorder (Strober and Carlson, 1982: 549–555). Antidepressants may induce hypomanic symptoms, though lithium therapy appears to be effective (Carlson and Strober, 1982: 549–555); Akiskal *et al*, 1985: 996–1003; Hsu and Starzynski, 1986: 596–599).

3) Substance abuse – Chemical dependency may represent a primary disorder, a coexisting condition, or a sequelae of depression. Recent epidemiologic studies have determined that early age of onset of a depressive or anxiety disorder more than doubles the likelihood of a later substance abuse disorder (Christie *et al*, 1988: 971–975). DeMilio (DeMilio, 1989: 1212–1214) reported that 53% of adolescents admitted to a substance abuse facility met diagnostic criteria for major depressive disorder at admission, and 35% remained clinically depressed after two week detoxification.

A coexisting substance abuse disorder can adversely affect the treatment and prognosis of a depressed adolescent (Bukstein *et al*, 1989: 1131–1141). Depressed adolescents who abuse alcohol frequently have psychotic symptoms, suicide attempts, and conduct problems (Ryan *et al*, 1987: 854–861). Antidepressants can have additive toxic effects when combined with alcohol and other drugs, and pharmacotherapy may be contraindicated if the adolescent cannot maintain sobriety. Although total abstinence is recommended, the occasional use of recreational drugs is to be expected. Urine drug monitoring and referral to Alcoholics Anonymous may be effective adjuncts to treatment.

4) Conduct disorder – Ryan and his colleagues (Ryan *et al*, 1987: 854–861) reported that 11% of their sample of adolescents with major depressive disorder had conduct problems of sufficient severity to have substantial disruptive effects on school and social functioning. The frequency of disruptive behavior within the family home may be even greater. Complaints by parents of lying, theft, running away, arguments, and a reluctance to participate in family activities are commonly encountered. Although depression may be a partial "explanation" of oppositional or antisocial behavior, it seldom constitutes an "excuse" for an infringement on the rights of others. Recurrent conduct problems are an indication for family therapy (DiGiuseppe, 1988: 183–214).

5) Anxiety disorders – Kashani *et al* (1987: 584–589) found a significant rate of coexisting anxiety and depressive disorders in a community sample of adolescents. Other studies also suggest an association between anxiety and depressive disorders, though the exact relationship remains unclear (Stavrakaki and Ellis, 1989: 791–802). The presence of panic attacks, severe social anxiety, phobias, or obsessive-compulsive symptoms may necessitate referral for specific cognitive, behavioral, or pharmacologic therapies.

6) Eating disorders – An association between depression and eating disorders has been suggested by a number of studies, though they appear to be distinct disorders (Swift *et al*, 1986: 290–299). The comorbidity of a depressive and eating disorder can create complex clinical problems. For instance, an organic brain syndrome can develop from severe malnutrition, rendering psychotherapy essentially ineffective. Most depressed anorexics require a multimodal treatment approach which includes weight and nutritional monitoring, individual, family, and/or group therapy, and behavioral contingencies such as bedrest, restriction of activities, or hospitalization if weight drops below the established goal range (Strober and Yager, 1985: 363–390).

Bulimic adolescents usually obscure their binge eating, purging, excessive exercise, and abuse of laxatives, cathartics, and diuretics from family, friends, and physicians (Fitzgerald *et al*, 1988: 119–123). These behaviors can lead to a variety of metabolic disturbances, including menstrual irregularities, electrolyte imbalance, and cardiac arrhythmias. Pharmacotherapy and cognitive-behavioral approaches appear to be effective treatments for both depression and bulimia (Fitzgerald *et al*, 1988: 119–123).

TREATMENT INTERVENTIONS

Supportive measures

1) Accurate empathy – Supportive psychotherapy is intended to mobilize the depressed teenager's adaptive response to life stresses. Supportive measures include empathic listening, examining alternatives and options, advice and encouragement, and providing accurate information. Unfortunately, many clinicians and other adults attempt to be helpful by minimizing the adolescent's problem: "You're just 16 – You have your whole life ahead of you" or "It's your first boyfriend, you'll get over him".

A feeling of being understood can lead to increased hope and a sense that things will begin to get better. Regular contact by telephone and frequent follow-up visits are valuable the initial stage of treatment. It is uncommon for depressed teenagers to abuse the privilege of phone calls to the physician.

2) Support groups—Many depressed adolescents feel isolated and fear being labeled by friends or family as weak or inadequate. Referral to adolescent group therapy where they meet other teens with similar problems can often be helpful. Many schools and churches have youth groups which provide an opportunity for socialization in a supportive environment. Most communities have support groups, such as the National Depressive and Manic Depressive Association (NDMDA), that can be located through the local mental health association of crisis center.

Environmental manipulations

1) School—Maintaining the depressed adolescent in an optimal school program is a complex issue. For many, their present program is appropriate. However, an adolescent enrolled in a highly academic program may be unable to keep up with the work during the acute phase of depression. Contact with school personnel to lessen the volume of work may be necessary. At times, a mismatch of student and school program is discovered during the evaluation and treatment of depression. The merits of changing schools must be balanced against the merits of staying in familiar territory. In general, homebound instruction is contraindicated for depressed adolescents because it reinforces a sense of inadequacy and withdrawal from the social and academic environment. Specialized school programs for emotionally disturbed students are preferable to homebound instruction for the student who cannot be maintained in a traditional educational program.

2) Parenting effectiveness—Many depressed adolescents describe frequent negative remarks by parents such "you're lazy" or "why can't you do anything right?" If a parent is making negative, critical statements, this should be identified and discussed. Although some adolescents say they "don't care" what their parents think, depressed adolescents tend to be especially sensitive to these comments on an emotional level. Parents can be encouraged to focus on the teenager's behavior and not attack them as a person. The treatment of the adolescent may lead to the discovery of untreated parental psychopathology or severe marital discord, and referral of a parent or couple for treatment may need to be discussed .

Building self-esteem

1) Negative thinking—Depressed adolescents typically have low self-esteem, as evidenced in comments such as "I'm boring", "I can't do anything right" or "I'm ugly". The physician can often assist in building self-esteem and may need to elicit the help of other adults to work on these issues. The first step to building self-esteem with depressed adolescents is to assist them in recognizing these negative self-statements. This can be facilitated by having the adolescent keep a log or record of their mood

and thoughts. Once negative thoughts are recognized, the adolescent can be assisted in modifying or correcting some of their negative distortions. It is generally unsuccessful to try to debate or persuade an adolescent into believing something else. However, adolescents can often be encouraged to examine the evidence for their statements and to consider alternatives. A depressed adolescent who says "I can't do anything right" is making an all or nothing statement. An approach which begins "We all do something well and other things not so well. Let's list some of the things you do well", can often facilitate a more realistic and less absolutistic self-evaluation.

2) Activities – A depressed teenager often needs encouragement to get involved in extracurricular activities in which they find a sense of enjoyment and success. Some teenagers will continue in activities in which they have little success or interest and eventually drop out of social activities altogether. The support of other adults is usually critical as the apathy, fatigue, and negative attitude of depressed adolescents often lead to failure to follow through in esteem building activities.

Managing medication problems

1) Compliance – Although the available research does not provide strong support for the efficacy of pharmacotherapy in adolescent depression (Ambrosini, 1987: 1247–1254; Campbell and Spencer, 1988: 269–279), most clinicians will employ a combined psychotherapy/pharmacotherapy approach in selected cases. Compliance with psychotropic medication has not been studied in adolescents, but there is evidence of high rates of noncompliance with oral contraceptives, which must also be taken on a daily basis for extended periods (Emans *et al*, 1987: 3377–3381).

2) Attitudes about medication – Attitudes of the physician, the adolescent, and the family exert a powerful influence on compliance, safety, and the efficacy of pharmacotherapy (Wright and Schrodt, 1989: 267–282). Patients who believe "medications are a crutch", "I'll become addicted", or "drugs are dangerous" are unlikely to agree to pharmacotherapy. Some adolescents (and their parents) fear that others will think they are "crazy" if they take medication. In contrast, when an adolescent and their family are educated about the psychobiology of depression and the risks and expected benefits of antidepressants, their acceptance of this treatment is improved.

3) Behavior factors – Improper or irregular compliance can be a problem even if the adolescent is willing to take medication and is reasonably well-informed. The lifestyle of many teenagers is unstructured, and as a result, they may "forget" to take their medication. Specific interventions may include reminder systems (checklists, divided pill boxes), pairing with a routine behavior (brushing teeth, going to bed), and the involvement of family members. This latter recommendation generally requires some discussion and mutual consent between the teenager and their parents, or medication issues may become a focus of intense conflict over control, autonomy, and privacy. Physicians should regularly monitor medication compliance and side effects with frequent appointments and phone contact. Certain "minor" side effects such as weight gain, tremor, or acne, may be very significant to an adolescent with low self-esteem. Compliance can be monitored by medication records or pill counts.

Antidepressant medications may unfortunately provide a readily accessible means of suicide, though the risk can be diminished by close follow-up and prescription of sublethal amounts.

Indications for hospitalization

The American Academy of Child and Adolescent Psychiatry (1989) has recently established guidelines for the hospitalization of adolescents. The decision to hospitalize should be based on either a personal examination of the teenager by the responsible physician, or a review of the findings of an appropriately trained and trusted clinician. Indications for impatient care include:

1) Risk of death or serious injury—In addition to serious suicidal ideation or attempt, dangerous behaviors may include a general recklessness and risk of accidental injury to self or others. Potentially life-threatening situations may be associated with severe eating disorders (e.g., severe dehydration or electrolyte imbalance) or substance abuse or dependence (e.g., accidental overdose, abstinence syndromes). Teenagers who runaway from home may be unable to provide food and shelter for themselves, and are at substantial risk of exploitation and victimization.

2) Significant pain or distress—Depressive symptomatology such as severe insomnia, overwhelming anxiety, agitation, or the presence of psychotic symptoms may warrant inpatient evaluation and treatment.

3) Significant disability of dysfunction—Severe or refractory depression can lead to significant impairment in interpersonal relations, family dysfunction, or academic failure. Depressed adolescents with poor insight, judgment, or impulse control may require the structure and intensity of the hospital in order for effective treatment to be initiated.

4) Complex case—Concurrent psychiatric or medical disorders (e.g., anorexia nervosa, substance abuse, diabetes) may also necessitate a hospital treatment program.

5) Failure of treatment at lower level of care—Some communities lack intensive outpatient programs for depressed adolescents, including partial hospitalization, multimodal treatment approaches, and special education programs. In other cases, there may be inadequate support from the family, as with a teenager who lives alone or with family members who are themselves significantly impaired by psychiatric or substance abuse problems. Outpatient care may be ineffective if the adolescent's behavior seriously disrupts family life or arouses destructive antagonism from family members.

Annotated bibliography of reading materials for depressed adolescents and their families

1) Pamphlets and Information Sheets
American Medical Association, "Patient Medication Instruction Sheet"

Patient medication instruction sheets are available for tricyclic antidepressant, monoamine oxidase inhibitors, lithium, and a variety of other psychotropic medications. They provide succinct, accurate information on the indications, contraindications, proper use of the medication, precautions and side effects.

American Psychiatric Association Division of Public Affairs "Let's Talk Facts About . . ." series, APA, 1400 K Street, N.W., Washington, D.C. 20005.
This series includes pamphlets on Depression, Manic-Depressive Illness, and Teen Suicide. Brief accurate information is presented on the diagnosis, etiology, and treatment, with suggestions for further reading and accessing other information resources.

Beck, A.T. and Greenberg, R.L. (1974) "Coping with Depression", New York: Institute for Rational Living, Inc.
This pamphlet describes the cognitive theory of depression and provides practical suggestions for recognizing cognitive distortions and replacing them with a more accurate and adaptive way of thinking.

Bohn, J. and Jefferson, J.W. (1988) "Lithium and Manic-Depression", Lithium Information Center, Department of Psychiatry, University of Wisconsin, Center for Health Sciences, 600 Highland Avenue, Madison, Wisconsin 53792.
This booklet provides extensive information on bipolar disorder and lithium therapy. The lithium work-up and maintenance regimen is discussed and the management of side effects is described. The Lithium Information Center also has a booklet on carbamezepine therapy for bipolar disorder.

2) Books

Benson, H. (1975) *The Relaxation Response*, New York: William Morrow.
This easily readable book offers specific detailed instructions for eliciting the relaxation response. Relaxation training has been shown to be very effective in reducing symptoms in depressed high school students (Reynolds and Coats, 1986: 653–660). Relaxation training may be enhanced by the use of audiotapes which are available through most bookstores.

Burns, D.D. (1980) *Feeling Good: The New Mood Therapy*, New York: William Morrow.
Feeling Good is one of the most popular self-help books currently available. It provides an easily readable and understandable explanation of the role of negative thinking in depression. Some depressed adolescents are unlikely to complete the entire book, although they may benefit from specific chapters on "love addiction", "approval addiction", and "building self-esteem".

Dinkmeyer, D., and McKay, G.D. (1983) *The Parent's Guide–Systematic Training for Effective Parenting of Teens*, Circle Plains, MN: American Guidance Service.

This self-instructional workbook provides practical insights into adolescent development and offers specific techniques for building self-esteem, resolving conflicts, discipline, and promoting responsible independence.

Lewinsohn, P.M. *et al* (1986) *Control Your Depression*, New York: Prentice-Hall Press.

This programmed workbook focuses on mood monitoring, social skills, increasing pleasant activities, controlling depressive thoughts, relaxation, and improving communication, negotiation, and problem solving skills. Lewinsohn and his colleagues (1989) have reported a significant reduction in depression scores following an eight-week "Coping with Depression" course presented in a group format. Sustained remission was found in 85% of the teenagers at two year follow-up.

Papolos, D.F. and Papolos, J. (1987) *Overcoming Depression*, New York: Harper and Row.

A very thorough, balanced resource book which provides up-to-date information on the diagnosis, etiology, pharmacotherapy, and psychotherapy of depression. Special chapters on the family, coping with hospitalization, and dealing with insurance companies are especially informative.

CONCLUSIONS

The treatment of depressed adolescents is often complex, occasionally frustrating, but generally very gratifying. Early recognition and intervention for depressive disorders decrease the toxic effect on the adolescent's physical, social, intellectual, and emotional development. The primary physician may be called upon to be a diagnostician, teacher, coach, advocate, mediator, pharmacologist, and referral agent. This chapter has reviewed practical aspects of the therapeutic alliance, diagnosis, evaluation, and treatment of depression in adolescents.

References

Aksikal, H.S. *et al* (1985) Affective disorders in referred children and younger siblings of manic-depressives. *Archives of General Psychiatry*, **42**, 996–1003.

Ambrosini, P.J. (1987) Pharmacotherapy in child and adolescent major depressive disorder, ed. H.Y. Meltzer. *Psychopharmacology: The Third Generation of Progress*, New York: Raven Press.

American Academy of Child and Adolescent Psychiatry (1989) Child and Adolescent Psychiatric Illness: Guidelines for Treatment Resources, Quality Assurance, Peer Review and Reimbursement, Washington, D.C.: American Academy of Child and Adolescent Psychiatry.

American Psychiatric Association Committee on Confidentiality (1987) Guidelines on confidentiality. *American Journal of Psychiatry*, **144**, 1522–1526.

Brent, D.A. *et al* (1987) Alcohol, firearms, and suicide among youth. *Journal of The American Medical Association*, **257**, 3369–3372.

Brent, D.A. *et al* (1988) Risk factors for adolescent suicide. *Archives of General Psychiatry*, **45**, 581–588.

Brown, S.L. *et al* (1982) Aggression, suicide and serotonin: relationship to CSF amine metabolites. *American Journal of Psychiatry*, **139**, 741–746.

Bukstein, O.G. *et al* (1989) Comorbidity of substance abuse and other psychiatric disorders in adolescents. *American Journal of Psychiatry*, **146**, 1131–1141.

Campbell, M. and Spencer, E.K. (1988) Psychopharmacology in child and adolescent psychiatry: A review of the past five years. *Journal of the American Academy of Child and Adolescent Psychiatry*, **27**, 269–279.
Carlson, G.A. and Strober, M.A. (1979) Affective disorders in adolescence. *Psychiatric Clinics of North America*, **2**, 511–526.
Christie, K.A. *et al* (1988) Epidemiologic evidence for early onset of mental disorders and higher risk of drug abuse in young adults. *American Journal of Psychiatry*, **145**, 971–975.
Crumley, F.E. (1982) The adolescent suicide attempt: a cardinal symptom of a serious psychiatric disorder. *American Journal of Psychotherapy*, **36**, 158–165.
Deykin, E.Y. *et al* (1985) A pilot study of the effect of exposure to child abuse or neglect on adolescent suicidal behavior. *American Journal of Psychiatry*, **142**, 1299–1303.
DiMilio, L. (1989) Psychiatric syndromes in adolescent substance abusers. *American Journal of Psychiatry*, **146**, 1212–1214.
DiGiuseppe, R.A. (1988) A cognitive-behavioral approach to the treatment of conduct disorder in children and adolescents, ed. N. Epstein *et al*, Cognitive-Behavioral Therapy With Families, New York: Brunner/Mazel.
Egeland, J.A. and Sussex, J.N. (1985) Suicide and family loading for affective disorders. *Journal of The American Medical Association*, **254**, 915–918.
Emans, S.J. *et al* (1987) Adolescent's compliance with the use of oral contraceptives. *Journal of the American Medical Association*, **257**, 3377–3381.
Fitzgerald, B.A. *et al* (1988) Bulimia nervosa. *Postgraduate Medicine*, **84**, 119–123.
Friedman, J.M.H. *et al* (1987) Prevalence of specific suicidal behaviors in a high school sample. *American Journal of Psychiatry*, **144**, 1203–1206.
Goetz, R.R. *et al* (1987) Electroencephalographic sleep of adolescents with major depression and normal controls. *Archives of General Psychiatry*, **44**, 61–68.
Haley, G.M.T. *et al* (1985) Cognitive bias and depression in psychiatrically disturbed children and adolescents. *Journal of Consulting and Clinical Psychology*, **53**, 535–537.
Holder, A.R. (1987) Minors' rights to consent to medical care. *Journal of The American Medical Association*, **257**, 3400–3402.
Hodgman, C.H. and Roberts, F.N. (1982) Adolescent suicide and the pediatrician. *Journal of Pediatrics*, **101**, 118–123.
Hsu, L.K.G. and Starzynski, J.M. (1986) Mania in adolescence. *Journal of Clinical Psychiatry*, **47**, 596–599.
Kalogerakis, M.G. (1986) Legal Issues. *American Psychiatric Association Annual Review*—Vol. 5, eds. Frances, A.J. and Hales, R.E., Washington, D.C.: American Psychiatric Press, Inc.
Kandel, D.B. and Davies, M. (1986) Adult sequelae of adolescent depressive symptoms. *Archives of General Psychiatry*, **43**, 255–262.
Kashani, J.A. *et al* (1987) Psychiatric disorders in a community sample of adolescents. *American Journal of Psychiatry*, **144**, 584–589.
Keller, M.B. *et al* (1982) Treatment received by depressed patients. *Journal of the American Medical Association*, **248**, 1848–1855.
Keller, M.B. *et al* (1986) Impact of severity and chronicity of parental affective illness on adaptive functioning and psychopathology in children. *Archives of General Psychiatry*, **43**, 930–937.
Kendall, P.C. *et al* (1989) Depression in children and adolescents: assessment issues and recommendations. *Cognitive Therapy and Research*, **13**, 109–146.
Klerman, G.L. and Weissman, M.W. (1989) Increasing rates of depression. *Journal of The American Medical Association*, **261**, 2229–2235.
Koenig, L.J. (1988) Self-image of emotionally disturbed adolescents. *Journal of Abnormal Child Psychology*, **16**, 111–126.
Kovacs, M. (1983) The Children's Depression Inventory: A self-rated depression scale for school-aged youngsters, University of Pittsburg School of Medicine, unpublished manuscript, April, 1983.
Levy, J.C. and Deykin, E.Y. (1989) Suicidality, depression, and substance abuse in adolescence. *American Journal of Psychiatry*, **146**, 1462–1467.
Lewinsohn, P.M. *et al* (1989) The Adolescent Coping With Depression Course, presented at the Annual Meeting of the Association for the Advancement of Behavior Therapy, Washington, D.C., November, 1989.
Meeks, J.E. (1980) The Fragile Alliance, 2nd ed., Malabar, Fla.: Robert E. Krieger Publishing.
McCauley, E. *et al* (1988) Cognitive attributes of depression in children and adolescents. *Journal of Clinical and Consulting Psychology*, **56**, 903–908.

Offer, D. (1987) In defense of adolescents. *Journal of the American Medical Association*, **257**, 3407–3408.

Pfeffer, C. R. (1988) Risk factors associated with youth suicide: a clinical perspective. *Psychiatric Annals*, **18**, 652–656.

Reynolds, W. M. and Coats, K. I. (1986) A Comparison of cognitive-behavioral therapy and relaxation training for the treatment of depression in adolescents. *Journal of Clinical and Consulting Psychology*, **54**, 653–660.

Rotheram-Borus, M. J. and Trautman, P. D. (1988) Hopelessness, depression, and suicidal intent among adolescent suicide attempters. *Journal of American Child and Adolescent Psychiatry*, **27**, 700–704.

Ryan, N. D. *et al* (1987) The clinical picture of major depression in children and adolescents. *Archives of General Psychiatry*, **44**, 854–861.

Schrodt, G. R., Jr. and Fitzgerald, B. A. (1987) Cognitive therapy with adolescents. *American Journal of Psychotherapy*, **41**, 402–408.

Schrodt, G. R., Jr. (1992) Cognitive therapy, Clinical Guide to Depression in Children and Adolescents, ed. M. Shafii and S. L. Shafii, Washington, D.C.: American Psychiatric Press, Inc.

Schrodt, G. R., Jr. *et al* (unpublished data) The negative cognitive triad in depressed adolescents.

Shafii, M. *et al* (1985) Psychological Autopsy of completed suicide in children and adolescents. *American Journal of Psychiatry*, **142**, 1061–1064.

Stavrakaki, C. and Ellis, J. (1989) The relationship of anxiety to depression in children and adolescents. *Psychiatric Clinics of North America*, **12**, 791–802.

Strober, M. and Carlson, G. (1982) Bipolar illness in adolescents with major depression. *Archives of General Psychiatry*, **39**, 549–555.

Strober, M. and Yager, J. (1985) A developmental perspective on the treatment of anorexia nervosa in adolescents. *Handbook of Psychotherapy for Anorexia Nervosa and Bulimia*, eds. D. M. Garner and P. E. Garfinkel, New York: Guilford Press.

Swift, W. J. *et al* (1986) The relationship between affective disorder and eating disorders: a review of the literature. *American Journal of Psychiatry*, **143**, 290–299.

Teri, L. (1982) Depression in adolescence: its relationship to assertion and various aspects of self-image. *Journal of Clinical Child Psychology*, **11**, 101–106.

Wright, J. H. and Schrodt, G. R., Jr. (1989) Combined Cognitive Therapy and Pharmacotherapy. *Handbook of Cognitive Therapy*. ed. A. Freeman *et al, New York: Plenum.*

16 The Psychopharmacology of Childhood and Adolescent Depression

Harold S. Koplewicz, Emily Klass and Vivian Kafantaris

Schneider Children's Hospital of Long Island Jewish Medical Center, New Hyde Park, New York 11042, USA

DEPRESSION: BACKGROUND AND INTRODUCTION

Definitions and epidemiology of mood disorders

Although the term "depression" is often used to describe a temporary state of mind, feeling, or attitude, the term "mood disorders" refers to specific psychopathological entities with particular associated features. Mood disorders can be diagnosed in adults, children and adolescents. The Diagnostic and Statistical Manual, Third Edition, Revised (DSM-III-R), developed by the American Psychiatric Association (1987), bifurcates this class of disorders into two main types: bipolar, in which at least one manic or hypomanic episode has occurred; and unipolar, in which only depression has occurred. Unipolar disorders are further delineated into major depressive disorder and dysthymia. Major depressive disorder (MDD) is defined as follows:

> Either depressed mood, (or possibly, in children or adolescents, an irritable mood) or loss of interest or pleasure in all, or almost all, activities, and associated symptoms, for a period of at least two weeks. The symptoms represent a change from previous functioning and are relatively persistent, that is, they occur for most of the day, nearly everyday, during at least a two-week period. The associated symptoms include appetite disturbance, change in weight, sleep disturbance, psychomotor agitation or retardation, decreased energy, feelings of worthlessness or excessive or inappropriate guilt, difficulty thinking or concentrating, and recurrent thoughts of death or suicidal ideation or attempts (DSM-III-R, 1987: 218–219). (See Table 16.1 for major criteria.)

Recent researchers report a prevalence of MDD of 0.3% in a general preschool population (Kashani and Ray, 1983: 233–238), with a rate of 1.8% in prepubertal children (Kashani *et al*, 1983: 1217–1223) and 4.7% in 14–16 year-old adolescents (Kashani *et al*, 1987: 932). Adult lifetime prevalence rates range from 4.1%–7.5% (Robins *et al*, 1984: 949–958).

Dysthymia is a unipolar syndrome with a more chronic course but less severe

Table 16.1 Diagnostic and Statistical Manual 3rd Edition, Revised (DSM-III-R)

Diagnostic Criteria for Major Depressive Episode

A) At least five of the following symptoms have been present during the same two-week period and represent a change from previous functioning; at least one of the symptoms is either: 1) depressed mood, or 2) loss of interest or pleasure.
   1) depressed mood (or can be irritable mood in children and adolescents) most of the day, nearly every day, as indicated either by subjective account or observation by others
   2) markedly diminished interest or pleasure in all, or almost all, activities most of the day, nearly every day
   3) significant weight loss or weight gain when not dieting, or decrease or increase in appetite nearly every day (in children, consider failure to make expected weight gains)
   4) insomnia or hypersomnia nearly every day
   5) psychomotor agitation or retardation nearly every day
   6) fatigue or loss of energy nearly every day
   7) feelings of worthlessness or excessive or inappropriate guilt nearly every day
   8) diminished ability to think or concentrate, or indecisiveness, nearly every day
   9) recurrent thoughts of death (not just fear of dying), recurrent suicidal ideation without a specific plan, or a suicide attempt or a specific plan for committing suicide

B) 1) It cannot be established that an organic factor initiated and maintained the disturbance
   2) The disturbance is not a normal reaction to the death of a loved one (Uncomplicated Bereavement)

Reprinted with permission, American Psychiatric Association (1987) Diagnostic and Statistical Manual of mental disorders, Third Edition-Revised, Washington, D.C.: APA, page 222.

clinical manifestation; only two rather than four symptoms associated with depression need to be present in order to make the diagnosis. Children and adolescents with this disorder experience a depressed, or frequently, irritable mood lasting most of the day and a majority of the week for at least one year, during which time the child is not without symptoms for more than two months. Dysthymia is analogous to a chronic viral syndrome. Major Depressive Disorder would resemble an acute infectious illness.

Bipolar disorders (also known as manic-depressive illness) are defined by the presence of at least one manic or hypomanic episode. A manic episode is defined by the DSM-III-R as:

> A distinct period during which the predominant mood is either elevated, expansive, or irritable, and there are associated symptoms of Manic Syndrome. The disturbance is sufficiently severe to cause marked impairment in occupational functioning or in usual social activities or relationships with others, or to require hospitalization to prevent harm to self or others. The associated symptoms include inflated self-esteem or grandiosity (which may be delusional), decreased need for sleep, pressure of speech, flight of ideas, distractibility, increased involvement in goal-directed activity, psychomotor agitation, and excessive involvement in pleasurable activities which have a high potential for painful consequences that the person often does not recognize (DSM-III-R, 1987: 214–215). (See Table 16.2 for major criteria.)

The lifetime prevalence of bipolar disorder in the adult general population is 1.2% (Weissman *et al*, 1988: 141–153). Rates of bipolar disorder in the prepubertal and adolescent populations have not yet been established. However, retrospective studies of bipolar adults confirm that the most common age of onset is between 15 and 19 years (Goodwin and Jamison, 1990: 128).

Table 16.2 Diagnostic and Statistical Manual, 3rd Edition, Revised (DSM-III-R)

Diagnostic Criteria for Manic Episode

A) A distinct period of abnormally and persistently elevated, expansive or irritable mood.

B) During the period of mood disturbance, at least three of the following symptoms have persisted (four if the mood is only irritable) and have been present to a significant degree:
1) inflated self-esteem or grandiosity
2) decreased need for sleep
3) more talkative than usual or pressure to keep talking
4) flight of ideas or subjective experience that thoughts are racing
5) distractibility
6) increase in goal-directed activity (either socially, at work or school, or sexually) or psychomotor gitation
7) excessive involvement in pleasurable activities which have a high potential for painful consequences

C) Mood disturbance sufficiently severe to cause marked impairment in occupational functioning or in usual social activities or relationships with others, or to necessitate hospitalization to prevent harm to self or others.

Reprinted with permission, American Psychiatric Association (1987) Diagnostic and Statistical Manual of mental disorders, Third Edition-Revised, Washington, D.C.: APA, page 217.

An adolescent with a first episode of major depression has a 20% risk of developing a manic episode in the next 3 to 4 years (Strober and Carlson, 1982: 549–555). Features which may predict subsequent manic episodes in a depressed adolescent include rapid onset of depression, the presence of delusions, slowing of movements and thought processes (psychomotor retardation), a family history of bipolar disorder and an abnormally elevated mood (e.g. hypomania) in response to treatment with antidepressants. Concurrent treatment with lithium and an antidepressant in a depressed adolescent with some of the above predictors of bipolarity may prevent a "flip" into mania.

Cyclothymia is a chronic condition (of at least one year) characterized by mood shifts of less magnitude than evidenced in bipolar disorder, however, the shifts between the depressed and hypomanic states are still clearly outside the normal limits. The onset for cyclothymia is reported to be in adolescence or in early adulthood, although there are case reports of prepubertal onset.

Treatment for the mood disorders incorporate the varying modalities of psychotherapy as well as pharmacologic intervention. Psychopharmacological treatment of unipolar depression will be discussed in this chapter. Psychotherapeutic interventions for children and adolescents are discussed comprehensively in Chapters 13, 14 and 15.

Presentation of mood disorders in children and adolescents

Until the 1970's mood disorders in children and adolescents were trivialized, believed to be masked by other disorders or simply not believed to be present in anyone but adults. More careful and parsimonious diagnostics and the use of structured interviewing techniques have resulted in unassailable evidence that both unipolar and bipolar disorders do exist in children and adolescents. Researchers have struggled in the past 20 years to clarify phenomenological and treatment issues of patients with these disorders which often have a recurrent course and a marked detrimental impact on life. Support for pharmacological interventions for depressed children and adolescents derives from the recent acknowledgement that not only does depression exist in these age groups, but that the syndrome is in many ways clinically equivalent to that in adulthood (Puig-Antich, 1987: 843).

Descriptive clinical studies make a strong case for the position that childhood, adolescent and adult MDD are phenomenologically similar (Strober *et al*, 1981: 281–290; Ryan *et al*, 1986: 854–861; Kutcher and Marton, 1989: 895–918), and the one follow-up study of adolescents with depressive symptomatology into adulthood, (Harrington *et al*, 1990: 465–473), is consistent with this view. Researchers do note, however, that there is some variability in the symptoms and presentation of MDD associated with developmental factors. Carlson and Kashani (1988: 1222–1225) compared clinical signs of depression reported from early infancy through adolescence and found that the basic clinical picture of depression is consistent regardless of age. There is only one study in which direct comparisons of depressed adolescents (n = 26; 15–18 years of age) with depressed adults (n = 27; 18–45 years of age) were conducted (Friedman *et al*, 1983: 37–43). Of thirty symptoms, only one (self pity for adolescents) significantly varied in the two age groups providing additional support for the hypothesized consistency of symptoms across age. Differences in presentation will be discussed below and a more comprehensive, and clinically applicable description is available in Chapter 1 by Schachter and Romano in this volume.

Prepubertal children with MDD, more frequently than their adolescent or adult counterparts, present comorbidity with phobias, anxiety disorders and somatic complaints. For these children, these other complaints may appear more salient both due to limitations on the types of verbal expression available to young children as well as the tendency for young children to be more reactive to exogenous events, and therefore less likely to be continually depressed. In adolescence, an irritable, negativistic or oppositional profile may emerge with the MDD, which again can appear more obvious than the sadness or anhedonia more typically associated with MDD in adults. Hopelessness and increased lethality of suicide attempts is more common in the adolescent depressives then in the prepubertals (Ryan *et al*, 1987: 854–861). Koplewicz and colleagues, (1990), in their study of 90 adolescent outpatients diagnosed with MDD, found that there was a large subgroup (84%) of patients with a comorbid and, in temporal terms, primary diagnosis of an anxiety disorder. A significant subgroup (44%) of the patients studied met criteria for "atypical" depression, characterized by mood reactivity, rather than a mood autonomous from external events as well as other symptoms at variance with a "classic" depressive presentation (e.g. hyperphagia, hypersomnia and extreme rejection sensitivity).

Because of the predominantly equivalent phenomenology of depressive symptoms across the age span, it might be posited that there is etiological equivalence as well. It is likely that there is a multifactorial model for the onset of depression in youth that is yet to be established. Noteworthy are the concordance rates for depression: for monozygotic twins, 76%; for monozygotic twins reared apart, 67%; and for dizygotic twins, 19%, attesting to a prominent but not singular role for heredity.

Biological findings in depressed children and adolescents are not yet well established and both consistencies and inconsistencies with adults have been discovered. Frequently, parents request a biologic "test" to diagnose depression in their child. Some markers for neuroendocrine dysregulation have been found (Puig-Antich, 1986: 867–874). The Dexamethasone Suppression Test (DST), in depressed children and adolescents, showed early promise (Carroll *et al*, 1981: 15–22), but has limitations and is not often used in clinical practice. In this test a dose of dexamethasone is given and cortisol levels are measured at standard intervals. Nonsuppression of cortisol levels following dexamethasone is believed to be a marker for depression. Analysis of pooled data from 13 prospective studies using the DST in depressed children and adolescents (Casat *et al*, 1989: 503–507), showed that adolescent results on this test are similar to those seen in adults, but differ from those in children. In adolescents the test has a sensitivity of 47% and specificity of 80%, which is similar to pooled data from DST studies in depressed adults which found overall sensitivity to be 43% and specificity 76.5% (Arana *et al*, 1985: 1193–1204). In children, however, the test has a 70% sensitivity, and a 70% specificity. The reasons for the test's increased sensitivity and decreased specificity in children are unknown. Another neuroendocrine marker is growth hormone (GH) secretion. Secretion of GH is increased during sleep in depressed prepubertal children and adolescents, though the total daily amount of hormone secreted is the same as in nondepressed children (Kutcher *et al*, 1988: 751–754; Puig-Antich *et al*, 1984a: 471–475). Depressed children also hyposecrete growth hormone in response to an insulin-induced hypoglycemia (Puig-Antich *et al*, 1984b: 455–460). The same is true of post-menopausal adult depressives. This abnormal response in growth hormone secretion remains even after the remission of the depression (Puig-Antich *et al*, 1984c: 471–475), though it is unclear if it is a true trait marker (with predictive value) or an aftermath of the first depressive episode. The sleep of depressed children, adolescents and adults has also been compared to normal controls using polysomnography. Shortened rapid eye movement (REM) latency has been found consistently in depressed adults. A shortened REM latency was also found in hospitalized depressed children compared to age-matched normal controls (Emslie *et al*, 1990: 119–124), and in depressed older adolescents (Lahmeyer *et al*, 1983: 1150–1153), but other studies have reported conflicting results.

PSYCHOPHARMACOLOGIC TREATMENT OF DEPRESSION

Response to pharmacologic interventions in adulthood and mechanisms of action

Cyclic antidepressants

The similar symptom constellation across the age spans has led to the expectation that treatments effective in adults should be effective in children and adolescents as well. The cyclic antidepressants are the standard somatic treatment for major depression in adults. They are effective in 60–70% of patients (Klein *et al*, 1980). Placebo response rates in studies of depressed adults range from 20 to 40%. To date, there are no satisfactory predictors of drug response in adults. Slight differences in chemical structure account for the varying treatment effects of chlorpromazine (Thorazine), a three-ringed phenothiazine which is an effective antipsychotic, and the tricyclic imipramine (Tofranil), an antidepressant. Tricyclic antidepressants (TCA's) developed subsequent to imipramine (amitriptyline, amoxapine, clomipramine, desipramine, doxepin, nortriptyline, protriptyline, trimipramine) are equally efficacious, but have different pharmacologic actions and side effect profiles. Other cyclic antidepressants which are effective in adults with MDD have different chemical structures, for example maprotiline, trazodone, and bupropion. The newest type of antidepressant, chemically unrelated to the tricyclics having two rings, are the selective serotonin reuptake inhibitors, fluoxetine (Prozac) and sertraline (Zoloft), and two not yet marketed in the United States, fluvoxamine and paroxetine.

Fluoxetine in particular has been reported to be as effective in treating MDD in adults as the more established antidepressants. Fluoxetine has fewer anticholinergic side effects and less weight gain and is possibly safer in overdose (Gelenberg *et al*, 1991).

Difficulties with fluoxetine include agitation and anxiety in many patients and a prolonged half-life (approximately 48 hours). It has been reported that children experience a similar side effect profile except that weight gain has also been documented (Riddle 1992: personal communication). The tricyclic antidepressants, and new antidepressants like fluoxetine have been widely accepted for use in depressed adults. Their use by psychiatrists as well as internists and family practitioners is widespread and founded on methodologically sound research studies in adults. Outgrowth of these findings have led to trials of these medications in both children and adolescents.

Monoamine oxidase inhibitors

Monoamine oxidase inhibitors (MAOI's) were first studied as anti-tubercular drugs and were found to have an antidepressant effect. Isocarboxazid (Marplan), phenelzine (Nardil) and tranylcypromine (Parnate) are the MAOI's marketed in the United States. The enzyme, monoamine oxidase, exists in two forms, MAO-A and B, the former primarily deaminates norepinephrine and serotonin, and the latter deaminates mostly dopamine and perhaps norepinephrine in humans. Currently available medications block both the A and B forms of the enzyme. Early in the use of MAOI's, it was discovered that patients who ingested foods rich in the amino acid tyramine (e.g. certain cheeses, aged or processed meats and beers) or who take prescription or over the counter medications containing stimulants or sympathomimetics could develop a hypertensive crisis. This resulted in a curtailment in the use of these medications as studies demonstrated the efficacy and greater safety of the tricyclic antidepressants. Clorgyline, (not yet available in the U.S.), is a selective inhibitor of MAO-A which is more effective, and may render the patient less sensitive to tyramine than currently available MAOI's.

However, a number of double-blind, placebo-controlled trials of MAOI's and TCA's in adults have clearly documented a subtype of depressed patients who respond in greater numbers to MAOI's than to the cyclic antidepressants—those with an "atypical" depression. For a complete review see Davidson *et al* (1981: 115–124), Leibowitz *et al* (1984: 669–677), and Quitkin, *et al* (1983).

Mechanism of action

Until recently, the mechanism of action for the cyclic antidepressants was thought to be the blocking of the reuptake of the neurotransmitters norepinephrine and serotonin, which increases their concentration in the synapse. In the case of currently available MAOI's, degradation of these and other neurotransmitters is irreversibly blocked, which also increases their concentration at the postsynaptic receptor. This theory, however, could not explain why some effective antidepressants were weak norepinephrine and serotonin reuptake inhibitors (i.e. bupropion), and why full antidepressant effect often takes weeks, when the reuptake blocking occurs immediately (Gelenberg *et al*, 1991). More recent theories involve the effect of antidepressants on the catecholamine receptors. One theory, that an excess of norepinephrine activity causes depression, postulates that antidepressants work by reducing the number of post-synaptic beta-adrenergic receptors and increasing alpha-adrenergic and serotonergic receptor sensitivity. Another theory postulates a decrease in the amount of serotonin available at post-synaptic or pre-synaptic sites. Additional neurotransmitters with postulated roles in antidepressant activity include acetylcholine and gamma-aminobutyric acid (GABA). It has become clear that there are complex interrelationships between the different neurotransmitters in the brain, leading in a certain interplay to depression.

Response to pharmacological intervention in prepubertal children

The use of antidepressants in depressed prepubertal children has been investigated to only a small extent and the efficacy of the drugs for this age group and diagnosis has been difficult to substantiate in double-blind placebo-controlled studies.

No antidepressant has been approved by the Food and Drug Administration (FDA) for use in children under the age of 12 for the treatment of depression. Imipramine (Tofranil) is approved by the FDA for administration to children ages 6–12 for the treatment of enuresis, and clomipramine (Anafranil) is approved for ages 10 and over for the treatment of obsessive-compulsive disorder.

Early open (Geller *et al*, 1983: 62–64) and placebo-controlled studies of amitriptyline (Kashani *et al*, 1984: 348–361) and imipramine (Petti and Law, 1982: 107–110; Weller *et al*, 1982: 506–508) in depressed children were favorable to drug effect. In Geller's study, all 12 prepubertal children were treated with nortriptyline and all met strict diagnostic criteria for MDD, as well as having a first degree family member with either an affective disorder or alcoholism; 8 patients completed the study with a marked diminution of scores on standard children's depression rating scales. In Weller's trial of imipramine in 11 children who met the diagnostic criteria for

MDD, children were first observed as inpatients without medication. They then received three weeks of 75 mg of imipramine, following which, depending on clinical response, children received three additional weeks of medication on an altered dose. For those children completing the final phase, 80% remitted and response was determined to be related to total plasma TCA level (IMI + DMI). Preskorn *et al* (1987: 128–133) in a preliminary study found that, of the prepubertal children included in the study, DST non-suppressors responded more favorably than DST suppressors to imipramine. This may also be true in adolescents (Robbins *et al*, 1989: 99–104).

Puig-Antich and his colleagues (1987: 81–89) studied 38 depressed prepubertal children, mostly outpatients, in a randomized double-blind, placebo-controlled study of imipramine. The researchers point out that 20% of the original sample improved without treatment during the two-week, no drug baseline and so were not included in the experimental treatment. Imipramine dosage of 5 mg/kg/day was attempted for five weeks with careful cardiac monitoring. The placebo response rate was very high (15/22 or 68%), not significantly different from response to imipramine (9/16 or 56%). The study was terminated early due to these poor results instead of completing the 60 subjects originally planned. For future studies in this population, the investigators recommended that placebo be given during the baseline period to eliminate the placebo responders from the experimental phase and that the dose be titrated to therapeutic serum level (above 150 ng/ml) rather than titrated to body weight.

Geller and colleagues (1989: 101–108) completed a well-designed random assignment, double-blind, placebo-controlled study of nortriptyline in 50 prepubertal depressed children, using a fixed plasma level design (80 ± 20 ng/ml). There was no statistically significant difference between response to drug (30.8%) and to placebo (16.7%).

The only controlled study of MAOI's in prepubertal children (Frommer, 1967: 729–732) combined phenelzine with chlordiazepoxide (Librium) and showed it to be superior to phenobarbital in 32 depressed children. No controlled studies employing the newer selective serotonin reuptake inhibitors in prepubertal depressed children have been published to date.

Poor response rates to medication in this population may in part be due to biological differences between children, adolescents and adults, small sample size, high placebo response rates and methodological issues. Research into subtyping, biological mechanisms, dosing and the relationship of drug efficacy to drug plasma level is expected to more clearly predict which depressed children would be drug responders. Presently common practice includes the administration of TCA's for prepubertal children when psychotherapy alone does not alleviate clear breakdown in the child's functioning. Concomitant supportive individual and/or family psychotherapy should always be provided.

Response to pharmacologic intervention in adolescents

The tricyclics amitriptyline, desipramine, imipramine and nortriptyline are approved for the treatment of depression for ages 12 and over. However, the problem of proving efficacy of the medication over placebo also exists in this age group.

The controlled studies of tricyclic antidepressants in adolescents are difficult to interpret because of the generally high placebo response, and the relatively small sample sizes. The relationship of clinical response to antidepressant plasma level found in some prepubertal studies has not been replicated in the adolescent population (Koplewicz *et al*, 1990; Ryan *et al*, 1986: 275–288). To date, results of six placebo-controlled studies in adolescents have been reported. The first and only controlled trial to study hospitalized adolescent subjects was a pilot study of amitriptyline, 200 mg/day for six weeks in 20 patients (13 female) ages 13–17. No statistically significant differences were found except on one depression checklist (Kramer and Feiguine, 1981: 636–644).

Geller and colleagues (1990: 85–90) entered 52 depressed adolescent outpatients into a ten-week double-blind placebo-controlled study of nortriptyline titrated to plasma levels of 80 ± 20 – ng/ml. The patient group had long duration of illness: greater than two years for 83% of the sample and greater than five years for 50% of the sample. Subjects also had high rates of comorbidity: separation anxiety in 52% and antisocial behavior in 44%. Despite this duration and severity of illness, one-third of the sample improved significantly during the two-week placebo washout phase and were not randomized to the double-blind phase. Interim analysis of the data after 31 subjects completed showed no statistically significant differences between response to nortriptyline (1/12 or 8.3%) and placebo (4/19 or 21.1%). Therefore, the study was terminated early.

Ryan and colleagues (1990) reported on an ongoing study of an eight week trial of amitriptyline versus placebo in adolescents who remained symptomatic after two weeks of placebo. A total of 25 cases were entered in the double-blind phase, 13 completed: 7 on amitriptyline (mean dose of 243 mg/day) and 6 on placebo. No differences were found between treatments on several indices: a) still meeting criteria for depression; b) 50% reduction on structured interview depression scale; c) mean scores on structured interview depression scale.

Boulos *et al* (1990: 59–65) entered 46 patients 15–20 years of age in a six-week placebo-controlled trial of desipramine in a fixed dose design (200 mg/day after a one-week placebo phase). Thirty patients completed the trial: 12 on desipramine and 18 on placebo. Almost half (47%) had concurrent anxiety disorders. Twenty percent had substance abuse disorder and 7% had conduct disorder. The only positive outcome reported for the treatment group was a 50% reduction in the Hamilton Depression Scale scores, a standard rating scale to measure depression in adults.

In a study recently completed by Koplewicz *et al* (1990), there is also no statistically significant advantage of drug (desipramine) over placebo in terms of rates of remission of the disorder, yet drug treatment was rated as superior on selected depression checklists administered to parent and child. Small sample size of treatment completers limits conclusions. A preponderance of patients had comorbid diagnoses particularly anxiety disorders, and almost half met criteria for "atypical" MDD.

A double-blind placebo-controlled study of fluoxetine with a one-week baseline period to eliminate early placebo responders, was completed in 30 depressed adolescent outpatients ages 13–18 (Simeon *et al*, 1990: 791–795). The target dose of 60 mg/day was reached during the second week of the study. Total treatment duration was seven weeks. Once again, there was no difference between active medication and placebo as two-thirds (66%) in each group improved.

In open studies, a less stringent measure of drug efficacy, results are mixed. In an uncontrolled study of depressed inpatients (Strober *et al*, 1990: 80–84) of 24 non-psychotic adolescents who received up to 300 mg/day of imipramine, 38% clearly improved; in contrast, only one of 10 psychotically depressed patients responded. Another uncontrolled trial of imipramine in 34 outpatients showed a 44% improvement rate, which is similar to that expected from placebo. There was no relationship between plasma level and clinical response (Ryan *et al*, 1986: 275–288).

In an open clinical trial of fluoxetine with 10 adolescents with MDD, who were refractory to desipramine (Klein *et al*, 1991: personal communication), 7 of 10 adolescents improved significantly with a ten-week trial on a mean daily dosage of 60 mg.

The strategy of augmentation of tricyclic response with lithium has been studied. Strober and his colleagues (1992: 16–20) examined lithium augmentation for 24 inpatients who had not responded to treatment with imipramine. In a three-week period, 10 (40%) showed some improvement, but only 2 had a marked response. Ryan and colleagues (1988: 371–376) reviewed their own results after adding lithium to a tricyclic in adolescents with inadequate response to the TCA alone after six to eight weeks. Six of 14 patients (44%) responded to the combination. Fluoxetine efficacy augmented with other pharmacological agents has been reported in patients with other psychiatric disorders, predominantly obsessive compulsive disorder (OCD). Lithium, clonazepam, clomipramine, haloperidol, fenfluramine and bupropion have been reported as efficacious augmentors of fluoxetine.

A retrospective chart review of adolescents with MDD treated with MAOI's alone or in combination with TCA's concluded that there is evidence for the utilization of MAOI's in adolescents as long as good dietary compliance can be maintained (Ryan *et al*, 1988: 755–758). The concern with children and adolescents is that many of their favorite foods such as processed meats, pizza and chocolate, contain significant amounts of tyramine and many prescription and over-the-counter medications commonly given to children and adolescents are contraindicated on MAOI's. Koplewicz *et al* (1990) found that a significant proportion of depressed adolescents met criteria for atypical depression, which may indicate the utility of MAOI's for this group.

At this time, based on the above research findings, it is difficult to recommend specific treatment for adolescents with MDD. Clinicians often choose to use antidepressants in an empirical way, particularly when the patient's life is severely compromised by the effects of the depression.

Guidelines for the administration of antidepressants

Physical and laboratory examinations to be conducted prior to treatment with an antidepressant are outlined in Table 16.3.

Table 16.3 Guidelines for the Administration of Antidepressants

Administration of antidepressants for the treatment of depression should be done by a child and adolescent psychiatrist. Prior to treatment, the parents should be informed that the Federal Drug Administration (FDA) has not approved any antidepressant for the treatment of depression for children under age 12. However, this type of medication has been FDA-approved for other indications such as enuresis. Results from the following should be obtained before administering any antidepressant:

1) height, weight, blood pressure and pulse
2) a complete blood cell count with differential
3) thyroid function test
4) determination of blood urea nitrogen (BUN), serum creatinine and electrolyte levels
5) liver function tests
6) electrocardiogram

Tricyclic antidepressants

The dosage is titrated clinically for imipramine, desipramine and amitriptyline with a maximum of 5 mg/kg/day. Nortriptyline is titrated to plasma levels in the range of 50–150 ng/ml which typically requires 0.5–2 mg/kg/day. Doses as high as 7 mg/kg of tricyclics have been used with close EKG and vital sign monitoring. In obese children, there may be a tendency to accumulate the drug in fatty tissue so caution should be used in dose increases. To insure compliance and help prevent cardiotoxicity and neurotoxicity, plasma levels should be monitored.

If there is clinical response within 8–10 weeks, treatment should continue for approximately 4–6 months before gradual tapering is attempted. It is best to expedite the measurement of treatment response by using standard depression rating scales at baseline and at two-week intervals during titration (see Chapter 14 for a discussion of useful rating scales).

Adverse effects

Tricyclic antidepressants have several short and long term side effects that justify monitoring. Most common are the anticholinergic effects which include dryness of the mouth, urinary retention, orthostatic hypotension and constipation. Tricyclic antidepressants lower the seizure threshold and, therefore, children and adolescents with neurological disorders would be at increased risk for seizures. Electrocardiographic changes have been reported to include increased heart rate, prolonged P-R interval, increased QRS duration and development of a right bundle branch block pattern, shortened QT interval, increased corrected QT and increased production of T wave changes (Bartels *et al*, 1991: 100–103). There is some controversy concerning the relationship between these cardiac changes and plasma level. Plasma levels greater than 500 ng/ml appear to create a higher risk for the development of increased P-R intervals, S-T segment suppression and diastolic blood pressure. Since plasma levels vary widely between children receiving the same dose of cyclic antidepressants, dose alone cannot predict cardiac effects. The sudden deaths of several prepubertal children treated with desipramine on surprisingly small doses has been reported (Abramowicz, 1990: 53; Riddle *et al*, 1991: 104–108). It has been hypothesized that children's cardiovascular systems are more sensitive to the effects of tricyclics. Death can also result from overdose; as little as one weeks' dose at therapeutic level can lead to death by cardiovascular toxicity. Prescription size should reflect this danger.

In order to minimize or prevent adverse effects, electrocardiogram (EKG) monitoring is necessary at each dose increase and at frequent intervals during dose elevation. (Extensive discussion of exact EKG parameters can be found in Ryan, 1990: 21–32). The anticholinergic side effects can be managed by dose reduction, sugar-free candy or gum; stool softeners should be used for constipation. Rashes are most likely due to the tartrazine, a yellow dye used, in the pill and the pharmacy may be contacted to determine if the particular strength of the antidepressant brand contains this substance. Seizures warrant discontinuation of the medication until an emergency seizure workup is completed.

Of great concern to adolescent patients is the potential weight gain resulting from treatment with TCA's, particularly from amitriptyline. Patients must be warned in advance and suggestions concerning weight control provided. Fluoxetine is less likely to cause weight gain; indeed adult reports indicate an average weight loss of two to four pounds.

Sudden withdrawal from TCA's which are highly anticholinergic, (Ryan, 1990: 21–32), may cause cholinergic rebound which may include symptoms of anxiety, malaise, sleep disturbance and gastrointestinal symptoms. These are transient and may be treated with a slower dose tapering should they arise.

The effects of CNS stimulants or depressants, anticholinergic drugs, thyroid medication, seizure potentiating drugs and phenytoin are enhanced with the use of heterocyclic antidepressants while the effects of clonidine and guanethidine can be decreased. Phenothiazines, methylphenidate and estrogen may also potentiate the effect of the heterocyclic antidepressants. Lithium, barbiturates, chloral hydrate and smoking may decrease effect. And, important for the adolescent population, marijuana in combination with the heterocyclics may bring on sinus tachycardia (Ryan, 1990: 21–32).

Selective serotonin reuptake inhibitors (SSRI)

The SSRI's currently available in the U.S. are fluoxetine (Prozac) and sertraline (Zoloft). Fluoxetine is available in 20 mg capsules and in oral solution, doses up to 80 mg/day are used. To minimize the common initial adverse effect of increased anxiety, agitation and insomnia, the daily dose is given in the morning and the initial dose may be 10 mg. Sertraline is used in doses up to 200 mg/day in children and adolescents.

Adverse effects

Fluoxetine is a generally well-tolerated antidepressant that has a low potential for lethality. Reports indicate that mortality has not occurred in patients taking several times the daily recommended dose. Common side effects include nausea, increased anxiety and insomnia. However, other adverse effects such as hypomania, transient psychotic episodes, disinhibition and akathisia, a disturbing sense of inner and motoric restlessness have been reported in children treated with fluoxetine at doses as low as 20 mg. Decreased dosage usually reverses these side effects. There has been controversy concerning increased suicidality in adults taking fluoxetine (Teicher, 1990: 207–210). Akathisia may be the suicide potentiator (Ruthschild and Loche, 1991: 491–493). Children have also been reported to show an emergence of self-destructive behavior once fluoxetine has been initiated (King *et al*, 1991: 179–186). While the lay press has sensationalized the potential adverse effects of fluoxetine, there is a plethora of case reports and open clinical trials indicating positive response to this medication with minimal or no adverse effects. The combination of tricyclic antidepressants and fluoxetine in adults has led to increased antidepressant plasma levels (Aranow *et al*, 1989: 111–113). Fluoxetine does not appear to have any adverse symptoms upon withdrawal and this may be performed abruptly.

Monoamine oxidase inhibitors

MAOI's are rarely used as first-line antidepressants in children and adolescents because of the high potential for adverse effects from dietary and medication interactions. However, they are very effective antidepressants and have been used safely in well-informed and compliant patients. Before initiating MAOI treatment one must allow for adequate regeneration of MAO enzyme when switching from a tricyclic or another MAOI. This regeneration takes at least one week and maybe as long as five weeks for the longer acting antidepressants such as fluoxetine. Therapeutic doses of isocarboxazid (Marplan) and tranylcypromine (Parnate) range from 10 to 30 mg; for phenelzine (Nardil) the range is from 45 to 90 mg/day for adults.

Adverse effects

The most serious and potentially life-threatening adverse effects of MAOI treatment are hypertensive and hypermetabolic crises. Hypertensive crisis most often follows the ingestion of food with a high tyramine content or medications with a pressor effect such as the stimulants, sympathomimetics (procaine, ephedrine and epinephrine) and many over-the-counter cold medications which contain phenylpropanolamine, pseudoephedrine and phenylephrine. Normally these exogenous pressor substances are broken down by the MAO in the gut, blood vessels and liver but with the irreversible inhibition of this enzyme by MAOI's these pressor substances circulate and may precipitate sudden rises in blood pressure. Symptoms of an impending hypertensive crisis include sudden severe headache which may be accompanied by retro-orbital pain, photophobia, nausea, vomiting, flushing and palpitations. These episodes may be treated with alpha- and beta-blockers, calcium channel blockers and the antipsychotic chlorpromazine (Thorazine).

Hypermetabolic crisis is a potentially life-threatening drug-drug interaction with an MAOI which may be caused by meperidine (Demerol), clomipramine (Anafranil) and fluoxetine (Prozac) when combined with MAOI's. Hyperpyrexia, hyperreflexia, muscle rigidity, seizures, hypotension and death may ensue.

Hepatocellular toxicity is another potentially serious adverse effect which may necessitate drug discontinuation. Less severe and more common adverse effects include postural hypotension, sexual dysfunction, edema and weight gain. One advantage to treatment with this class of drugs is that they do not slow cardiac conduction or have other direct cardiac effects so they can be used in patients with bundle-branch block or second degree A-V block. After four to six months of successful symptom suppression the drug dose may be gradually tapered to avoid a withdrawal syndrome, and discontinued.

Lithium

Lithium is FDA approved for children over age 12 for the treatment of bipolar illness. However, its safety and efficacy has been studied in other disorders in children under 12 including conduct disorder with aggressiveness and explosiveness (Campbell *et al*, 1984: 650–656). Dosage in children over age 5 is similar to that used in adults, i.e., 600 to 2700 mg/day, in divided doses. Children have a higher renal lithium clearance and a shorter elimination half-life than adults (Vitiello *et al*, 1988: 355–359).

There are no published reports on the optimal therapeutic range for lithium in children but clinical usage does not normally exceed serum levels of 1.4 mEq/L. In a report of 48 children treated for behavior disorders with lithium, the most common adverse effects were weight gain, stomachache, vomiting, nausea, tremor, enuresis and weight loss (Campbell *et al*, 1991: 373–380). Weight gain is of particular concern in the adolescent population, with reports of weight gain of as much as 30 pounds. This weight gain however, seems to reverse itself after one year of maintenance medication (Kutcher, 1991:personal communication). Signs of lithium toxicity which warrant medication discontinuation and further medical evaluation include: slurred speech, muscle weakness, twitching, ataxia, and impaired consciousness. Lithium levels increase into the toxic range when the patient is dehydrated. Children must be continually reminded to drink plenty of liquids, particularly in the summer months.

FUTURE OF PHARMACOLOGICAL INTERVENTIONS FOR CHILDREN AND ADOLESCENTS

Depression is a debilitating disorder for adolescents and young children, yet research into the phenomenology and treatment of this disorder is relatively recent and quite sparse. MDD is rare in prepubertal children, but when it does occur, it can be severe and recurrent and bring marked deviation from normal development. In adolescence, rates of depression increase markedly, approximating those in adulthood. Different forms of psychotherapy have been used for treatment with variable success. Research into pharmacological interventions is still in its infancy. The rarity of the disorder, high placebo response rate, adverse side effects and, most probably, a general disinclination to medicate children with psychiatric problems, have been obstacles. In clinical practice, certain children and adolescents have had an excellent response to medication.

The future of psychopharmacologic intervention for depressed children and adolescent hinges on:

1) Continued research into the neurochemical basis of depression. As the relationship of neurotransmitter functioning to various psychiatric illnesses is more clearly understood it will become possible to specify sites and mechanisms for interventions.

2) Explicit subtyping in terms of comorbidity, phenomenology and biology. Diagnostic comorbidity patterns and biological markers may change with age and, therefore, the relationship between the comorbid disorders must be clarified. Research studies suggest that certain subtypes respond differently to different types of antidepressant treatment (e.g. the "atypical" depressives in adulthood respond more frequently to the MAOI's than the TCA's).

3) The development of antidepressants that are specific to particular neurotransmitter systems. The serotonergic specific reuptake inhibitors are promising in terms of their effectiveness in adults.

4) Better understanding of the mechanisms of action of the antidepressants for children, including dosing and drug effect in relationship to plasma level, and effect of pharmacologic augmentation.

References

Abramowicz, M. (1990) Sudden death in children treated with a tricyclic antidepressant. *The Medical Letter on Drugs and Therapeutics*, **32**, p. 53.

American Psychiatric Association (1987) *Diagnostic and Statistical Manual of Mental Disorders—Revised (DSM-III-R)*, 3rd. ed., revised, Washington, D.C.: American Psychiatric Association.

Arana, G.W., Baldessarini, R.J. and Ornsteen, M. (1985) The dexamethasone suppression test for diagnosis and prognosis in psychiatry: Commentary and review. *Archives of General Psychiatry*, **42**, pp. 1193-1204.

Aranow, A.B., Hudson, J.I., Pope, H.G. Jr., Grady, T.A., Laage, T.A., Bell, I.R. and Cole, J.O. (1989) Elevated antidepressant plasma levels after addition of fluoxetine. *American Journal of Psychiatry*, **146**, pp. 911-913.

Bartels, M.G., Varley, C.K., Mitchell, J. and Stamm, S.J. (1991) Pediatric cardiovascular effects of imipramine and desipramine. *Journal of the American Academy of Child and Adolescent Psychiatry*, **30**, pp. 100-103.

Boulos, C., Kutcher, S., Marton, P., Simeon, J., Ferguson, B. and Roberts, N. (1991) Response to desipramine treatment in adolescent major depression. *Psychopharmacology Bulletin*, **27**, pp. 59-65.

Campbell, M., Silva, R.R., Kafantaris, V., Locascio, J.J., Gonzalez, N.M., Lee, D. and Lynch, N.S. (1991) Predictors of side effects associated with lithium administration in children. *Psychopharmacology Bulletin*, **27**, pp. 373-380.

Campbell, M., Small, A.M., Green, W.H., Jennings, S.J., Perry, R., Bennett, W.G. and Anderson, L. (1984) Behavioral efficacy of haloperidol and lithium carbonate: A comparison in hospitalized aggressive children with conduct disorder. *Archives of General Psychiatry*, **41**, pp. 650-656.

Carlson, G.A. and Kashani, J.H. (1988) Phenomenology of major depression from childhood through adulthood: Analysis of three studies. *American Journal of Psychiatry*, **145**, pp. 1222-1225.

Carroll, B.J., Feinberg, M., Greden, J.F., Tarika, J., Albala, A.A., Haskett, R.F., James, N.M., Kronfol, Z., Lohr, N., Steiner, M., de Vigne, J.P. and Young, E. (1981) A specific laboratory test for the diagnosis of melancholia: Standardization, validation, and clinical utility. *Archives of General Psychiatry*, **38**, pp. 15-22.

Casat, C.D., Arana, G.W. and Powell, K. (1989) The DST in children and adolescents with major depressive disorder. *American Journal of Psychiatry*, 146, pp. 503-507.

Davidson, J., Weiss, J., Sullivan, J., Turnbull, C. and Linnoila, M. (1981) A placebo controlled evaluation of isocarboxazid in outpatients. *Monoamine oxidase inhibitors—The state of the art*, M.B.H. Youdim and E.S. Paykel (Eds), New York: John Wiley and Sons.

Emslie, C.J., Rush, A.J., Weinberg, W.A., Rintelmann, J.W. and Roffwarg, H.P. (1990) Children with major depression show reduced rapid eye movement latencies. *Archives of General Psychiatry*, **47**, pp. 119-124.

Friedman, R. C., Hurt, S. W., Clarkin, J. F., Corn, R. and Aronoff, M. S. (1983) Symptoms of depression among adolescents and young adults. *Journal of Affective Disorders*, **5**, pp. 37–43.
Frommer, E. A. (1967) Treatment of childhood depression with antidepressant drugs. *British Medical Journal*, **1**, pp. 729–732.
Gelenberg, A. J., Bassuk, E. L. and Schoonover, S. C. (1991) *The Practitioner's Guide to Psychoactive Drugs*, New York: Plenum Medical Book Company.
Geller, B., Cooper, T. B. and Graham, D. L. (1990) Double-blind placebo-controlled study of nortriptyline in depressed adolescents using a 'fixed plasma level' design. *Psychopharmacology Bulletin*, **26**, pp. 85–90.
Geller, B., Cooper, T. B. and McCombs, H. G. (1989) Double-blind placebo-controlled study of nortriptyline in depressed children using a 'fixed plasma level' design. *Psychopharmacology Bulletin*, **25**, pp. 101–108.
Geller, B., Perel, M. J., Knitter, E. F., Lycaki, H. and Sarooki, Z. (1983) Nortriptyline in major depressive disorders in children: Response, steady-state plasma levels, predictive kinetics and pharmacokinetics. *Psychopharmacology Bulletin*, **19**, pp. 62–64.
Goodwin, F. K. and Jamison, K. R. (1990) *Manic-Depressive Illness*, New York: Oxford University Press, Inc.
Harrington, R., Fudge, H., Rutter, M., Pickles, A. and Hill, J. (1990) Adult outcomes of childhood and adolescent depression. *Archives of General Psychiatry*, **47**, pp. 465–473.
Kashani, J. H. and Carlson, G. A. (1987) Seriously depressed preschoolers. *American Journal of Psychiatry*, **144**, pp. 348–350.
Kashani, J. H., Carlson, G. A., Beck, N. C., Hoeper, E. W., Corcoran, C. M., McAllister, J. A., Fallahi, C., Rosenberg, T. K. and Reid, J. C. (1987) Depression, depressive symptoms and depressed mood among a community sample of adolescents. *American Journal of Psychiatry*, **144**, pp. 931–934.
Kashani, J. H., McGee, R. O., Clarkson, S. E. Anderson, J. C., Walton, L. A., Williams, S., Silva, P. A., Robins, A. J., Cytryn, L. and McKnew, D. H. (1983) Depression in a sample of 9-year old children. *Archives of General Psychiatry*, **40**, pp. 1217–1223.
Kashani, J. and Ray, J. S. (1983) Depressive symptoms among preschool-age children. *Child Psychiatry and Human Development*, **13**, pp. 233–238.
Kashani, J. H., Shekim, W. O. and Reid, J. C. (1984) Amitriptyline in children with major depressive disorder: A double-blind crossover pilot study. *Journal of the American Academy of Child Psychiatry*, **23**, pp. 348–361.
King, R. A., Riddle, M. A., Chappell, P. B., Hardin, M. T., Anderson, G. M., Lombroso, P. and Scahill, L. (1991) Emergence of self-destructive phenomena in children and adolescents during fluoxetine treatment. *Journal of the American Academy of Child and Adolescent Psychiatry*, **30**, pp. 179–186.
Klein, D. F., Gittelman, R., Quitkin, F. and Rifkin, A. (1980) *Diagnosis and Drug Treatment of Psychiatric Disorders: Adults and Children*, 2nd edition. Baltimore: Williams and Wilkins.
Klein, R. G. (1991) Personal Communication.
Koplewicz, H., Klass, E. and Klein, R. (1990) Preliminary data of a study of the efficacy of desipramine in the treatment of adolescents with major depressive disorder. Presented at the 30th Annual Meeting of the New Clinical Drug Evaluation Unit, Key Biscayne, Florida.
Kramer, A. D. and Feiguine, R. J. (1981) Clinical effects of amitriptyline in adolescent depression: A pilot study. *Journal of the American Academy of Child Psychiatry*, **20**, pp. 636–644.
Kutcher, S. P. and Marton, P. (1989) Parameters of adolescent depression: A review. *Psychiatric Clinics of North America*, **12**, pp. 895–918.
Kutcher, S. P., Williamson, P., Silverberg, J., Marton, P., Malkin, D. and Malkin, A. (1988) Nocturnal growth hormone secretion in depressed older adolescents. *Journal of the American Academy of Child and Adolescent Psychiatry*, **27**, pp. 751–754.
Lahmeyer, H. W., Poznanski, E. O. and Bellur, S. N. (1983) EEG sleep in depressed adolescents. *American Journal of Psychiatry*, **140**, pp. 1150–1153.
Liebowitz, M. R., Quitkin, R. M., Stewart, J. W., McGrath, P. J., Harrison, W., Rabkin, J., Tricamo, E., Markowitz, J. S. and Klein, D. F. (1984) Phenelzine v. imipramine in atypical depression: A preliminary report. *Archives of General Psychiatry*, **41**, pp. 669–677.
Petti, T. and Law, W. (1982) Imipramine treatment of depressed children: A double-blind pilot study. *Journal of Clinical Psychopharmacology*, **2**, pp. 107–110.
Preskorn, S. H., Weller, E. B., Hughes, C. W., Weller, R. A. and Bolte, K. (1987) Depression in prepubertal children: Dexamethasone nonsuppression predicts differential response to imipramine vs. placebo. *Psychopharmacology Bulletin*, **23**, pp. 128–133.
Puig-Antich, J., Goetz, R. and Davies, M. (1984) Growth hormone secretion in prepubertal children with

major depression: II. Sleep – related plasma concentrations during a depressive episode. *Archives of General Psychiatry*, **4**, pp. 463-466.

Puig-Antich, J. (1986) Biological factors in prepubertal major depression. *Pediatric Annals*, **15**, pp. 867-874.

Puig-Antich, J., Novacenko, H., Davies, M., Chambers, W. J., Tabrizi, M. A., Krawiec, V., Ambrosini, P. J. and Sachar, E. J. (1984) Growth hormone secretion in prepubertal children with major depression: I. Final report on response to insulin-induced hypoglycemia during a depressive episode. *Archives of General Psychiatry*, **41**, pp. 455-460.

Puig-Antich, J., Novacenko, H., Davies, M., Tabrizi, M.A., Ambrosini, P., Goetz, R., Bianca, J., Goetz, D. and Sachar, E. J. (1984b) Growth hormone secretion in prepubertal children with major depression: III. Response to insulin-induced hypoglycemia after recovery from a depressive episode and in a drug-free state. *Archives of General Psychiatry*, **41**, pp. 471-475.

Puig-Antich, J. (1987) Affective disorders in children and adolescents: Diagnostic validity and psychobiology. *Psychopharmacology – The Third Generation of Progress*, ed. H.Y. Meltzer, New York: Raven Press.

Puig-Antich, J., Perel, J.M. and Lupatkin, W. (1987) Imipramine in prepubertal major depressive disorders. *Archives of General Psychiatry*, **44**, pp. 81-89.

Quitkin, F.M., Liebowitz, M.R., McGrath, P.J., Harrison, W., and Rabkin, J.G. (1983) A trial of deprenyl in atypical depression. Paper presented at the meeting of American Psychiatric Association, New York, May, 1983.

Riddle, M.A. (1992) Personal Communication.

Riddle, M.A., Nelson, J.C., Kleinman, C.S., Rasmusson, A., Leckman, J.F., King, R.A. and Cohen, D.J. (1991) Sudden Death in children receiving Norpramin: A review of three reported cases and commentary. *Journal of the American Academy of Child and Adolescent Psychiatry*, **30**, pp. 104-108.

Robbins, D.R., Alessi, N.E. and Cotler, M.V. (1989) Treatment of adolescents with major depression: Implications of the DST and the melancholic clinical subtype. *Journal of Affective Disorders*, **17**, pp. 99-104.

Robins, L.N., Helzer, J.E., Weissman, M.M., Orvaschel, H., Gruenberg, E., Burke, J.D. Jr. and Reiger, D.A. (1984) Lifetime prevalence of specific psychiatric disorders in three sites. *Archives of General Psychiatry*, **41**, pp. 949-958.

Ruthschild, A.J. and Loche, C.A. (1991) Re-exposure to fluoxetine after serious suicide attempts by three patients: The role of akathesia. *Journal of Clinical Psychiatry*, **52**, pp. 491-493.

Ryan, N.D. (1990a) Heterocyclic antidepressants in children and adolescents. *Journal of Child and Adolescent Psychopharmacology*, **1**, pp. 21-32.

Ryan, N.D. (1990b) Amitriptyline vs. placebo in adolescent depression. Presented at Child Depression Consortium, Pittsburgh, PA. September, 1990.

Ryan, N.D., Meyer, V., Dachille, S., Mazzie, D. and Puig-Antich, J. (1988) Lithium antidepressant augmentation in TCA-refractory depression in adolescents. *Journal of the American Academy of Child and Adolescent Psychiatry*, **27**, pp. 371-376.

Ryan, N.D., Puig-Antich, J., Cooper, T., Robinovich, H., Ambrosini, P., Davies, M., King, J., Torres, D. and Fried, J. (1986), Imipramine in adolescent major depression: Plasma level and clinical response. *Acta Psychiatrica Scandinavia*, **73**, pp. 275-288.

Ryan, N.D., Puig-Antich, J., Robinovich, H., Fried, J., Ambrosini, P., Meyer, V., Torres, D., Dachille, S. and Mazzie, D. (1988) MAOI's in adolescent major depression unresponsive to tricyclic antidepressants. *Journal of the American Academy of Child and Adolescent Psychiatry*, **27**, pp. 755-758.

Ryan, N.D., Puig-Antich, J., Ambrosini, P., Robinovich, H., Robinson, D., Nelson, B., Iyengar, S. and Twomey, J. (1987) The clinical picture of major depression in children and adolescents. *Archives of General Psychiatry*, **44**, pp. 854-861.

Ryan, N.D. and Puig-Antich, J. (1986) Affective illness in adolescence. *American Psychiatric Association Annual Review, Vol. 5*, eds. R.E. Hales, A.J. Frances, Washington DC: American Psychiatric Press.

Simeon, J.G., Dinicola, V.F., Ferguson, H.B. and Copping, W. (1990) Adolescent depression: A placebo-controlled fluoxetine treatment study and follow-up. *Progress in Neuropsychopharmacology and Biological Psychiatry*, **14**, pp. 791-795.

Strober, M. and Carlson, G. (1982) Bipolar illness in adolescents with major depression: Clinical, genetic and psychopharmacologic predictors in a three-four year prospective follow-up investigation. *Archives of General Psychiatry*, **39**, pp. 549-555.

Strober, M., Freeman, R. and Rigali, J. (1990) The pharmacotherapy of depressive illness in adolescence: An open label trial of imipramine. *Psychopharmacology Bulletin*, **26**, pp. 80-84.

Strober, M., Freeman, R., Rigali, J., Schmidt, S. and Diamond, R. (1992) The pharmacotherapy of depressive illness in adolescence: II. Effects of lithium augmentation in nonresponders to imipramine. *Journal of the American Academy of Child and Adolescent Psychiatry*, **31**, pp. 16–20.

Strober, M., Green, J. and Carlson, G. (1981) Phenomenology and subtypes of major depressive disorder in adolescence. *Journal of Affective Disorders*, **3**, pp. 281–290.

Teicher, M.H., Glod, C. and Cole, J.O. (1990) Emergence of intense suicidal preoccupations during fluoxetine treatment. *American Journal of Psychiatry*, **147**, pp. 207–210.

Vitiello, B., Behar, D., Malone, R., Delaney, M.A., Ryan, P.J. and Simpson, G.M. (1988) Pharmacokinetics of lithium carbonate in children. *Journal of Clinical Psychopharmacology*, **8**, pp. 355–359.

Weissman, M.M., Leaf, P.J., Tischler, G.L., Blazer, D.G., Karno, M., Bruce, M.L. and Florio, L.P. (1988) Affective disorders in five United States communities. *Psychological Medicine*, **18**, pp. 141–153.

Weller, E.B., Weller, R.A., Preskorn, S.H. and Glotzbach, R. (1982) Steady-state plasma imipramine levels in prepubertal depressed children. *American Journal of Psychiatry*, **139**, pp. 506–508.

Index

For Product Safety Concerns and Information please contact our EU representative GPSR@taylorandfrancis.com Taylor & Francis Verlag GmbH, Kaufingerstraße 24, 80331 München, Germany

Batch number: 10726294

Printed by Printforce, the Netherlands